Guide to Hawk Watching in North America

Help Us Keep This Guide Up to Date

Every effort has been made by the author and editors to make this guide as accurate and useful as possible. However, many things can change after a guide is published—trails are rerouted, regulations change, techniques evolve, facilities come under new management, etc.

We would love to hear from you concerning your experiences with this guide and how you feel it could be improved and kept up to date. While we may not be able to respond to all comments and suggestions, we'll take them to heart and we'll also make certain to share them with the author. Please send your comments and suggestions to the following address:

The Globe Pequot Press
Reader Response/Editorial Department
P.O. Box 480
Guilford, CT 06437

Or you may e-mail us at:
editorial@GlobePequot.com

Thanks for your input, and happy travels!

A FALCON GUIDE®

Guide to Hawk Watching in North America

Donald S. Heintzelman

FALCON®

GUILFORD, CONNECTICUT
HELENA, MONTANA
AN IMPRINT OF THE GLOBE PEQUOT PRESS

_A_FALCONGUIDE ®

Photos: All photos and illustrations by the author unless otherwise noted.
Text design: Josh Comen

Library of Congress Cataloging-in-Publication Data

Heintzelman, Donald S.
  Guide to hawk watching in North America / by Donald S. Heintzelman.– 2nd ed.
    p. cm.
  Includes bibliographical references (p.   ).
  ISBN 0-7627-2670-9
  1. Birds of prey–North America. 2. Bird watching–North America. I. Title.
  QL696.F3H46 2004
  598.9'44'097–dc22

                                                                    2004040541

Manufactured in the United States of America
First Globe Pequot Edition/First Printing

For Robert and Anne MacClay

Contents

Checklist of North American Hawks...xii

Preface xiii

Species Accounts...1

    New World Vultures: Family Cathartidae 1

    Ospreys: Family Pandionidae 9

    Kites, Hawks, Eagles, Harriers: Family Accipitridae 12

    Caracaras and Falcons: Family Falconidae...52

Hawk Identification and Study 63

    Size 63

    Shape 63

    Flight Style and Behavior 65

    Distance from Observer 67

    Viewing Angle...67

    Light Conditions..68

    Habitat 68

    Geographic Range and Location 68

    Date 69

    Length of Observation Period 69

    Experience of Observer 69

    Miscellaneous Factors 69

Types of Hawk Watching 71

    Watching Hawks Migrate 71

    Summer Hawk Watching 71

    Winter Hawk Watching 72

Field Equipment..73

    Binoculars 73

    Telescope...74

    Decoys 74

    Cameras and Video Cameras 75

Field Clothing..75
Other Equipment 75

The Migration Seasons..77
Spring Hawk Migrations...77
Autumn Hawk Migrations 77

Mechanics of Hawk Flights 83
General Weather Conditions...83
Deflective Updrafts 83
Lee Waves 84
Thermals...85
Thermal Streets..86
Squall Lines..86
Leading-Lines 86

U.S. Hawk Migration Watch Sites....................................89
Alabama 89
Alaska 90
Arizona 92
Arkansas 94
California 94
Colorado...97
Connecticut 98
Delaware...101
Florida 103
Georgia 106
Idaho...107
Illinois...107
Indiana 108
Iowa 109
Kentucky...111
Maine 111
Maryland 116
Massachusetts 124
Michigan...133
Minnesota...137

Mississippi...140
Montana 140
Nevada 141
New Hampshire 142
New Jersey 145
New Mexico 158
New York 159
North Carolina 173
Ohio 188
Oregon 190
Pennsylvania 191
Rhode Island...216
South Carolina 216
Tennessee 217
Texas...219
Utah 223
Vermont 227
Virginia...231
Washington...258
West Virginia 259
Wisconsin 264
Wyoming 268

Canadian Hawk Migration Watch Sites 269
Alberta 269
British Columbia 269
Manitoba 270
New Brunswick..271
Nova Scotia...273
Ontario...274
Quebec 282

Bald Eagle Viewing Areas...287
Eagle Watching Etiquette 288
Alaska 289
California 297
Colorado...299

Connecticut 300

Delaware 301

Florida 302

Idaho...306

Illinois..306

Iowa 311

Kansas 320

Kentucky..320

Maryland 321

Massachusetts 322

Minnesota 322

Missouri 328

Montana 330

Nebraska 331

Nevada 332

New Jersey 333

New Mexico 333

New York 335

Oklahoma 339

Oregon 343

Pennsylvania 343

South Dakota 346

Tennessee 348

Texas 349

Utah 350

Vermont 351

Virginia..352

Washington..353

West Virginia 358

Wisconsin 359

British Columbia 362

Other Raptor Viewing Areas 367

Alaska 367

California 368

Florida 369

Idaho..372

Indiana 374

Kentucky...375

Maryland 375

Mississippi..376

Nebraska 376

Nevada 377

New Jersey 379

New Mexico 382

Pennsylvania 383

Texas 385

Vermont 390

Ontario 391

Yukon 392

Appendix: Vagrant North American Raptor Sightings 395

References and Suggested Reading 396

Index 410

About the Author 425

Checklist of North American Hawks

- ○ Black Vulture
- ○ Turkey Vulture
- ○ California Condor
- ○ Osprey
- ○ Hook-billed Kite
- ○ Swallow-tailed Kite
- ○ White-tailed Kite
- ○ Snail Kite
- ○ Mississippi Kite
- ○ Bald Eagle
- ○ White-tailed Eagle
- ○ Steller's Sea-Eagle
- ○ Northern Harrier
- ○ Sharp-shinned Hawk
- ○ Cooper's Hawk
- ○ Northern Goshawk
- ○ Crane Hawk
- ○ Gray Hawk
- ○ Common Black-Hawk
- ○ Harris's Hawk
- ○ Roadside Hawk
- ○ Red-shouldered Hawk
- ○ Broad-winged Hawk
- ○ Short-tailed Hawk
- ○ Swainson's Hawk
- ○ White-tailed Hawk
- ○ Zone-tailed Hawk
- ○ Red-tailed Hawk
- ○ Ferruginous Hawk
- ○ Rough-legged Hawk
- ○ Golden Eagle
- ○ Collared Forest-Falcon
- ○ Crested Caracara
- ○ Eurasian Kestrel
- ○ American Kestrel
- ○ Merlin
- ○ Eurasian Hobby
- ○ Aplomado Falcon
- ○ Gyrfalcon
- ○ Peregrine Falcon
- ○ Prairie Falcon

Preface

A quarter century has passed since the first (1979) edition of *A Guide to Hawk Watching in North America* was published. During those years much has been learned about raptor biology, identification, and the locations where these spectacular birds concentrate during their seasonal migrations. The latter two aspects of raptor study constitute the primary focus of this second edition of the guide: I have included improved identification field marks than were available in 1979, and many more raptor migration and other watch sites—especially in the American West—than were known a quarter century ago. In addition, I've provided new chapters discussing Bald Eagle watching (especially during winter), as well as other raptor viewing areas unrelated to migration. The result is that this Globe Pequot edition of *Guide to Hawk Watching in North America* has come of age.

In addition to the many books already used as references in the first (1979) edition of *Guide to Hawk Watching in North America,* the following more recently published books were also consulted in preparing this Globe Pequot edition: American Ornithologists' Union, *Check-List of North American Birds* (seventh edition) and *The Birds of North America;* Stanley H. Anderson and John R. Squires, *The Prairie Falcon;* David R. Barber, Craig R. Fosdick, Laurie J. Goodrich, and Stacy Luke, *Hawk Mountain Sanctuary Migration Count Manual;* Eric C. Bolen and Dan Flores, *The Mississippi Kite;* T. Bosakowski, *The Northern Goshawk: Ecology, Behavior, and Management in North America;* William J. Boyle Jr., *A Guide to Bird Finding in New Jersey;* Cindy B. Brashear and Philip K. Stoddard, *Autumn Raptor Migration Through the Florida Keys with Special Focus on the Peregrine Falcon;* Cindy Kilgore Brown, *Vermont Wildlife Viewing Guide;* Bureau of Land Management, *Snake River Birds of Prey National Conservation Area/Idaho Visitor's Guide;* Tom J. Cade, *The Falcons of the World;* Tom J. Cade, James H. Enderson, C. G. Thelander, and Clayton M. White, *Peregrine Falcon Populations: Their Management and Recovery;* Allen Chartier and Dave Stimac, *Hawks of Holiday Beach* (second edition); Jeanne L. Clark, *Nevada Wildlife Viewing Guide;* William S. Clark and Brian K. Wheelers, *A Field Guide to Hawks of North America* (second edition); Tim Cullinan, *Important Bird Areas of Washington;* Mark Damian Duda, *Virginia Wildlife Viewing Guide* and *West Virginia Wildlife Viewing*

Guide; Sheryl De Vore, *Birding Illinois;* Pete Dunne, Debbie Keller, and Rene Kochenberger, *Hawk Watch: A Guide for Beginners;* Pete Dunne, David Sibley, and Clay Sutton, *Hawks in Flight: The Flight Identification of North American Migrant Raptors;* James Ferguson-Lees and David A. Christies, *Raptors of the World;* J. M. Gerrard and G. R. Bortolotti, *The Bald Eagle;* Fran Hamerstrom, *Harrier: Hawk of the Marshes;* David Hancock, *The Bald Eagle of Alaska, BC and Washington;* Donald S. Heintzelman, *The Migrations of Hawks* and *Hawks and Owls of Eastern North America;* David Houston, *Condors and Vultures;* Laura Jackson, *Iowa Wildlife Viewing Guide;* Paul A. Johnsgard, *Hawks, Eagles, and Falcons of North America: Biology and Natural History;* John Kemper, *Birding Northern California;* Paul Kerlinger, *Flight Strategies of Migrating Hawks;* Frank Knight, *New York Wildlife Viewing Guide;* Joseph Knue, *Nebraska Wildlife Viewing Guide;* Dan Kunkle, *Bake Oven Knob Autumn Hawk Count Manual;* Jim Lockyer, *Rose Tree Park Hawk Watch Site Manual;* William G. Lord, *Blue Ridge Parkway Guide* (Vols. I and II); Carolyn Hughes Lynn, *Kentucky Wildlife Viewing Guide;* Jane Susan MacCarter, *New Mexico Wildlife Viewing Guide;* Ted Murin and Bryan Pfeiffer, *Birdwatching in Vermont;* Ralph A. Palmer, *Handbook of North American Birds* (Vols. 4 and 5); Roger Tory Peterson and Virginia M. Peterson, *A Field Guide to the Birds of Eastern and Central North America* (fifth edition); Laurie Pettigrew, *New Jersey Wildlife Viewing Guide;* Alan F. Poole, *Ospreys: A Natural and Unnatural History;* C. R. Preston, *Wild Bird Guides: Red-tailed Hawk;* Charles E. Roe, *North Carolina Wildlife Viewing Guide;* Phil T. Seng and David J. Case, *Indiana Wildlife Viewing Guide;* David Allen Sibley, *The Sibley Field Guide to Birds of Eastern North America* and *The Sibley Field Guide to Birds of Western North America;* R. E. Simmons, *Harriers of the World: Their Behaviour and Ecology;* Marcus B. Simpson Jr., *Birds of the Blue Ridge Mountains;* Noel Snyder and Helen Snyder, *The California Condor: A Saga of Natural History and Conservation;* Karen Steenhof, *Snake River Birds of Prey National Conservation Area 1994 Annual Report;* Jay Michael Strangis, *Birding Minnesota;* Lars Svensson, Peter J. Grant, Killian Mullarney, Roland H. Wauer, and Mark A. Elwonger, *Birding Texas;* W. E. Clyde Todd, *Birds of Western Pennsylvania;* Judith A. Toups and Jerome A. Jackson, *Birds and Birding on the Mississippi Coast;* Tom

Vezo and Richard L. Glinski, *Birds of Prey in the American West;* Brian K. Wheeler, *Raptors of Eastern North America* and *Raptors of Western North America;* Brian K. Wheeler and William S. Clark, *A Photographic Guide to North American Raptors;* Mel White, *Guide to Birdwatching Sites/Eastern U.S.;* Dan Zetterström, *Birds of Europe;* and Jorje I. Zalles and Keith L. Bildstein, *Raptor Watch: A Global Directory of Raptor Migration Sites.*

Along with the journals named in the original edition of this book, the following journals were consulted and useful information secured for use in this edition of the guide: *American Hawkwatcher, Annals of Carnegie Museum, Association of Southeast Biologists Bulletin, Audubon Magazine, Hawk Mountain News, HMANA Hawk Migration Studies, International Hawkwatcher, Loon, Narragansett Naturalist, OFO News, Passenger Pigeon, Pennsylvania Birds, Proceedings of Hawk Migration Conference IV, Prothonotary, Raptor Research,* and *Western Birds.*

National Park Service maps for the Skyline Drive in Shenandoah National Park and the Blue Ridge Parkway, and the Hawk Migration Association of North America's (HMANA) *John Anthony Alderman Guide to Hawk Watching on the Blue Ridge Parkway* also contained important information including names of overlooks and their elevations that was useful in preparing selected watch site descriptions for North Carolina and Virginia. The Ferry Bluff Eagle Council's *Eagle Watcher's Guide to Sauk City and Prairie du Sac Wisconsin* also provided important information about key Bald Eagle watching locations (and off-limits areas) in those villages, and in New Jersey The Raptor Trust's brochure *The Raptor Trust* provided basic information about that organization's raptor rehabilitation and education activities.

To make a uniform evaluation of the importance of raptor migration watch sites, data from each site were compared with one of the following rating scales. Hawk Mountain Sanctuary, Pennsylvania, provided the baseline data from which the two scales were prepared. Whenever possible I used the average number of hawks observed per hour for an entire season to evaluate and rate a site. If that information was unavailable, I used the average number of hawks observed per day. In some instances neither of these data were available. Then I used my judgment, rooted in nearly fifty years of field experience studying hawk migrations, to arrive at a site's rating.

Hawks-Per-Hour Rating Scale

Watch Site Rating	Average Number of Hawks Observed per Hour
Poor	0–11
Fair	12–22
Good	23–33
Excellent	34 or more

Hawks-Per-Day Rating Scale

Watch Site Rating	Average Number of Hawks Observed per Hour
Poor	0–46
Fair	47–92
Good	93–138
Excellent	139 or more

Only one raptor migration watch site in North America consistently and vastly exceeds these criteria—the Hazel Bazemore County Park Hawk Watch (near Corpus Christi, Texas). It is classified as a "world class" watch site, in a category similar to several sites in Mexico and Costa Rica.

I also include a number of roadside overlooks potentially useful as hawk observation sites along the Skyline Drive in Shenandoah National Park in Virginia and the Blue Ridge Parkway in North Carolina and Virginia. These are not evaluated and are indicated as "Experimental (not evaluated)" for spring and autumn. However, my examination of these sites indicates they provide views suitable for hawk watching purposes. They should be carefully investigated to determine their actual value for hawk watching and raptor migration monitoring.

Although many black-and-white photographs used in this second edition of the guide are my own, several additional photographers kindly allowed use of one or more of their photos. They are: Ryan Brady, Rodney Davis, Mark A. McConaughy, Sue A. Ricciardi, and Fred Tilly. I extend a special note of appreciation to each.

In addition to the many people providing helpful information or assistance during the preparation of the first edition of this guide, the following people also contributed to this second edition: Audie Bakewell, Bob

Barnhurst, Dave Carman, Juliana Clausen, Hal Cohen, Tim Cullinan, Cecily Fritz, Marcel Gahbauer, Alan C. Gregory, Meg Hahr, Jim Harleman, Dave Helzer, Stephen W. Hoffman, Dan Kunkle, Jim Lockyer, Andrew Mason, Mark A. McConaughy, Leslie McFarlane, Justin Monetti, Clark Moore, Joe O'Connell, Tim Oksiuta, Ron Pittaway, Bill Purcell, Karen Steenhof, Fred Tilly, Diane M. Von Eschen, and Joseph Yoder. The Northern Shenandoah Valley Aududon Society and the Wildlife Information Center, Inc., also provided helpful assistance and information.

The task of preparing the second edition of *Guide to Hawk Watching in North America* was substantial. I express my appreciation to each person who assisted in this effort toward conservation education on behalf of birds of prey in North America.

Donald S. Heintzelman
Allentown, Pennsylvania

Species Accounts

New World Vultures
Family Cathartidae

New World vultures are large black or dark brown carrion-eating birds. The Turkey Vulture is widespread, the Black Vulture less so. One species, the California Condor, is critically endangered but has been reintroduced into the wild in California and Arizona.

Black Vulture *(Coragyps atratus)*

Wingspread: 54 to 63 inches.

Length: 23 to 27 inches.

Field Recognition: A common vulture, especially of the southern United States, represented by the subspecies *C. a. atratus* in North America. *Adult (sexes similar)*—Large black bird with large whitish patch on underside (smaller on upperside) of each wing near tip. Tail short, barely extending beyond rear edge of wings; tip square. Naked head blackish-gray; neck more or less corrugated. Eyes and feet dark brown; legs whitish; narrow bill brownish-black with lighter tip. *Juvenile (sexes similar)*—Similar to adults but plumage duller, neck smooth (not corrugated as in adult), and all-black bill. *Chick*—Covered with thick buffy (not white) natal down. Naked head similar to juvenile.

Flight Style: Several rapid flaps, then short glide. Generally soars less than Turkey Vultures, but when soaring tends to reach higher altitudes without the tipping or rocking that characterizes Turkey Vultures. Sometimes their legs hang down or dangle when soaring or gliding.

Voice: Variety of hissing, rasping snarls when cornered; otherwise silent.

Nest: None constructed. Eggs deposited on the ground, on leaves or in other litter, in caves, hollow stumps, hollow logs, on bare ground underneath tangles of vines, or in other protected and sheltered places.

Eggs:	2 (rarely 1 or 3), pale gray-green with a few dark brown blotches. Incubation period 28 to 39 days.
Maximum Reported Longevity:	25 years, 6 months.
Food:	Carrion. Rarely kills young or injured animals, domestic or wild; occasionally eats rotting fruit or vegetables.
Habitat:	Much the same as for Turkey Vulture, except not occurring at higher elevations. Sometimes gathers in large numbers to feed upon carrion.
North American Range:	Southern United States west to southeastern Texas and extreme southern Arizona; expanding range northward into southern New England. Isolated individuals or vagrants reported in California, Maine, Minnesota, New Mexico, North Dakota, Wisconsin, and in Canada in New Brunswick, Newfoundland, Nova Scotia, Ontario, Prince Edward Island, Quebec, Saskatchewan, and Yukon.

Black Vulture nest and eggs.

Turley Vultures usually hold their wings in a distinctive V or dihedral when soaring.

Turkey Vulture *(Cathartes aura)*

Wingspread: 68 to 72 inches.

Length: 26 to 32 inches.

Field Recognition: A common vulture represented in North America by sub-species *C. a. septentrionalis* in the East, *C. a. meridionalis* in most of the West, and *C. a. aura* in the Southwest; however, subspecies *not recognizable* in field. *Adult (sexes similar)*—Large, nearly eagle-sized dark brown bird; appears black at a distance. Wings grayish or silvery on undersides of primaries and secondaries, giving bird two-toned appearance. Wings usually held in a distinctive V or dihedral when bird is in flight; head also frequently pointed down rather than extending forward. Tail relatively long, extending well beyond rear edge of wings; tip rounded or sometimes wedge-shaped, but sometimes damaged. Naked head reddish-crimson with short blackish bristles visible only at very close range. Eyes grayish-brown; bill ivory white; cere red; legs and feet fleshy-whitish. *Juvenile (sexes similar)*—Similar to adults, but naked head grayish-black. In some recently fledged birds, ring of white down circles base of neck. Front of bill black, but back portion ivory white. *Chick*—Covered with white natal down; head naked and dark as in juvenile.

Flight Style: Tilts or rocks from side to side when soaring. Occasional wingbeats slow, deep, and powerful, but appear labored, similar to those of an eagle.

Voice: Various hisses and grunts when bird is cornered; otherwise silent.

Nest: None constructed. Eggs deposited on the ground, sometimes on leaf or other litter, in caves, cliffs, hollow logs, and similar protected places.

Eggs: 2 (rarely 1 or 3), dull or creamy white with brown blotches. Incubation period 38 to 40 days.

Maximum Reported Longevity: 16 years, 10 months.

Food: Carrion (especially small animals); rarely rotting fruits or vegetables.

Habitat: Widespread in open country. Perches on posts, tall dead trees, limbs of living trees, electric towers, wires, fences, and on or near dead animals on ground.

North American Range: Southern Canada south throughout contiguous United States.

California Condor *(Gymnogyps californianus)*

Wingspread: 8.5 to 9.5 feet.

Length: 43 to 55 inches.

Field Recognition: Huge; eagles much smaller in comparison. Seven very long primaries extend outward from long wings like fingers. Legs whitish, with reddish upper tarsal joint. Subtle changes occur continually in condor's plumage until it reaches adult stage, resulting in too much variation in developmental plumage to allow precise determination of age. Birds sometimes can be placed in one of following approximate age classes adapted from Koford (*The California Condor,* 1953) and Wilbur (*California Fish and Game,* 1975, 61: 144–148), although not all fall exactly

California Condor at a California nest site. Photo by Carl B. Koford/U.S. Fish and Wildlife Service.

into any one category. *Adult (sixth year or older)*—Black with orange or yellow head or neck; pure white under-wing coverts. *Subadult (fourth and fifth year)*—Black, head sooty with well-defined ring of pale pink skin on neck of early-fourth-year birds (so-called ring-necked birds); exact age at which pink ring begins to appear and progress outward until entire neck is pink and head changes to orange is somewhat variable, but transition may begin toward end of third year. By late fourth or early fifth year, neck is entirely pink. Underwing coverts white, more or less similar to adults', but have distinctive dark patch in center of white near body. Difficulty in distinguishing this plumage from that of some immatures at a distance or in unfavorable light leads some experienced condor observers to refer to subadult birds and early immatures as "light immature" birds. *Immature (first to third year)*—Considerable variability in plumage patterns makes it difficult, and sometimes impossible, to determine accurately the precise age of birds in this age class. However, second- and third-year birds are black with grayish heads. In many birds underwing coverts mostly tawny or brown (so-called "dark immature" birds) rather than mottled white. (Several captive birds had underwing coverts mottled with much white and some brown but no typical "dark" state; the reason for this discrepancy is unknown.) Later in immature stage, perhaps late in third year, "ring-necked" plumage begins to appear as transition into difficult-to-recognize subadult plumage. First-year birds are best recognized by erratic flight rather than plumage, although they are black with a gray head and neck but without the ring-necked feature of older birds. Eyes brown. Underwing coverts white, irregularly mottled with brown, having distinctive dark patch in center near body, giving birds an appearance deceptively similar to subadult condors. Some experienced condor observers refer to these birds as "light immature" condors. When soaring, tip of tail slightly pointed rather than smoothly rounded as in adults. *Chick*—Covered with white natal down, changing at about 20 days to dark gray down. At about 55 days black juvenal plumage begins to appear. By about 30 weeks most of juvenal (first-year) plumage is in place. Head naked.

California Condor in overhead flight. Photo by Fred Sibley/U.S. Fish and Wildlife Service.

California Condor in flight. Photo by U.S. Forest Service.

Flight Style: Soars for hours on broad, flat wings (almost airplane-like) without the rocking and tilting exhibited by the much smaller Turkey Vulture in areas inhabited by condors. Golden Eagles also occur in areas inhabited by condors but are smaller. In head-on or rear views, condor's primaries appear brush-like at tips. Soaring condors sometimes flex wings upward about 90 degrees then backward about 45 degrees at wrists in so-called double dip, requiring 1 to 2 seconds to complete (slower than in other raptors) before continuing normal soaring activity. The purpose of the double dip is to increase speed, lose elevation, or avoid stall; as many as 26 consecutive double dips have been seen within 5- to 15-second intervals when a condor flew into a strong wind. Not infrequently soaring condors produce steady hissing whistle due to action of air upon wings. Whistle sometimes audible up to distances of 100 yards. Other styles of flight, including flex-gliding and flapping, also used. Condors generally remain on roosts until much later in morning than do vultures or eagles.

Voice: Usually silent but occasionally hisses and grunts.

Nest: None constructed. Egg deposited in cliff cavity, cave, pothole, or cave-like hollow in large tree (rarely). Captive-bred California Condors now have been reintroduced into parts of their historic breeding range in Arizona and California.

Eggs: 1, greenish-white to dull white. Very large. Incubation period about 42 days.

Maximum Reported Longevity: At least 21 years; detailed information for wild birds unavailable.

Food: Carrion (chiefly cattle but sometimes deer and other animals).

Habitat: Mostly mountains but occasionally grasslands and other open areas.

North American Range: Southern California and Grand Canyon in Arizona.

Ospreys
Family Pandionidae

The single species of Osprey, primarily a fish-eating species, occurs throughout the world. It is again common in many parts of North America after having seriously declined in numbers during the DDT era in the mid-twentieth century.

Osprey *(Pandion haliaetus)*

Wingspread:	54 to 72 inches.
Length:	21 to 26 inches.
Field Recognition:	Eagle-like hawk with long wings, generally associated with aquatic ecosystems. *Adult (male)*—Typical example of subspecies *P. h. carolinensis* of North America, large, dark brown above, and white below. Black patch extends through cheeks and eyes, contrasting with white head. Breast varies from pure white on some birds to slightly streaked with brown on others. Wrist black. Sometimes confused with Bald Eagles, but Ospreys' white underparts separate them. Nonmigratory birds of southern Florida (Florida Bay and Everglades National Park) closer in color to *P. h. ridgwayi,* of Bahamas and coastal Yucatán and northern Belize; exhibit exceptional whiteness, often white breasts, sometimes almost completely white heads. Eyes vivid yellow; cere, legs, and feet grayish-blue. *Adult (female)*—Similar to male, but with breast always boldly streaked with brown. *Juvenile*—Similar to adults, but with white spotting on back and upper surface of wings. *Chick*—Covered with pale pinkish-buff natal down.
Flight Style:	Soars on updrafts with wings deeply bent or crooked (an excellent characteristic). Long wings appear bowed when seen head-on. When soaring in thermal, however, wings and tail fully spread to achieve maximum lift. Commonly hovers over water when fishing.

Osprey nest in a dead cedar tree along coastal New Jersey.

Voice: Melodious series of *chewk-chewk-chewk* or *tchip-tchip-tchip* whistles uttered while fishing; ringing *kip-kip-kip-kiweeek-kiweeek* alarm note; various other notes.

Nest: Large stick structure placed near top of dead or living tree, post, utility pole or tower, duck hunting blind, billboard, roof, tank, channel buoy, or other elevated structure; occasionally on ground. Nests repaired and used year after year.

Eggs: 3 (rarely 1 to 4), white to pinkish-cinnamon with numerous reddish-brown blotches. Incubation period 37 (34 to 40) days.

Maximum Reported Longevity: 26 years, 2 months.

Food: Mostly fish; rarely injured birds; frogs and crustaceans.

Habitat: Ponds, lakes, rivers, coastal areas. Commonly migrates along coastlines and inland mountains.

North American Range: Nearly cosmopolitan. From northern Canada and Alaska south (in winter) to West Indies, Central America, and South America. Ospreys in southern Florida are nonmigratory.

Osprey nest and eggs.

Kites, Hawks, Eagles, Harriers
Family Accipitridae

Most diurnal birds of prey belong to this large raptor family whose species are diverse in habits and structure. The birds are further divided into several subfamilies.

Hook-billed Kite *(Chondrohierax uncinatus)*

Wingspread: 32 to 38 inches.

Length: 15 to 20 inches.

Field Recognition: Medium-sized kite with unusually long, thick, strongly hooked bill. All adults (regardless of color morph) have white irises, yellow patch in front of each eye, cere bright pea green, and feet bright yellow to orange. The distinctive wings are broad and paddle-shaped, caused by the shape of the wings pinching in at their attachment to the body. Several color phases, sexual differences, and age and individual variations occur. Subspecies *C. u. aquilonsis* reaches extreme southwestern United States. *Adult male (normal morph)*—Slaty gray on head and upperparts, lighter gray below; lightly marked with white bars on body but boldly barred with white on undersides of primaries. Tail blackish-gray with two broad, pale gray bars and narrow white tip. *Adult female (normal morph)*—Head gray, buffy collar on back of neck, body brown above with rufous below with bold whitish bars; undersides of primaries gray or rufous-gray with white bars. Tail bars narrower than in male. *Adult (black morph)*—Completely black (both sexes) with tail marked by 1 broad white bar. Black morph birds fairly common. *Juvenile (normal morph)*—White with black cap and back, tail with gray tip and 3 or 4 narrow pale gray and/or white bars. *Juvenile (black morph)*—Entirely brownish-black. *Chick*—Covered with long white down, washed pinkish on crown, back, and wings.

Flight Style: Generally secretive forest bird; soars occasionally on long elliptical or paddle-shaped wings. Typical flight alternates flaps with short glides, but wings somewhat bowed when soaring and gliding. Usually flies low over treetops.

Voice: Musical whistle similar to oriole's song; screams and harsh chatters or rattles when alarmed; also loud, shrill screams.

Nest: Stick-and-twig structure placed in tree.

Eggs: 2 (1 to 3), creamy white blotched with chocolate brown. Incubation period about 35 days.

Maximum Reported Longevity: Information unavailable.

Food: Chiefly land (tree) snails; rarely frogs, salamanders, and insects.

Habitat: Lower forest canopy, dense undergrowth in swampy areas, occasional dry tropical forest and even temperate areas up to elevations of 6,000 feet or more.

North American Range: Rio Grande Valley in extreme southern Texas (Santa Ana National Wildlife Refuge, Bentsen–Rio Grande Valley State Park, and area below Falcon Dam). Hook-billed Kites in southern Texas are nonmigratory.

Swallow-tailed Kite (Elanoides forficatus)

Wingspread: 45 to 54 inches.

Length: 20 to 25 inches.

Field Recognition: An unmistakable kite with a long, deeply forked, black tail. *Adult (sexes similar)*—Head and undersides of body white. Back, flight feathers of wings, and tail dark gray; distinct interconnecting, white patches on back when perched; tail deeply forked. In North American subspecies *E. f. forficatus,* upperside of wings has purplish gloss. Eyes dark brown; cere bluish; bill black; legs and feet pale bluish-gray. *Juvenile (sexes similar)*—Similar to adult, but back feathers tipped with white; white body narrowly streaked with black. *Chick*—Covered with buffy white natal down, darker on nape and breast.

Flight Style: Graceful and buoyant soaring and gliding, sometimes in flocks of as many as 50 birds. Occasional wingbeats are slow.

Voice: Repetitious, high-pitched *eee* or *kee;* also hissing, high-pitched whistle.

Nest: Twig, pine needle, and Spanish moss structure placed at top of tall, slender trees.

Eggs: 2, white or creamy white, boldly blotched with dark reddish-brown or various shades of dark brown. Incubation period about 28 days (in Florida).

Maximum Reported Longevity: Information unavailable.

Food: Large flying insects, birds (nestlings), bats, snakes, lizards, tree frogs, and occasionally other items.

Habitat: Swampy forests, montane pine woods, marshland, and near lakes and rivers.

North American Range: South Carolina southward along Atlantic coast, and along parts of Gulf coast; most of Florida; winters in South America (rarely a few birds in Florida during December and January). Extralimital or occasional records from Arizona, Colorado, Massachusetts, Michigan, New Hampshire, New Mexico, New York, Pennsylvania, Vermont, Wisconsin, and in Canada from Manitoba, Nova Scotia, Ontario, and Saskatchewan; also Bermuda.

White-tailed Kite *(Elanus leucurus)*

Wingspread: 37 to 40 inches.

Length: 14 to 17 inches.

Field Recognition: Falcon-like, medium-sized, white kite. *Adult (sexes similar)*—Subspecies *E. l. majusculus,* of North America, with very bold and distinctive black shoulders on the grayish upperside of each wing, but only small black carpal patches on the otherwise white undersides of the wings. Seen from above, the white head contrasts with the darker uppersides of the wings. Undersides of body and wings white, with dark wrist patch on each wing. Wings pointed; whitish tail long. Eyes orange-rufous to scarlet. Bill black. Cere, legs, and feet yellow. *Juvenile (sexes similar)*—Head and body streaked with orange-brown; otherwise similar to adult. *Chick*—Covered with dull white to pinkish-buff natal down, followed by second bluish down.

Flight Style: Gull-like and graceful with wings often held in dihedral. Frequently hovers, then dives (with wings elevated) at prey when it is seen.

Voice: Chirped or whistled *kewp;* also *eee-grack.*

Nest: Stick-and-twig structure placed in trees and shrubs.

Eggs: 4 or 5 (rarely 3 to 6), white to creamy white, boldly and extensively blotched with brown. Incubation period 30 to 32 days.

Maximum Reported Longevity: 5 years, 11 months.

Food: Mice, other small mammals, small birds, lizards, and amphibians.

Habitat: River valleys, marshes, grasslands, and foothills that are open.

North American Range: Common in southern and coastal California, Gulf coast of Texas; also occurs along Gulf coast of Louisiana and Mississippi, and in southern Florida, southern Arizona, and expanding into Oregon coastal areas. Extralimital or occasional records from Idaho, Illinois, Indiana, Iowa, Maryland, Massachusetts, Missouri, Nevada, New Mexico, New York, North Dakota, Tennessee, Utah, Virginia, Wisconsin, and Wyoming, and in Canada in British Columbia.

Snail Kite *(Rostrhamus sociabilis)*

Wingspread: 41 to 45 inches.

Length: 17 to 19 inches.

Field Recognition: Medium-sized kite with proportionately broader wings than other North American kites; bill very slender and strongly hooked. Social, sometimes forming large groups. Florida subspecies *R. s. plumbeus* endangered. *Adult (male)*—Slaty black with white upper and lower tail coverts, white rump, square or slightly forked black tail with narrow white tip and broad white basal area. Eyelids and area in front of eyes flame scarlet; iris carmine; bill black; legs apricot-orange. *Adult (female)*—Brown above with white forehead and throat; sometimes whitish line behind eye. Dusky brown below, heavily blotched with rufous or white circular marks; rump white; tail brown with narrow white tip and broad white basal area. *Subadult (male)*—Similar to adult male, but upperparts tinged with fuscous. Broad cinnamon-buff streaking on chin, throat, breast, and middle abdomen. Breast streaks dark rufous shading to deep chestnut. *Subadult (female)*— Similar to adult female but with white and black streaks on top of head and nape; whitish to pinkish-buff upperparts heavily streaked with fuscous-black. Thighs also cinnamon-buff, as are underwing coverts, also having brownish-black streaks. *Juvenile (sexes similar)*—Similar to subadult female but more richly colored and darker. Chestnut brown streaked with darker brown, yellow, and white; throat and conspicuous line behind eye white; tail as in adults. Upper tail coverts light buffy; tail brownish-black on upperside, with broad cinnamon-buff tip. Juvenile retains plumage through first winter, during which time plumage fades, assuming subadult plumage following summer or autumn. *Chick*—Covered with buffy natal down tinged with cinnamon on crown, wings, and rump; second down thicker and darker grayish-brown.

Flight Style: "Floppy," suggesting heron's wingbeat; less graceful than most other kites. When hunting snails, kites fly slowly over marsh at low altitude, moving back and forth searching for prey. When snail is seen, kite drops swiftly and clutches prey with talons, then carries snail to well-used feeding perch where it is extracted and swallowed whole.

Voice: Cackling *kor-ee-ee-a kor-ee-ee-a* cry.

Nest: Bulky, somewhat flattened stick platform, lined with leaves, vines, and Spanish moss, placed from 3 to 15 feet above water in shrubs, trees, saw grass.

Eggs: 3 (rarely 1 to 6), white extensively blotched with brown. Incubation period 24 to 30 days.

Maximum Reported Longevity: 14 years, 8 months.

Food: Almost entirely freshwater snails of genus *Pomacea* (in Florida *P. paludosa*); rarely mites, midge larvae, and plant debris. All may have been eaten accidentally while swallowing snails.

Habitat: Freshwater marshes, open swamps, large lakes, and rivers where *Pomacea* snails occur.

North American Range: Southern peninsular Florida in six freshwater ecosystems: (1) Kissimmee River Valley, (2) St. Johns River, (3) northern and western sides of Lake Okeechobee, (4) Loxahatchee Slough, (5) Everglades including parts of Loxahatchee National Wildlife Refuge, and (6) Big Cypress National Preserve. Extralimital records from Georgia and Texas (the latter perhaps from Mexico).

Mississippi Kite *(Ictinia mississippiensis)*

Wingspread: 29 to 33 inches.

Length: 13 to 17 inches.

Field Recognition: Dark, falcon-like raptor with long, pointed wings and outer primary much shorter than others. Females average considerably larger than males. *Adult*—Head pale gray, somewhat darker in female. Back and uppersides of wings dark gray, but secondaries white on upper surface. Underparts paler gray; tail completely black. Eyes scarlet; legs orange-yellow with grayish top of toes. *Juvenile*—Head pale grayish with dark streaks. Undersides of body heavily streaked with brown. Tail dark with 3 or 4 lighter bars and lighter tip. Eyes brown. *Chick*—Covered with white natal down tinged with buff on upperparts.

Flight Style: Graceful, smooth, and buoyant, with wings extended flat or a slight dihedral; sometimes slow with much easy flapping. Resembles medium-sized gull at times. Frequently seen in flocks that, during migration, can become large (200 or more birds).

Voice: *Phee-phew; kee-ee.*

Nest: Twig structure, or old crow's nest, lined with green leaves or twigs, placed from 10 feet above ground to crotch or fork high in tall tree.

Eggs: 2 (1 to 3), white to pale bluish-white. Incubation period 30 (29 to 32) days.

Maximum Reported
Longevity: 11 years, 2 months.

Food: Mainly insects; rarely birds, bats, lizards, frogs, and fish.

Habitat: Wooded creek bottoms, wooded areas adjacent to farm-land, and open shrubland.

North American
Range: Population and range expanding. Nests locally in southern and south-central United States (Kansas, Iowa, Tennessee, and South Carolina southward to northwestern Florida, Gulf coast west to Arizona). Some winter in South America. Winter range poorly known because of confusion in distinguishing this species from very similar Plumbeous Kite *(Ictinia plumbea)* of Central and South America. Extralimital records from California, Colorado, Maine, Massachusetts, Michigan, Minnesota, Nevada, New Jersey, New York, Ohio, Pennsylvania, Wisconsin, Wyoming, and in Canada from Nova Scotia, Ontario, and Saskatchewan.

Bald Eagle *(Haliaeetus leucocephalus)*

Wingspread: 72 to 98 inches.

Length: 30 to 43 inches.

Field Recognition: Large eagle with robust head and neck extending well beyond leading edge of wings when seen in flight; lower tarsi (legs) unfeathered (feathered on Golden Eagle). Usually associated with aquatic ecosystems. *Adult (sixth year or older)*—Typical individual of subspecies *H. l. leuco-cephalus,* of southern United States, unmistakable with dark brown body (black at distance) and pure white head and tail. Some sixth-year birds have white heads with sprinkle of brown remaining on rectrices and occasionally nape. Pattern may persist for some time. Alaskan and Canadian subspecies *H. l. alascensis* similar to southern form but larger. In all cases females larger than males. Eyes, bill, legs, and feet bright yellow. Bill larger and more robust than that of Golden Eagle. *Juvenile and immatures*—Bald Eagles not yet adult are extremely variable in color and pattern of plumage. The following age groups and plumage descriptions are adopted from the field studies of Southern (*Wilson Bulletin,* 1964, 76: 121–137) and Sherrod, White, and Williamson (*Living*

Bird, 1976, 15: 145–146). *Subadult (fifth year)*—Plumage similar to adults, but with sprinkling of brown on most of white rectrices; this may not be visible except with high-magnification binoculars or telescopes. Some crown and nape feathers have brown tips; sometimes entire crown still brown. Iris yellowish. At distance, without binoculars, observers can mistake these birds for adults although head appears somewhat darker. *Late immature (fourth year)*— Body primarily brown on dorsal surface. Breast also brown, but some dull white may be visible on belly. Throat light brown or whitish; sides of head and possibly forehead dull white. Crown and nape often dull white with brown-tipped feathers (sometimes largely brown). Dark brown eyeline sometimes extends ahead of and behind each eye. Bill yellow on basal half; iris brownish. *Immature (third and second years)*—In third-year birds throat has some white; breast remains brown, resulting in

Immature Bald Eagle.

obvious but perhaps narrow band on breast. Belly and lower breast whitish to white. In some birds white areas very large, in others small and flecked with brown. Dorsal surface dark brown mottled with occasional white patch or scattered white feathers (may have brown tips). Most common location for white back patch between wings, where it resembles white V on perched bird. Coverts often spotted with white; crown generally dark brown, but sometimes feathers have tawny tip. White may begin to show on sides of head or throat (usually throat first), but crown and nape are usually dark. Some yellow present at base of bill. Iris brown. Considerable variation in third-year plumage. In second-year birds belly and lower breast generally light tawny brown; upper breast darker, possibly with band or bib. Upper surface of body dark brown mottled with white. Sometimes a few white feathers are visible on the belly and throat (perhaps incoming feathers of third-year plumage). Some white in tail, perhaps more than in first year. Bill and iris brown. Legs and feet yellow. *Juvenile (first year)*—Upper and lower sides of body uniformly dark brown except for occasional white portion on one or more feathers. Primaries, secondaries, and upper-wing coverts dark or darker than body color, but buffy or whitish underwing lining extends outward on each wing from body toward primaries. Crown sometimes darker than rest of body. Rectrices brown, often with grayish-white varying from a sprinkling to coverage of about 60 percent of central rectrices. Less white visible on dorsal side of tail. Bill horn brown. Iris light brown. Legs yellowish. *Chick*—Natal down smoky gray; second down dark brown.

Flight Style: Wingbeat slow and labored. Similar to Golden Eagle, but when seen approaching head-on wings usually held more level, whereas Golden Eagle frequently shows slight dihedral in flight profile. Head and neck larger and more robust compared with Golden Eagle.

Voice: Harsh *kark-kark-karl* or *kleek-kik-ik-ik-ik-ik* cackle.

Nest: Massive stick structure lined with pine needles or similar softer material; located near water most of time. Nest placed high in large tree, on rocky overlook, or occasionally on ground if high supporting structures unavailable.

Eggs: 2 (occasionally 1 to 4), dull white. Incubation period 35 days.

Maximum Reported Longevity: 29 years, 7 months.

Food: Fish (usually alive but sometimes as carrion); occasionally birds and mammals.

Habitat: Coastal areas, large rivers and lakes, during winter at open water below dams, and (during migration) along mountain ridges and other inland areas.

Range: North America from Alaska and Canada south to Baja California and Florida.

White-tailed Eagle (*Haliaeetus albicilla*)

Wingspread: 78 to 92 inches.

Length: 31 to 36 inches.

Field Recognition: Rare; robust sea eagle sometimes confused with Bald Eagle. *Adult (sexes similar)*—Typical individual of subspecies *H. a. albicilla* of Eurasia grayish-brown with yellowish-brown head (palest in worn plumage and odd birds; not white) and pure white wedge-shaped tail (sometimes rounded or square-tipped in worn plumage). Eyes, legs, and feet yellow; bill and cere pale yellow. Greenland subspecies *H. a. groenlandicus* slightly larger than *albicilla*. *Immature*—Brown, mottled with whitish on throat and breast; wings brown without whitish undersides as in immature Bald Eagle. Tail brown and wedge-tipped. In second-year birds webs of rectrices show distinctive whitish centers not present in Bald Eagles of similar age. Bill dark with base pale and larger than in Bald Eagle. Eyes brown. Feet and legs yellow. *Chick*—Covered with buffy-gray down; second down coarse and dark grayish-buff.

Flight Style: Soars and glides on long, broad, flat wings that may show slight dihedral when thermal soaring (never as marked as in Golden Eagle). Large head extends forward in front of wings as far as tail extends behind them. Tip of tail may appear somewhat rounded when spread in soaring flight.

Numerous shallow and rapid wingbeats, usually followed by short period of soaring or gliding.

Voice: Barking *gri-gri-gri or krick-krick-krick.* Additional calls for each sex under certain circumstances.

Nest: Huge stick structure lined with green vegetation and placed high in tree, on crag, or even on ground.

Eggs: 2 (sometimes 1 to 4), dull white. Incubation period estimated at 35 to 45 days, perhaps around 37 to 40 days.

Maximum Reported Longevity: Information unavailable.

Food: Fish (dead or alive), waterbirds, mammals, and carrion.

Habitat: Usually seacoasts; occasionally river valleys and inland lakes.

North American Range: Extremely rare in North America, mostly in Alaska. Skeletal remains found in American Harbor (Cumberland Sound), Alaska, October 1877. Two adults observed flying over Henderson Valley, Attu Island (extreme western Aleutians), Alaska, May, 27, 1977, and remaining in area through July 16, 1977; also bred on Attu. Another record from Shemya, Aleutian Islands. In eastern North America an immature off Nantucket Lightship, Massachusetts, November 14, 1914.

Northern Harrier *(Circus cyaneus)*

Wingspread: 40 to 54 inches.

Length: 17.5 to 24 inches.

Field Recognition: Widely distributed harrier represented in North America by subspecies *C. c. hudsonius;* some taxonomists consider this race a separate species. Individuals of all ages (except chicks) have *conspicuous white rump patch.* Long wings frequently form slight dihedral; wing tips usually appear pointed but occasionally can appear rounded. *Adult (male)*—Ashy gray on upperparts, white on underside with some cinnamon spots; wing tips black. Eyes orange-yellow. Cere, legs, and feet yellow. *Adult (female)*—Brown on upperparts, lighter brown on underside with heavy brown streaks. Eyes brownish-yellow to yellow. Cere, legs,

Adult male Northern Harrier. Photo by Fred Tilly.

and feet yellow. *Immature male (second year)*—Brownish above but largely whitish on underside, mottled with buffy markings on chest; wings and tail similar to adult male. *Immature female (second year)*—Similar to juvenile but with faint cinnamon spots on breast sometimes visible at distance. *Juvenile (both sexes)*—First-year birds similar to adult female, but undersides uniformly pale cinnamon and lack spots or streaks on belly or lower chest. Eye in male grayish-brown to yellowish; brown in females. *Chick*—Covered with white natal down tinged with buff and dark ring around each eye; second down buffy brown.

Flight Style: Unsteady; frequently rocks, tips, and zigzags on updrafts. Also quarters low over marshes and fields. Sometimes hovers briefly while hunting. During migration, wing positions sometimes appear deceptively similar to those of the Peregrine Falcons with which these harriers sometimes are confused by inexperienced hawk watchers.

Voice: Nasal *pee pee pee* or *chu-chu-chu* whistle.

Nest: Reed, grass, and small-stick structure placed on ground in marshes among reeds, tall weeds, or low shrubs.

Eggs: 5 (sometimes 4 to 6; rarely 8 to 12), dull white or pale bluish-white occasionally slightly blotched with brown. Incubation period 30 to 32 (28 to 36) days.

Maximum Reported Longevity: 16 years, 5 months.

Food: Small mammals, birds, small reptiles, frogs, insects, and crustaceans.

Habitat: Coastal areas, freshwater and saltwater marshes, meadows, prairies, fields, grasslands, and (during migration) along mountain ridges and Great Lakes shorelines.

North American Range: Breeds from edge of Alaskan and Canadian boreal forests south to California, Texas, and Virginia; winters south to Cuba and (rarely) northern South America. Extralimital records from Labrador, northern Quebec; Bermuda and Bahamas.

Sharp-shinned Hawk (Accipiter striatus)

Wingspread: 20 to 27 inches.

Length: 10 to 14 inches.

Field Recognition: Smallest North American accipiter. Eyes proportionately larger than in other North American accipiters, giving somewhat pop-eyed appearance when seen at close range; feature can sometimes help in distinguishing immature Sharp-shins from immature Cooper's Hawks if used in combination with other field marks. Legs very thin compared with much thicker legs of Cooper's Hawk. *Adult*— Widespread continental subspecies *A. s. velox* bluish-gray on upperparts and whitish with reddish-brown bars on underside. Wings short and rounded; long tail has 3 gray bars and narrow white tip that can be notched, square, or occasionally slightly rounded. Subspecies *A. s. perobscurus,* of Queen Charlotte Islands, British Columbia, slightly darker than *velox*. However, *A. s. suttoni,* of forested mountains of southern Arizona, New Mexico, and portions of Mexico, is strikingly different from *velox:* paler below with attractive wash of rufous on undersides and unbarred rufous thighs. Eye red (variable in some subspecies); cere, legs, and feet yellow. *Juvenile*—Brown above, white below, with bold brown streaks formed by small drop-shaped brown spots. Streaks usually cover most of the underside, whereas in many (but not all) juvenile Cooper's Hawks, streaking covers only the anterior half or three-quarters of the underside. Suggestion of pale eyebrow line seen on some birds; this is not a useful field mark and should not be confused with the similar mark on Cooper's Hawks and especially on Northern Goshawks. As birds begin to acquire adult plumage, some barring and streaking appear on breast. Eye yellow, changing to orange; cere, legs, and feet yellowish. *Chick*—Covered with creamy white or yellowish down followed by second, longer white down with some grayish on back.

Identification Note: Field marks published to aid in flight identification of some Sharp-shinned Hawks (large females) and some Cooper's Hawks (small males) based upon relative extent to which head of bird protrudes from, or is tucked into, shoulders (Brett and Nagy, *Feathers in the Wind*, 1973; Clark and Wheeler, *A Field Guide to Hawks of North America*, 2001; see also Berardi,

Adult Sharp-shinned Hawk with a square-tipped tail. Photo by Fred Tilly.

HMANA Hawk Migration Studies, 2003, 28 [2]: 19–25). Head tucked deeply into shoulders, bird is considered Sharp-shin; head protrudes extensively from shoulders, considered Cooper's Hawk. However, degree to which hawk's head is tucked into, or protrudes from, shoulders varies considerably depending upon size of bird, flight style, position of wings at any particular moment, and wind conditions. While field mark generally applies to some Sharp-shinned Hawks (birds with tips of tail notched or square), mark does not seem to apply consistently to many large female Sharp-shins or to some Cooper's Hawks. Therefore, use head-to-shoulder profile cautiously, in combination with other field marks discussed under appropriate species accounts, to arrive at identification of accipiters. Impossible to identify some birds correctly; when in doubt, never hesitate to list bird as unidentified. Cooper's Hawks less common than Sharp-shinned Hawks, especially in East.

Flight Style: Several rapid wingbeats, then brief period of sailing, followed by more wingbeats. Soars in thermals occasionally with wings and tail fully spread. In general, lighter and more buoyant flight than exhibited by other accipiters.

Voice: Thin, repeated *kik-kik-kik* cackle higher in pitch than in larger accipiters.

Nest: Large twig platform, usually on branch or in crotch of conifer but occasionally in oak tree, lined with twigs, strips, or chips of bark.

Eggs: 4 or 5 (occasionally 3 to 8), white or bluish-white with brown and/or purple marks. Incubation period 30 to 35 days.

Maximum Reported Longevity: 19 years, 11 months.

Food: Mostly small birds, but occasionally small mammals, lizards, and insects.

Habitat: Normally forests and woodlands, but during migration coastlines, mountains, and Great Lakes shorelines. Sometimes visits urban, suburban, and rural backyard bird feeders during spring and autumn migrations, and, in winter, to prey on songbirds. Some Sharp-shins accidentally fly into plate glass windows and are injured or killed.

Range: Tree line of North America southward throughout the
United States. Extralimital records from northern Alaska
north of tree line.

Cooper's Hawk (Accipiter cooperii)

Wingspread: 27 to 36 inches.

Length: 14 to 20 inches.

Field Recognition: Most difficult of accipiters to identify. Intermediate in size
between Sharp-shinned Hawk and Northern Goshawk.
Essentially a larger version of the Sharp-shin but with
much thicker legs, and a tail longer in proportion to rest
of body as compared with Sharp-shinned Hawk; tip of tail
usually well rounded. Some large immature Cooper's
Hawks similar in appearance to small immature Northern
Goshawks, but Cooper's Hawk tail usually more rounded,
with undertail coverts unmarked. Northern Goshawk has
more heft, heavier wingbeats, broader wings, and shorter

Immature Cooper's Hawk in flight. Photo by Fred Tilly.

tail. In addition, some Cooper's Hawks have narrow white eyebrow line similar to some immature Northern Goshawks' line but much less conspicuous. Nevertheless observers should be cautious about confusing this line with that of Northern Goshawk. *Adult (male)*—Bluish-gray on upperparts (darkest on back) with black cap; whitish below, richly marked with reddish-brown bars, tending to give birds richer appearance than usually smaller Sharp-shinned Hawk. Tail bluish-gray with 3 black bands and narrow, white, well-rounded tip. Eye red; cere yellow; legs and feet deep yellow. *Adult (female)*—Similar to adult male but back browner than bluish-gray. Considerably larger than male, sometimes almost size of small Northern Goshawk. *Juvenile*—Brown above, white below marked with fine to broad dark brown streaks, *or* with bold, dark brown club-shaped spots, making it easy to confuse these birds with juvenile Northern Goshawks. Streaks or spots usually cover upper half or three-quarters of underside of body; occasional bird has most of underside well marked. Juvenal plumage larger and less compact that adult plumage, giving young birds larger appearance. Eye pale grayish to pale yellow; legs and feet yellow. *Chick*—Covered with short creamy white natal down, soon replaced with short silky white down.

Flight Style: Similar to Sharp-shinned Hawk but wingbeats sufficiently slower to enable experienced observers to recognize differences in many instances. Usually more direct flight than that of Sharp-shinned Hawk, and soars (with slight dihedral) more than Sharp-shin.

Voice: Harsh, staccato *ca-ca-ca-ca* cackling; dozens of additional calls used in specific situations.

Nest: Large twig platform, lined with hemlock, oak, or maple bark, placed in crotch of tree or on limb next to trunk.

Eggs: 3 to 5 (rarely 1 to 7), pale sky blue fading to dirty white, occasionally spotted lightly. Incubation period 34 to 36 days.

Maximum Reported Longevity: 13 years, 10 months.

Food: Medium-sized birds (particularly starlings, flickers, and meadowlarks), small mammals (including Red Squirrels and chipmunks), lizards, amphibians, and large insects.

Habitat: The most adaptable of our North American accipiters in selection of habitats. Mature forested and wooded areas, large woodlots, riverine woodland, canyons, and even Sonoran Desert. Some Cooper's Hawks also now nest in urban and suburban areas. During migration, along coastlines, mountain ridges, and Great Lakes shorelines.

North American Range: Southern Canada south to Gulf coast and northwestern Mexico. Extralimital sight records from southeastern Alaska.

Northern Goshawk *(Accipiter gentilis)*

Wingspread: 40 to 47 inches.

Length: 20 to 26.5 inches.

Field Recognition: The largest of the North American accipiters. *Adult*— Subspecies *A. g. atricapillus,* distributed widely in North America, dark bluish-gray or grayish on upperparts and pale grayish-white on undersides marked with fine dark bars. Dark cap and cheek, bold white eyebrow line are distinctive. Adults and immatures sometimes show unusually conspicuous white undertail coverts. Wings proportionately longer and broader than other accipiters. Tail unusually long, tip slightly to moderately rounded. Iris red to orange; cere and legs yellow. Subspecies *A. g. laingi,* on islands off British Columbia coast, similar to *atricapillus* but slightly darker, particularly in immature plumage; subspecies *A. g. apache,* of southern Arizona and New Mexico mountains (and northwestern Mexico), differs from *atricapillus* only by being somewhat larger and with heavier feet. *Juvenile*—Brown on upperparts, usually with bold white eyebrow (juvenile Cooper's, Red-shouldered, and Broad-winged Hawks also have pale eyebrows); whitish on undersides with heavy brown streaking formed by bold, dark brown drop-shaped marks. White undertail coverts also have bold, dark brown drop-shaped marks lacking in other accipiters. Eye varying shades of yellow. Legs and feet yellow. If bird is seen perched at close range, this feature may help distinguish juvenile Northern Goshawk from juvenile Cooper's Hawk; probably not

Nestling Northern Goshawks in a nest in southern Vermont.

helpful for birds in flight. *Chick*—Covered with short white natal down, later changing to longer woolly down tinged with gray on back.

Flight Style: Usually several heavy flapping wingbeats, then brief period of gliding, followed by more wingbeats. Heavier and more direct flight than exhibited by smaller accipiters. Sometimes soars; at times its flight is deceptively similar to that of the Gyrfalcon.

Voice: *Ca-ca-ca-ca* or *kuk-kuk-kuk* screamed in alarm; occasionally other calls used at nest.

Nest: Large, flat, stick platform, sometimes used for several years in succession, placed in crotch of tall tree or on limb from 30 to 60 feet above ground.

Eggs: 2 to 4 (1 to 5), dirty white or pale bluish. Incubation period 32 (28 to 38) days.

Maximum Reported
Longevity: 16 years, 4 months.

Food: Large and medium-sized mammals and birds. In New York and Pennsylvania, Red Squirrels and American Crows important food items; other species taken in much smaller numbers.

Habitat: Forests (especially large stands of old-growth trees in American West) and extensive woodlands. Coastlines, mountain ridges, and Great Lakes shorelines during migration.

North American
Range: Holarctic; from tree line south to southern Appalachians in East, and Mexico in West. Except for mountains of Arizona and New Mexico, where these hawks breed, usually reaches southeastern and Gulf coast states only during periodic invasions every 10 to 12 years.

Gray Hawk *(Asturina nitida)*

Wingspread: 32 to 38 inches.

Length: 16 to 18 inches.

Field Recognition: A small, rare, local, rather trusting tropical and subtropical soaring hawk; somewhat accipiter-like with a long tail, and similar in flight style. Represented in North America by subspecies *A. n. plagiatus. Adult (male)*—Ashy gray above, whitish below with dark gray barring. Tail coverts white, tail black with white tip and 2 or 3 bold white bands suggesting that of Broad-winged Hawk. Dark tip on outer primaries. Eyes dark brown; bill bluish-black; cere, legs, and feet yellowish-orange. *Adult (female)*— Darker gray above than in adult male; fine barring on undersides including leg feathers. *Juvenile*—Dark brown above, with bold, light superciliary line, white cheeks, buffy below with dark brown streaks on throat and upper breast, and belly spotted. Rump white. Tail long and brown with numerous dark bands and narrow white tip; longer than in adult birds. Bill large. Cere and legs also less vivid than in adults. *Chick*—Covered with white natal down with gray tinge on back.

Flight Style: Fast, similar to accipiters with several quick flaps followed by a glide; sometimes soars at low altitudes.

Voice: An unusually vocal southwestern raptor. Loud, high-pitched *cree-ee-ee* or *cree-eer* somewhat similar to that of Broad-winged Hawk; voice also resembles peacock.

Nest: Crow-nest-sized twig or stick structure, lined with green vegetation, placed high in tree or mesquite but hidden by leaves.

Eggs: 2 (occasionally 1 to 3 or 4), white or pale blue, generally unmarked, but sometimes slightly spotted. Incubation period 32 to 34 days.

Maximum Reported Longevity: Information unavailable.

Food: Mostly lizards, but sometimes small birds, rodents, and insects.

Habitat: Riverine forests and groves in semi-arid regions with numerous cottonwood trees adjacent to areas with giant mesquite; also occasionally nests in yards of some rural homes near Nogales and Patagonia, Arizona. Sometimes seen in the Patagonia–Sonoita Creek Preserve and San Pedro National Conservation Area in Arizona, and Big Bend National Park in southern Texas.

North American Range: Small, local, fragmented populations in southern and southwestern Texas, as well as southeastern Arizona; also casual in southern New Mexico. Extralimital record from Kansas.

Common Black-Hawk *(Buteogallus anthracinus)*

Wingspread: 40 to 48 inches.

Length: 20 to 23 inches.

Field Recognition: Large, black, unusually wide-winged hawk of American Southwest. Usually spends much time perched and concealed amid vegetation. Subspecies *B. a. anthracinus* occurs in North America. *Adult (sexes similar)*—Sooty black (tinged with brown in worn plumage); tail appears short with broad white band in middle and narrow white tip. In flight wings unusually wide with light base-of-primaries area on underside of each wing. Eyes brown. Bill black with some yellow at base. Cere, long legs, and feet yellow. *Juvenile (sexes similar)*—Brownish-black above with streaks of rufous, buffy, and white. Underparts whitish to buffy-orange; strongly streaked with black on breast. Black tail has white bands and white tip. Eyes brown. Cere and legs yellow. *Chick*—Covered with white natal down on head and breast, grayish elsewhere.

Flight Style: Powerful and swift; occasionally soars and glides like buteo with wings held flat. Tail also fanned when soaring. Legs sometimes dangle while bird is in flight.

Voice: High-pitched, weak *quee-quee-quee*.

Nest: Stick nest, lined with smaller twigs and green vegetation, placed in trees from 15 to 100 feet above ground. Nest sometimes used for several years in succession.

Eggs: 1 (occasionally 2 or 3), grayish-white slightly spotted with dull brown. Incubation period 37 to 39 days.

**Maximum Reported
Longevity:** 13 years, 6 months.

Food: Crabs, fish, frogs, snakes, insects, rodents, and rarely birds.

Habitat: Riverine woodland (in North American portion of range). Elsewhere in its range prefers coastal lowlands with mixed savanna or grassland, dunes, lagoons, and ponds.

**North American
Range:** Mexico–U.S. border from Arizona to Texas (locally north to Utah). Extralimital records from California, Florida, Minnesota, and Nevada.

Harris's Hawk *(Parabuteo unicinctus)*

Wingspread: 40 to 45 inches.

Length: 17.5 to 24 inches.

Field Recognition: Unusually tame, social hawk of Southwest sometimes perched in pairs on cactus, mesquite, tree, or other object. Sometimes up to a dozen engage in cooperative hunting during winter. *Adult (sexes similar)*—Typical individual of subspecies *P. u. harrisi*, of southern Texas southward, sooty with chestnut shoulders, thighs, and underwing coverts.

Harris's Hawk in Arizona. Photo by Willis Peterson/U.S. Fish and Wildlife Service.

Rump and undertail coverts white. Tail sooty with tip and basal half white. *P. u. superior,* of southeastern California and southwestern Arizona, slightly larger and darker than *harrisi.* Tends to perch conspicuously. Eyes brown; bill gray with black tip; cere, legs, and feet yellow. *Juvenile (sexes similar)*—Brownish above, light below with buffy streaking, and tail banded. *Chick*—Covered with buffy natal down that changes in about a week to a rich brown roughly the color of an adult's shoulder. Some authors state that the dark plumage fades rapidly to pure white.

Flight Style: Generally rapid, direct flight when disturbed. Occasionally soars in wide circles high overhead.

Voice: Loud *iirr* when alarmed; several other calls given during nesting cycle.

Nest: Stick structure, lined with fresh sprigs of vegetation, placed in tree, high shrub, or Saguaro cactus.

Eggs: 3 or 4 (sometimes 1 to 5), unmarked white. Sometimes second clutch deposited in same nest or one nearby after first nesting effort of season completed. Incubation period 31 to 36 days.

Maximum Reported Longevity: 14 years, 11 months.

Food: Rabbits, small mammals, birds, lizards, and insects. Apparently snakes are not taken, or rarely even when abundant.

Habitat: Chaparral, Sonoran Desert, riverine wooded areas, and savanna country; golf courses in Tucson, Arizona.

North American Range: In United States confined to Mexican border from southeastern California (occasionally) and southeastern Arizona to southwestern Texas. Extralimital records (some escaped from falconers) from Colorado, Florida, Iowa, Kansas, Louisiana, Missouri, Nevada, New Jersey, New York, Ohio, Oklahoma, and Utah.

Red-shouldered Hawk *(Buteo lineatus)*

Wingspread: 32 to 50 inches.

Length: 17 to 24 inches.

Field Recognition: Moderate-sized soaring hawk with richly colored rufous underside plumage in adults and distinctive. "window" near tip of primaries. *Adult (both sexes)*—The most widely distributed eastern subspecies, *B. l. lineatus,* is blackish-brown on upperparts with reddish shoulder patches on the uppersides of the wings, crescent-shaped "windows" (areas of translucence) in the primaries when seen in flight (especially when backlighted), richly colored reddish or rufous underparts, and a vividly banded black-and-white tail. Eyes brown. Cere, legs, and feet yellow. *B. l. alleni,* of Florida (except extreme southern part) and westward along Gulf coast to eastern Texas, somewhat smaller and paler than *lineatus*. *B. l. extimus*, of extreme southern Florida and Keys, even smaller than *alleni* and noticeably paler to field observers than *lineatus*. *B. l. texanus*, of south-central Texas coast south to Mexico City, somewhat smaller than eastern *lineatus* and more rufous. Isolated lowland riverine valley subspecies *B. l. elegans*, of southern Oregon south to northern Baja California, even more rufous than *texanus* on undersides but less rufous on back. *Juvenile (both sexes)*—Brown above with white eyebrow line similar to that of juvenile Northern Goshawk (with which these birds are sometimes confused), white on underparts with heavy brown streaks, tinge of rufous on shoulders, and translucent "windows" (especially when backlighted) on wings when seen in flight. *Chick*—Covered with buffy-white natal down.

Flight Style: Rapid wingbeats often followed by brief sail. More or less suggests accipiter's flight. Occasionally soars in thermals.

Voice: Distinctive *kee-aah* or *kee-oow* scream, with second syllable more prolonged and lower in pitch than first.

Nest: Twig-and-stick platform in large tree (or palmetto in Florida); occasionally abandoned hawk, crow, or squirrel nest is used.

Eggs: 3 (sometimes 2 to 4), whitish blotched with brown, chestnut, and lilac. Incubation period 33 days.

Maximum Reported Longevity: 19 years, 11 months.

Food: Varied; small mammals, snakes, lizards, turtles, frogs, toads, small birds, grasshoppers, crayfish, occasional other items (including suet at bird feeders).

Habitat: Broken wet forest or wooded areas and lowland riverine valleys.

North American Range: Southeastern Canada south to Florida Keys and westward to eastern Texas, Oklahoma, Nebraska, Iowa, central Minnesota, most of Wisconsin, and northern Michigan; isolated from coastal Oregon south to Baja California, central California–Nevada border area, and southeastern California–Arizona border area. Occasional records from Idaho, Montana, Utah, and Washington, and in Canada from Manitoba and Saskatchewan.

Broad-winged Hawk (Buteo platypterus)

Wingspread: 32 to 39 inches.

Length: 13.5 to 19 inches.

Field Recognition: Chunky, crow-sized eastern soaring hawk represented by subspecies *B. p. platypterus* in North America. *Adult (normal morph)*—Brown on upperparts, throat white, chest chestnut, underparts white barred with brown. Tail distinctive with 2 white and 2 black bands. Large light area (cere and small portion of forehead) behind bill suggests headlight when hawk is seen head-on. Eye light reddish-hazel; bill bluish-black; cere, legs, and feet yellow. *Adults (dark morph)*—Completely sooty brown body but tail same as on normal morph. Underside of extended wing distinctive with white or light primaries and secondaries with dark border, and dark brown underwing coverts. Extremely rare. A few dark morph individuals observed migrating southward past Point Diablo near San Francisco, California, and occasionally in midwestern and northeastern United States. *Juvenile (normal morph)*—Brown above, white below with brown streaks. *Juvenile (dark morph)*—Body sooty brown with underside of extended wing similar to adult dark morph, but tail with numerous narrow gray bands rather than 2 white and 2 black bands. *Chick*—Covered with short dusky white natal down.

Flight Style: Wings of gliding birds seen head-on are bowed slightly downward. Frequently forms large flocks or "kettles" in thermals during migration, then glides to new thermals and repeats process. Western Swainson's Hawks also use this technique; sometimes species form mixed flocks in Southwest and Central America. During breeding season individual birds sometimes seen soaring in wide circles over eastern forests and wooded areas.

Voice: Shrill, high-pitched *pweeeeee* or *ker-wee-eeee* whistle.

Nest: Twig-and-stick platform, sometimes repaired hawk, crow, or squirrel nest, placed in trees at heights ranging from 3 to 90 feet above ground. Oak and pine chips, as well as green sprigs, line nest.

Eggs: 2 or 3 (rarely 1 to 4 or 5), dull creamy white blotched with brown. Incubation period 28 to 31 days.

Broad-winged Hawk nest and eggs.

Maximum Reported
Longevity: 16 years, 1 month.

Food: Small mammals, snakes, toads, frogs, large insects, occasionally small birds, and other items.

Habitat: Deciduous forests and woodlands. Also mixed forests.

North American
Range: Deciduous and mixed forests from central Alberta eastward across southern Canada to Nova Scotia and southward to Florida and Texas. Some birds stray westward to Great Plains; during autumn very large numbers migrate south across the Detroit, Michigan, area and Hazel Bazemore County Park near Corpus Christi, Texas; rare autumn migrant down Pacific coast.

Short-tailed Hawk (Buteo brachyurus)

Wingspread: 35 to 37 inches.

Length: 14 to 17 inches.

Field Recognition: Small (crow-sized) hawk of Central and South America barely reaching North America. A few hundred individuals of the subspecies *B. b. fuliginosus* occur in Florida. *Adult (light morph)*—Head, back, and primaries dark, contrasting with otherwise white throat and body; small whitish area on lower forehead behind bill. Tail grayish-brown with narrow white tip, broader black band behind tip, and 3 or 4 additional narrow black bands (broken or reduced in older birds). Bill black; eyes brown; cere, legs, and feet yellow. *Adult (dark morph)*—Entirely sooty black to chocolate brown with small whitish area on lower forehead and conspicuous white area on underside of each wing. *Juvenile (normal morph)*—Buffy and similar to immature Broad-winged Hawk. *Juvenile (dark morph)*—Similar to dark morph adult but with more bands on tail. Partly concealed white or buffy body feathers sometimes make undersides appear spotted. *Chick*—Covered with creamy white natal down.

Flight Style: Soars on motionless wings. When hunting, sometimes hangs motionless in midair, then stoops.

Voice: High-pitched scream intermediate between that of Red-shouldered Hawk and Broad-winged Hawk.

Nest: Large stick-and-twig structure, lined with green leaves, placed from 8 to 90 feet above ground in cypress, gum, or magnolia trees, mangroves, or Cabbage Palms.

Eggs: 2 (sometimes 1 or 3), pale bluish-white often blotched with brown. Incubation period approximately 34 to 39 days.

Maximum Reported Longevity: Information unavailable.

Food: Rodents, birds, lizards, and insects.

Habitat: Usually cypress and mangrove swamps, occasionally pine areas and open terrain.

North America Range: There is a small, peninsular Florida population. These birds occur in central and southern part of state (rarely in northern Florida) from late February through early October. From mid-October through early February, the population apparently migrates southward to the extreme southern part of the Florida mainland, with substantial numbers wintering within and close to Everglade National Park, and a few in the Keys. Casual in southern Texas, and extralimital in southeastern Arizona.

Swainson's Hawk *(Buteo swainsoni)*

Wingspread: 47 to 57 inches.

Length: 19 to 22 inches.

Field Recognition: Common soaring hawk of Great Plains and West with notably long, pointed wings. Occurs in light, dark, and rufous color morphs; light morph birds are most common. Intermediate color forms occur between all color morphs. *Adult (light morph)*—Head, back, chest, and primaries dark brown, contrasting with otherwise light to whitish underparts. Tail light with numerous narrow, dark bands and wider, dark subterminal band. Eye brown; bill blackish; cere pale greenish-yellow; legs and feet light yellow. *Adult (dark morph)*—Rare; entirely blackish except for light throat, forehead, undertail coverts, and cloudy or dark buffy wing linings. *Adult (rufous morph)*—Somewhat like dark morph but lighter brown on underparts with rusty brown blotches and bars. *Juvenile*—Dark brown above, light rufous below with brown chest and much brown streaking. Birds also have whitish eyebrow line. *Chick*—Covered with white natal down.

Flight Style: Forms large flocks or "kettles" (sometimes mixed with Broad-winged Hawks) during migration. Soars with wings held in slight V or dihedral; also hovers in strong winds.

Voice: Long, shrill *kreeeeeer* whistle.

Nest: Large twig, grass, and weed structure lined with bark, green leaves, down, and other materials, placed in giant cactus, low tree, cliff, rocky pinnacle, or on ground.

Eggs: 2 (rarely 1 to 3 or 4), white with pale brown markings. Incubation period 34 to 35 days.

Maximum Reported Longevity: 19 years, 7 months.

Food: Insects (especially orthoptera), rodents, bats, reptiles, amphibians, and some birds (injured or young).

Habitat: Mixed deciduous-coniferous parklands, rangeland and foothills, grassland, and plains. During migration hawks sometimes occur over high meadows and mountain ridges in Rockies.

North American Range: Great Plains and West from interior Alaska south to northern Mexico; does not occur along coastal plain of Pacific coast. A few individuals regularly seen in East and Midwest during spring and autumn migrations. Extralimital records from Indiana, Maryland, Massachusetts, Michigan, New York, North Carolina, Pennsylvania, and Virginia, and in Canada from Nova Scotia, Ontario, and Quebec. Winters in pampas of Argentina; however, a few immature Swainson's Hawks winter in southern Florida.

White-tailed Hawk *(Buteo albicaudatus)*

Wingspread: 48 to 54 inches.

Length: 20 inches.

Field Recognition: Large, stocky, tropical and subtropical hawk with long, somewhat pointed wings. Represented in North America by subspecies *B. a. hypospodius*. *Adult (male)*—Slaty gray above, undersides and rump white, wings slaty gray with rufous shoulders and white underwing linings; dark wing tips, tail white with fairly wide blackish subterminal band and very narrow white tip. Eyes brown; cere pale yellow-green; bill black; legs and feet yellow. *Adult (female)*—Somewhat darker than male, with more rufous on wings. *Juvenile*—Brownish-black, white upper breast, somewhat lighter on undersides of primaries, tail light (darker in Swainson's Hawks) with white uppertail coverts. Outstretched wings of juveniles notably thinner than those of adults, with long and pale bar on underside wing coverts, and wing tips extending beyond tail on perched birds. Juveniles variable in coloration ranging from completely dark (with light tail) to somewhat similar to juvenile Red-tailed Hawks. *Chick*—Covered with buffy natal down washed with smoky brown on head and wings; blackish around each eye. Appearance distinctively different from chicks of other hawks.

Flight Style: Uses slow, continuous wingbeats, and also soars high over-head with noticeable dihedral or, at other times, low over ground; also hovers and kites while hunting. Sometimes attracted to fires.

Voice: High-pitched, tinkling, *ke-ke-ke-ke* cackle.

Nest: Large twig nest mixed with dry grass, lined with green mesquite sprigs or similar material, placed 5 to 15 feet above ground in small tree or bushes.

Eggs: 2 (sometimes 1 to 3 or 4), white; sometimes spotted with lavender or brown. Incubation period 29 to 32 days.

Maximum Reported Longevity: Information unavailable.

Food: Rabbits, rodents, birds (rarely), snakes, lizards, frogs, vari-ous insects, and occasionally carrion.

Habitat: Coastal prairie (in Texas), chaparral, and open grassy range.

North American Range: Casual in coastal Texas, and juveniles in southwestern Louisiana; a few records from Arizona and New Mexico.

Zone-tailed Hawk *(Buteo albonotatus)*

Wingspread: 47 to 53 inches.

Length: 18.5 to 21.5 inches.

Field Recognition: Slender, solitary, grayish-black (black at distance) hawk of American Southwest sometimes confused with Turkey Vulture. *Adult (sexes similar)*—Grayish-black with under-sides of wings two-toned (similar to Turkey Vulture); dark tail offset by 3 bands and narrow white tip (no bands on Turkey Vulture tail). Small whitish-gray area on forehead behind cere. Eyes brown; bill horn-colored at base and black at tip; cere, mouth corners, legs, and feet yellow. *Juvenile*—Similar to adult but black with varying numbers of white spots scattered on underside; tail marked with numerous bands (absent in Turkey Vulture). *Chick*—Cov-ered with grayish natal down.

Flight Style: Similar to Turkey Vulture (with which it is often com-pared and occasionally associates in flight), with notable dihedral when soaring and rocking, but sluggish compared with vultures. Aggressive when defending nests, sometimes striking human intruders.

Voice: Feeble squealing whistle similar to Red-tailed Hawk's.

Nest: Bulky stick platform with green leaves placed 25 to 100 feet above ground in pine, cottonwood, or mesquite (rarely).

Eggs: 2 (rarely 1 or 3), bluish-white or white, occasionally slightly spotted. Incubation period 28 to 34 days.

Maximum Reported Longevity: Information unavailable.

Food: Lizards, frogs, small fish, and sometimes small mammals and birds.

Habitat: Mountains with coniferous woodland, dry country, canyons in mountains, and hilly riparian areas with cottonwood and sycamore trees.

North American Range: Southwestern border of United States on middle slopes of coniferous mountains, and upland riparian habitat in Arizona, New Mexico, and southwestern and southern Texas; locally in southern California. Extralimital records from Louisiana and Nevada, and in Canada from Nova Scotia.

Red-tailed Hawk *(Buteo jamaicensis)*

Wingspread: 46 to 58 inches.

Length: 19 to 25.5 inches.

Field Recognition: Widespread, common soaring hawk with broad wings and tail. Extremely variable in color—especially in western North American subspecies. Pure or partial albinos, and very dark brown (black at distance) individuals, sometimes seen among various subspecies. *Adult*—Typical individual of eastern subspecies *B. j. borealis*, which ranges westward to Great Plains, brown above and white below with vivid, reddish-chestnut tail (lighter on underside) and conspicuous belly band of dark streaks. In some birds belly band very faint or lacking entirely. Seen head-on, light cere at base of bill and light wrist area on leading edge of each wing frequently produce "headlights," visible at great distance in some birds. Western subspecies differ considerably from eastern race. *B. j. calurus*, of much of West, often resembles *borealis*, but light morph has rufous wash on underside; most individuals, even very dark or black ones, recognized by darker belly and upper breast, enclosing paler area on midbreast. *B. j. harlani*, breeding in Alberta, British Columbia, and Alaska, occurs in dark (often black) color morph with body black or dark sooty, wing lining black flecked with white, wing tips dark, primaries and secondaries light on underside edged with dark border, and tail grayish with dusky (not red) mottling, blending into broad, dark subterminal band. Rarer light (sometimes almost white) color morph also occurs in which body is white with narrow, dark belly band and tail similar to that of dark morph birds; some *harlani* show mixture of characteristics of both color morphs. *B. j. alascensis*, of southeastern Alaska south to Queen Charlotte Islands, resembles eastern *borealis* but is smaller. *B. j. kriderii*, of Great Plains, pale with tail much paler red than in eastern race. *B. j. fuertesi*, of southern Texas, New Mexico, and parts of adjacent Mexico, usually darker on upperside but pale and white below with little or no belly band compared with eastern race. *B. j. umbrinus*, of Florida peninsula and Bahamas, similar to eastern *borealis* but has dark bars near shafts of rectrices and is smaller. *Juvenile*— Similar to adult, but tail grayish-brown (in typical eastern bird) with narrow blackish bars instead of rich reddish-chestnut as in adult. Enormous variation in western birds. *Chick*—Covered with grayish or buffy-white natal down, later changing to woolly white down.

Flight Style: Frequently soars on partly folded wings on updrafts along mountains and bluffs; sometimes uses a quick wingbeat then glides, but also sometimes uses slow, deep wingbeats. Tail not spread. At other times soars in thermals in wide circles with wings and tail spread completely. While hunting, may hover briefly or hang motionless in midair.

Voice: Hoarse, rasping *tsee-eeee-arrr* scream lasting 2 or 3 seconds.

Nest: Large twig-and-stick platform, lined with bark, cornstalks, and similar material, placed in trees, cacti, towers, ledges, rock pinnacles, and similar places.

Eggs: 2 or 3 (rarely 1 to 4 or 5), whitish to bluish-white blotched with brown. Incubation period 28 to 35 days.

Red-tailed Hawk hanging in midair while hunting. Photo by Fred Tilly.

Maximum Reported
Longevity: 28 years, 10 months.

Food: Varied; rodents, rabbits, snakes (including rattlesnakes), lizards, birds (especially pheasants), and occasionally other items.

Habitat: Mountains, woodland, deserts, fields, agricultural areas, other open country, and recently urban parks and buildings on which nests are constructed.

North American
Range: Tree line of North America south to Mexican border. Occasional in Bermuda.

Ferruginous Hawk *(Buteo regalis)*

Wingspread:	56 inches.
Length:	22.5 to 25 inches.
Field Recognition:	The largest and most reclusive of the North American buteos or soaring hawks; occasionally perches on ground. Two color morphs. *Adult (light morph)*—Brown to rufous or rusty above streaked with white, rufous on back and shoulders, and dark wing tips. White below with some narrow dark streaks on chest and belly. Rufous thighs, marked with black bars, form conspicuous V on underside when bird observed overhead in flight. Tail whitish washed with ash. Legs feathered to toes (in all ages and color morphs). Eyes pale yellow; cere and gape bright yellow; bill dark horn; legs and feet yellow. *Adult (dark morph)*—Entirely dark brown except for wings and tail, which resemble light morph birds. *Juvenile*—Dark brown or rufous on upperparts and white below (including thighs on light morph), with some darker flecks. Rump white. Tail grayish, occasionally with several faint dusky bars. Dark morph juveniles dark above and dark rufous below. *Chick*—Covered with white natal down, washed with gray on crown and back. Later thicker white down develops.
Flight Style:	Heavy, sluggish, eagle-like wingbeats, but soars well with dihedral when aloft. Sometimes zigzags low over ground similar to Northern Harrier. Occasionally hovers.
Voice:	Loud *kree-a* or harshly uttered gull-like *kaah kaah.*
Nest:	Large stick structure lined with sagebrush roots, bones, horse or cow dung, placed amid hillside boulders or rock outcroppings, in bush, in small trees, or on windmills, utility line towers, or abandoned farmhouses in remote areas away from human activity and presence.
Eggs:	3 or 4 (1 to 8), bluish-white blotched with brown. Incubation period 32 to 33 days.
Maximum Reported Longevity:	17 years, 11 months.
Food:	Ground squirrels, Prairie Dogs, rabbits, mice, birds (occasionally), snakes, and insects.

Habitat: Open prairie and (in winter) mixed pineries and grassy glades.

North American Range: Breeds from eastern Washington and southern Alberta, Saskatchewan, and Manitoba southward to eastern Oregon, Nevada, New Mexico, Texas, and Oklahoma. Winters from southwestern United States southward to northern Mexico (including Baja California). Extralimital or casual records from Alabama, Arkansas, Florida, Illinois, Indiana, Louisiana, Michigan, Mississippi, Missouri, Virginia, Wisconsin, and in Canada from Ontario.

Rough-legged Hawk *(Buteo lagopus)*

Wingspread: 48 to 56 inches.

Length: 19 to 24 inches.

Field Recognition: A large soaring hawk represented in North America by the subspecies *B. l. sanctijohannis.* Rough-legs are extremely variable in color, forming gradations between light-colored birds and completely melanistic individuals (*Condor*, 1955, 57: 313–346). For field identification purposes, however, light and dark morphs are recognized. Sex of some adults recognized by differences in pattern of bands on tail. Likewise, juveniles distinguished from adults by pattern of band on tail; sex apparently impossible to determine. See illustration. Wings and tail on all individuals slightly longer than on other buteos. *Adult (light morph)*—Tawny on head and chest, with considerable variation in amount of black on belly. Distinctive black wrist patch on upper- and underside of each wing; usually trailing edge of wings' underside boldly lined with black. Broad black band, separated into lighter and darker segments, near tip of white tail in females; band variable in extent and pattern. Males tend to have 1 broad band and 2 to 4 clear-cut narrower black bands near tip of white tail. Tail band pattern also variable. Legs feathered to toes (in birds of all ages and color morphs). Eyes brown to yellow. Cere yellow. Bill dark horn. Legs and feet yellow. *Adult (dark morph)*—Black with much white on undersides of wings. Intermediates also occur between these two

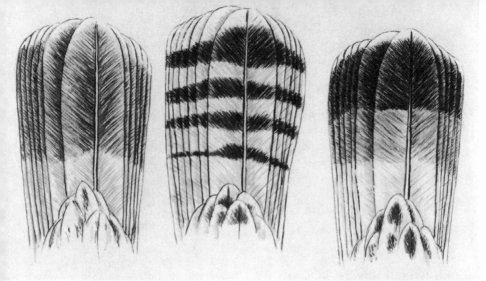

Tail patterns of Rough-legged Hawks. Juvenile (left), adult (center), and adult female (right). Drawings by Rod Arbogast.

color morphs. *Juvenile*—Similar to adults, but usually paler on upperside and underside. Sometimes underside snow white except for black or dark belly band (which can cover entire belly), black wrist patch on underside of each wing, and black wing tips. In some juveniles black trailing edge of underside of wings is much less prominent or extensive than in adults, or lacking almost entirely. Broad, dark subterminal tail band also less defined than in adult males, but suggests tail band pattern of some adult females unless seen clearly. *Chick*—Covered with pale grayish-brown natal down, later replaced with darker, thicker gray down.

Flight Style: Soars on updrafts with dihedral visible; also uses some flapping and more wrist action than in other buteos. Frequently hovers when hunting, sometimes with legs extended downward.

Voice: Loud *kle-kle-kle-kle-ree-hee* screech.

Nest: Stick nest lined with green vegetation and placed on rocky ledge or available tree.

Eggs: 3 or 4 (sometimes 1 to 7), white blotched with brown. Incubation period 31 days.

Maximum Reported Longevity: 17 years, 9 months.

Food: Small mammals (especially lemmings on Arctic nesting grounds) and small birds. *Microtus* voles replace lemmings in hawk's diet on winter range. Carrion also sometimes consumed during winter.

Habitat: Arctic tundra and coastlines in summer. Marshes, coastal dunes, open fields, farmland, prairies, and open expanses at airports in winter.

North American Range: Holarctic; breeds between latitudes 61 degrees and 76 degrees north, and winters southward through southern three-quarters of contiguous United States (for subspecies *B. l. sanctijohannis*). Casual or extralimital records from central and western Aleutians, South Carolina, and in Canada from St. Lawrence Island; also Bermuda.

Rough-legged Hawk nest and nestlings. Photo by Fred Tilly.

Golden Eagle *(Aquila chrysaetos)*

Wingspread: 75 to 94 inches.

Length: 30 to 41 inches.

Field Recognition: A large, brown (black at a distance) eagle with legs feathered to the toes in birds of all ages. Golden Eagles most abundant in American West. Subspecies *A. c. canadensis* occurs in North America. Eagles variable in plumage; not all individuals conform exactly to age-class descriptions provided here, based on studies of Jollie (*Auk*, 1947, 64: 549–576) and Spofford (*The Golden Eagle in the Trans-Pecos and Edwards Plateau of Texas*, 1964: 45–46); see also Smith (*HMANA Hawk Migration Studies*, 2002, 27 [2]: 30–31). Usually they are applicable. *Adult (fifth year or older)*—Large brown bird (lighter than immatures and juveniles but often black at distance or in poor light); patchy appearance formed by irregular dark and lighter brown feathers. Under favorable circumstances, and at close range, golden coloration of nape is seen. In some adults old, worn feathers on upperside of wings may produce white area near back; leading edge of each wing may also be whitish. Base of tail may show traces of white until bird is 7 years old. Eyes hazel. Bill black. Cere and feet yellow. *Immature (second to fourth year)*—Dark brown with large, conspicuous white patch on underside of each wing but often without white patch on upperside of each wing after second year. Broad white basal tail band covers about half length of tail. Youngest birds show most white on wings and tail. *Juvenile (first year)*—Similar to immatures but very dark chocolate brown or even blackish with somewhat larger white patch on underside and upperside of each wing; broad white basal tail band covers two-thirds (or more) length of tail, and black terminal band narrower than in immature. *Chick*—Covered with white or pale gray natal down; second down thicker and white.

Flight Style: Soars on updrafts on broad wings with slight dihedral. Occasional wingbeats powerful and labored. In dives sometimes exceeds speed of stooping Peregrine Falcons.

Voice: Yelping *kya* or *weeo-hyo-hyo-hyo* bark.

Golden Eagle. Photo by Karl Maslowski/U.S. Fish and Wildlife Service.

Nest: Large, sometimes made of massive branches and sticks, lined with sprigs of vegetation, placed in trees or on cliffs, ledges, or crags. New nests on ledges may be mere scrapes but after some years of use become impressive structures.

Eggs: 2 (sometimes 1 to 4), dull white blotched with brown. Incubation period 41 to 45 days.

Maximum Reported Longevity: 23 years, 10 months.

Food: Mammals (sometimes including large mammals such as deer and antelopes), carrion (wild or domestic animals during winter), occasionally birds, snakes, lizards, turtles, and fish.

Habitat: Mountains, canyons, cliffs and rocky outcrops, foothills, deserts, farmland, and coastal areas.

North American Range: Holarctic. In North America ranges south to Mexico in the American West; in East, south through northern half of continental United States. There is a small Appalachian and Canadian breeding population in eastern North America. Birds from this population are seen at eastern hawk migration watch sites during autumn. During winter, sometimes ranges south to Florida Keys.

Caracaras and Falcons
Family Falconidae

Caracaras, although classified in the same family as falcons, are rather terrestrial birds and are more vulture-like than falcon-like in habits. Falcons are long-winged raptors with pointed wing tips and long tails. They are streamlined birds with direct and swift flight.

Crested Caracara (Caracara cheriway)

Wingspread: 48 inches.

Length: 20 to 25 inches.

Field Recognition: Long-legged scavenger of open scrublands and prairies. *Adult (sexes similar)*—In subspecies *C. c. auduboni* of

North America, face red, crown and short crest black, wings and upperparts dark brown, sides of head and throat white, underparts whitish with dark brown bars, belly brownish-black, and tail long and white with wide dark terminal band. Large light patch appears on each wing near somewhat blunt tip when bird is in flight. Eyes brown. Bill whitish but bluish at base. Long legs and feet yellow. Sometimes associates with vultures. *Juvenile (sexes similar)*—Similar to adult but generally browner and dingier in appearance with streaks on lower breast (rather than bars as in adults) and some light spots on upperwing coverts. *Chick*—Covered with pinkish-buff natal down, considerably darker on crown and back.

Flight Style: Resembles raven's flight; irregular or zigzagging but with rapid wingbeats alternating with gliding. Appearance swift and graceful. Soars on flat wings.

Voice: Harsh *trak-trak-trak-trak* cackle.

Nest: Crude structure of sticks placed in dense branches of trees, palm fronds, or cacti.

Eggs: 2 or 3 (1 to 4), pinkish-white to white vividly covered with reddish-brown markings. Incubation period 30 to 33 days. May rarely deposit second clutch in same season.

Maximum Reported Longevity: 26 years, 2 months.

Food: Carrion and live prey of various sorts, including small mammals, birds, reptiles (especially horned lizards), amphibians, insects, worms, and other prey. Vegetable matter also eaten occasionally.

Habitat: Open scrubland, prairies, and pastures.

North American Range: Central Florida, southern Arizona, and central and southern Texas. Extralimital records from California, Louisiana, Mississippi, New Jersey, New Mexico, New York, Oregon, Pennsylvania, Washington, Wyoming, and in Canada from Ontario.

American Kestrel *(Falco sparverius)*

Wingspread:	20 to 24.5 inches.
Length:	8.75 to 12 inches.

Field Recognition: Our smallest and most colorful falcon (about the size of an American Robin); strongly sexually dimorphic in coloration. *Adult (male)*—Typical individual of widely distributed North American subspecies *F. s. sparverius* has rusty back, 2 "sideburns" or "whiskers" on each side of head, and fairly large black patch or "false eye" on each side of nape; top of head grayish with chestnut cap, cheeks and throat white, wings bluish-gray on upperside with row of white spots along back edge, underparts whitish or buffy white with black spots. Tail chestnut with broad black subterminal band and narrow white tip. Individuals of subspecies *F. s. paulus*, of South Carolina south to Florida and southern Alabama, somewhat smaller than *sparverius* with fewer spots below. Eyes dark brown; cere, orbit, legs, and feet yellow. *Adult (female)*—Similar to adult male but wings brownish, back duller chestnut, underparts streaked with dark brown (not spotted). Tail duller chestnut with numerous narrow, black bands. *Juvenile (male)*—Difficult to distinguish in field from adult males, but usually tip of tail brownish (rather than white); more black barring on back in region of shoulders, and considerable longitudinal black streaking on upper breast or chest, tending to widen into broad spots along flanks. *Juvenile (female)*—Extremely difficult to distinguish from adult female in field unless bird is in hand and examined critically. Usually, however, brown and gray areas on crown or top of head less defined than in adult females (although some adults show this characteristic). Black subterminal band on tail not well defined or unusually wide (use caution when applying field mark because tips of many migrating American Kestrels broken or damaged). *Chick*—Covered with snow-white, fluffy natal down followed by thicker, dirty-white second down.

Flight Style: More buoyant and less direct than medium-sized falcons, with occasional periods of gliding or soaring between wingbeats. Frequently hovers or kites when hunting. When stooping, wings sometimes folded into distinctive sickle shape.

American Kestrel eggs in nest box.

Voice: Loud *klee-klee-klee-klee-klee* often repeated rapidly, some *chuck-chuck-chuck* calls, and sometimes other sounds.

Nest: Natural cavities in trees, old woodpecker holes, nest boxes, small openings in barns and other buildings, and similar locations.

Eggs: 4 or 5 (sometimes 1 to 7), white to pinkish-white covered with brownish spots or blotches. Incubation period 28 to 35 days, often 31 days.

Maximum Reported Longevity: 14 years, 8 months.

Food: Small mammals (especially *Microtus* voles), insects, occasionally small birds and other items.

Habitat: Urban and rural areas, deserts, prairies, wooded riverine ecosystems, agricultural areas, and other open areas.

North American Range: North America south of tree line throughout the continent. Extralimital records from northern and southwestern Alaska.

Merlin *(Falco columbarius)*

Wingspread: 23 to 26.5 inches.

Length: 10 to 13.5 inches.

Field Recognition: Small, dark, jay-sized falcon varying by subspecies in the amount of underpart streaking. *Adult (male)*—Typical example of subspecies *F. c. columbarius*, so-called Taiga Merlin of boreal forests, has bluish-gray upperparts but lighter underparts (becoming darker in eastern birds) with some streaking. Tail has several black bands, bordered by narrow white bands, broader black subterminal band, and white tip. *F. c. richardsonii*, so-called Prairie Merlin of northern prairies and aspen woodland, strikingly paler than other Merlin races in North America. *F. c. suckleyi*, so-called Black Merlin of Pacific Northwest (darkest of three North American subspecies), very dark on back (almost black) and underparts. Eyes brown. Cere, orbit, legs, and feet yellow. Bill grayish-black. *Adult (female)*—Brown on upperparts with heavily streaked (varying in subspecies) underparts. Tail brown with 3 or 4 narrow whitish bands. *Juvenile (sexes similar)*—Similar to adult female. *Chick*—Covered with creamy white natal down followed by second light grayish to dark grayish-brown down.

Flight Style: Swift and direct with "rowing" wingbeats. Usually flies low over ground or just above treetops, providing clue to identification during migration.

Voice: Harsh, high-pitched *ki-ki-ki-ki-kee* uttered rapidly; other calls also used.

Nest: Either scrape on ground or old nest of crow placed from 5 to 60 feet above ground.

Eggs: 5 or 6 (sometimes 1 to 8), light buffy, covered with reddish-brown, purplish, and chocolate markings. Incubation period 28 to 32 days.

Maximum Reported Longevity: 11 years, 11 months.

Food: Mostly small birds such as larks, pipits, and finches; occasionally small mammals, snakes, lizards, and other items.

Habitat: Forested areas, shorelines of remote lakes, coasts, river valleys, marshes, and open areas; now breeding in urban areas in parts of Canada. Some Merlins now winter in various urban areas in Canada and the United States.

North America Range: Holarctic. Breeds from north of tree line, and openings in boreal forests, southward to Oregon, Colorado, northern Great Plains states (Minnesota and Wisconsin), northern New York, and northern New England; also some Canadian and Great Lakes urban areas. Winters in much of contiguous United States, but less so in midwestern states, southern New England, and inland parts of Middle Atlantic and northern southern states; expanding during winter into some urban areas. Many winter in Central and South America, and the West Indies.

Aplomado Falcon *(Falco femoralis)*

Wingspread: 40 inches.

Length: 15 to 18 inches.

Field Recognition: Rare, boldly marked medium-sized falcon with an unusually long tail, commonly seen in pairs, represented by subspecies *F. f. septentrionalis* in U.S.–Mexico border area. *Adult (sexes similar)*—Bluish-gray on upperparts, crown darker, head pattern distinctive with bold black line on each side of head and light stripe behind each eye. Throat white; chest nearly white, light gray, tawny, or deep cinnamon, often with evenly scattered streaking. Black cummerbund on belly shows varying numbers of horizontal white bars (sometimes absent, restricted to upper and middle parts of cummerbund, or evenly distributed over entire black band). Thighs cinnamon. Tail black with 5 or 6 white bands and white tip. Eyes dark brown surrounded by yellow orbit. Bill light gray at base but blackish-gray at tip. Cere, legs, and feet yellow. *Juvenile (sexes similar)*—Lead gray on upper parts similar to adults, but upper beast streaked more heavily than in adults. Cummerbund rarely has white bars found on adults. Eyes brown; cere and orbit bluish-gray, but gradually changes to yellow. Legs and feet yellow. *Chick*—Covered with white down.

Flight Style: Flight profile distinctive—long tail and long, narrow wings (much narrower in secondary region than in Peregrine Falcon, Prairie Falcon, or Merlin). Flight swift, graceful, and easy. Sometimes hovers when hunting, but not as easily or as long as American Kestrel. May land on ground (when in pursuit of prey) or on low scrub.

Voice: High-pitched cackling; also *eek* uttered several seconds apart.

Nest: Old nests of other birds such as White-necked Ravens, often in yucca or mesquite.

Eggs: 2 or 3 (rarely 4), pale white or pinkish-white covered with blotches or spots of brown. Incubation period 31 to 32 days.

Maximum Reported Longevity: 12 years (in captivity).

Food: Birds, large insects, small mammals, and lizards.

Habitat: Open plains with mesquite, cactus, and yucca (especially *Yucca elata*).

North American Range: On the U.S.–Mexico (Arizona, New Mexico, and Texas) border. Now rare in United States; formerly more common.

Gyrfalcon *(Falco rusticolus)*

Wingspread: 44 to 52 inches.

Length: 20 to 25 inches.

Field Recognition: Large Arctic falcon, variable in color, with dark, gray, and white color morphs (along with variety of intermediate color forms). Wing tips usually slightly rounded compared with smaller falcons. Gyrfalcons tend to perch on ground rather than elevated perches. *Adult (dark morph)*—Varies from completely dark slaty blue in some birds to pale brownish-gray with much whitish marking on body and numerous tail bands. Eyes brown. Cere, legs, and feet yellow. *Adult (gray morph)*—Intermediate (somewhat lighter in color) between dark morph and white morph birds. Dark above and white below, with dark flecks and spots on underside. *Adult (white morph)*—Spectacular large white falcon with flecks of brownish-gray on upperparts, but white on underside of body. In some birds tail barred;

in others, unbarred. *Juvenile (dark morph)*—Variable, but many birds dark brown on upperparts with various streaks and/or spots, throat whitish, and underparts dark with spots and streaking. Cere, legs, and feet bluish-gray. *Juvenile (gray morph)*—Variable, but typically dark grayish-brown, with pale eyebrow line and darker line extending back from back of eye. Tail brown with numerous pale and darker bands. *Juvenile (white morph)*—Similar to white morph adult but with some streaking on undersides. Cere, legs, and feet bluish-gray. *Chick*—Covered with creamy white natal down.

Flight Style: Slow, gull-like wingbeats as if made entirely by hands, but flight deceptively fast. Often flies close to ground. Sometimes hovers briefly. When soaring, wings usually slightly bowed or held level; occasionally dihedral seen.

Voice: Harsh *kyek-kyek-kyek* or *hyaik-hyiak-hyiak*; also *ke-a-ke-a*, which becomes rattling scream.

Nest: Merely scrapes on ledge or cliff, often in gorge; old nests of Rough-legged Hawks and Common Ravens also used.

Eggs: 4 (sometimes 1 to 7), buffy or pale yellowish-white spotted with dark reds. Incubation 35 to 36 days.

Maximum Reported Longevity: 13 years, 6 months.

Food: Mainly birds such as grouse and ptarmigan, but seabirds and ducks also taken frequently. Small mammals may form more of diet for immature birds during winter.

Habitat: Arctic coasts, mountains, tundra, and river valleys in summer. In winter along mountains, coastal regions, airports, and other open terrain.

North American Range: Arctic portions of North America. Gyrfalcons occasionally wander south into the northern contiguous United States as rare winter visitors. A handful of records indicate these birds occasionally migrate past some eastern hawk migration watch sites during autumn. Casual or extralimital during winter in California, Colorado, Delaware, Illinois, Indiana, Kansas, Missouri, Ohio, Oklahoma, Oregon, Pennsylvania, Tennessee, Utah, and Virginia; also in Bermuda.

Peregrine Falcon *(Falco peregrinus)*

Wingspread:	38 to 46 inches.
Length:	15 to 20 inches.
Field Recognition:	Splendid medium-sized falcon admired universally. *Adult (male)*—Typical individual of widespread North American subspecies *F. p. anatum* is slaty-backed and dark-capped and -cheeked, producing a hooded (or even dark helmet) appearance; creamy underparts offset by dark narrow, horizontal bars. Subspecies *F. p. pealei*, of Pacific Northwest, darker and more boldly marked than *anatum*. Tundra subspecies *F. p. tundrius*, of tundra biome from tree line north to 77 degrees north latitude, smaller and paler on upperparts than other North American subspecies, with white cheeks and one distinctive "sideburn" on each side of head. Uniform barred or spotted pattern on underside of wings when seen in flight. Eyes brown. Orbit and cere bright yellow to yellow-greenish. Bill pale bluish. Legs and feet bright yellow. *Adult (female)*—Considerably larger than adult male, and somewhat darker. *Juvenile*—Brown on upperparts and heavily streaked on underside (rather heavily washed with cinnamon in some females). "Sideburn" distinctive; feathering on thighs streaked vertically rather than barred horizontally, as in adults. Eyes brown. Orbit and cere greenish-yellow. Legs and feet greenish-yellow to bluish-gray. *Chick*—Covered with white natal down; second down longer and woolly.
Flight Style:	Fast with quick "rowing" wingbeats. Soars with wings held flat and tail spread. Stoops (vertical dives) at fantastic speeds.
Voice:	Sharp *hek-hek-hek* repeated rapidly. *Witchew-witchew* in vicinity of eyrie. Some other calls also used.
Nest:	Usually scrape on ledge on cliff, ledge on tall building or bridge in urban environments, or old hawk nest.
Eggs:	3 or 4 (sometimes up to 6), pinkish-white to creamy white with rich brown blotches. Incubation period 33 to 37 days.
Maximum Reported Longevity:	19 years, 3 months.
Food:	Mostly birds of various sizes; rarely a few mammals and other items.

Peregrine Falcon.

Habitat: Cliffs overlooking rivers, open areas, tundra, coastlines, and other high places close to aquatic ecosystems. During migration, appears over marshes, lakes, ponds, and rivers with concentrations of ducks, shorebirds, and other birds; also seen along mountain ridges and Atlantic, Gulf, and Pacific coastlines.

North American Range: Cosmopolitan. In North America from Arctic southward through United States. Many reintroduction programs ongoing in Canada and U.S.

Prairie Falcon *(Falco mexicanus)*

Wingspread: 40 to 42 inches.

Length: 17 to 20 inches.

Field Recognition: Intermediate-sized falcon, similar to but slightly smaller than Peregrine Falcon. *Adult (sexes similar)*—Pale brown above, very light below with darker spots. When passing overhead, *boldly distinctive black axillaries* (feathers on armpits) extend outward from body almost half length of wing. Narrow brownish-black mustache on face. Eyes dark brown. Bill horn-bluish, yellow at base. Cere, orbits (areas around eyes), legs, and feet yellow. *Juvenile (sexes similar)*—Reddish-brown on upperparts, buffy on undersides marked with heavy streaks. *Chick*—Covered with pure white natal down.

Flight Style: Swift, using powerful wingbeats. Occasionally soars. Usually flies at low to moderate elevations. Juvenile birds sometimes hover clumsily, or fly along slowly like harrier, while hunting.

Voice: Shrill *kik-kik-kik-kik-kik* yelp repeated frequently.

Nest: Scrape on ledge with overhang on cliff in foothills or abandoned stick nest of another bird.

Eggs: 4 or 5 (sometimes 1 to 8), pinkish-white to white heavily marked with browns or cinnamon. Incubation period 29 to 39 days.

Maximum Reported Longevity: 17 years, 3 months.

Food: Small and medium-sized mammals (especially ground squirrels) and birds (especially Horned Larks) often captured on ground. Occasionally lizards and insects.

Habitat: Cliffs and canyons in treeless country, deserts, prairies, and plains; tundra on high western mountains.

North American Range: Interior North America from British Columbia, Alberta, Saskatchewan, and western North Dakota south to Baja California, Arizona, New Mexico, and northern Texas. Casual records from Illinois, Kentucky, Michigan, Minnesota, Mississippi, Ohio, Tennessee, and Wisconsin, and in Canada from Manitoba and Ontario. Extralimital records from Alabama, Georgia, Florida, and South Carolina.

Hawk Identification and Study

More than a quarter century ago, when the first edition of this book was published, much was known about the identification of diurnal birds of prey. Today even more is known about the fine points of raptor identification. With the aid of a modern field guide, hawk watchers and ornithologists can identify correctly most raptors they see. However, I can't stress too strongly that it is not always possible to identify every raptor. Occasionally even experts are unable to identify some birds for one reason or another.

When a diurnal raptor is seen, remember that a number of factors determine whether the bird can be identified correctly. The most important considerations include size and shape of the bird, flight style and behavior, distance of the bird from the observer, angle at which the bird is seen, prevailing light conditions, habitat in which the bird is found, range of the bird and the geographic location where it is seen, date and length of time the bird is observed, experience of the observer, and other factors.

Size

Birds of prey exhibit marked sexual dimorphism in respect to size. Usually females are about one-third larger than males. This partly accounts for the range in wingspreads and lengths of some species. Some raptors are also sexually dimorphic in respect to color; others exhibit several strikingly different color morphs.

Shape

Equally important, a hawk's shape can vary tremendously depending on its manner of flight. For example, a Broad-winged Hawk circling in a thermal will spread its wings and tail fully to achieve maximum lift. However, the same bird gliding from a thermal a few minutes later, or soaring on updrafts along a mountain, will not spread its tail and may not extend its wings fully. The result is that the bird will appear deceptively different in

Adult Broad-winged Hawk thermal soaring with wings and tail extended.

Adult Broad-winged Hawk gliding from a thermal.

Kettle of Broad-winged Hawks soaring in a thermal.

each situation and may cause difficulty and confusion among inexperienced hawk watchers. Therefore, always consider the shape of the bird in relation to the type of flight being used when attempting to arrive at an identification.

Flight Style and Behavior

The flight style and behavior exhibited by a hawk are frequently critical in identifying the bird. Many species have distinctive flight or behavior characteristics such as peculiar wingbeats or an unusual manner in which the

An Osprey's long wings held in their distinctive crooked position while using deflective updrafts.

wings are held. For example, accipiters commonly use a distinctive flap-flap-flap-glide pattern, which varies enough among Sharp-shinned Hawks, Cooper's Hawks, and Northern Goshawks to allow experienced hawk watchers generally to identify each species correctly. In comparison, when dozens of migrating Broad-winged Hawks mill aloft within a thermal, this type of migratory behavior provides an excellent aid to the correct identification of these birds in eastern North America—and similarly for identification of Swainson's Hawks in western North America. Mixed flocks of migrating Broad-winged Hawks and Swainson's Hawks are sometimes also seen during autumn along coastal Texas and elsewhere in the West.

However, flight style is only one of a range of characteristics that allow a skilled observer to identify a particular raptor correctly.

Head-on view of an Osprey showing distinctive bowed wings. Photo by Fred Tilly.

Distance from Observer

The distance at which a hawk is observed can be important in determining whether the bird can be identified correctly: It may not be possible to see essential field marks for some species at great distances. For example, if you are watching migrating hawks and see a large, immature accipiter in the distance, the bird could be either a large, immature, female Cooper's Hawk or a small, immature, male Northern Goshawk. It might be impossible to identify the bird if it fails to come close enough to distinguish any conspicuous white eyebrow line. On the other hand, most migrating Ospreys can be identified at great distances because of the distinctive crooked position in which they hold their long wings when soaring on updrafts along mountains and coastlines, or the distinctive bowed position of their wings when seen head-on.

Viewing Angle

The angle at which a hawk is seen can play another important role in determining whether it can be identified. Looking toward the back of a bird as it flies away is the most difficult angle because few, if any, field marks are then visible. Frequently such birds can't be identified correctly. Sometimes head-on or side views can also cause difficulty.

Light Conditions

The prevailing light conditions under which you see a raptor are extremely important. A common species may be easy to identify in good light, but the same species may have to be considered unidentified when seen in poor light. The task is even greater when the light is bad and the bird is seen at a great distance. Caution, therefore, is always in order when looking at hawks in poor light.

Sometimes problems occur when a hawk is observed in bright sunlight. For example, if a buteo is circling overhead and viewed against the sun, it is possible that "windows" (light translucent areas) will be seen in the wings. However, this does not necessarily mean that the bird is a Red-shouldered Hawk (the species generally associated with windows in its wings). Almost any species can show windows when viewed under such conditions. Wait until the bird moves into a more favorable position before identifying it.

Habitat

Except during migration, the habitat in which you see a hawk can be a valuable clue to the bird's identity. During spring and summer, for example, a Northern Goshawk is expected to occur in forests or large tracts of woodland, an Osprey in or close to aquatic ecosystems, and an American Kestrel in farmland or other open areas.

Geographic Range and Location

The geographic range of a species and location where a raptor is seen also offer important clues to a bird's identity. Some species are restricted to specific locations and rarely seen elsewhere. For example, Snail Kites now are confined to parts of central and southern Florida. Yet, much to the delight of birders, raptors sometimes stray from their normal ranges. Thus a Zone-tailed Hawk was photographed in Nova Scotia! Such occurrences are unusual; be very skeptical and careful when attempting to identify a raptor suspected of being outside its normal geographic range. Also keep in mind that some strays are merely birds held in captivity by falconers and have escaped. If jesses (leather straps) are attached to the legs of the bird, this indicates that it has escaped from a falconer.

Date

The date or time of year is another factor to consider when identifying birds of prey. A much larger number of species can be expected to occur in many areas during the spring and autumn migration seasons than during winter or summer.

Length of Observation Period

Although it might seem obvious, the length of time a hawk is observed should also be considered when identifying a bird. The longer you can observe a bird, the greater the possibility that you will identify it correctly. This can be a more important factor in some species than in others. For example, you need only a brief glance at a Swallow-tailed Kite to determine its identity, but considerable study may be necessary to identify some immature hawks or rare color morphs of some individuals.

Experience of Observer

Another important factor in determining whether a hawk can be identified correctly is the field experience of the observer. Inexperienced observers frequently make mistakes that lead to incorrect identification. For example, many novice hawk watchers mistake the white undertail coverts of many hawks for the white rump of Northern Harriers. Similarly, the "windows" that appear in the wings of some hawks lead many observers to identify such birds as Red-shouldered Hawks when they may be other species.

Miscellaneous Factors

A variety of other factors can influence your efforts at identifying hawks. Among them are the availability, type, and magnification of the binoculars being used. Under poor light conditions, for example, an expensive pair of binoculars may enable an observer to clearly identify essential field marks that another person using binoculars of lesser quality may not be able to see. Weather conditions, including rain and snow, fog and mist, haze and air pollution, can be influential, as can the opinions of companions. Thus many factors must be actively or passively considered before you can arrive at the final identification of a hawk. In most instances the process of considering these varied factors requires only a few seconds to complete, and the more experience you have, the faster the process of identifying most diurnal raptors.

Types of Hawk Watching

Watching hawks can be separated into at least three common types of activities: watching hawks migrating during spring or autumn, summer hawk watching, and winter hawk watching. The most popular of these is migration watching, but the others have both increased in popularity in some areas.

Watching Hawks Migrate

Hawk watchers are particularly active during the spring and autumn migration seasons—the times when the greatest variety of species of diurnal birds of prey can be seen with the least amount of effort.

In the East much of this activity is done from well-known raptor concentration lookouts or watch sites. And in the West, where fewer watch sites have been discovered, hawk watchers and birders use such sites and often drive along roads looking for birds of prey perched on utility poles, wires, trees, tall shrubs, cacti, and other elevated objects.

In the Southwest and probably elsewhere in the western states, raptors tend to concentrate in agricultural areas or on range with good grass, but avoid overgrazed areas of Creosote Bush and rabbitbrush. Thus observers can concentrate their raptor viewing efforts on productive areas and bypass poor ones. As new hawk migration watch sites are discovered in the West, however, they doubtless will become special gathering places for hawk watchers.

Summer Hawk Watching

Summer hawk watching is entirely different from watching hawks migrating in spring or autumn. Since most summer activities focus on nesting birds, few people spend much time watching hawks during this season. Watching nesting hawks is a sensitive activity—there is danger of causing damage to, or loss of, nesting efforts. Unless you are engaged in ornithological research, raptor nests should not be visited or disturbed. On the other hand, after raptor nesting activities are completed, hawk watchers sometimes have opportunities to observe recently fledged birds of prey as they disperse from their natal locales. These birds provide opportunities to observe and study juvenal plumages that are strikingly different from adult plumage for most raptor species.

However, other areas can sometimes be used for summer raptor viewing without disturbing the birds. For example, raptors can be observed in the Snake River Birds of Prey National Conservation Area in Idaho. Similarly, Ospreys can be seen along parts of coastal New Jersey and the Chesapeake Bay area of Maryland—including some birds with nests on distant support structures.

Winter Hawk Watching

Watching hawks during winter is rapidly gaining in popularity. It can in turn be separated into two types of activities: roadside raptor viewing and visiting raptor conservation areas.

Roadside raptor viewing is easily enjoyed by driving along rural and other lightly traveled roads looking for birds of prey perched on trees, utility poles and wires, or other elevated objects. American Kestrels can also be seen hunting grassy areas at intersections of interstate or other highways; some buteos hunt along the sides of such highways or in open, adjacent fields.

Visiting raptor concentration areas in winter can be more rewarding especially where large numbers of Bald Eagles gather to feed in open pools of water below dams and locks on rivers such as the upper Mississippi and other locations. *Since Bald Eagles are very sensitive to human disturbance at most winter concentration areas, they should never be approached closely*. In locations such as Lake Barkley State Resort Park and the Land Between the Lakes Recreation Area in Kentucky, and Reelfoot Lake State Park in Tennessee, where formal eagle watching programs are operated in winter, regulations assure that the birds will not be disturbed by the numerous visitors who come each year to watch them. But at eagle concentration areas where formal viewing programs do not exist, and where regulations do not prevent people from approaching the birds too closely, we have an obligation and responsibility to remain at least 0.25 mile away from these birds.

Field Equipment

Selection of the correct field equipment is essential for successful and enjoyable hawk watching. The items mentioned here are especially useful to birders interested in recreational hawk watching; those engaged in serious field studies of diurnal birds of prey will find additional types of equipment necessary.

Binoculars

Good binoculars are necessary for hawk watching, and birders use a wide assortment of brands and types. For recreational hawk watching, 7 x 35, 7 x 50, or 8 x 40 birding binoculars are adequate. But if more detailed field studies are planned as part of a research project, many experienced hawk watchers prefer 10X binoculars because they frequently permit more rapid and accurate hawk identification under unfavorable viewing conditions.

Binoculars are essential hawk watching equipment.

Telescopes

It is useful to have a telescope available at hawk migration watch sites, as well as at raptor wintering areas, to identify birds seen at a distance or under dim light conditions. An instrument equipped with a 20X eyepiece is adequate, although higher magnification is occasionally helpful. If few people are present on a watch site, the telescope can be mounted on a tripod for support. However, many experienced observers prefer to mount their telescopes on gunstocks or shoulder supports if they intend to visit the more popular watch sites, because such mounting makes a scope more maneuverable.

Decoys

Many hawk watchers place a papier-mâché Great Horned Owl on a long pole in an upright position at the watch sites they visit. Some species of raptors such as Sharp-shinned Hawks, Cooper's Hawks, and Northern Goshawks are attracted to decoys and dart within a few feet of both decoys and observers. These can be among the most memorable of hawk watching experiences.

Northern Goshawk attacking an owl decoy. Photo by Fred Tilly.

Cameras and Video Cameras

Many hawk watchers also enjoy taking photographs, or videos, of migrating hawks or raptors seen during other seasons of the year. For conventional photographs, I recommend using a 35mm single-lens reflex camera equipped with a 400mm or 500mm telephoto lens. Some digital cameras also accept these long telephoto lenses; the same lenses might be usable on both digital and photographic cameras if you carefully select brands and models.

When using video cameras or digital camcorders, I recommend a model with built-in image stabilization and a lens that provides a minimum of 10X *optical* magnification (the higher the optical magnification, the better).

Field Clothing

Weather conditions at hawk migration watch sites are extremely variable, and they dictate the type of field clothing that is suitable. For example, air temperatures soar into the nineties during August and September at some of the watch sites, but below-freezing readings are not uncommon at the same spots during November and early December. Therefore, it is important to dress correctly.

Whenever in doubt, carry an extra jacket or sweater with you on visits to the more northern watch sites. A cap for protection from the sun or a hood during the colder part of the season is also recommended. Normal hiking boots or shoes with rubber soles are ideal. Gloves, too, are necessary during cold weather. Some hawk watchers also put a raincoat or poncho into their packs.

Other Equipment

A backpack, knapsack, or day pack or bag is useful when visiting a watch site because lunches, thermoses, field guides, cameras, hand tally counters, thermometers, and other items can be carried easily while allowing free use of the hands. Some hawk watchers also use a walking stick when climbing to remote mountain sites. A pillow or cushion is useful to sit on, because many mountain watch sites are covered with rocks or boulders. A folding aluminum beach chair can be taken to watch sites that are easily reached by vehicle—folding chairs are not recommended for remote areas, because it's difficult carrying them, and crowds of people often gather at some of these spots.

It is helpful to carry and use a copy of the pocket-sized *All-Weather Hawk Watcher's Field Journal*, designed with a raptor checklist and formatted especially for writing down raptor sightings and GPS receiver determination of a watch site's exact geographic location. In some parks and many national wildlife refuges, checklists are also available. Special field data forms, such as those distributed by the Hawk Migration Association of North America, are also used in research projects. Lunch and a beverage must be taken to most watch sites, since it is generally impossible to buy food or beverages there. Of course, all waste paper, beverage cans, and other litter always must be carried back with you at the end of the day for proper disposal.

The pocket-sized All-Weather Hawk Watcher's Field Journal.
Photo courtesy of J. L. Darling Corporation.

The Migration Seasons

Hawk migrations in North America occur during fairly well-defined temporal periods in spring and autumn, and are related to weather conditions, geographic landscape features, and other factors.

Spring Hawk Migrations

The northward spring hawk migrations in North America usually are not as spectacular or concentrated in most locations as the famous autumn flights. Nevertheless, large spring flights can be seen at a few locations, particularly along the southern shorelines of Lakes Erie and Ontario, and modest flights also occur at a number of other locations in the East including some important autumn watch sites.

There are also a few locations in the West where impressive numbers of migrating hawks can be seen in spring. Perhaps the best spots are in southern Texas near the Santa Ana National Wildlife Refuge on the Mexican border. For the most part, however, spring hawk flights tend to be more dispersed, and perhaps at higher altitudes, than their autumn counterparts.

March, April, and May are the most important months for watching hawk migrations, with mid- to late April being especially important. Sometimes flights of several thousand Broad-winged Hawks are seen during a single day during this period in Texas, as well as along the southern shoreline of Lake Ontario in New York. In the Great Lakes region, the best concentration spots seem to be located where fingers of land extend into a lake a short distance west of the lookout. In Texas various watch sites along the Rio Grande seem to be particularly favorable points for hawks migrating northward.

Autumn Hawk Migrations

Autumn hawk migrations in eastern North America are among the most extraordinary animal spectacles in the world. For more than three months, tens of thousands of vultures, Ospreys, Northern Harriers, eagles, hawks, and falcons follow the Atlantic, Gulf, and Pacific coastlines, inland mountain ridges, and northern and western Great Lakes shorelines southward en route to their ancestral wintering grounds. As they do so, they offer hawk

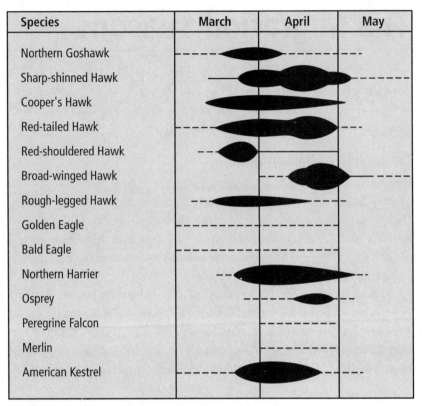

Species	March	April	May
Northern Goshawk			
Sharp-shinned Hawk			
Cooper's Hawk			
Red-tailed Hawk			
Red-shouldered Hawk			
Broad-winged Hawk			
Rough-legged Hawk			
Golden Eagle			
Bald Eagle			
Northern Harrier			
Osprey			
Peregrine Falcon			
Merlin			
American Kestrel			

Spring Hawk Flights—Eastern North America.

watchers, birders, ornithologists, naturalists, and scientists opportunities to observe and enjoy these flights at scores of watch sites. To large numbers of outdoor and wildlife enthusiasts, watching autumn hawk flights is a highlight of the year's activities—certainly a time to look forward to.

Although the autumn hawk migration season extends from early August through early to mid-December, the bulk of the flights occur from September through November. Within this three-month period, the season can be further divided into three major segments based on the peak migration periods of Broad-winged Hawks, Sharp-shinned Hawks, and Red-tailed Hawks. These are the three most abundant species seen at most hawk migration watch sites. In parts of the West, the Swainson's Hawk replaces the Broad-winged Hawk, whereas in other places the two species sometimes form mixed flocks.

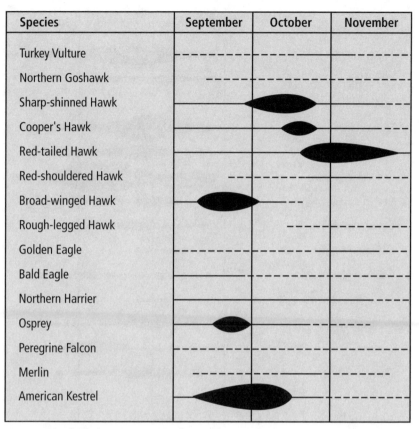

Species	September	October	November
Turkey Vulture			
Northern Goshawk			
Sharp-shinned Hawk			
Cooper's Hawk			
Red-tailed Hawk			
Red-shouldered Hawk			
Broad-winged Hawk			
Rough-legged Hawk			
Golden Eagle			
Bald Eagle			
Northern Harrier			
Osprey			
Peregrine Falcon			
Merlin			
American Kestrel			

Autumn Hawk Flights—Eastern North America.

September is noted for Broad-winged Hawk flights, which frequently peak during the middle of the month. Such flights, sometimes containing many thousands of hawks, occur between September 11 and 24, with September 16 or 17 often producing exceptional flights. At Hawk Mountain in Pennsylvania, for example, 11,392 hawks (mainly Broad-wings) were counted on September 16, 1948. Similar or larger counts have been recorded at lookouts in New Jersey. However, those numbers pale when you consider the 95,499 Broad-wings counted on September 15, 1984, at the Holiday Beach Migration Observatory in southwestern Ontario, Canada.

In addition to September's spectacular Broad-wing flights, Bald Eagles migrate southward in small numbers during late August and throughout

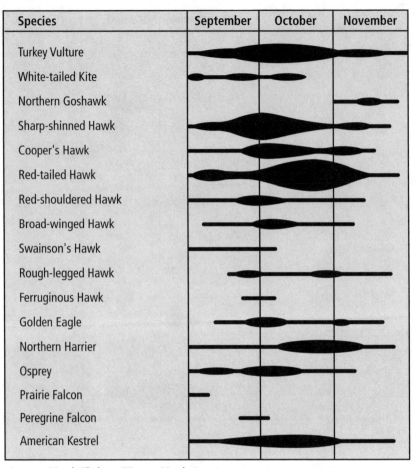

Species	September	October	November
Turkey Vulture			
White-tailed Kite			
Northern Goshawk			
Sharp-shinned Hawk			
Cooper's Hawk			
Red-tailed Hawk			
Red-shouldered Hawk			
Broad-winged Hawk			
Swainson's Hawk			
Rough-legged Hawk			
Ferruginous Hawk			
Golden Eagle			
Northern Harrier			
Osprey			
Prairie Falcon			
Peregrine Falcon			
American Kestrel			

Autumn Hawk Flights—Western North America. Adapted from data supplied by Laurence C. Binford.

September, with occasional stragglers from the northern subspecies appearing in late November and December. Ospreys are notable components of the September hawk flights, the largest numbers appearing during mid- to late September.

October is the second important period in the autumn hawk migration season. Sharp-shinned Hawks are the most abundant migrants from early to mid-October, but they become less numerous later in the month. Adding zest to the season, however, are lesser numbers of other species, including Northern Harriers, Cooper's Hawks, Northern Goshawks,

Golden Eagles, American Kestrels, Merlins, and Peregrine Falcons. On October 16, 1970, at Cape May Point, New Jersey, an extraordinary flight of about 25,000 American Kestrels was seen! In addition to hawks, thousands of Canada Geese are seen during October at the hawk migration watch sites; thrushes, kinglets, vireos, wood warblers, blackbirds and grackles, and finches and sparrows are also seen.

From the end of October to early November, the largest and most majestic hawks reach peaks of abundance in their southward migrations. On any cold day with northwest winds in early November, large numbers of Red-tailed Hawks are likely to be seen—especially along the Appalachian Mountains and the northern and western shorelines of the Great Lakes. Adding more excitement to these flights are lesser numbers of Northern Harriers, Northern Goshawks, Red-shouldered Hawks, sometimes Rough-legged Hawks, Golden Eagles, and occasionally other species. Golden Eagles are the highlights of the eastern hawk watching season. Indeed, every visitor to an eastern hawk migration watch site hopes to see one of these regal birds, although only approximately 150 or fewer are counted each year even at the best of the eastern sites. And although these birds are very common in many western locations, they are no less spectacular. Nevertheless, dedicated eastern hawk watchers can see Golden Eagles eventually if they make repeated visits to places such as Bake Oven Knob, Hawk Mountain, or Waggoner's Gap in Pennsylvania. Perhaps you will be lucky on your first visit and see a Golden Eagle immediately. If you select the correct day in mid- to late October or early November, it is possible. And if you fail on your first trip, try again. To see the King of Birds is worth the effort!

Mechanics of Hawk Flights

In addition to knowing when to visit a hawk lookout during the migration seasons, your chances of seeing a good hawk flight are improved through an understanding of the basic mechanics of hawk flight. Among the most important factors are weather conditions, especially local weather conditions such as deflective updrafts and thermals, along with so-called leading-lines.

General Weather Conditions

During springtime in the East, the largest hawk flights seem to occur on southerly winds accompanied by a drop in barometric pressure, a rise in air temperature, and the westerly approach of a low-pressure area and a cold front. In the West, particularly in the Rio Grande area of southern Texas, large concentrations of northward-migrating hawks sometimes develop along parts of the Texas border when strong northern winds occur.

Large autumn hawk flights also tend to occur in the wake of certain weather features. This is particularly true in the East; a pronounced low-pressure area first covers southern New England and upstate New York, followed a day or two later by the passage of a strong cold front across the East or Northeast. The front is accompanied by brisk northwest, north, or west winds. This combination of wind and weather usually produces ideal hawk flight conditions, but occasionally good flights also occur on eastern and southerly winds.

Deflective Updrafts

The cold, brisk, northwest surface winds that usually occur after the passage of a strong cold front create excellent flight conditions for migrating hawks because they strike the sides of mountains and are deflected upward. These deflective updrafts are perfect for the soaring flight used by accipiters, buteos, and other hawks. In addition to creating strong updrafts along the inland mountains, northwest winds tend to concentrate hawks at certain geographic bottlenecks such as Cape May Point, New Jersey. Apparently the hawks are unwilling to cross Delaware Bay unless the wind changes direction. However, they sometimes follow the New Jersey side of

When surface winds strike the sides of mountains, they are deflected upward. Migrating hawks soar and glide on these deflective updrafts.

the bay northward until they can cross at a narrow spot despite the north-westerly winds. At other times under northwesterly wind conditions, hawks tend to make large circles in the vicinity of Cape May Point and are probably counted repeatedly as they circle the tip of the cape. Such activity provides excellent recreational hawk watching opportunities but makes it difficult to count birds accurately. When the wind changes direction, however, the birds readily cross Delaware Bay and continue their southward migrations.

Lee Waves

Lee waves, undulatory movements of air downwind from an obstacle such as a mountain, are apparently used by migrating hawks at times, but not much is known about the relationship of these local weather features to hawk migrations.

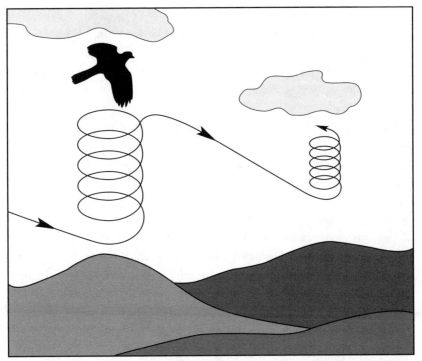

Migrating Broad-winged Hawks and Swainson's Hawks enter thermals in large numbers during migration, ride them aloft, then glide downward to another thermal and repeat the process.

Thermals

Thermals (bubbles of warm air rising into the atmosphere) are also especially important to migrating Broad-winged Hawks and Swainson's Hawks. Indeed, it is this dependence upon thermals that causes hundreds of Broad-wings, for example, to gather in milling flocks called "kettles"— extraordinary spectacles that hawk watchers eagerly look forward to seeing.

In the eastern United States and Canada, most raptors occasionally use thermals, but Broad-winged Hawks are the only raptors that are particularly thermal-dependent during migration. But in the West, Swainson's Hawks also use thermals extensively, and the two species sometimes kettle in mixed flocks in southern Texas, Mexico, and Central American en route to or from their winter ranges.

The use of thermals by hawks enables these birds to migrate over vast distances while expending very little energy. This is accomplished by entering thermals and remaining in them as they rise into the atmosphere. When the warm air in the thermals begins to cool and the thermals dissipate in the form of cumulus clouds, the hawks leave and begin long, downward glides sometimes extending for several miles until another thermal is located. Then the process is repeated. In this manner, Broad-winged Hawks migrate cross-country drifting on the wind, or they move down the great folds of the Appalachians or around the shorelines of the Great Lakes, thence around the Gulf of Mexico and through Central America into their South American winter range.

Thermal soaring is one of the most effective and practical methods of flight used by migrating hawks. Sometimes Broad-winged Hawks also use combinations of thermals and updraft soaring, as do other species, when cross-country flights are taken over mountains and valleys. At such times hawks may drift across valleys on thermals, but may change direction and use deflective updrafts along mountains when they are encountered before resorting to thermal soaring.

Thermal Streets

Under certain conditions thermals and wind combine to produce long, parallel lines of thermals and clouds called thermal streets. Migrating hawks can soar and glide in lines extending several miles in length along the streets, although this is probably relatively uncommon.

Squall Lines

Occasionally migrating hawks soar on updrafts occurring in front of squall lines. The squalls are neighboring thunderstorms arranged in a line parallel to, and in front of, an advancing cold front. In one instance about 4,300 hawks were observed soaring on updrafts in front of an advancing squall line.

Leading-Lines

In various parts of eastern North America, prominent geographic features such as the shorelines of the Great Lakes, Appalachian Mountain ridges, and the Atlantic coastline extend unbroken for long distances. Scientists refer to these natural features as leading-lines (or diversion-lines). When soaring hawks encounter such leading-lines during migration, they fre-

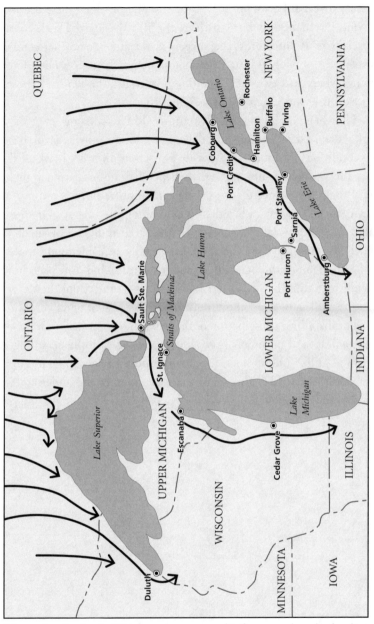

Many migrating hawks follow prominent geographic features such as the shorelines of large lakes, mountain ridges, or coastlines when they are encountered. Such natural features are called leading-lines or diversion-lines. During autumn, for example, thousands of migrating hawks follow the northern and western shorelines of the Great Lakes rather than flying across these major water obstacles.

quently divert at least a portion of their migration along these features for varying distances. For birds such as the Broad-winged Hawk, which is especially reluctant to cross large expanses of water, the northern and western shorelines of the Great Lakes act as major autumn leading-lines. In spring, when the hawks are migrating northward, the southern shorelines of Lakes Erie and Ontario play a similar role.

Elsewhere, as along the Kittatinny Ridge crossing part of New York–New Jersey–Pennsylvania, deflective updrafts provide favorable soaring conditions for buteos and a wide assortment of other hawks. Falcons, however—which are not particularly dependent upon soaring as their primary flight style—occur in much larger numbers during autumn along the Atlantic coastline rather than inland along the ridges. Many of these migrating falcons take advantage of the large numbers of small birds, which also migrate along the coast, as a readily available food supply.

Although ornithologists differ about the role wind drift plays in influencing migrating hawks to use leading-lines—some think hawks follow them regardless of wind conditions, others because of wind conditions—in all probability a combination of the two factors, especially strong northwest winds and prominent geographic features, influences migrating hawks to utilize leading-lines. Like many aspects of hawk migrations, however, additional field studies may produce a more refined understanding of leading-line phenomena.

U.S. Hawk Migration Watch Sites

Alabama

Dauphin Island (near Mobile)

Spring Flights: Information unavailable.

Autumn Flights: Fair.

Watch Site Description: A hook-shaped barrier beach island in the Gulf of Mexico just south of Mobile.

Access: From Mobile, drive south on State Route 163 across the causeway and bridge to the eastern part of Dauphin Island. Details are unavailable regarding the best hawk watching spots, but exposed areas near the eastern end of the island presumably are satisfactory. Such spots include the dunes along the Gulf, the Audubon Bird Sanctuary, and the Indian shell-mound area on the bay side of the island—which is less than a mile wide.

References: *American Birds*, 1971, 25 (3): 539–540; *Alabama Birds* (University of Alabama Press, 1976); *A Guide to Hawk Watching in North America* (Pennsylvania State University Press, 1979).

Fort Morgan State Park (near Gull Shores)

Spring Flights: Information unavailable.

Autumn Flights: Fair.

Watch Site Description: The western end of a narrow peninsula projecting westward from the eastern side of Mobile Bay. Hawk watching is done anywhere on the bay side of the park. The migrating hawks approach from the east in autumn and sometimes kettle overhead before crossing the bay to Dauphin Island on the western side of the bay.

Access: From the junction of State Routes 59 and 180 at Gull Shores, turn right (west) onto Route 180 and continue for about 21 miles to the end of the road. The last mile is in Fort Morgan State Park. Migrating hawks sometimes concentrate at the tip of the peninsula. Additional hawk watching information within the park may be available from park officials.

References: *Alabama Birds* (University of Alabama Press, 1976); *A Guide to Hawk Watching in North America* (Pennsylvania State University Press, 1979); *Raptor Watch* (BirdLife International and Hawk Mountain Sanctuary, 2000).

Alaska

Current knowledge of raptor migration flight-lines, corridors, and concentration areas in Alaska is very limited, and few productive hawk watching locations are known and accessible by road. Those presented here appear to be the most important. However, birders, hawk watchers, and ornithologists have many opportunities to do exploratory hawk watching to identify and evaluate new raptor migration watch sites in this state.

Because the route number designations of Alaskan highways are marked at the beginning and end, but rarely between those points, *be absolutely certain* you are on the correct highway before driving very long distances to very remote locations. In addition, do not fail to purchase a copy of the *MILEPOST Trip Planner* for more detailed Alaska highway travel information. Almost exclusively, Alaskans recognize highways by their name rather than route numbers when discussing directions.

Glenn Highway (between Chickaloon and Eureka)

Spring Flights: Fair.

Autumn Flights: Fair.

Watch Site Description: Various roadside pullovers along a section of State Route 1 (Glenn Highway) between mileposts 76 just east of

Chickaloon and approximately 126 at Eureka from which raptor migrations sometimes are observed. Remain alert for migrant Red-tailed Hawks, Rough-legged Hawks, and Golden Eagles—especially in the area between King and Sheep Mountains.

Access: From Anchorage, drive northeast on State Route 1 (Glenn Highway) to Chickaloon at milepost 76. From here, continue eastward on Route 1 to milepost 128 at Eureka, stopping along the way at roadside pullovers to check for migrating hawks. Several tourist facilities are available along the Glenn Highway: King Mountain Lodge (gas, food, and lodging) at milepost 76.2; Long Rifle Lodge (gas and lodging) at milepost 102.2; Sheep Mountain Lodge (cabins, food, and telephone) at milepost 113.5, and Eureka Lodge (gas, lodging, and telephone) at milepost 128.

Reference: *Raptor Research*, 1984, 18 (1): 10–15.

Gunsight Mountain Hawkwatch (near Eureka, 60 miles west of Glennallen)

Spring Flights: Fair

Autumn Flights: Information unavailable.

Watch Site Description: Two roadside pullovers along State Route 1 (Glenn Highway) between mileposts 118 and 121 (as measured from Anchorage) at Eureka Summit (elevation 3,322 feet) provide vistas over the spectacular Alaskan landscape. The milepost 118.9 pullover is used regularly by local hawk watchers because it gives observers closer overhead views of raptors and more protection from bitterly cold winds. However, the milepost 120.2 pullover provides a better view toward the north and better detection of distant flying raptors. Both pullovers are good for seeing several color morphs of Red-tailed Hawks, along with Rough-legged Hawks and Golden Eagles. Small numbers of other raptor species are also seen. Late March to very early May is the best hawk watching period. Alaska is remarkable for the largest known concentration of the distinctive Harlan's subspecies of the Red-tailed Hawk, and Gyrfalcons are seen annually.

Access: From Glennallen, drive west on State Route 1—Glenn Highway—to either roadside pullover at mileposts 118.9 and 120.2 from which hawk watching is done. This is a remote area, but outhouse facilities are available at milepost 118.5 on the north-side pullover.

Reference: *HMANA Hawk Migration Studies*, 2003, 28 (2): 77–78.

Long Lake Cliffs (near Chickaloon)

Spring Flights: Information unavailable.

Autumn Flights: Fair.

Watch Site Description: A large public parking lot at milepost 85.3 on State Route 1 (Glenn Highway) at the Long Lake State Recreation Area. Migrating raptors use thermal soaring and deflective updrafts at the cliffs adjacent to this pullover. Hawk watchers observe from the parking lot. Outhouse facilities are available at this site.

Access: From Anchorage, drive northeast on State Route 1 (Glenn Highway) to milepost 85.3; park in the lot at the Long Lake State Recreation Area.

Reference: None.

Arizona

Grand Canyon National Park—South Rim (north of Flagstaff)

Spring Flights: Information unavailable.

Autumn Flights: Fair (Lipan Point) and poor (Yaki Point).

Watch Site Description: Two watch sites—Lipan Point and Yaki Point—on the South Rim of the Grand Canyon provide stunning vistas overlooking the canyon. Both sites are used for autumn hawk watching. Sharp-shinned Hawks, Cooper's Hawks, Red-tailed Hawks, and American Kestrels are seen most frequently, but all diurnal raptors found in the area appear in lesser numbers during autumn.

Access: From Flagstaff, south of Grand Canyon National Park, drive north on U.S. Route 180/State Route 64 to the South Entrance to Grand Canyon National Park. Alternatively, if arriving from Cameron toward the east, drive west on Route 64 to the East Entrance to the park. Enter at either location by paying a $20 per-vehicle entrance fee (or using one of several types of passes—National Park Pass, Golden Eagle Pass, Golden Access Pass, and so on). Then continue ahead to the Canyon View Information Plaza from the South Entrance, or the Desert View campground/store area from the East Entrance.

Additional information can be secured from either location, and restrooms are also available. There are many activities, services, and facilities available in the park, including ranger programs, lodging, a campground, food services, a bookstore, gift shops, and a shuttle bus to transport visitors to various parts of the park.

Please note, however, that hawk watchers are warned *not* to stand on exposed points during thunderstorms with lightning activity, which may occur in early September. Shelters are *not* available at Yaki Point or Lipan Point.

To reach Yaki Point from March 1 through November 30, board one of the free park shuttle buses at the Canyon View Information Plaza to go to, and return from, the point. Private vehicles are not permitted at the Yaki Point except during the three winter months, when they may drive to the Yaki Point parking area. To do so, head *east* on Desert View Drive for about 2 miles from its intersection with the South Entrance Road, turn north onto a park road intersecting with Desert View Drive, and continue for about 1 mile to the parking area for Yaki Point. The watch site overlooking the canyon is a short walk from the parking area. A portable restroom is available at Yaki Point.

To reach Lipan Point by private vehicle at any time of year (using a shuttle bus is not necessary) from the Desert View campground and store/gas station inside the park, a short distance northeast of the East Entrance, head west on Desert View Drive for approximately 3 miles, then continue north a short distance on an access road to the Lipan Point parking area. The watch site is a short walk from the parking area. No portable restroom is provided at Lipan Point.

References: *Raptor Watch* (BirdLife International and Hawk Mountain Sanctuary, 2000); *HMANA Hawk Migration Studies*, 2001, 27 (1): 46–47; 2002, 28 (1): 176–177, 200–202.

Arkansas

Petit Jean State Park (near Pontoon)

Spring Flights: Information unavailable.

Autumn Flights: Fair.

Watch Site Description: Any elevated area in the park with exposed views over the adjacent landscape. Migrations of Sharp-shinned Hawks and Broad-winged Hawks are reported from this park. Ask at the park office or headquarters for current hawk migration and hawk watching information.

Access: From Pontoon, drive east on State Route 154 for about 4 miles to the park entrance. Follow signs to the office or headquarters.

References: *A Guide to Bird Finding West of the Mississippi* (Oxford University Press, 1981); *The Migrations of Hawks* (Indiana University Press, 1986).

California

Borrego Valley Hawk Watch (near Borrego Springs)

Spring Flights: Good.

Autumn Flights: Information unavailable.

Watch Site
Description: The corner of a valley floor, surrounded by desert vegetation, with unobstructed visibility in all directions. The Santa Rosa and San Jacinto mountain ranges in southern California converge near the watch site, and migrating raptors fly through two canyon passes (Coyote Canyon and Hell Hole Canyon).

Access: From the junction of Di Giorgio Road and Palm Canyon Drive, in Borrego Springs in southern California, drive north on Di Giorgio Road for 2.5 miles to the watch site on the west side of the road.

References: None.

Golden Gate Raptor Observatory (Point Diablo near San Francisco)

Spring Flights: Fair

Autumn Flights: Excellent.

Watch Site
Description: Two 900-foot hills (Cross Hill and Bunker Hill) located 0.4 mile apart, but connected by a saddle-like ridge, overlooking the mouth of San Francisco Bay.

- Cross Hill, the northeastern site, has a broad, flat parking lot at its summit along with what looks like a cross. It is best used for watching spring hawk migrations.

- Bunker Hill, the southwestern site, has numerous cement bunkers and platforms on its summit and is the best spot from which to watch autumn hawk migrations.

Access: From San Francisco, follow U.S. Route 101 north across the Golden Gate Bridge. Upon leaving the bridge, take the Alexander Avenue exit toward Sausalito, but rather than continue directly to that town, proceed only about 50 yards and turn left under U.S. 101 as if returning to San Francisco. Just before rejoining U.S. 101, turn right uphill on a paved road into the Golden Gate National Recreation Area (GGNRA). Proceed 1.2 miles to the first Y intersection. To reach Cross Hill, park here and walk about 50 yards down the right-hand road to a narrow dirt road that goes to the top of the hill at the "cross"; this road is closed to motorized vehicles and presents a steep walk. To reach Bunker Hill, drive left at the Y intersection for 0.6 mile to the first crest, where a sign announces BEGIN ONE-WAY ROAD (in the direction you are going). Park here and walk several hundred yards up a narrow, gated road to the highest point on the northeast end.

From the north on U.S. 101, the Alexander Avenue exit is not marked as such, but is simply called SAUSALITO; another sign points to the GGNRA. There are other Sausalito exits, but this is the only one in sight of the Golden Gate Bridge. Immediately upon leaving the highway, turn left onto the same GGNRA road just described.

References: *Birding*, 1977, 9 (1): 29–30; *A Guide to Hawk Watching in North America* (Pennsylvania State University Press, 1979); *The Migrations of Hawks* (Indiana University Press, 1986); *Raptor Watch* (BirdLife International and Hawk Mountain Sanctuary, 2000); *HMANA Hawk Migration Studies*, 2001, 27 (1): 13, 29, 31; 2002, 28 (1): 206–208.

Kern Valley Turkey Vulture Festival (near Lake Isabella)

Spring Flights: Information unavailable.

Autumn Flights: Excellent Turkey Vulture flights.

Watch Site Description: The Kern River Preserve is owned by Audubon California. An annual festival is devoted to observing, enjoying, and understanding autumn migrations of Turkey Vultures and other raptors from late September through early October.

Access: From the town of Lake Isabella, drive northeast on State Route 178 through the communities of Mount Mesa and South Lake to the junction with Sierra Way on the left. Continue on Route 178 for 1.1 miles farther, looking for a wooden sign on the left side of the road that reads AUDUBON CALIFORNIA'S KERN RIVER PRESERVE. Turn left onto an unpaved road just before reaching the sign, then continue slowly for 0.2 mile on this road (watching for cattle in the field; do not stop or park) until you reach the preserve's parking area.

References: *HMANA Hawk Migration Studies*, 2001, 27 (1): 29, 34; Kern River Preserve at www.kernriverpreserve.org.

Kern Valley Vulture Watch (near Weldon)

Spring Flights: Information unavailable.

Autumn Flights: Excellent Turkey Vulture flights.

Watch Site Description: The north-facing slope of a rounded hill (elevation 2,950 feet) providing a 360-degree view of the Kelso Creek section of the South Fork Valley at the southern end of the Sierra Nevada. The site is owned by ARK, a nonprofit organization, and is used from late September through early October for watching migrating Turkey Vultures, which also roost in cottonwood-willow riparian forest in the valley below the watch site. See also Kern Valley Turkey Vulture Festival for related activities.

Access: The Kern Valley Vulture Watch is located 5 miles south of Weldon, Kern County, California. From Weldon, and the junction of State Route 178 and Kelso Valley Road, drive south on Kelso Valley Road for 4.9 miles and park in a wash along the side of the road. Then walk *back* for 0.1 mile in the direction from which you came to a small trail. Follow this trail to the right for about 150 feet up the hillside to the watch site.

References: *Western Birds*, 1996, 27: 48–53; *HMANA Hawk Migration Studies*, 2000, 27 (1): 29; 2002, 28 (1): 208.

Colorado

Dinosaur Ridge Raptor Migration Station (near Morrison)

Spring Flights: Poor.

Autumn Flights: Information unavailable.

Description: A hogback a short distance south of Interstate 70 on the
western side of metro Denver. The site separates the
prairie from the foothills. This site is especially noted for
seeing migrating Ferruginous Hawks (more than 250 during one season).

Access: From Interstate 70 near Morrison, take exit 259, then
drive south to a Park & Ride parking lot on the southeast
corner of the junction of I–70 and State Route 26. Park,
then walk uphill on a two-track trail to a gate. Turn sharp
right, follow the trail to the ridge crest, and continue left
to the watch site.

Reference: HMANA Web site at www.hmana.org.

Connecticut

Bald Peak (near Salisbury)

Spring Flights: Information unavailable.

Autumn Flights: Good.

Watch Site
Description: A rocky ridge with a 360-degree view.

Access: From Hartford, drive north on U.S. Route 44 to Salisbury
(in the northwestern corner of the state), then follow
Mount Riga Road for about 4.1 miles to the Bald Peak
parking area (about 0.3 mile beyond South Pond). Five
minutes are required to walk from the parking area to a
large rock ledge.

References: *A Guide to Hawk Watching in North America* (Pennsylvania State University Press, 1979); *The Migrations of Hawks*
(Indiana University Press, 1986).

Bluff Head (in North Guilford)

Spring Flights: Poor.

Autumn Flights: Excellent.

Watch Site
Description: A rocky bluff rising some 350 feet above the surrounding deciduous forests with unrestricted visibility from the north through the south, but with visibility toward the west blocked by woodland.

Access: From exit 58 off the Connecticut Turnpike (Interstate 95) in Guilford, drive north on State Route 77. At 4.3 miles cross State Route 80, continuing north on Route 77. At 6.9 miles Lake Quonnipaug will be seen on the right. At 8.5 miles you will pass Great Hill Road on the left. From this junction, go 0.3 mile; on the left there is an unpaved parking area beneath large pine trees. Park here and take the blue trail (blazes painted on trees) up the steep talus slope. This path leads about 1.5 miles to the top of Bluff Head. The trail is very steep at the start up the talus, and you will pass several overlooks before you reach the final summit.

References: *A Guide to Hawk Watching in North America* (Pennsylvania State University Press, 1979); *The Migrations of Hawks* (Indiana University Press, 1986).

Hammonasset Beach State Park (near Madison)

Spring Flights: Information unavailable.

Autumn Flights: Good.

Watch Site
Description: A seaside park from which considerable numbers of migrating raptors are observed during September and October.

Access: From Madison, drive east on U.S. Route 1 for a short distance to the entrance to Hammonasset Beach State Park. Enter the park and go to the edge of the ocean, selecting an exposed spot with good views of the surrounding landscape and seascape from which to observe migrating hawks. Ask at the park headquarters for updated information regarding the most favorable spots to engage in hawk watching.

Reference: *The Migrations of Hawks* (Indiana University Press, 1986).

Lighthouse Point Park (in New Haven)

Spring Flights: Poor.

Autumn Flights: Good (sometimes excellent).

Watch Site Description: A large, open field atop a knoll about 300 yards north of the park's beach.

Access: From Interstate 95 at New Haven, take exit 50 (Main Street East Haven); at the second traffic light, turn right onto Townsend Avenue. Continue on Townsend Avenue for 2.2 miles to the traffic light at Lighthouse Point Road. Turn right and follow Lighthouse Point Road for 0.1 mile into the park. Park in the southernmost parking lot. Then walk north to the large field atop the knoll adjacent to the parking lot from which observations are made. Or observe from the parking lot.

References: *Auk*, 1895, 12: 259–270; *A Guide to Hawk Watching in North America* (Pennsylvania State University Press, 1979); *The Migrations of Hawks* (Indiana University Press, 1986); *HMANA Hawk Migration Studies*, 2001, 27 (1): 139–141; 2002, 28 (1): 86–88.

Quaker Ridge (Audubon Center of Greenwich)

Spring Flights: Information unavailable.

Autumn Flights: Excellent.

Watch Site Description: An exposed area directly across from the center's lodge and adjacent to the main driveway. This site may be most useful for watching Broad-winged Hawk migrations during September. The Audubon Center of Greenwich is a facility owned and operated by the National Audubon Society.

Access: From New York or points north, follow Interstate 684 to exit 3 (or exit 3-N if you are coming from the south); leave the highway there and continue north on New York State Route 22 to a traffic light. Turn right onto State Route 433 and continue 2 miles to John Street. The Audubon Center is on the corner.

If arriving via the Merritt Parkway, leave the parkway at exit 28 (Round Hill Road), then continue north on Round Hill Road for 1.4 miles to John Street. Turn left and drive 1.4 miles to the corner of Riversville Road and the center.

Those approaching via Interstate 95 (Connecticut Turnpike) should leave the turnpike at exit 3 and turn onto Arch Street. Immediately after passing the Railroad Avenue traffic light, turn left onto Soundview Drive and continue to Field Point Road. Turn right onto Field Point Road and continue to Brookside Drive (the first left). Turn onto Brookside Drive and proceed 0.6 mile to Glenville Road. Turn left and drive to Glenville. Turn right at the traffic light onto Riversville Road and proceed 4.4 miles to John Street. The center is on the corner.

This facility is open Tuesday through Saturday, 9:00 A.M. to 5:00 P.M.; closed Sunday, Monday, and holiday weekends. When autumn hawk watches occur on holiday weekends, special arrangements are made to allow hawk watchers entrance to the center. For more information, write to the Audubon Center of Connecticut, 613 Riversville Road, Greenwich, CT 06830.

References: *A Guide to Hawk Watching in North America* (Pennsylvania State University Press, 1979); *The Migrations of Hawks* (Indiana University Press, 1986); *HMANA Hawk Migration Studies*, 2001, 27 (1): 142–144; 2002, 28 (1): 94–95.

Delaware

Brandywine Creek State Park (near Wilmington)

Spring Flights: Information unavailable.

Autumn Flights: Fair.

Watch Site Description: A stone wall overlooking Brandywine Creek and adjacent to the main parking lot in the park.

Access: From Wilmington, 3 miles to the south, drive north on State Route 100 to the junction with State Route 92.

Enter the park. Then continue to the main parking lot and stone wall adjacent to it.

References: *Delaware Conservationist*, 1969, 13 (4): 3–13; *A Guide to Hawk Watching in North America* (Pennsylvania State University Press, 1979); *The Migrations of Hawks* (Indiana University Press, 1986).

Cape Henlopen State Park (near Lewes)

Spring Flights: Poor (sometimes fair).

Autumn Flights: Fair.

Watch Site Description: The top of a bunker just south of the tip of the peninsula, within the park, extending into Delaware Bay.

Access: In Lewes, Delaware, drive east on U.S. Route 9/Cape Henlopen Drive for 1 mile to the park entrance at 42 Cape Henlopen Drive. A $2.50-per-vehicle entrance fee is

Hawk watchers in autumn using the hawk watching platform in Cape Henlopen State Park, Delaware. Photo by Bruce Lantz.

charged for vehicles from Delaware ($5.00 for out-of-state vehicles) from April through October. Annual passes are available at the park office. After passing the fee booth, follow signs to the nature center and continue past it to the point where the road turns left. Continue past the bathing beaches and bathhouse to the next entrance on the right leading to the picnic pavilion and Battery Hunter. Park, climb the steps to the top of the bunker, and watch from there. Signs and other information regarding hawk watching are posted there. Good westerly winds produce the best hawk flights.

References: *The Migrations of Hawks* (Indiana University Press, 1986); *HMANA Hawk Migration Studies*, 2001, 27 (1): 186–187; 2002, 27 (2): 107; 2002, 28 (1): 49–50.

Florida

Canaveral National Seashore (near Titusville)

Spring Flights: Information unavailable.

Autumn Flights: Fair (occasionally good to excellent).

Watch Site Description: The top of the old NASA camera pad No. 10, or its immediate vicinity, from which observers have clear views over the coast and surrounding barrier beach island. In October Sharp-shinned Hawks and Peregrine Falcons migrate past the spot. Occasionally other species are also seen.

Access: From Interstate 95 near Titusville, drive east on State Route 402 for about 12 miles to Playalinda Beach at the southeastern end of Canaveral National Seashore. Once there drive north on the beach road for about 5 miles to the camera pad near the end of the road. Drive onto the pad and observe from there. Bird watchers are allowed on the pad despite the sign asking people to stay off. However, check with park rangers before using the pad because it is an active NASA facility.

References: *A Guide to Hawk Watching in North America* (Pennsylvania State University Press, 1979); *The Migrations of Hawks* (Indiana University Press, 1986).

Destin

Spring Flights: Information unavailable.

Autumn Flights: Fair.

**Watch Site
Description:** A vantage point behind a shopping center.

Access: From Destin, drive to a point along U.S. Route 98 just before the highway meets the bridge crossing East Pass. The shopping center is located along the north side of the highway. Park and walk to the vantage point behind the center. Observe from there.

Reference: *A Guide to Hawk Watching in North America* (Pennsylvania State University Press, 1979).

Everglades National Park

Spring Flights: Information unavailable.

Autumn Flights: Poor to fair.

**Watch Site
Description:** A large lawn in front of the park's visitor center at Flamingo. There are excellent views in all directions. Some hawks also are seen in the Royal Palm Hammock area, as well as elsewhere along the park's roads. Everglades National Park is not a major raptor migration watch site, but it is notable as a location where small numbers of wintering immature Broad-winged Hawks and a few Swainson's Hawks (along with more common buteos) are seen. A few rare Short-tailed Hawks also are seen in the Flamingo area, and sometimes elsewhere in the park, from mid-October through early February. Days in November with northwest winds sometimes are productive for seeing Swainson's and Short-tailed Hawks.

Access: From the junction of U.S. Route 1 (the Florida Turnpike) and State Route 9336 at Florida City south of Miami, follow Route 9336 and directional signs to the entrance to Everglades National Park. Pay the entrance fee, enter the park, and drive for about 37 miles to its southern end at Flamingo. Park at the visitor center and use the lawn in front of the center as a hawk migration watch site. The Royal Palm Hammock area is located within the park a few miles from the park's entrance. Follow directional signs to reach it.

References: *The Migrations of Hawks* (Indiana University Press, 1986); HMANA Web site at www.hmana.org.

Grassy Key (in Curry Hammock State Park near Marathon)

Spring Flights: Poor.

Autumn Flights: Excellent.

Watch Site
Description: A balcony on a building (bathhouse) in Curry Hammock State Park providing excellent views toward the north and south.

Access: On U.S. Route 1 at mile marker 56 (just north of Marathon), drive into the park and continue on the main road to a T intersection. Turn right and continue to the bathhouse. Hawk watching is done from a second-floor balcony.

References: *Living Bird,* 2001, 20 (4): 32–38; *HMANA Hawk Migration Studies,* 2002, 28 (1): 35; *Autumn Raptor Migration Through the Florida Keys with Special Focus on the Peregrine Falcon* (Florida Fish and Wildlife Conservation Commission, 2001); *HMANA Hawk Migration Studies,* 2002, 28 (1): 37.

Key West Area

Spring Flights: Information unavailable.

Autumn Flights: Good (sometimes excellent).

Watch Site
Description: No specific site in the Key West area can be recognized as a hawk migration watch site, but kettles of Broad-winged Hawks are seen occasionally over the Key West area in October. Birders should remain alert and look for these hawk flights from time to time.

Access: From the southern Florida mainland, drive south on U.S. Route 1 to Key West.

References: *A Guide to Hawk Watching in North America* (Pennsylvania State University Press, 1979); *The Migrations of Hawks* (Indiana University Press, 1986).

Georgia

Cumberland Island National Seashore (near St. Marys)

Spring Flights: Information unavailable.

Autumn Flights: Poor.

Watch Site Description: A barrier beach island along which migrating Peregrine Falcons, Merlins, American Kestrels, and other raptors stop to rest and feed. Although the overall rating of this watch site is poor, as many as 125 Peregrine Falcons have been reported in one season along the beaches (chiefly the first two weeks in October). The stone jetty at the southern end of the island is a suitable observation point as well as the middle and northern sections of the beaches.

Access: From the junction of Interstate 95 and State Route 40 near Kingsland, follow Route 40 eastward to St. Marys, where a National Park Service passenger ferry (toll) transports visitors to Cumberland Island. The schedule for departure may vary; current information is available from the Cumberland Island National Seashore, P.O. Box 806, St. Marys, GA 31558.

Upon reaching the island and the visitor center, you can walk to the middle or northern sections of the beaches to look for falcons or walk 3.5 miles south to the rock jetty and observe from there. However, special care should be taken not to walk on the dunes to prevent dune damage. Overnight camping is permitted at selected sites on the island by reservation. Details can be secured from the park headquarters.

References: *A Guide to Hawk Watching in North America* (Pennsylvania State University Press, 1979); *The Migrations of Hawks* (Indiana University Press, 1986).

Idaho

Lucky Peak (near Boise)

Spring Flights: Information unavailable.

Autumn Flights: Fair.

Watch Site Description: A southwest-facing ridge from which hawk watchers have views over the adjacent landscape. The hawk migration watch site is part of the Idaho Bird Observatory located on the Boise River Wildlife Management Area.

Access: From Boise, drive north on State Route 21 for 12 miles. At the junction with the Highland Valley Road (about 0.5 mile before a cafe on the left), turn left onto Highland Valley Road and continue for 8 miles up this road (vehicles should have high underside clearance), following the *E* mark at each fork.

References: *HMANA Hawk Migration Studies*, 2001, 27 (1): 70–71; HMANA Web site at www.hmana.org.

Illinois

Chicago

Spring Flights: Poor.

Autumn Flights: Fair.

Watch Site Description: Exposed locations along the lakefront, including the vicinity of Northwestern University, with unrestricted visibility. Some exploratory hawk watching will be necessary along the city's lakefront to find the best raptor migration watch sites during spring and autumn.

Access: Various parks and open space areas along U.S. Route 41 along much of the Chicago lakefront, and also Sheridan Road, which extends northward from U.S. 41 along the lakefront, including the vicinity of Northwestern University.

Reference: *The Migrations of Hawks* (Indiana University Press, 1986).

Illinois Beach State Park (near Waukegan)

Spring Flights: Information unavailable.

Autumn Flights: Fair.

Watch Site Description: The south shore of Lake Michigan, from which observers have exposed views of migrating hawks.

Access: From Waukegan, drive north on State Route 42 (Sheridan Road) for 4.5 miles. Then turn right onto Beach Road and continue into the park. The Lake Michigan shore is reached via a nature trail from a parking lot in the nature preserve portion of the southern section of the park. Additional details may be available from park authorities.

References: *A Guide to Bird Finding East of the Mississippi* (Oxford University Press, 1977); *A Guide to Hawk Watching in North America* (Pennsylvania State University Press, 1979); *The Migrations of Hawks* (Indiana University Press, 1986); *HMANA Hawk Migration Studies*, 2001, 27 (1): 83; 2002, 28 (1): 158–160.

Indiana

Indiana Dunes National Lakeshore (near Michigan City)

Spring Flights: Good (sometimes excellent).

Autumn Flights: None.

Watch Site Description: The top of a bare dune known locally as Mount Baldy. Hawks follow an east-to-west direction, with Sharp-shinned Hawks and Red-tailed Hawks being observed most commonly in late March and April.

Access: From Michigan City, drive west on U.S. Route 12 for a few miles to the Mount Baldy area of the national lakeshore. Leave your vehicle in the parking area closest to

Mount Baldy, then walk along the trail leading to the top of the dune, from which hawk watching is done. Maps of the area are available at the federal information center located along U.S. 12 a few miles west of the Mount Baldy Area.

References: *A Guide to Hawk Watching in North America* (Pennsylvania State University Press, 1979); *The Migrations of Hawks* (Indiana University Press, 1986).

Indiana Dunes State Park (near Michigan City)

Spring Flights: Good (sometimes excellent).

Autumn Flights: None.

Watch Site
Description: The top of Mount Tom or the south rim of the Beach-house Blowout. Hawks follow an east-to-west direction, with Sharp-shinned Hawks and Red-tailed Hawks being observed most commonly in late March and April.

Access: From Michigan City, drive west on U.S. Route 12 for several miles past the Mount Baldy Area of Indiana Dunes National Lakeshore to the entrance to Indiana Dunes State Park (an entrance fee is charged). Obtain a park map at the entrance, then drive to the parking lot near Mount Tom or Trail 8. Park here, then walk to the top of Mount Tom. Alternatively, drive to the parking lot along the beach, then walk east on Trail 10 along the beach to the blowout. Observe from there.

References: *A Guide to Hawk Watching in North America* (Pennsylvania State University Press, 1979); *The Migrations of Hawks* (Indiana University Press, 1986).

Iowa

Effigy Mounds National Monument (near Marquette)

Spring Flights: Information unavailable.

Autumn Flights: Good to excellent.

Watch Site
Description: Overlooks providing views over bottomland hardwood forests along the Mississippi River. The Fire Point Overlook is particularly useful for autumn hawk watching and winter Bald Eagle viewing along the river.

Access: From the junction of U.S. Route 18 and State Route 76 at Marquette, drive north on Route 76 for 3.7 miles to the entrance to the national monument on the right side of the highway. Secure current hawk and eagle watching information at the park's headquarters, as well as directions to the Fire Point Overlook.

Reference: *Iowa Wildlife Viewing Guide* (Falcon Press Publishing, 1995).

Hitchcock Nature Area (near Crescent)

Spring Flights: Information unavailable.

Autumn Flights: Good.

Watch Site
Description: Hawk watching is done from the Hitchcock Nature Area lodge, which provides views across the Missouri River Valley. Several other nearby spots also are used for hawk watching; inquire at the lodge for information about them. An excellent diversity of raptor species is reported from this location. Mid-September through late October is the best hawk watching period.

Access: From the junction of Interstate 680 and State Route 988 near Crescent, follow Route 988 into town, then drive north on State Route 183 for about 4.5 miles to the junction with Page Lane. Turn west onto Page Lane and continue for 0.2 mile to Ski Hill Loop. Turn north onto Ski Hill Loop and continue for 0.3 mile to the entrance to the Hitchcock Nature Area. Turn into the nature area and follow the road to the lodge, where hawk watching is done.

References: *Iowa Wildlife Viewing Guide* (Falcon Press Publishing, 1995); *HMANA Hawk Migration Studies*, 2001, 27 (1): 84–85, 99–101; HMANA Web site at www.hmana.org; also www.virtualbirder.com.

Kentucky

High Rocks (near Whitesburg)

Spring Flights: Information unavailable.

Autumn Flights: Fair.

Watch Site Description: A little-used watch site on Pine Mountain in the Bad Branch State Nature Preserve with views toward the north and northeast. The largest hawk flights occur on northwest winds.

Access: From Whitesburg, drive northwest on State Route 15 to the junction with State Route 931. Turn left onto Route 931 and continue for a few miles to the Pine Mountain Wildlife Area.

Reference: *Raptor Watch* (BirdLife International, 2000).

Maine

Beech Mountain (near Southwest Harbor)

Spring Flights: Information unavailable.

Autumn Flights: Good.

Watch Site Description: Any suitable spot on the top of Beech Mountain with an exposed view of the surrounding landscape. Limited use of this site has indicated that good hawk migrations occur here.

Access: A trail leading from a parking lot to the top of Beech Mountain, on Mount Desert Island, provides access to this site. In Southwest Harbor or at various Acadia National Park visitor centers, request more specific access information for hiking to the top of Beech Mountain.

References: *HMANA Newsletter*, 1979, 4 (2): 10–13; *1980* and *1982 Hawk Migration New England Hawk Watch* reports (Connecticut Audubon Council, 1980, 1982); *The Migrations of Hawks* (Indiana University Press, 1986).

Bradbury Mountain State Park (near Pownal)

Spring Flights: Information unavailable.

Autumn Flights: Good.

Watch Site Description: A bare granite mountaintop providing hawk watchers with excellent views of migrating birds. Mid-September to mid-October is the best hawk watching period.

Access: From the town of Pownal, drive north on State Route 9 for a short distance to the park entrance. Alternatively, from Durham drive south on Route 9 for several miles to the park entrance. Enter and drive to the main parking lot near the top of the mountain. Park here, then take a short ten-minute hike to the mountaintop following directional signs.

References: *A Guide to Hawk Watching in North America* (Pennsylvania State University Press, 1979); *The Migrations of Hawks* (Indiana University Press, 1986).

Casco Bay Area (near Cooks Corner)

Spring Flights: Information unavailable.

Autumn Flights: Fair to good.

Watch Site Description: The vicinity of South Harpswell at the end of the peninsula on which it is located, and along the shoreline of Casco Bay (particularly near the head of the bay). Some exploration is necessary in this area.

Access: From the junction of U.S. Route 1 and State Route 123 near Cooks Corner (near Brunswick), drive south on Route 123 to the South Harpswell area and explore the region for migrating hawks.

References: *American Birds*, 1974, 28 (1): 113–114; *A Guide to Hawk Watching in North America* (Pennsylvania State University Press, 1979); *The Migrations of Hawks* (Indiana University Press, 1986).

Cutler Area

Spring Flights: Information unavailable.

Autumn Flights: Fair.

Watch Site Description: Raptor migrations sometimes are seen opportunistically along State Route 191 between Cutler and West Lubec.

Access: From Cutler, drive north on State Route 191 while remaining alert for migrating raptors.

References: *A Birder's Guide to the Coast of Maine* (Down East Books, 1981); *The Migrations of Hawks* (Indiana University Press, 1986).

Kittery Point (near Kittery)

Spring Flights: Information unavailable.

Autumn Flights: Probably fair to good.

Watch Site Description: Any suitable spot with an exposed view as close to the tip of Kittery Point as possible. More than 400 Sharp-shinned Hawks have been reported migrating past this site in late September.

Access: From the junction of U.S. Route 1 and State Route 103 at Kittery, drive east on Route 103 to Kittery Point. Park in a suitable location and explore the coastline as close to Kittery Point as possible, watching for migrating hawks.

References: *American Birds*, 1976, 30 (1): 29–36; *The Migrations of Hawks* (Indiana University Press, 1986).

Monhegan Island

Spring Flights: Information unavailable.

Autumn Flights: Fair.

Description: The top of an open field near the eastern shore, beyond the last buildings of the village, where the island's only main road ends. Sharp-shinned Hawks pass overhead.

Access: From the wharf, follow the main road to the right. Continue through the village and along the harbor, then continue on the road as it turns inland and eventually ends at the top of the field near the eastern shore.

References: *Bird Islands Down East* (Macmillan, 1941): 114; *A Guide to Hawk Watching in North America* (Pennsylvania State University Press, 1979).

Mount Agamenticus (near Ogunquit)

Spring Flights: Poor.

Autumn Flights: Fair.

Watch Site Description: The summit of Mount Agamenticus, from which hawk watchers have good views of passing birds.

Access: From the center of Ogunquit, drive south on U.S. Route 1 for 0.4 mile to Agamenticus Road. Turn right (west) onto Agamenticus Road and continue about 2 miles to a stop sign. Turn right and drive a short distance to Mountain Road on the left. Turn onto Mountain Road and continue 1.5 miles, then turn right onto a road and continue 0.6 mile to a large parking area on the summit of the mountain. The distance from U.S. 1 to the mountain summit is about 6.1 miles.

References: *A Guide to Hawk Watching in North America* (Pennsylvania State University Press, 1979); *The Migrations of Hawks* (Indiana University Press, 1986).

Mount Cadillac in Acadia National Park (near Bar Harbor)

Spring Flights: Information unavailable.

Autumn Flights: Fair.

Frenchman Bay seen from the summit of Mount Cadillac, Acadia National Park, Maine.

**Watch Site
Description:** The top of Mount Cadillac, from which observers enjoy superb views over Frenchman Bay and the Gulf of Maine.

Access: From Bar Harbor, drive into the park and follow the directional signs to the summit of Mount Cadillac. Park in the lot at the summit and observe from there, or walk about 200 yards along the North Ridge Trail to the site from which hawk counting is done.

References: *A Guide to Hawk Watching in North America* (Pennsylvania State University Press, 1979); *The Migrations of Hawks* (Indiana University Press, 1986); *HMANA Hawk Migration Studies*, 2001, 27 (1): 127; 2002, 28 (1): 108.

Popham Beach State Park (south of Bath)

Spring Flights: Information unavailable.

Autumn Flights: Probably fair.

**Watch Site
Description:** The south coastline of the park.

Access: From the junction of U.S. Route 1 and State Route 209 at Bath, drive south on State Route 209 for a number of miles to Popham Beach State Park. Enter the park, leave your vehicle in a designated area, and explore the southern coast, watching for migrating raptors following the coastline. Raptor migration data are unavailable for this site, but based on its geographic location it is possible that raptor migrations can be seen here.

References: None.

Maryland

Assateague Island National Seashore/Assateague State Park (near Berlin)

Spring Flights: Information unavailable.

Autumn Flights: Fair.

**Watch Site
Description:** The dunes and outer beach areas along the length of the island are famous as a Peregrine Falcon flyway.

Access: To enter Assateague Island National Seashore/Assateague State Park from Berlin, drive east on State Route 376 to the junction with State Route 611, then continue south on Route 611 into the park.

References: *Raptor Research News*, 1971, 5: 31–43; *Journal of Wildlife Management*, 1972, 36: 484–492; *A Guide to Hawk Watching in North America* (Pennsylvania State University Press, 1979).

Bay Hundred Peninsula (near Fairbank)

Spring Flights: None.

Autumn Flights: Fair.

Watch Site Description: A narrow peninsula extending southward into the Chesapeake Bay with largely rural land that is either wooded or under cultivation.

Access: From Easton, follow State Route 33 west to St. Michaels, then head west and south on the Bay Hundred Peninsula to its tip near the village of Fairbank. Hawk watching is done from Route 33 near the southern tip of the peninsula anywhere adjacent to open habitats with good visibility. Do not trespass!

References: *A Guide to Hawk Watching in North America* (Pennsylvania State University Press, 1979); *The Migrations of Hawks* (Indiana University Press, 1986).

Fort Smallwood Park (near Pasadena)

Spring Flights: Good.

Autumn Flights: Poor.

Watch Site Description: The shoreline of the Chesapeake Bay in a park near the confluence of the Patapsco River and the bay. Hawk watchers enjoy good to excellent views in all directions. Ospreys, Northern Harriers, and Sharp-shinned Hawks are important components of spring hawk migrations at this watch site.

Access: From Pasadena and the intersection of State Route 100 east and State Route 607, turn left onto Route 607 and continue for two traffic lights. At the second light turn right onto State Route 173 (Fort Smallwood Road); continue for about 3 miles to the end of the road and entrance to the park. Pay an entrance fee at the booth near the park entrance, turn left onto the loop road, turn

Hawk watchers at Fort Smallwood, Maryland. Photo by Sue A. Ricciardi.

right at a T intersection, and continue to a parking lot located on the right side of the fort. Park in this lot, then walk south past a pavilion to a gate. Continue through the gate for about 200 yards to a point where you encounter a broad view (an old shack may be at that spot). Enjoy hawk watching from a suitable spot in the vicinity of the shack along the Chesapeake Bay. Many hawk watchers bring a folding chair for comfort.

Fort Smallwood Park is open to the public from mid-April to mid-November. Entrance to the park at other times of the year is uncertain, and there are no visitor facilities available during the closed period.

References: *The Migrations of Hawks* (Indiana University Press, 1986); *HMANA Hawk Migration Studies*, 2002, 27 (2): 103–105.

Hooper Island (near Church Creek)

Spring Flights: None.

Autumn Flights: Good.

Watch Site Description: A group of three long, narrow islands (Upper, Middle, and Lower Hooper Islands) bordered on the east by the Honga River and on the west by Tar and Chesapeake Bays. Hawk watching can be done at various spots on the three-part island, and observers will sometimes find it necessary to drive down the island group looking for migrating birds in various directions. At other times hawk watchers can station themselves at spots south of Hoopersville, in the center of Middle Hooper Island, around Ferry Point at the southern end of Upper Hooper Island, just west of Fishing Creek, or north of Honga just before the Hooper Island Road crosses onto Upper Hooper Island. *Warning*: The residents of Hooper Island have a long and sometimes fierce tradition of independence and have been known to shoot at strangers who are trespassing. They also have a tradition of shooting and eating migrating hawks and other birds—let the hawk watcher beware!

Access: From Cambridge, follow State Route 16 south to Church Creek. Then follow State Route 335 south to Hooper Island and the villages of Honga, Fishing Creek, and Hoopersville.

References: *Bulletin Natural History Society of Maryland*, 1935, 5 (7): 34–40; *A Guide to Hawk Watching in North America* (Pennsylvania State University Press, 1979); *The Migrations of Hawks* (Indiana University Press, 1986).

Kent Island (near Stevensville)

Spring Flights: None.

Autumn Flights: Fair.

Watch Site Description: A narrow island extending southward into the Chesapeake Bay with largely rural land that is wooded or under cultivation.

Access: From Grasonville, drive west on U.S. Routes 50/301 to the town of Stevensville. Then continue south on State Route 8 as far as possible on Kent Island toward its southern tip. Hawk watching is done from the highway near the tip—anywhere adjacent to open habitats with good visibility. *Do not trespass on private property.*

References: *A Guide to Hawk Watching in North America* (Pennsylvania State University Press, 1979); *The Migrations of Hawks* (Indiana University Press, 1986).

Roth Rock Fire Tower (near Oakland)

Spring Flights: None.

Autumn Flights: Good.

Watch Site Description: A fire tower on the crest of Backbone Mountain providing unrestricted views in all directions.

Access: From Oakland, drive south on U.S. Route 219 to Red House. Then continue east on U.S. Route 50 for 2.5 miles. Turn south there onto a paved road and continue for 1 mile to the top of Backbone Mountain. Then turn right and continue for another mile on a steep, stony road to the fire tower.

References: *A Guide to Hawk Watching in North America* (Pennsylvania State University Press, 1979); *The Migrations of Hawks* (Indiana University Press, 1986).

Sandy Point State Park (near Annapolis)

Spring Flights: Fair.

Autumn Flights: Fair.

Watch Site Description: A point extending into the Chesapeake Bay.

Access: From Annapolis, drive northeast on U.S. Route 50 for about 7 miles to the park, which is located at the western end of the Chesapeake Bay Bridge. Enter the park and ask at the headquarters where the best spots are located for hawk watching.

References: *American Birds*, 1976, 30 (1): 48; *A Guide to Hawk Watching in North America* (Pennsylvania State University Press, 1979); *The Migrations of Hawks* (Indiana University Press, 1986).

Table Rock (near Red House)

Spring Flights: Information unavailable.

Autumn Flights: Fair.

Watch Site Description: A small pullover or clearing along the side of a road.

Access: From the junction of U.S. Routes 50 and 219 near Red House (about 10 miles southwest of Oakland), drive east on U.S. 50 for about 2 miles, then turn right onto Table Rock Road near the crest of the mountain. Just after entering Table Rock Road, pull into the small roadside pullover, or clearing, on the right side of the road and observe hawk migrations from here.

Reference: Maryland Ornithological Society Web site at www.mdbirds.org/hawkwatch.html.

Town Hill Hawk Watch (near Hancock)

Spring Flights: Information unavailable.

Autumn Flights: Probably fair.

Watch Site Description: A long, roofed shelter providing excellent views across the valley to the east.

Access: From Hancock, drive west on Interstate 68, continuing past Sidling Hill. When you reach the Washington–Allegany county line, continue for 3 miles to the junction of I–68 and U.S. Route 40. Turn onto U.S. 40 and continue to the summit of Town Hill. Look for the Town Hill Inn on the right. The hawk watching site is on the left across the road from the inn.

Reference: Maryland Ornithological Society Web site at www.mdbirds.org/hawkwatch.html.

Turkey Point in Elk Neck State Park (near North East)

Spring Flights: Information unavailable.

Autumn Flights: Fair.

Watch Site Description: An exposed location with views of the surrounding area.

Access: From the junction of Interstate 95 and State Route 272 near North East, leave I–95 at exit 100 and drive south on Route 272 to its terminus. Enter Elk Neck State Park, leave your vehicle in a suitable location, and walk about a mile to the Turkey Point site, where hawk watching is done. Hawk watching continues from early September through late November.

References: *HMANA Hawk Migration Studies*, 2001, 27 (1): 183–184; 2002, 28 (1): 47–49; Maryland Ornithological Society Web site at www.mdbirds.org/hawkwatch.html.

Washington Monument State Park (near Boonsboro)

Spring Flights: Fair.

Autumn Flights: Fair.

Watch Site Description: The top of a stone tower in the park.

Access: From Boonsboro, follow Alternate (old) U.S. Route 40 to the top of South Mountain. Then turn left onto a road opposite an inn and continue for a mile to Washington Monument State Park. Enter the park and drive to a parking lot near the stone tower. Walk to the tower via a trail and climb to the top. The park is sometimes called Monument Knob State Park.

References: *Atlantic Naturalist*, 1951, 6: 166–168; 1966, 21: 161–168; *A Guide to Hawk Watching in North America* (Pennsylvania State University Press, 1979); *The Migrations of Hawks* (Indiana University Press, 1986); *HMANA Hawk Migration Studies*, 2001, 27 (1): 188–189; 2002, 28 (1): 46–47.

Observation tower, Washington Monument State Park, Maryland.

Massachusetts

Barre Falls (near Gardner)

Spring Flights: Fair.

Autumn Flights: Poor to fair.

Watch Site Description: The parking lot on a south-facing hill overlooking the Ware River Valley. The watch site provides a 180-degree view toward the east.

Access: From the junction of State Routes 2 and 68 (exit 23) at Gardner, drive south on Route 68 to the junction with State Route 62. Turn right (west) onto Route 62 and continue for about 2 miles to the entrance to the Barre Falls Dam on the left. Enter and continue to the unpaved parking lot on the left. Hawk watching is done from this lot.

References: *HMANA Hawk Migration Studies*, 2001, 27 (1): 132–133; 2002, 27 (2): 96–100, 102, 122; 2002, 28 (1): 106–107; 2003, 28 (2): 30, 34–40.

Blueberry Hill (near Granville)

Spring Flights: Poor.

Autumn Flights: Good.

Watch Site Description: The summit of a hill, known locally as Blueberry Hill, from which migrating hawks are observed.

Access: From Westfield, drive south on U.S. Route 202 to the junction with State Route 57 near Southwick. Turn west onto Route 57 and continue through Granville to North Lane 2 (a right turn about 3 miles west of Granville). Turn right (north) onto North Lane 2 and continue for about a mile to Blueberry Hill on your right. Park at the bottom of the hill. Then walk about 0.25 mile to the summit, from which hawk watching is done.

References: *Bird Observer of Eastern Massachusetts*, 1977, 5 (4): 107–111; *A Guide to Hawk Watching in North America* (Pennsylvania State University Press, 1979); *The Migra-*

tions of Hawks (Indiana University Press, 1986); *HMANA Hawk Migration Studies*, 2001, 27 (1): 136; 2002, 28 (1): 103–104.

Bolton Flats Hawk Watch (near Bolton)

Spring Flights: Information unavailable.

Autumn Flights: Excellent.

Watch Site Description: The spring watch site is the top of a small hill beside a pond. The autumn watch site is the top of a grassy hill at a roadside pullover. Migrating Broad-winged Hawks are the primary attractions at this watch site, although various other raptors are also seen in small numbers. The site is located on a wildlife management area owned and operated by the commonwealth of Massachusetts. Hunting limits hawk watching activities on the property from October into December.

Access: From the junction of Interstate 495 and State Route 117 in Bolton, drive west on Route 117 to the junction with State Route 110, then continue a short distance farther on Route 117 to the entrance to the Bolton Flats Wildlife Management Area. Enter and park in a suitable spot. Then walk on a trail to a small hill adjacent to a pond from which hawk watching is done in spring. Autumn hawk watching is done from another site reached by driving west on Route 117 *past* the entrance to the Bolton Flats Wildlife Management Area for a few hundred yards to a small roadside pullover on the left. Park here and walk to the top of a grassy hill at the pullover. Watch hawk migrations from this hilltop.

References: *Raptor Watch* (BirdLife International and Hawk Mountain Sanctuary, 2000); HMANA Web site at www.hmana.org.

Fisher Hill (near Westhampton)

Spring Flights: Poor.

Autumn Flights: Good.

Watch Site
Description: The exposed top of a hill, at an elevation of 1,309 feet, providing an unrestricted view in all directions.

Access: At the junction of State Routes 9 and 66 in Northampton, drive west on Route 66 for 10.4 miles to a house on the right side of the highway. On the left, just beyond the house, is an unpaved road. Park near this road and walk up it for about 0.25 mile to the exposed summit, from which hawk watching is done.

References: *A Guide to Hawk Watching in North America* (Pennsylvania State University Press, 1979); *The Migrations of Hawks* (Indiana University Press, 1986).

Martha's Vineyard

Spring Flights: None.

Autumn Flights: Poor.

Watch Site
Description: The shoreline along the southeastern end of Chappaquiddick Island and the entire southern shore of Martha's Vineyard as far as Squibnocket Point and Zacks Cliffs serve as a migration route for limited numbers of Peregrine Falcons during autumn.

Access: Various roads on the island pass within close proximity to portions of the shorelines previously mentioned. Some walking and searching for favorable observation spots will be necessary, but avoid trespassing on private property. Most visitor accommodations on the island are available by reservation only.

References: *A Guide to Hawk Watching in North America* (Pennsylvania State University Press, 1979); *The Migrations of Hawks* (Indiana University Press, 1986).

Mount Everett State Reservation (near South Egremont)

Spring Flights: Information unavailable.

Autumn Flights: Good.

Watch Site
Description: An exposed summit of the mountain from which hawk watchers may view migrating hawks.

Access: From South Egremont, drive west on State Routes 23/41, following signs pointing toward Jug End Resort. At the point a short distance from South Egremont where the two routes separate, follow Route 41 a little farther, then turn right (Route 41 turns left) onto another road marked by a sign pointing to Mount Everett and Jug End Resort. Continue to the first crossroad, then drive straight ahead, uphill, for 2.8 miles to a fork. Follow the left fork in the road (a sign there points to Bash Bish Falls and Copake Falls, New York) for 3 miles to the entrance to Mount Everett State Reservation on the left. Drive to the parking lot near the summit of the mountain, then walk to the top of the mountain.

References: *Journal Hawk Migration Association*, 1975, 1 (1): 8; *A Guide to Hawk Watching in North America* (Pennsylvania State University Press, 1979); *The Migrations of Hawks* (Indiana University Press, 1986).

Mount Tom State Reservation (near Holyoke)

Spring Flights: Poor.

Autumn Flights: Good.

Watch Site
Description: Observations are made from an open steel tower on the summit of Goat Peak within the reservation.

Access: From Interstate 91, take the Easthampton exit and follow State Route 141 north for 2.3 miles to the reservation entrance. Turn right and continue 1.5 miles into the reserve to the Goat Peak parking lot. Then walk along a well-used trail to the Goat Peak observation tower.

References: *Bulletin Massachusetts Audubon Society*, 1937, 21: 5–8; *A Guide to Hawk Watching in North America* (Pennsylvania State University Press, 1979); *The Migrations of Hawks* (Indiana University Press, 1986).

Upridge view from Goat Peak, Mount Tom State Reservation, Massachusetts.

Mount Wachusett State Reservation (at Princeton)

Spring Flights: Information unavailable.

Autumn Flights: Excellent.

Watch Site Description: A 2,006-foot-high mountain providing views of Boston to the east and the Berkshire Mountains to the west. No single spot provides good views in all directions, but the watch site facing Leominister seems to be the best for hawk watching, followed by the view to the right of the fire tower (especially good for accipiters). Broad-winged Hawks are the most common raptors, followed by Sharp-shinned Hawks and lesser numbers of other species.

Access: From Boston, drive west on State Route 2 to the junction with State Route 140 in Westminster. Turn south onto

Route 140 and continue to Wachusett Lake. At this point turn right onto Mile Hill Road and follow the signs to Mount Wachusett Ski Area. Approximately 0.5 mile past the ski area, you will arrive at the entrance to the reservation on the right. Enter and drive to the summit of the mountain, following the reserve's paved road. This road usually is open by 8:00 A.M. (although it is marked as opening at 10:00 A.M.) and remains open until dusk. After October 30 the road is closed for the season. Park at the top of the mountain and walk to the hawk watching sites previously described.

References: *Bird Observer of Eastern Massachusetts*, 1977, 5 (4): 107–111; *A Guide to Hawk Watching in North America* (Pennsylvania State University Press, 1979); *The Migrations of Hawks* (Indiana University Press, 1986); *HMANA Hawk Migration Studies*, 2001, 27 (1): 134–135; 2002, 28 (1): 104.

Mount Watatic (near Ashburnham)

Spring Flights: Information unavailable.

Autumn Flights: Excellent.

Watch Site Description: The summit of a mountain with views of the surrounding landscape.

Access: From Ashburnham and the junction of State Routes 12 and 101, turn right onto Route 101 and continue to the junction with State Route 119. Turn left onto Route 119, and continue for 0.7 mile to a steep trail leading off the right side of the road at a power line. Follow the trail for about thirty minutes to the summit of Mount Watatic, where hawk watching is done. Alternatively, drive west on Route 119 for 0.8 mile to a parking area off the side of the road and leave your vehicle there. Then follow either of two trails—the Blueberry Ledge Trail or the Nutting Hill Trail—to the summit of Mount Watatic. The walk using these trails requires from forty-five to sixty minutes.

References: *Raptor Watch* (BirdLife International and Hawk Mountain Sanctuary, 2000); HMANA Web site at www.hmana.org.

Parker River National Wildlife Refuge (on Plum Island)

Spring Flights: Good.

Autumn Flights: Information unavailable.

Watch Site Description: A barrier beach island, the southern half of which forms part of the Parker River National Wildlife Refuge. Most migrating hawks can be seen from the Hellcat Swamp Dunes Observation Platform, or from the main parking lot (Lot No. 1). Sharp-shinned Hawks and American Kestrels are the most commonly observed species, but other species including some Merlins also can be expected.

Access: From Boston, follow U.S. Route 1 north for about 35 miles to Hanover Street in Newbury. Turn right onto Hanover Street (which becomes Rolfe's Lane at the first set of traffic lights) and drive to the harbor. Turn right there onto Water Street, which becomes the Plum Island Turnpike, and follow it to Plum Island. Once on the island, turn at the first right and follow this road to the refuge entrance. Enter and continue driving to the main parking lot or another spot you select to watch migrating hawks.

References: *Bird Observer of Eastern Massachusetts*, 1978, 6 (1): 10–22; *A Guide to Hawk Watching in North America* (Pennsylvania State University Press, 1979); *The Migrations of Hawks* (Indiana University Press, 1986); *Raptor Watch* (BirdLife International and Hawk Mountain Sanctuary, 2000); *HMANA Hawk Migration Studies*, 2002, 27 (2): 121.

Pilgrim Heights (in North Truro on Cape Cod)

Spring Flights: Poor to fair.

Autumn Flights: Information unavailable.

Watch Site Description: The top of a ridge or hill within Cape Cod National Seashore, providing a vista over a river valley toward the east and northeast, coastal heath toward the west, and dunes and the Atlantic Ocean toward the east. Spring hawk watching is done during April and May, with the best period being late April and early May.

Access: At the Pilgrim Heights section of Cape Cod National Seashore along U.S. Route 6 at North Truro, leave your vehicle in the parking area on the east side of the road just south of the Provincetown–Truro town line. Then walk on an interpretive trail to the second (northernmost) overlook, from which hawk watching is done.

References: *Raptor Watch* (BirdLife International and Hawk Mountain Sanctuary, 2000); *HMANA Hawk Migration Studies,* 2002, 27 (2): 120–121.

Province Lands State Reservation (near Provincetown)

Spring Flights: Fair.

Autumn Flights: Information unavailable.

Watch Site Description: The observation deck of the visitor center from which falcons can be seen over the outer beach, or the summit of High Dune from which clear views in all directions are enjoyed.

Access: In Provincetown, at the outer tip of Cape Cod, follow U.S. Route 6 to Race Point Road. Turn left onto Race Point Road and continue driving to the visitor center, from which hawk watching can be done. Alternatively, stop at the Beech Forest parking lot (the first on the left) after turning from U.S. 6 onto Race Point Road. Park here, then walk on the trail to the south of Wood Duck Pond (to your left when facing the pond from the parking lot) to a section of split-rail fence on the south side of the trail. Turn south along the sandy trail. Then pass through scrub pine to the summit of High Dune (the highest point in the area), from which observations are made.

References: *Bird Observer of Eastern Massachusetts,* 1978, 6 (2): 40–47; *A Guide to Hawk Watching in North America* (Pennsylvania State University Press, 1979); *The Migrations of Hawks* (Indiana University Press, 1986).

Quabbin Reservoir (near Belchertown)

Spring Flights: Information unavailable.

Autumn Flights: Good.

Watch Site Description: A lookout tower with nearby picnic and parking facilities.

Access: From Ware, drive west on State Route 9 for 7.25 miles to the Winsor Dam entrance to Quabbin Reservoir. Enter, then drive to the parking lot near the observation tower. After parking, walk to the tower or open areas nearby and observe from there.

References: *Journal Hawk Migration Association*, 1975, 1 (1): 8; *A Guide to Hawk Watching in North America* (Pennsylvania State University Press, 1979); *The Migrations of Hawks* (Indiana University Press, 1986).

Round Top (in Athol)

Spring Flights: Poor.

Autumn Flights: Good.

Watch Site Description: An exposed summit of a 1,207-foot-high hill from which unrestricted observations in all directions are possible. Hawk watching is done from a picnic table at the highest point on the hill.

Access: From the center of Athol, drive east on Main Street until Athol Memorial Hospital appears on the right. At the sign ATHOL CONSERVATION AREA, turn left onto Bearsden Road and follow it north for about a mile to a fork in the road. Take the right fork, following the ATHOL CONSERVATION AREA signs to a point where the road is unpaved. Park here at a suitable spot. Then walk along the road to a sign on the right reading ROUND TOP PATH. Follow this well-marked trail for about 0.5 mile to the summit of the exposed hill and the picnic table from which hawk watching is done.

References: *A Guide to Hawk Watching in North America* (Pennsylvania State University Press, 1979); *The Migrations of Hawks* (Indiana University Press, 1986).

Michigan

Brockway Mountain (near Copper Harbor)

Spring Flights: Good.

Autumn Flights: Information unavailable.

**Watch Site
Description:** The exposed, treeless summit of an east-to-west ridge at the northern end of the Keweenaw Peninsula.

Access: From the twin cities of Hancock and Houghton, drive north on U.S. Route 41 for about 24 miles to Phoenix (a "ghost town" of about a dozen houses along the highway). At Phoenix turn left onto State Route 26 and continue for about 2 miles to the village of Eagle River. Remain on Route 26 for another 8 miles to Eagle Harbor, where the road makes a sharp right followed by a sharp left, and continue for 4.5 miles to the point in which the highway crosses a small stone bridge over the Silver River. Route 26 bears left here, while the Brockway Mountain Drive bears right; follow the Brockway Mountain Drive for about 5 miles to the top of the mountain. At times, early in the season, the road may not yet be clear of snow, and it is sometimes necessary to walk for several miles to the summit. Be prepared for very cold, windy weather on top of the mountain.

References: *Birding*, 1977, 9 (2): 79–80; *A Guide to Hawk Watching in North America* (Pennsylvania State University Press, 1979).

Lake Erie Metropark (near Rockwood)

Spring Flights: Information unavailable.

Autumn Flights: Excellent.

**Watch Site
Description:** An exposed area near a boat launch overlooking the Detroit River and its surroundings areas at the mouth of the Detroit River. This is a major autumn migration

watch site for Broad-winged Hawks (several hundred thousand Broad-wings are counted in a season), as well as for far smaller numbers of Turkey Vultures, Sharp-shinned Hawks, Red-tailed Hawks, and American Kestrels. Lake Erie Metropark is used for autumn hawk watching under all wind conditions *except* north winds. Members of Southeastern Michigan Raptor Research coordinate raptor counting at this site. When north winds occur, use the nearby Point Mouille State Game Area (see below).

Access: From Detroit, drive south on Interstate 75 to exit 27 (Rockwood). Leave I–75 here and head east on Huron River Drive for 2.3 miles to the junction with West Jefferson Road. Turn left (north) onto West Jefferson Road and continue a short distance to the entrance of Lake Erie Metropark on the right. There is a $4.00 fee to enter the park. Enter the park and drive to the boat-launch area. Hawk watching is done here on the south side of the boat slips—*except* on days with strong northerly winds. On those days, hawk watchers gather at the nearby Point Mouille State Game Area boat-launch area (see below).

References: *The Migrations of Hawks* (Indiana University Press, 1986); *Raptor Watch* (BirdLife International and Hawk Mountain Sanctuary, 2000); *Birding*, 2001, 33 (5): 403–406; *HMANA Hawk Migration Studies*, 2002, 28 (1): 161–163; 2003, 29 (1): 12.

Lakeport State Park (near Port Huron)

Spring Flights: Good.

Autumn Flights: Fair.

Watch Site Description: A picnic area in Lakeport State Park providing open views of the south shoreline of Lake Huron.

Access: From Lakeport (a few miles north of Port Huron), drive south for a short distance on State Route 25 to Lakeport State Park. Enter the park and continue to the picnic area overlooking Lake Huron, from which hawk watching is done.

References: *Audubon Field Notes,* 1961, 15 (4): 405–409; 1963, 17 (4): 404–407; 1966, 20 (4): 511–513; *A Guide to Hawk Watching in North America* (Pennsylvania State University Press, 1979); *The Migrations of Hawks* (Indiana University Press, 1986); *Raptor Watch* (BirdLife International and Hawk Mountain Sanctuary, 2000).

Point Mouille State Game Area (near Rockwood)

Spring Flights: Information unavailable.

Autumn Flights: Excellent.

Watch Site Description: The exposed parking lot and boat-launch area of a wildlife management area near the mouth of the Detroit River. This is a major autumn migration watch site for Broad-winged Hawks (several hundred thousand Broad-wings are counted in a season), but much smaller numbers of Turkey Vultures, Sharp-shinned Hawks, Red-tailed Hawks, and American Kestrels are reported as well. This site is used when strong northerly winds occur. When winds from other directions occur, use the Lake Erie Metropark watch site (described above) for hawk watching.

Access: From Detroit, drive south on Interstate 75 to exit 27 (Rockwood). Leave I–75 here and head east on Huron River Drive for 2.3 miles to the junction with West Jefferson Road. Turn right (south) onto West Jefferson Road and continue for several miles to Campau Road. Turn left onto Campau Road (the sign for this road is on the right side of the highway), and drive for about 2 miles to the entrance to the Point Mouille State Game Area. Enter and continue to the boat-launch area and parking lot. Hawk watching is done near the observation platform.

References: *Birding,* 2001, 33 (5): 403–406; *HMANA Hawk Migration Studies,* 2002, 28 (1): 163; 2003, 29 (1): 12.

Straits of Mackinac (near Mackinaw City)

Spring Flights: Good.

Autumn Flights: Fair.

**Watch Site
Description:** Areas with exposed views west of Mackinaw City along Wilderness Park Drive.

Access: From the Lower Peninsula, drive north on Interstate 75 to the last exit off the interstate before the Mackinac Bridge. Take this exit to Wilderness Park Drive and travel west from the city limits for a mile or two; good hawk watching is possible in this area.

References: *Jack-Pine Warbler*, 1965, 43: 79–83; *A Guide to Hawk Watching in North America* (Pennsylvania State University Press, 1979).

Whitefish Point Bird Observatory (near Paradise)

Spring Flights: Good.

Autumn Flights: Fair.

**Watch Site
Description:** A parking lot near the lighthouse, the road leading to the point, or a platform on a dune west of the road near the shoreline.

Access: From the Lower Peninsula, cross the Straits of Mackinac on Interstate 75 and continue northward to its junction with State Route 123. Turn onto Route 123 and continue north to Paradise. Then follow an unnumbered road north for about 12 miles to Whitefish Point.

References: *Jack-Pine Warbler*, 1965, 43: 79–83; *A Guide to Hawk Watching in North America* (Pennsylvania State University Press, 1979); *The Migrations of Hawks* (Indiana University Press, 1986); *Raptor Watch* (BirdLife International and Hawk Mountain Sanctuary, 2000); *HMANA Hawk Migration Studies*, 2002, 27 (2): 64–65, 76–77; 2003, 28 (2): 46.

Minnesota

Eagle Ridge (in La Crescent)

Spring Flights: Experimental (not evaluated).

Autumn Flights: Experimental (not evaluated).

Watch Site Description: A roadside pullover on a high bluff along Scenic Drive providing excellent views over the Mississippi River and Lock & Dam No. 7.

Access: In La Crescent, take Elm Street to Scenic Drive, then continue north on Scenic Drive to the roadside pullover. Park and observe from here. Alternatively, follow Mackintosh Road to the watch site.

Reference: HMANA Web site at www.hmana.org.

Hawk Ridge Nature Reserve (in Duluth)

Spring Flights: Fair.

Autumn Flights: Excellent.

Watch Site Description: Bluffs rising 600 to 800 feet above the shoreline of Lake Superior in Duluth. The most important spot, the Main Overlook, is along Skyline Parkway. Hawk Ridge is especially notable for large autumn flights of Bald Eagles, Sharp-shinned Hawks, Broad-winged Hawks, Red-tailed Hawks, and American Kestrels.

Access: From the junction of Interstate 35 and 26th Street/London Road in Duluth, take the 26th Street/London Road (State Route 61) exit and continue northeast on London Road to the junction with 43rd Street. Turn left onto Glenwood Street and continue 0.8 mile to the top of the first hill you encounter and the junction with Skyline Parkway. Turn sharply right onto Skyline Parkway and continue a mile to the HAWK RIDGE NATURE RESERVE sign.

Hawk watchers along Skyline Parkway, Hawk Ridge Nature Reserve, Duluth, Minnesota.

Park along the road and observe near the sign. During the autumn migration season, hawk watchers are almost always found here.

References: *Wilson Bulletin*, 1966: 79–87; *A Guide to Hawk Watching in North America* (Pennsylvania State University Press, 1979); *The Migrations of Hawks* (Indiana University Press, 1986); Hawk Ridge home page at www.hawkridge.org/direct.htm.

Paradise Point (near Reno)

Spring Flights: Information unavailable.

Autumn Flights: Fair.

Watch Site Description: The top of a bluff near the Mississippi River in Richard J. Dorer Memorial Hardwood State Forest, Crooked Creek township, Houston County, Minnesota. Hawk watchers have superb, unrestricted views toward the north, east, and west—which make this watch site useful for hawk watching purposes—but a somewhat restricted view toward the south.

Access: From the junction of State Highway 26 and Township Road 105 in Reno, drive north for 1.5 miles on Township Road 105 to a trailhead on the right side of the road. Park and walk on the trail to an old quarry and a ridge of rock that's used for hawk watching.

References: *The Migrations of Hawks* (Indiana University Press, 1986); *Loon*, 1996, 68: 158–164.

West Skyline Hawk Count (in Duluth)

Spring Flights: Excellent.

Autumn Flights: Not used during autumn.

Watch Site Description: Two locations are used for the West Skyline Hawk Count: Rice's Point Scenic Overlook provides an excellent view over the Duluth–Superior Harbor, and Thompson Hill looks over the adjacent landscape. Thompson Hill is a secondary location used when east and northeast winds prevail.

Access: Directions for visiting these locations follow.

- *Rice's Point Scenic Overlook.* From the junction of Interstate 35 and U.S. Route 53, drive north on U.S. 53 and continue uphill to West Skyline Drive. Turn right onto West Skyline Drive, continue past the Enger Municipal Golf Course on the left, then on past Hank Jensen Road on the left. After passing Hank Jensen Road, continue toward the Harbor Overlook below the Enger Tower Park. The hawk migration watch site is the Rice's Point Marker/Plaque Scenic Overlook overlooking the Duluth–Superior Harbor.

- *Thompson Hill.* To reach this location from the north, follow Interstate 35 in Duluth to exit 149 (Boundary Avenue/Proctor). Take exit 149, turn left at the end of the ramp, continue over the interstate, then turn right onto West Skyline Drive (the next right turn). Continue on West Skyline Drive for about 0.75 mile to Thompson Hill, located a short distance below the Thompson

Hill rest stop. When coming from the south, take exit 149 (Boundary Avenue) off I–35 and turn right at the end of the ramp. Continue to the next right, turn onto West Skyline Drive, and continue as per the previous directions.

References: *Loon*, 1998, 70: 47–52; *HMANA Hawk Migration Studies*, 2002, 27 (2): 73; 2003, 28 (2): 57–58; 2003, 28 (2): 46.

Mississippi

Fort Hill (in Vicksburg)

Spring Flights: Fair.

Autumn Flights: Fair.

Watch Site
Description: The top of a mountain providing a panoramic view of the surrounding landscape. The watch site is in Vicksburg National Military Park.

Access: In Vicksburg, follow directional signs to the Vicksburg National Military Park. Secure further directions there for visiting Fort Hill.

Reference: *Raptor Watch* (BirdLife International and Hawk Mountain Sanctuary, 2000).

Montana

Bridger Mountains Hawk Watch (near Bozeman)

Spring Flights: Information unavailable.

Autumn Flights: Poor to good.

Watch Site
Description: This watch site, the crest of a ridge above the Bridger Bowl Ski Area, is noted for the large numbers of Golden Eagles seen there—especially during early October. Ideal autumn hawk watching conditions occur on warm days with prevailing southeast or southwest winds.

Access: From Bozeman, drive north about 12 miles to the Bridger Bowl Ski Area. Park in a suitable area, then walk up a foot trail that begins on the south side of a shack for the top ski lift and extends around switchbacks for the final 200 feet to the ridge summit, identified by some radio antennas and a small building. A spot about 0.25 mile north of the radio antennas is ideal, with excellent views toward east and west, but almost any spot along the ridge crest can also be used for hawk watching.

References: *Birding*, 1991, 23 (4): 197–204; *HMANA Hawk Migration Studies*, 2001, 27 (1): 69; 2002, 28 (1): 196–197.

Rogers Pass Overlook (near Wolf Creek)

Spring Flights: Poor to fair.

Autumn Flights: Fair.

Watch Site Description: A roadside pullover from which observers have excellent views of the surrounding landscape. The watch site is especially noted for *large numbers of migrating Golden Eagles*, and some Bald Eagles, seen during March on cold southwest winds. Eagle flights are scattered during April.

Access: From the junction of Interstate 15 (exit 228) and U.S. Route 287 at Wolf Creek, drive north on U.S. 287 to the junction with State Route 200. Turn left (west) onto State Route 200 and continue to the top of Rogers Pass (elevation 5,610 feet). Look for a large roadside pullover 0.3 mile southwest of a road maintenance facility, and 1.2 miles southwest of the Middle Fork of the Dearborn River.

References: *Birding*, 1991, 23 (4): 197–204; *HMANA Hawk Migration Studies*, 2002, 27 (2): 38–39, 55; 2003, 28 (2): 61.

Nevada

Goshute Mountain (south of Wendover)

Spring Flights: Information unavailable.

Autumn Flights: Good to excellent.

**Watch Site
Description:** A mountain summit with wide vistas.

Access: From Interstate 80 north of Wendover, drive into town to Alternate U.S. Route 93, then continue south on U.S. 93 for about 25 miles to an old, unused highway maintenance facility on the west side of the highway. Turn west onto another road at this point, passing a pond, and continue to a T intersection (and perhaps BLM signs). Turn right at the T and continue for a few miles to a rough road from the left marked by a WILDERNESS STUDY AREA sign. Turn left onto this road and continue to a parking lot. Leave your vehicle there and hike for about 2.5 miles to the Goshute Mountain watch site (elevation about 10,000 feet—some 2,000 feet higher in elevation than the parking lot). Be very prepared for rugged hiking and cold, windy weather.

References: *HMANA Hawk Migration Studies*, 2001, 27 (1): 72–74; Virtual Birder Web site at www.virtualbirder.com.

New Hampshire

Little Round Top (near Bristol)

Spring Flights: None.

Autumn Flights: Good.

**Watch Site
Description:** An exposed summit of a hill with good views in all directions except southwest.

Access: From Interstate 93 near Bristol, leave the interstate at exit 23, drive into the center of Bristol, then drive south on State Route 3A to a firehouse and rescue squad building in the middle of a fork in the road near the edge of the town. Follow the right fork (High Street) up a hill, then turn right at the next fork onto New Chester Mountain Road (look for Slim Baker Lodge and sometimes HAWK WATCH signs). Follow this road as far as possible, ignoring all roads that turn sharply right, to the Slim Baker Conservation Area and Day Camp. Park at a suitable spot near the main building. Then walk for ten to fifteen minutes along a trail or old road with some steep sections to the lookout on the northeast corner of the hilltop. Hawk watching is done slightly below a large wooden cross and outdoor chapel.

References: *A Guide to Hawk Watching in North America* (Pennsylvania State University Press, 1979); *HMANA Hawk Migration Studies*, 2001, 27 (1): 129; 2002, 28 (1): 100–101.

Peaked Hill (near New Hampton)

Spring Flights: Poor.

Autumn Flights: Poor.

Watch Site Description: A vista from a road overlooking large fields.

Access: From Interstate 93 near Bristol, take exit 23 and follow State Route 104 toward Bristol. Cross a bridge, and at the next right, turn onto River Road. Drive to the fork, keep right, then continue to and take the next *sharp* left turn. Drive up the hill past the last farmhouse and stop at a cattle gate on the left. Remain on the side of the road at this spot and look over the fields on both sides of the road for migrating hawks.

References: *A Guide to Hawk Watching in North America* (Pennsylvania State University Press, 1979); *HMANA Hawk Migration Studies*, 2002, 27 (2): 122.

Pitcher Mountain (near Keene)

Spring Flights: Information unavailable.

Autumn Flights: Fair.

Watch Site Description: A broad, treeless mountain summit (elevation 2,153 feet) providing a 360-degree view. A fire tower is located on the summit.

Access: From Keene, in southern New Hampshire, drive north on State Route 10 to the junction with State Route 9, then continue north on Route 9 to the junction with State Route 123. Turn left (west) onto Route 123 and continue through Stoddard to the entrance to the Pitcher Mountain parking lot (marked by a sign along the right side of Route 123) about 2 miles past Stoddard. Park in the lot and walk to the summit of the mountain—a five- or ten-minute walk.

Reference: *A Guide to Hawk Watching in North America* (Pennsylvania State University Press, 1979).

South Pack Monadnock Mountain (near Peterborough)

Spring Flights: Information unavailable.

Autumn Flights: Fair.

Watch Site Description: A mountain summit providing exposed views of migrating hawks toward the north and west.

Access: From Peterborough, drive east on State Route 101 for a few miles to the Miller State Park entrance. Enter the park (there is a modest entrance fee) and drive to the summit of the mountain (South Pack Monadnock). Park and walk north for several hundred feet on the Wapack Trail to the spot from which hawk watching is done.

References: *Bird Observer of Eastern Massachusetts*, 1977, 5 (4): 107–111; *A Guide to Hawk Watching in North America* (Pennsylvania State University Press, 1979).

Uncanoonuc Mountain (near Goffstown)

Spring Flights: None.

Autumn Flights: Good.

Watch Site Description: A parking lot with visibility restricted by trees.

Access: From Main Street in Goffstown, drive on Mountain Road, keeping left around two sharp curves at two intersections. Turn left again onto Mountain Summit Road, following it to the top of the mountain. Park near the fire tower.

Reference: *A Guide to Hawk Watching in North America* (Pennsylvania State University Press, 1979).

New Jersey

Cape May Point State Park

Spring Flights: None.

Autumn Flights: Excellent.

Watch Site Description: An elevated platform adjacent to a large parking lot in front of the lighthouse, exposed areas between the platform and the front of the lighthouse, and miscellaneous other areas in the vicinity of the lighthouse or within the village of Cape May Point. The latter locations are determined by watching the flight paths of the hawks on a particular day.

Access: Drive south on the Garden State Parkway to its terminus just north of the town of Cape May, then continue ahead for about 2 miles on State Route 109 (Lafayette Street in Cape May) to its end at a stop sign. From here, go right

Hawk watchers at Cape May Point, New Jersey.

onto Perry Street, and continue for another 0.4 mile to the traffic light at Broadway and Sunset Boulevard. Follow Sunset Boulevard south for 1.7 miles to Lighthouse Avenue, then turn left and continue for 0.7 mile to Cape May Point State Park. The lighthouse toward which you are heading makes an excellent landmark. Enter, park in the large lot, then walk to the nearby hawk watching plat-form—or remain in the parking lot and watch migrating hawks from there.

References: *Auk*, 1936: 393–404; *Bird Studies at Old Cape May* (Dover Publications, 1965); *New Jersey Audubon*, 1977, 3 (7–8): 114–124; *A Guide to Hawk Watching in North America* (Pennsylvania State University Press, 1979); *The Migrations of Hawks* (Indiana University Press, 1986); *HMANA Hawk Migration Studies*, 2001, 27 (1): 184–186; 2002, 28 (1): 69–70.

Chimney Rock Hawk Watch (near Martinsville)

Spring Flights: Information unavailable.

Autumn Flights: Fair to good.

Watch Site
Description: A platform in Washington Valley Park from which hawk watchers have views over the surrounding landscape.

Access: From Interstate 287 at Martinsville, take the U.S. Route 22 exit and drive east for about 1 mile to a jug handle for Vosseler Avenue. Turn right onto the jug handle, then left onto Vosseler Avenue, and cross U.S. 22. Continue for about 0.6 mile to the top of a hill and look for Miller Lane on the left. Turn left onto narrow Miller Lane and drive about 0.5 mile to the parking lot for the hawk watching site. Park here, enter the trail at the far end of the lot, and walk to the watch site.

References: *The Migrations of Hawks* (Indiana University Press, 1986); *HMANA Hawk Migration Studies*, 2002, 28 (1): 76–77; Rutgers University Web site at www.eden.rutgers.edu/ ~cmagarel/chimney_rock/directions.html.

Greenbrook Sanctuary (near Tenafly)

Spring Flights: Information unavailable.

Autumn Flights: Excellent.

Watch Site Description: A parking lot near the entrance to the sanctuary, or the edge of the pond in the middle of the sanctuary.

Access: From Clinton Avenue (the main east-to-west street) in Tenafly, drive east on Clinton Avenue to State Route 9W (a T intersection). Turn left (north) onto Route 9W and drive about 0.5 mile to the first road leading to the right (the sanctuary entrance). Turn right and proceed about 300 feet to the gate. Enter after meeting the sanctuary naturalist (by prior arrangement only, through the Palisades Nature Association, P.O. Box 155, Alpine, NJ 07620) and continue to the watch sites previously described.

References: *A Guide to Hawk Watching in North America* (Pennsylvania State University Press, 1979); *The Migrations of Hawks* (Indiana University Press, 1986).

Higbee Beach Wildlife Management Area (near Cape May)

Spring Flights: Information unavailable.

Autumn Flights: Good to excellent.

Watch Site Description: On some days with prevailing northwest winds, hawks shift their flight-line from the tip of Cape May Point and migrate northward along the New Jersey side of Delaware Bay. Under such conditions, one of the best hawk migration watch sites is located along Higbee Beach north of Cape May Point. You can sit or stand behind the beach or along the shore and watch the migrating hawks pass by. Frequently large numbers of songbirds also appear here under similar weather conditions.

Access: From the town of Cape May at the southern terminus of the Garden State Parkway, drive through town and follow Sunset Boulevard toward Cape May Point for about 2 miles. Then turn right onto Bayshore Road and continue for 1.8 miles to Higbee Beach Road (the second paved road, marked with a DEAD END sign). Turn left (west) onto Higbee Beach Road and continue to the end of the pavement. Park, then walk along a road through a wooded area to the nearby beach. Migrating hawks and other birds can be observed at various locations here.

References: *Auk*, 1936: 393–404; *Bird Studies at Old Cape May* (Dover Publications, 1965); *A Guide to Hawk Watching in North America* (Pennsylvania State University Press, 1979); *The Migrations of Hawks* (Indiana University Press, 1986).

High Point State Park (near Sussex)

Spring Flights: Information unavailable.

Autumn Flights: Fair.

Watch Site
Description: An exposed ridge crest with a huge monument. Observe from the vicinity of the monument's base.

Access: In extreme northwestern New Jersey. From Sussex, drive north on State Route 23 for about 10 miles into High Point State Park, then follow marked park roads to the monument. Alternatively, from Interstate 84 at Port Jervis, New York, drive south on Route 23 to the park.

References: *Annotated List of Birds of High Point State Park and Stokes State Forest* (Dryden Kuser, 1962); *A Guide to Hawk Watching in North America* (Pennsylvania State University Press, 1979); *The Migrations of Hawks* (Indiana University Press, 1986).

Montclair Hawk Lookout Sanctuary

Spring Flights: Poor to fair.

Autumn Flights: Excellent.

Watch Site
Description: An exposed cliff edge and field overlooking a quarry and surrounding landscape.

Montclair Hawk Lookout Sanctuary, New Jersey.

Access: From exit 151 (Watchung Avenue) off the Garden State Parkway near Montclair, drive west on Watchung Avenue for about 2.1 miles to Upper Mountain Road, then turn right onto Upper Mountain Avenue. Remain on this street for about 0.75 mile, then turn left onto Bradford Avenue. Continue on Bradford Avenue for about 0.25 mile to Edgecliff Road (the second street on the right). Turn onto Edgecliff and continue for about 0.3 mile to the top of the hill. Just before reaching Crestmont Road, drive into a small parking lot on the right beside the road; leave your vehicle here. Then walk to the staircase located just before the parking lot and climb the stairs to the watch site.

References: *A Guide to Hawk Watching in North America* (Pennsylvania State University Press, 1979); *The Migrations of Hawks*

(Indiana University Press, 1986); *Raptor Watch* (BirdLife
International and Hawk Mountain Sanctuary, 2000);
HMANA Hawk Migration Studies, 2001, 27 (1): 156–158;
2002, 27 (2): 116–117; 2002, 28 (1): 70–72.

Palisades Interstate Parkway (near Alpine)

Spring Flights: Information unavailable.

Autumn Flights: Excellent.

**Watch Site
Description:** This parkway is a scenic road along the Hudson River in
northern New Jersey extending northward from the
George Washington Bridge. Two autumn raptor migration
watch sites are available along the parkway:

- *Alpine Boat Basin.* This watch site is reached from the
Palisades Interstate Parkway and offers satisfactory
autumn hawk watching.

- *State Line Lookout.* Located on the New Jersey–New
York border, this is another satisfactory autumn hawk
watching site.

Access: From the junction of the last New Jersey exit off Interstate
95 and the Palisades Interstate Parkway, drive north on
the Palisades Interstate Parkway (U.S. Route 9W) for 7.5
miles to exit 2. Leave the parkway at exit 2 and continue
east for 1 mile to the junction with Henry Hudson Drive.
The entrance to the Alpine Boat Basin is on the left. Turn
into the boat basin and watch for migrating hawks from
any exposed spot with suitable views over the landscape.

To reach the State Line Lookout, return to the parkway
and continue driving north to exit 3. Take this exit and
follow the secondary road to the roadside overlook. Watch
for migrating hawks from here.

References: *The Migrations of Hawks* (Indiana University Press, 1986);
New Jersey Wildlife Viewing Guide (Falcon Publishing,
1998).

Raccoon Ridge (near Blairstown)

Spring Flights: Fair.

Autumn Flights: Excellent.

Watch Site Description: Two exposed ridge crests on top of the Kittatinny Ridge from which hawk watchers can look over the surrounding landscape.

Access: From Blairstown, drive west on State Route 94 for several miles to a sign pointing to the Yards Creek Pump Storage Station. Drive to the gate of the station, secure permission to enter from the guard on duty, and continue to a small picnic area. Park here and walk uphill on a paved road until you reach a spot where power lines meet the road. Leave the road and walk north along the obvious power-line cut, cross two small streams, and climb the south slope of the ridge. The last part of this climb is extremely steep and involves vigorous effort. Once on top of the ridge, walk eastward along the Appalachian Trail for a few

Northeast view from Raccoon Ridge, New Jersey.

hundred feet to an exposed area (the Upper Lookout) identified by several small steel remnants from an old fire tower.

Alternatively, after crossing the second stream and beginning to climb the south slope of the ridge, follow an old log road leading to the right of the power-line cut. Continue on this road uphill to the top of the mountain. This brings you to the Lower Lookout. To visit the Upper Lookout, walk west on the Appalachian Trail for about 0.25 mile to the spot previously mentioned. Either site is suitable for hawk watching.

References: *New Jersey Nature News*, 1972, 27 (1): 22–28; *A Guide to Hawk Watching in North America* (Pennsylvania State University Press, 1979); *The Migrations of Hawks* (Indiana University Press, 1986); *Raptor Watch* (BirdLife International and Hawk Mountain Sanctuary, 2000); *HMANA Hawk Migration Studies*, 2001, 27 (1): 162–163; 2002, 28 (1): 75–76.

Rifle Camp Park (near Clifton)

Spring Flights: Information unavailable.

Autumn Flights: Excellent.

Watch Site Description: The lawn of a nature center in Rifle Camp Park from which hawk watchers have unrestricted views from the northeast to the southwest, and slightly restricted views in other directions. The park is located on top of the Watchung Mountains.

Access: From exit 154 off the Garden State Parkway near Clifton, drive west on U.S. Route 46 for about 3 miles to the Great Notch exit, which leads off U.S. 46 onto Rifle Camp Road. Drive north on Rifle Camp Road for about 2 miles to the Rifle Camp Park entrance. Enter the park and drive to the nature center building; hawk watching is done from the lawn outside the building. Additional information, water, and restroom facilities are available at the nature center.

References: *A Guide to Hawk Watching in North America* (Pennsylvania State University Press, 1979); *The Migrations of Hawks* (Indiana University Press, 1986).

Sandy Hook (near Highlands)

Spring Flights: Poor.

Autumn Flights: Information unavailable.

Watch Site Description: Exposed areas along the eastern side of the park or other open areas near the heliport parking area.

Access: From exit 117 (Route 36, Keyport) off the Garden State Parkway near Matawan, drive east for 13 miles on State Route 36 through Highlands, then take the exit on the right just before a bridge and follow the signs under the bridge for about 0.3 mile the entrance to Sandy Hook and the Gateway National Recreation Area. Enter the park, drive about 1.8 miles to the visitor center, and park. Then walk to the boardwalk and look for migrating hawks from there.

Alternatively, drive north to the ranger station/gatehouse. On request, the ranger will issue to you a birder's map, rules, and an automobile pass. Drive north through the park (following the map) to the parking area marked HELI-PORT PARKING AREA. Park here and observe from open areas near the helicopter landing site (helofield), or walk eastward to Battery Gunnison on the eastern side of the peninsula and observe from open areas about 500 feet south of Battery Gunnison. Additional information can be obtained by writing to Gateway National Recreation Areas, Sandy Hook Unit, P.O. Box 437, Highlands, NJ 07732.

References: *A Guide to Hawk Watching in North America* (Pennsylvania State University Press, 1979); *The Migrations of Hawks* (Indiana University Press, 1986); *HMANA Hawk Migration Studies*, 2002, 27 (2): 114–115.

Scott's Mountain Hawk Watch Site (near Phillipsburg)

Spring Flights: Poor.

Autumn Flights: Good to excellent.

Scott's Mountain Hawk Watch Site, New Jersey.

Watch Site

Description: A paved parking lot overlooking a reservoir and surrounding fields and woodland with the Kittatinny Ridge far to the north in the distance.

Access: From the junction of U.S. Route 22 and County Route 519 north, just east of Phillipsburg, turn north onto Route 519 and drive for 2.8 miles to Fox Farm Road on the right. Turn right onto Fox Farm Road (then look for a small MERRILL CREEK sign at a Y in the road and keep right) and drive for 2.7 miles, then turn right at a FISHING AREA sign and continue a very short distance up a steep hill to a parking lot overlooking the Merrill Creek Reservoir. Watch hawk migrations from here.

References: *A Guide to Hawk Watching in North America* (Pennsylvania State University Press, 1979); *The Migrations of Hawks* (Indiana University Press, 1986); *HMANA Hawk Migration Studies*, 2001, 27 (1): 161, 162; 2002, 28 (1): 76.

Skyline Ridge (near Oakland)

Spring Flights: Information unavailable.

Autumn Flights: Excellent.

Watch Site Description: An outcropping of rocks on a ridge from which observers look over the Wanque Valley toward the west, New York State toward the northwest, and High Mountain and New York City toward the southeast. Trees block visibility toward the northeast.

Access: From Oakland, drive west on State Route 208 to the end of the highway in Oakland. At the point where Route 208 ends, continue straight onto West Oakland Avenue. Cross the Ramapo River and continue about 0.13 mile to a T in the road. Turn right at the T onto Skyline Drive and continue on this road to a point where it begins to descend the western slope of the ridge. Look for an open area (a gas pipeline) and perhaps a LEAVING OAKLAND sign. Park at a suitable spot near the pipeline (and perhaps the sign), or continue a short distance down the road and park on the left side across from a RINGWOOD sign. From here, walk down Skyline Drive to a LIONS CLUB sign. Then go left over a guardrail and hike up a short, steep incline to the rocks from which observations are made.

References: *A Guide to Hawk Watching in North America* (Pennsylvania State University Press, 1979); *The Migrations of Hawks* (Indiana University Press, 1986).

Sunrise Mountain (near Newton)

Spring Flights: Information unavailable.

Autumn Flights: Good.

Watch Site Description: An exposed area on the Appalachian Trail, part of which is covered by an open-sided shelter. Unrestricted views are secured toward the south and northwest, but the view northeast is slightly limited.

Access: From Newton, drive north on U.S. Route 206 to Stokes State Forest, then follow directional signs to the Sunrise

View from Sunrise Mountain, New Jersey.

Mountain overlook. Park in the lot and walk along a well-used trail to the open-sided shelter over the Appalachian Trail. The walk takes about five minutes.

References: *A Guide to Hawk Watching in North America* (Pennsylvania State University Press, 1979); *The Migrations of Hawks* (Indiana University Press, 1986).

Wildcat Ridge Hawk Watch (near Boonton)

Spring Flights: Information unavailable.

Autumn Flights: Excellent.

**Watch Site
Description:** A northern New Jersey mountain watch site with a south-facing platform providing open vistas over an adjacent valley and the surrounding landscape, including the Manhattan skyline toward the east.

Access: From the Rockaway/Hibernia exit (37) off Interstate 80, leave the interstate and turn left (north) at the traffic light onto Green Pond Road (County Route 513). Continue on Green Pond Road for 6.3 miles, then turn right at the Marcella Community Club onto Upper Hibernia Road (which eventually becomes unpaved) and continue for 2.7 miles to a white gravel parking lot on the right side of the road and a sign for the Wildcat Ridge Wildlife Management Area. Park, and follow the directions provided below.

From the junction of Interstate 287 and State Route 23 near Riverdale, drive north on Route 23 for 8.9 miles to the La Rue and Green Pond Road exit. Cross Route 23, drive south a short distance, and turn right onto Green Pond Road. Continue on this road for 5.1 miles, then turn left onto Upper Hibernia Road (across from the Marcella Community Club). Continue on Upper Hibernia Road (which becomes unpaved) for 2.7 miles to a white gravel parking lot on the right side of the road and a sign for the Wildcat Ridge Wildlife Management Area. Park here, then walk to two white gateposts just beyond the parking lot and follow the trail to a point just before a yellow gate. Turn right and follow the orange-blazed trail to the watch site. The 1-mile hike requires about twenty-five minutes.

References: *HMANA Hawk Migration Studies*, 2001, 26 (2): 31; 2001, 27 (1): 159–160; 2002, 27 (2): 117–119; 2002, 28 (1): 77–79.

New Mexico

Manzanos Mountains Hawk Watch (near Albuquerque)

Spring Flights: Information unavailable.

Autumn Flights: Poor to fair.

Watch Site Description: A ridge crest overlooking the Rio Grande Valley to the west and shortgrass prairie on the east.

Access: From Albuquerque, drive east on Interstate 40 to the Tijeras exit. Leave I–40 at its junction with State Route 14, and drive south on Route 14 for approximately 45 miles to Manzano. Enter the town and turn right onto the first road opposite a church. Follow this road for a short distance, then turn right at a fork and continue another 9 miles past the New Canyon Campground to the Capilla Peak fire tower road. Turn onto the fire tower road and park at safe location along the road about 200 yards south of the fire tower. Then hike northwest across a meadow and continue on a trail for about 0.75 mile along the ridge crest to the hawk migration watch site.

References: *Birding*, 1991, 23 (4): 197–204; *HMANA Hawk Migration Studies*, 2001, 27 (1): 48; 2002, 28 (1): 202–203.

Sandia Mountains Hawk Watch (near Albuquerque)

Spring Flights: Poor to fair.

Autumn Flights: Information unavailable.

Watch Site Description: A watch site at an elevation of 7,400 feet overlooking the surrounding landscape.

Access: From Albuquerque, drive east on Interstate 40, leave I–40 at the Carnuel exit, and keep left over the interstate highway. Then continue for about a mile and turn left onto Montecello Drive (a taxidermy shop marks this turn). Drive on Montecello to Allegre Drive, turn left onto Allegre, and continue to Siempre Verde. Turn right onto Siempre Verde and continue to the 3-Gun Spring Trailhead. Park here and hike up the 3-Gun Spring Trail to the Forest Service boundary fence. Then take a branch trail to the right and follow it for about 1.5 miles to the hawk migration watch site. This involves a climb of about 1,000 feet. Hawk watchers usually are present on the lookout daily from March 10 to May 10. Peak hawk flights occur during mid-April.

References: *Birding,* 1991, 23 (4): 197–204; *HMANA Hawk Migration Studies,* 2002, 27 (2): 34, 51–53; 2003, 28 (2): 61.

New York

Bear Mountain State Park (near Nyack)

Spring Flights: Information unavailable.

Autumn Flights: Fair.

Watch Site Description: An overlook just beyond the main parking area on top of Bear Mountain; unobstructed views are available in all directions.

Access: From Nyack, drive west on Interstates 287/87 to the Palisades Interstate Parkway, then head north on the parkway to the Bear Mountain Bridge traffic circle. Stop at the main complex of buildings just off (west of) the bridge circle to inform the park superintendent and/or park police that you will be spending the day on top of Bear Mountain and will drive there via Perkins Memorial Drive. After leaving the headquarters, drive 1.5 miles west on Seven Lakes Drive (the road in front of the headquarters building) to a sign pointing to Perkins Memorial Drive. Turn right onto the drive, pass through an open gate, and continue to the top of the mountain. Leave your vehicle in the main parking area and walk to the lookout previously described. Observe from there.

If you are approaching on the Palisades Interstate Parkway, you can leave the parkway at exit 15 to reach Perkins Memorial Drive but will still need to drive 2.3 miles to the park headquarters at the bridge circle before returning to the road leading to the top of the mountain.

References: *A Guide to Hawk Watching in North America* (Pennsylvania State University Press, 1979); *HMANA Hawk Migration Studies*, 2001, 27 (1): 149–150; 2002, 28 (1): 79–80.

Belvedere Castle (in Central Park in New York City)

Spring Flights: Information unavailable.

Autumn Flights: Good.

**Watch Site
Description:** Hawk watching is done (especially on northwest winds) from two towers in Belvedere Castle—an impressive medieval-type building in the middle of Central Park from which observers have excellent views of the park and migrating raptors. Turtle Pond and the Great Lawn are immediately north of Belvedere Castle, and the Shakespeare Garden is west of it.

Access: From the 79th Street entrance to Central Park on the east, or the 81st Street entrance on the west, enter the park in Midtown Manhattan and walk approximately halfway across the park to impressive Belvedere Castle, from which hawk watching is done. The building is open from Wednesday through Monday, 11:00 A.M. to 4:00 P.M. For additional information, telephone the castle at (212) 772–0210.

There is no vehicle parking available in Central Park. You will have to park in a public lot or garage (which are expensive) near the park, such as on West 83rd Street between Columbus and Amsterdam Avenues, and walk to the park.

References: *Raptor Watch* (BirdLife International and Hawk Mountain Sanctuary, 2000); *HMANA Hawk Migration Studies*, 2001, 27 (1): 150–152; 2002, 28 (1): 82–83.

Bonticou Crag (near New Paltz)

Spring Flights: Fair.

Autumn Flights: Information unavailable.

Watch Site
Description: The summit of a bald knob with good views toward the east and south but somewhat restricted views toward the southwest and northwest.

Access: From exit 18 (New Paltz) off the New York State Thruway, drive west on State Route 299 (Main Street) to the Wallkill River Bridge. Cross the bridge, making the first right turn after it. Then take the first left turn and follow the signs to Lake Mohonk. At the top of the mountain (about 4 miles from the bridge), turn into Lake Mohonk Mountain House gatehouse and park. Secure a grounds pass (day fee charged), then walk from the gatehouse northeast on Bonticou Road for 1.5 miles to the yellow-marked trail at the foot of Bonticou Crag. Follow the yellow markings to the crag, which is about 200 feet high and consists of very steep boulders. The climb to the top requires hands and feet plus rubber-soled shoes or hiking boots. Those not in good physical condition should not attempt this climb. Once on top of the crag, observe from there.

Reference: *A Guide to Hawk Watching in North America* (Pennsylvania State University Press, 1979).

Braddock Bay State Park (near Greece)

Spring Flights: Excellent.

Autumn Flights: None.

Watch Site
Description: The parking lot of the park known locally among hawk watchers as Hawk Lookout.

Access: From the Lake Ontario State Parkway on the north side of Rochester, drive west for several miles to the East Manitou Road exit ramp. Leave the parkway here and turn right at the stop sign, then drive about 500 feet to the Braddock Bay State Park entrance. Enter the park and drive another 0.4 mile to the lot from which hawk watching is done.

References: *California Condor*, 1972, 7 (5): 9–10; *A Guide to Hawk Watching in North America* (Pennsylvania State University Press, 1979); *HMANA Hawk Migration Studies*, 2002, 27 (2): 67–69, 82–84; 2003, 28 (2): 46.

Cattaraugus Creek (near Irving)

Spring Flights: Good.

Autumn Flights: None.

Watch Site Description: The mouth of Cattaraugus Creek (for flights of accipiters) or higher ground nearby (for flights of Broad-winged Hawks).

Access: From exit 58 off Interstate 90 near Irving, turn right onto State Route 5. Cross Cattaraugus Creek, then turn left and continue to an underpass. Beyond this, turn left again, following the road to the northeast side of the creek's mouth; large flights of migrating Sharp-shinned Hawks are sometimes seen from here. Alternatively, return to Route 5 and continue west for about a mile, then drive south on Allegheny Road to higher ground near Lake Erie. Here flights of Broad-winged Hawks are seen.

Reference: *A Guide to Hawk Watching in North America* (Pennsylvania State University Press, 1979).

Derby Hill (near Mexico)

Spring Flights: Excellent.

Autumn Flights: None.

Watch Site Description: An exposed field on a ridge near the shoreline of Lake Ontario (the North Lookout, used with prevailing easterly to westerly winds), or a parking lot (the South Lookout, used with prevailing northerly winds) beside a road 1.2 miles south of the North Lookout.

Access: From Mexico, drive north on State Route 3 for 4.5 miles to the junction with State Route 104B. Turn west onto Route 104B and continue for 0.5 mile to the corner of Sage Creek Drive (marked by a barn with twin silos). Turn right onto Sage Creek Drive and continue north for 0.2 mile to a parking lot on the left—the South Lookout. To reach the North Lookout, continue driving north on

Hawk watchers at Derby Hill, New York.

Sage Creek Drive (passing Sage Creek Marsh on the left) for another 1.2 miles to a parking lot on the right near the top of the hill (and a cottage, which is the headquarters and small gift shop). This is the entry point for the North Lookout. Park in the parking lot (if full, park along the side of the road) and walk a short distance to the watch site, following the signs. The North Lookout is about 100 feet from a cliff overlooking Lake Ontario.

References: *Kingbird*, 1966, 16 (1): 5–16; *Wilson Bulletin*, 1966: 88–110; *A Guide to Hawk Watching in North America* (Pennsylvania State University Press, 1979); *HMANA Hawk Migration Studies*, 2002, 27 (2): 69, 86–88; 2003, 28 (2): 46; Onondaga Audubon Society Web site at www.onondagaaudubon.org.

Fire Island (Robert Moses State Park near Babylon)

Spring Flights: None.

Autumn Flights: Good.

Watch Site Description: The beach on dunes at Democrat Point at the western end of the island. Alternatively, any narrow spot along the beach with an unobstructed view across the width of the island is also satisfactory.

Access: From Babylon, drive east on State Route 27A then south on the Robert Moses Causeway across Captree State Park and the Fire Island Inlet into Robert Moses State Park. If parking areas Nos. 4 and 5 are open, leave your vehicle in No. 5 and walk eastward toward the lighthouse. If they are closed, park in area No. 3. To visit Democrat Point, park in area No. 2 and walk to the western end of the island.

References: *Kingbird*, 1963, 13 (1): 4–12; *A Guide to Hawk Watching in North America* (Pennsylvania State University Press, 1979); *HMANA Hawk Migration Studies*, 2001, 27 (1): 144–145; 2002, 28 (1): 92–94.

Fishers Island

Spring Flights: None.

Autumn Flights: Fair.

Watch Site Description: The top of Mount Chocomount, about three-quarters of the way down the island, or just to the west of a small bluff near the east end of Beach Pond at Middlefarm Flats about halfway down the island.

Access: Fishers Island ferryboats (the *Mystic Isle* or the *Olinda*) leave from the vicinity of the old railroad station at the foot of State Street in New London, Connecticut.

References: *Auk*, 1922: 488–496; *A Guide to Hawk Watching in North America* (Pennsylvania State University Press, 1979).

Fort Tilden (in Brooklyn)

Spring Flights: Information unavailable.

Autumn Flights: Good.

Watch Site Description: The vicinity of the visitor center at Fort Tilden (part of the Breezy Point Site, Gateway National Recreation Area).

Access: From exit 11 south of the Belt Parkway in southern Brooklyn, drive east on Flatbush Avenue for about a mile to the tollbooths for the Marine Parkway Bridge. Pay the toll, cross the bridge, then follow the right fork of the road heading toward Breezy Point. At the first traffic light after taking the right fork, turn left into Fort Tilden. Continue straight ahead to a stop sign. Turn left at the sign and continue to the visitor center (the first building on the right).

Reference: *Raptor Watch* (BirdLife International and Hawk Mountain Sanctuary, 2000).

Four Mile Creek State Park (near Ransomville)

Spring Flights: Good.

Autumn Flights: Information unavailable.

Watch Site Description: Any exposed area with unrestricted views along the Lake Ontario shoreline. Some experimental hawk watching is needed at this site. Park officials may be able to provide updated information regarding the best spots to use for hawk watching purposes.

Access: From Ransomville, drive northwest on State Route 93 to the junction with State Route 18, then follow Route 18 north and east to the entrance to Four Mile Creek State Park. Enter the park and drive to any exposed area with good views along the lake shoreline.

References: *Prothonotary*, 1966, 32 (5): 63–64; 1969, 35 (8): 116–118; 1970, 36 (5): 65–68; *The Migrations of Hawks* (Indiana University Press, 1986).

Franklin Mountain Hawkwatch (near Oneonta)

Spring Flights: Fair.

Autumn Flights: Fair.

Watch Site Description: The upper, north-facing slope of a hill (elevation 2,000 feet) on the Delaware–Otsego Audubon Society Sanctuary overlooking Oneonta, New York, the Susquehanna River Valley, and surrounding hills. Marked hiking trails also extend through various habitats in the sanctuary. Mid-October through November, on days with prevailing north and northwest winds, is the best time for seeing Red-tailed Hawks and Golden Eagles.

Access: From Interstate 88 eastbound, near Oneonta, take exit 14. Turn right, drive straight ahead to a traffic light, and cross State Route 28. Then immediately turn left at a T onto Southside Drive and continue for 0.8 mile. Turn right onto Swart Hollow Road and continue for 1.5 miles, then turn sharply right onto Grange Hall Road. Continue for 0.2 mile and turn sharply left into a driveway. Park on the right side. Walk to the barn, turn left, and continue on a path up the hill. The hawk watching site is approximately halfway up the hill (not at the top).

From westbound lanes on I–88, take exit 15. At the bottom of the ramp, turn left, drive to a traffic light near a McDonald's, and turn right. Continue 0.7 mile to the third traffic light, then turn left and follow the directions as above from Southside Drive.

References: *Kingbird*, 1977, 27: 74–79; *A Guide to Hawk Watching in North America* (Pennsylvania State University Press, 1979); *HMANA Hawk Migration Studies*, 2001, 27 (1): 146–147; 2002, 28 (1): 98–100.

Hamburg Hawk Watch (near Hamburg)

Spring Flights: Excellent.

Autumn Flights: None.

Watch Site

Description: A flat lake plain on the shoreline at the east end of Lake Erie. The watch site is inside Lakeside Memorial Park (formerly Lakeside Cemetery).

Access: At Hamburg take exit 57 (Hamburg/Camp Road) off Interstate 90 (New York State Thruway) and turn right onto State Route 75 (Camp Road). Continue through an intersection with a traffic light (at U.S. Route 20) for about 0.5 mile to the entrance to Lakeside Memorial Park on the left. Enter and continue to the watch site on a large area of lawn halfway along a road leading into woodland. The watch site can be seen from the Camp Road entrance to the park.

References: *HMANA Hawk Migration Studies*, 2000, 26 (2): 69; 2001, 27 (2): 67, 85–86; 2002, 27 (2): 67, 85–86; 2003, 28 (2): 46.

Hook Mountain (near Nyack)

Spring Flights: Excellent.

Autumn Flights: Excellent.

Watch Site

Description: An exposed clearing on the summit of a ridge crest.

Access: From the New York Thruway, drive north on U.S. Route 9W (near Nyack) for 2 miles. Park in a "dump" on the right side of the road near the bottom of a hill, or in suitable spots beside the road near the top of the hill. Then walk uphill or downhill from the respective parking area to several telephone cable markers. Enter the trail on the right (when walking uphill) and follow the blue blazes for a considerable distance to the lookout. The hike requires about twenty-five minutes and is a very strenuous climb most of the way. Those in poor physical condition should not attempt this climb.

References: *A Guide to Hawk Watching in North America* (Pennsylvania State University Press, 1979); *HMANA Hawk Migration Studies*, 2001, 27 (1): 153–154; 2002, 27 (2): 119; 2002, 28 (1): 84–85.

Hook Mountain, New York.

Jones Beach (on Long Island)

Spring Flights: None.

Autumn Flights: Fair.

**Watch Site
Description:** An exposed area near the southwest corner of Zach's Bay between the bay and a fishing station.

Access: From the Long Island Expressway or the Southern State Parkway, drive south on Meadowbrook State Parkway into Jones Beach State Park. Within the park, drive east on Ocean Parkway to parking field No. 4 or 6 (5 is closed during autumn). Then walk to the Zach's Bay area, where hawk watching is done.

References: *Kingbird*, 1958, 8 (2): 42–43; 1960, 10 (4): 157–159; *A Guide to Hawk Watching in North America* (Pennsylvania State University Press, 1979).

Lenoir Hawk Watch (in Yonkers)

Spring Flights: Information unavailable.

Autumn Flights: Fair to good.

Watch Site Description: A field (the "Great Lawn") in the Lenoir Nature Preserve west (in front) of the Lenoir Mansion overlooking the Hudson River and the Palisades. The preserve is on the east side of the river. Hawk watching is done from September through November.

Access: From the Saw Mill River Parkway in Yonkers, take exit 9 (Executive Boulevard) and drive west on Executive Boulevard across Nepperhan Avenue to North Broadway. Turn right onto North Broadway and continue 0.25 mile to Dudley Street. Turn left onto Dudley, continue a short distance, then turn left into the parking lot for the Lenoir Nature Preserve. Walk uphill from the parking lot to the nature center, and secure directions to the site from which hawk watching is done. If the nature center is closed, walk past the center to a T in the paved trail, then go either right or left on a trail around Dragonfly Pond and continue to the Gazebo. From here, walk south across the Great Lawn to the hawk migration watch site. Take a folding beach chair for comfortable hawk watching. The nature preserve is open to the public Wednesday through Sunday, 10:00 A.M. to 5:00 P.M.

References: *HMANA Hawk Migration Studies*, 2001, 27 (1): 154–155; Hudson River Audubon Society Web site at www.hras.org.

Mount Peter (near Greenwood Lake)

Spring Flights: None.

Autumn Flights: Good.

Hawk watchers at Mount Peter, New York.

Watch Site

Description: An exposed rocky outcropping and clearing on a ridge crest.

Access: From Greenwood Lake, drive north on State Route 17A for about 2 miles to a restaurant. Park here and walk about 200 feet to the ridge crest behind the restaurant's parking lot. Observe from there.

References: *Kingbird*, 1967, 17 (3): 129–142; 1969, 19 (4): 200–203; *A Guide to Hawk Watching in North America* (Pennsylvania State University Press, 1979); *HMANA Hawk Migration Studies*, 2001, 27 (1): 155–156; 2002, 28 (1): 85–86.

New Trapps Watch Site (near New Paltz)

Spring Flights: Information unavailable.

Autumn Flights: Fair.

Watch Site Description: An exposed rocky knob on the crest of the Shawangunk Mountain ridge. There is unlimited visibility toward the east and northwest. The view toward the northeast is along the ridge crest across a small gap.

Access: From exit 18 (New Paltz) off the New York Thruway, drive west on State Route 299 to the junction with U.S. Route 44/State Route 55. Turn right and continue about 1.5 miles to the Trapps Bridge (the only bridge over the highway). Park near the bridge, pay a nominal entrance fee, and enter the Mohonk Trust Preserve by walking about 200 feet southwest on the carriage road (Trapps Road) to the beginning of the Millbrook Range Trail, identified by three blue dots on a tree. Follow the blue-marked trail up steep rock slabs for about 700 feet to the ridge crest. The watch site is marked by a bronze NATIONAL OCEAN SURVEY benchmark.

Reference: *A Guide to Hawk Watching in North America* (Pennsylvania State University Press, 1979).

Oneida Watch Site

Spring Flights: None.

Autumn Flights: Good.

Watch Site Description: The crest of a lightly traveled road with good views toward the west, north, and east.

Access: From the Verona exit off Interstate 90 (exit 33 off the New York Thruway), drive south on State Route 365 to State Route 5, then east on Route 5 to State Route 26. Turn south onto Route 26 and continue for 6.7 miles to the intersection of Knoxboro Road. Turn right (west) onto Knoxboro Road and continue for 2.2 miles uphill to Hatella Road (marked by a small stone block building on the northwest corner). Turn right (north) onto Hatella Road and continue for 1.6 miles, passing the county dump, to a point where the road makes a sharp turn to the west. Park along the side of the road in a safe spot. The watch site is located at the top of the hill.

References: *Kingbird*, 1977, 27 (2): 82–85; *A Guide to Hawk Watching in North America* (Pennsylvania State University Press, 1979).

Port Jervis Watch Site

Spring Flights: Information unavailable.

Autumn Flights: Good.

Watch Site Description: A roadside pullover and overlook along the westbound lanes of Interstate 84 about 2 miles east of Port Jervis. Good views are enjoyed toward the west, north, and northeast. This watch site should be particularly good on days with prevailing northwest or north winds.

Access: From Port Jervis, drive east on Interstate 84 to the top of the mountain, where several roadside pullover areas will be seen. To reach the overlook used for hawk watching from the westbound lanes, it is necessary to drive eastward to the next exit. Leave I–84 here, reverse direction, enter the interstate again heading west, and return to the overlook on top of the mountain. Park and observe here or a few hundred feet west of the end of the overlook, at which point the visibility is better.

Reference: *A Guide to Hawk Watching in North America* (Pennsylvania State University Press, 1979).

Storm King Mountain (near Cornwall-on-Hudson)

Spring Flights: Poor.

Autumn Flights: Good.

Watch Site Description: An exposed rocky area on the south side of the top of Storm King Mountain overlooking U.S. Route 9W. There are unrestricted views in all directions.

Access: From the George Washington Bridge linking New York City with New Jersey, drive north on the Palisades Interstate Parkway to the Bear Mountain Bridge circle, then continue north on U.S. Route 9W for 9.6 miles to a parking lot on the right side of the road. (From Newburgh, drive south on U.S. 9W for about 5 miles.) Then hike along a trail (well marked with yellow paint) beginning on the west side of the parking lot and continue on the main trail to the top of the mountain. Observe from the spot previously described. The last half of the trail requires strenuous climbing.

References: *Enjoying Birds Around New York City* (Houghton Mifflin, 1966); *A Guide to Hawk Watching in North America* (Pennsylvania State University Press, 1979).

North Carolina

Various sites along coastal North Carolina, and inland along the Blue Ridge Parkway, have produced hawk flights during autumn. However, much remains to be learned about spring and autumn raptor migrations along the North Carolina part of the Blue Ridge Parkway. Hopefully this book can help fill in some existing gaps in our knowledge about raptor migrations in North Carolina's part of the southern Appalachians.

Blue Ridge Parkway

In addition to raptor migration watch sites of known importance along the Blue Ridge Parkway in North Carolina, some additional roadside overlooks are potentially useful locations for hawk watching and raptor migration study. Some of the latter are included here as *experimental* watch sites. I encourage hawk watchers and ornithologists to conduct hawk counts at these overlooks to determine their value as raptor migration monitoring sites during spring and/or autumn.

Blue Ridge Parkway roadside overlooks, and other watch sites along this spectacular road, are presented from north to south to correspond with handout parkway maps provided by the National Park Service, as well as the two-volume *Blue Ridge Parkway Guide* (Menasha Ridge Press, 2002). North Carolina's section of the Blue Ridge Parkway begins at approximately milepost 216.9 at the Cumberland Knob Visitor Center, and ends at milepost 469 at the Oconaluftee River Bridge and entrance to Great Smoky Mountains National Park near Cherokee, North Carolina.

Mahogany Rock Overlook (near Sparta)

Spring Flights: Information unavailable.

Autumn Flights: Good.

Watch Site Description: A roadside overlook, elevation 3,436 feet, along the Blue Ridge Parkway. Hawk watchers observe from folding chairs or their vehicles, scanning overhead or along the sides of the mountain for approaching hawks. Northeast winds tend to produce the largest hawk flights.

Access: Along the Blue Ridge Parkway at milepost 235.1, with the nearest access via U.S. Route 21. From the junction of U.S. 21 and the Blue Ridge Parkway, drive south on the parkway to the Mahogany Rock Overlook at milepost 235.1, from which hawk watching is done.

References: *Raptor Watch* (BirdLife International and Hawk Mountain Sanctuary, 2000); *Birds of the Blue Ridge Mountains* (University of North Carolina Press, 1992); *John Anthony Alderman Guide to Hawk Watching on the Blue River Parkway* (Hawk Migration Association of North America, no date); *HMANA Hawk Migration Studies*, 2002, 28 (1): 41.

Thunder Hill Overlook (near Boone and Blowing Rock)

Spring Flights: Information unavailable.

Autumn Flights: Good to excellent.

Watch Site Description: An east-facing roadside overlook, elevation 3,800 feet, along the Blue Ridge Parkway providing a view into the adjacent Blackberry Valley.

Thunder Hill Overlook, at milepost 290.5 on the Blue Ridge Parkway, North Carolina.

Access: Along the Blue Ridge Parkway at milepost 290.5, with the nearest access via U.S. Route 221. From the junction of U.S. 221 and the Blue Ridge Parkway, drive north on the parkway to the east-facing Thunder Hill Overlook, from which hawk watching is done. Alternatively, if you are approaching from Blowing Rock, drive west on U.S. Route 321 to the junction with the Blue Ridge Parkway, then head north on the parkway to the Thunder Hill Overlook.

References: *The Migrations of Hawks* (Indiana University Press, 1986); *Birds of the Blue Ridge Mountains* (University of North Carolina Press, 1992); *John Anthony Alderman Guide to Hawk Watching on the Blue River Parkway* (Hawk Migration Association of North America, no date).

Bear Den Overlook (near Linville Falls)

Spring Flights: Experimental (not evaluated).

Autumn Flights: Experimental (not evaluated).

Watch Site Description: A roadside overlook at an elevation of 3,359 feet, providing views of the adjacent mountain-and-valley landscape.

Access: Along the Blue Ridge Parkway at milepost 323.1, with the nearest access via U.S. Route 221. From the junction of U.S. 221 and the Blue Ridge Parkway, drive south for a few miles on the parkway to the east-facing Bear Den Overlook.

References: None.

View from Bear Den Overlook, at milepost 323.1 on the Blue Ridge Parkway, North Carolina.

North Cove Overlook (near Spruce Pine)

Spring Flights: Experimental (not evaluated).

Autumn Flights: Experimental (not evaluated).

Watch Site Description: A roadside overlook at an elevation of 2,815 feet, providing views of the adjacent mountain-and-valley landscape.

Access: Along the Blue Ridge Parkway at milepost 327.3, with the nearest access via State Route 226. From the junction of Route 226 and the Blue Ridge Parkway, drive north for a few miles on the parkway to the east-facing North Cove Overlook.

References: None.

View from North Cove Overlook, at milepost 327.3 on the Blue Ridge Parkway, North Carolina.

Green Knob Overlook (near Marion)

Spring Flights: Experimental (not evaluated).

Autumn Flights: Experimental (not evaluated).

Watch Site Description: A roadside overlook at an elevation of 4,761 feet, providing views of the adjacent mountain-and-valley landscape.

Access: Along the Blue Ridge Parkway at milepost 350.4, with the nearest access via State Route 80. From the junction of Route 80 and the Blue Ridge Parkway, drive south for a few miles on the parkway to the east-facing Green Knob Overlook.

References: None.

Ridge Junction Overlook (near Marion)

Spring Flights: Experimental (not evaluated).

Autumn Flights: Experimental (not evaluated).

Watch Site Description: A roadside overlook at an elevation of 5,160 feet, providing views of the adjacent mountain-and-valley landscape.

Access: Along the Blue Ridge Parkway at milepost 355.4, with the nearest access via State Route 80. From the junction of Route 80 and the Blue Ridge Parkway, drive south for a few miles on the parkway to the Ridge Junction Overlook.

References: None.

Mount Mitchell (near Marion)

Spring Flights: Information unavailable.

Autumn Flights: Excellent.

Watch Site Description: The highest mountain peak east of the Mississippi River, with a summit elevation of 6,684 feet. Hawk watching can be done from the observation tower or its vicinity at

View toward Mount Mitchell at approximately milepost 355 on the Blue Ridge Parkway, North Carolina.

the summit of Mount Mitchell within the park. Some large flights of Broad-winged Hawks are reported from this site during September.

Access: From the junction of State Route 80 and the Blue Ridge Parkway, drive south for about 15 miles on the parkway to the junction with State Route 128 between mileposts 350 and 360. Turn west onto Route 128, which leads into Mount Mitchell State Park and the summit of the mountain. Entrance to the park is free. A museum, a gift shop, restrooms, picnic areas, and a restaurant are available for visitor use.

Reference: *The Migrations of Hawks* (Indiana University Press, 1986).

Craggy Dome Overlook (near Asheville)

Spring Flights: Experimental (not evaluated).

Autumn Flights: Experimental (not evaluated).

Watch Site Description: A roadside overlook at an elevation of 5,640 feet, providing views of the adjacent mountain-and-valley landscape.

Access: Along the Blue Ridge Parkway at milepost 364.6, with the nearest access via U.S. Route 70. From the junction of U.S. 70 and the Blue Ridge Parkway, drive north on the parkway to the west-facing Craggy Dome Overlook.

Reference: *John Anthony Alderman Guide to Hawk Watching on the Blue River Parkway* (Hawk Migration Association of North America, no date).

Craggy Gardens Visitor Center (near Asheville)

Spring Flights: None.

Autumn Flights: Good.

Craggy Gardens Visitor Center, at milepost 364.6 on the Blue Ridge Parkway, North Carolina.

Watch Site

Description: A large roadside parking lot and overlook at an elevation of 5,220 feet, providing views of the adjacent mountain-and-valley landscape. A visitor center with a small gift shop as well as a drinking fountain, picnic area, and restrooms are available to the public.

Access: Along the Blue Ridge Parkway at milepost 364.6, with the nearest access via U.S. Route 70. From the junction of U.S. 70 and the Blue Ridge Parkway, drive north on the parkway to the Craggy Gardens Visitors Center, which provides east- and west-facing overlooks.

References: *A Guide to Bird Finding East of the Mississippi* (Oxford University Press, 1977); *A Guide to Hawk Watching in North America* (Pennsylvania State University Press, 1979); *The Migrations of Hawks* (Indiana University Press, 1986); *Birds of the Blue Ridge Mountains* (University of North Carolina Press, 1992).

East Fork Overlook (near Waynesville)

Spring Flights: Experimental (not evaluated).

Autumn Flights: Experimental (not evaluated).

East Fork Overlook, at milepost 418.3 on the Blue Ridge Parkway, North Carolina.

Watch Site Description: A roadside overlook at an elevation of 4,930 feet, providing views of the adjacent mountain-and-valley landscape.

Access: Along the Blue Ridge Parkway at milepost 418.3, with the nearest access via U.S. Route 276. From the junction of U.S. 276 and the Blue Ridge Parkway, drive south on the parkway to the East Fork Overlook.

References: None.

Devil's Courthouse (near Rosman)

Spring Flights: Experimental (not evaluated).

Autumn Flights: Experimental (not evaluated).

View of Devil's Courthouse from its nearby parking lot at milepost 422.4 on the Blue Ridge Parkway, North Carolina.

Watch Site
Description: The top of an impressive, exposed, rocky summit called the Devil's Courthouse, elevation 5,461 feet, providing panoramic views of the surrounding Broad, Pigeon River, and Tuckaseigee Valley landscapes.

Access: Along the Blue Ridge Parkway at milepost 422.4, with the nearest access via State Route 215. From the junction of Route 215 and the Blue Ridge Parkway, drive north on the parkway to the Devil's Courthouse parking lot at milepost 422.4, then walk on the well-marked trail to the top of the Devil's Courthouse.

Reference: *John Anthony Alderman Guide to Hawk Watching on the Blue River Parkway* (Hawk Migration Association of North America, no date).

Richland Balsam Overlook (near Waynesville)

Spring Flights: Experimental (not evaluated).

Autumn Flights: Experimental (not evaluated).

Watch Site
Description: A large roadside overlook at an elevation of 6,053 feet (the highest overlook on the parkway), providing views of the adjacent mountain-and-valley landscape.

Access: Along the Blue Ridge Parkway at milepost 431.4, with the nearest access via U.S. Routes 23/74. From the junction of U.S. 23/74 and the Blue Ridge Parkway, drive north on the parkway to the large parking lot at the Richland Balsam Overlook, from which hawk watching can be done.

References: None.

Yellow Face Overlook (near Waynesville)

Spring Flights: Experimental (not evaluated).

Autumn Flights: Experimental (not evaluated).

Watch Site Description: A roadside overlook at an elevation of 5,610 feet, providing views of the adjacent mountain-and-valley landscape.

Access: Along the Blue Ridge Parkway at milepost 450, with the nearest access via U.S. Routes 23/74. From the junction of U.S. 23/74 and the Blue Ridge Parkway, drive south on the parkway to the Yellow Face Overlook, from which hawk watching can be done. Alternatively, if you are approaching from the south and the junction of U.S. Route 19 and the Blue Ridge Parkway, drive north on the parkway to the Yellow Face Overlook.

References: None.

Bodie Island Lighthouse (near Nags Head)

Spring Flights: Information unavailable.

Autumn Flights: Fair.

Watch Site Description: The edge of pine woodland around the Bodie Island Lighthouse. The spot is a staging area only for migrating accipiters.

Access: From Manns Harbor, drive east on U.S. Route 64 to Nags Head, then continue about 5 miles south from Nags Head to the wooded area around the lighthouse. Observe from any open area around the site. Stop at the nearby visitor center for current hawk watching opportunities and maps and literature about the area.

References: *Association of Southeast Biologists Bulletin*, 1978, 25 (2): 53–54; *A Guide to Hawk Watching in North America* (Pennsylvania State University Press, 1979); *North Carolina Wildlife Viewing Guide* (Falcon Press Publishing, 1992).

Buxton Woods (near Buxton)

Spring Flights: Information unavailable.

Autumn Flights: Fair.

**Watch Site
Description:** The edge of a wooded area located about 0.5 mile south-west of the Cape Hatteras Lighthouse. Most hawks are seen from midafternoon to dusk. Accipiters are most common.

Access: From Manns Harbor, drive east on U.S. Route 64 for a few miles to the junction with State Route 12, then follow Route 12 south to Buxton. The wooded area is located about 0.5 mile southwest of the nearby lighthouse. Observe from any open area along the ocean side of the site.

References: *Association of Southeast Biologists Bulletin*, 1978, 25 (2): 53–54; *A Guide to Hawk Watching in North America* (Pennsylvania State University Press, 1979).

Fort Macon State Park (near Morehead City)

Spring Flights: Information unavailable.

Autumn Flights: Fair.

**Watch Site
Description:** The top of sand dunes on a barrier beach island, provid-ing views over the island and nearby ocean and sound. Accipiters and falcons, including Peregrine Falcons, are seen most frequently. Hawks approach from the north end of the island and often fly only 4 to 6 feet above the ground; observers must remain alert to avoid missing the birds. Late September to mid-October is the best observa-tion period.

Access: From Morehead City, drive south for a short distance to the park. Continue to the visitor parking lot, then walk to and climb the highest dune southeast of the lot. Observe from there.

References: *Association of Southeast Biologists Bulletin*, 1978, 25 (2): 53–54; *A Guide to Hawk Watching in North America* (Pennsylvania State University Press, 1979).

Hatteras Island (on the Outer Banks)

Spring Flights: Information unavailable.

Autumn Flights: Fair.

Watch Site Description: The tops of sand dunes at two narrow sections of a barrier beach island. Many hawks tend to fly only 4 to 6 feet above the island, and observers must remain alert or the birds can be overlooked. Late September to mid-October is the best observation period for Ospreys, accipiters, harriers, and falcons (Peregrine Falcons).

Access: From the village of Hatteras, drive north on State Route 12 for about 0.5 mile to a narrow section of the island. Park, climb to the top of a high dune, and observe from there. Alternatively, drive south from Hatteras on Route 12 to the Ocracoke Island Ferry Terminal. Then continue another 0.25 mile south of the terminal to the end of the paved road. Park, climb to the top of a high dune, and observe from there. Special care must be taken to avoid damaging the vegetation on the dunes.

References: *Association of Southeast Biologists Bulletin*, 1978, 25 (2): 53–54; *A Guide to Hawk Watching in North America* (Pennsylvania State University Press, 1979).

Pea Island (on the Outer Banks)

Spring Flights: Information unavailable.

Autumn Flights: Fair.

Watch Site Description: Exposed areas or the tops of sand dunes on a barrier beach island. Late September to mid-October is the best hawk watching period. Many hawks tend to fly only 4 to 6 feet above the island; observers must remain alert or the birds can be overlooked. Mostly accipiters, harriers, and falcons are seen here. Occasionally Peregrine Falcons appear.

Access: From Manns Harbor, drive east on U.S. Route 64 to the junction with State Route 12. Drive south on Route 12 for a few miles. Cross the Oregon Inlet Bridge and observe from a point about 0.25 mile east of the south end of the bridge. Alternatively, drive to the headquarters building on Pea Island National Wildlife Refuge somewhat farther south on Route 12 and observe from open areas near the headquarters building. A third possible site is reached by driving south on Route 12 to the southern end of the Pea Island National Wildlife Refuge, where you can observe from a narrow portion of the island.

References: *Association of Southeast Biologists Bulletin*, 1978, 25 (2): 53–54; *A Guide to Hawk Watching in North America* (Pennsylvania State University Press, 1979); *North Carolina Wildlife Viewing Guide* (Falcon Press Publishing, 1992).

Pilot Mountain State Park (near Pilot Mountain)

Spring Flights: Information unavailable.

Autumn Flights: Good.

Watch Site Description: The summit of a mountain providing spectacular views over the surrounding landscape.

Access: At the junction of U.S. Route 52 and State Route 268, at exit 134 off U.S. 52, leave that highway and follow signs to Pilot Mountain State Park. Enter the park, stop at the park office for current hawk watching updates and maps, then leave your vehicle in a designated area and hike to the summit of Pilot Mountain, from which hawk watching is done.

References: *The Migrations of Hawks* (Indiana University Press, 1986); *North Carolina Wildlife Viewing Guide* (Falcon Press Publishing, 1992).

Ohio

Crane Creek State Park (near Oak Harbor)

Spring Flights: Good to excellent.

Autumn Flights: Information unavailable.

Watch Site Description: Any unrestricted views along the Lake Erie shoreline within the park, or perhaps Locust Point just east of the park. Some experimental hawk watching is necessary to locate the best spots.

Access: From Oak Harbor, drive north on State Route 19 to the junction with State Route 2, then turn left (west) and continue a short distance to the park's entrance. Drive into the park and go to any exposed spot along the Lake Erie shoreline that provides unrestricted views.

References: *American Birds*, 1980, 34 (5): 781–785; *The Migrations of Hawks* (Indiana University Press, 1986).

Lakewood Park (in Cleveland)

Spring Flights: Good.

Autumn Flights: None.

Watch Site Description: A landfill projecting into Lake Erie that offers a fine view of bluffs toward the east and west.

Access: From Interstate 80 (south of Cleveland), drive north on Interstate 71 into the city to the junction with 130th Street. Drive north on 130th Street to State Route 10 (Lorain Avenue). Then turn east onto Route 10 and continue to West 117th Street. Turn onto West 117th Street and continue north to Lake Avenue. Turn left (west) onto Lake Avenue and continue to the intersection of Belle Avenue. Turn right into Lakewood Park and drive to the landfill extending into the lake.

References: *Cleveland Bird Calendar*, 1962, 58 (3): 28–33; *A Guide to Hawk Watching in North America* (Pennsylvania State University Press, 1979).

Perkins Beach (in Cleveland)

Spring Flights: Good.

Autumn Flights: None.

Watch Site Description: The top of bluffs overlooking Lake Erie, particularly the top of the rise to the right of West Boulevard.

Access: Follow the directions to Lakewood Park (see above) as far as Lake Avenue, at which point turn right (east) onto the avenue. Continue to West Boulevard (West 100th Street). Then turn left (north) and continue to the lakefront area formerly known as Perkins Beach. Currently this is the western edge of Edgewater Park.

References: *Cleveland Bird Calendar*, 1962, 58 (3): 28–33; 1963, 59 (3): 28–31; *A Guide to Hawk Watching in North America* (Pennsylvania State University Press, 1979).

South Bass Island (near Port Clinton)

Spring Flights: Fair.

Autumn Flights: None.

Watch Site Description: Exposed areas at Lighthouse Point at the extreme southern tip of the island. Most hawk flights occur between April 10 and early May.

Access: By ferry from the mainland. The ferryboats leave from the mainland village of Catawba Island, docking on South Bass Island a short distance east of Lighthouse Point; there are also ferries departing from Port Clinton.

Reference: *A Guide to Hawk Watching in North America* (Pennsylvania State University Press, 1979).

Oregon

Bonney Butte (near Government Camp)

Spring Flights: Information unavailable.

Autumn Flights: Fair.

Watch Site Description: The top of a ridge with views over the landscape on the east side of Mount Hood. Hawk watchers typically sit on folding chairs after arriving on the butte. The site is especially useful for seeing Sharp-shinned Hawks and Cooper's Hawks, but Red-tailed Hawks, Golden Eagles, and Merlins are also observed regularly; over the years, eighteen migrant raptor species have been reported at Bonney Butte.

Access: From Government Camp, drive south on U.S. Route 26 to the junction with State Route 35. Turn north onto Route 35 and continue for 4.5 miles across the White River to the White River East Snow Park. Turn right (south) here onto Forest Service Road 48 (paved) for 7 miles to the junction with Forest Service Road 4890. Turn left onto FR 4890 (look for the marker *after* you turn onto the road) and continue for 3.75 miles to the junction with Forest Service Road 4891. Turn left onto FR 4891, a rough road, following the signs for 4 miles to Bonney Meadows Campground. Restroom facilities here are the only ones available in the area. From the campground, continue to a spur road with a gate. Park at a suitable spot and walk on the gated spur road for about 0.25 mile to the summit of Bonney Butte, from which hawk watching is done.

References: *Raptor Watch* (BirdLife International and Hawk Mountain Sanctuary, 2000); *Audubon Warbler*, 2003, 67 (8): 13 (Audubon Society of Portland).

Dutchman's Peak (near Ashland)

Spring Flights: Information unavailable.

Autumn Flights: Fair to good.

Description: A peak in Rogue River National Forest rising above a long, east-to-west ridge above the Bear Creek drainage. An unrestricted view is enjoyed from the top of the ridge. Hawk watchers put folding chairs on the open hillside and wait for hawks to appear as they funnel up various canyons and draws in the vicinity of Dutchman's Peak.

Access: From exit 6 (Ashland Ski Area) off Interstate 5 south of Ashland, near the California border, drive west on clearly marked Forest Service Road 20 and continue past the ski area for a number of miles to the junction with Forest Service Road 22. Continue on FR 20 to the junction with Forest Service Road 800. Turn right and continue for about 1 mile to Dutchman's Peak. You will come to a gate about 0.5 mile after turning onto FR 800. If the gate is closed, you may have to park at a suitable spot and walk the remaining 0.5 mile to Dutchman's Peak, from which hawk watching is done.

Special Note: Before venturing far into national forest areas, secure a road map of the Rogue National Forest to avoid becoming lost in remote areas. Stop at, or write to, the headquarters at the following address: Rogue River National Forest, P.O. Box 520, 333 West 8th Street, Medford, OR 97501; (541) 858–2200. In addition, be sure your vehicle has adequate fuel before driving to Dutchman's Peak.

Reference: *Raptor Watch* (BirdLife International and Hawk Mountain Sanctuary, 2000).

Pennsylvania

Bake Oven Knob (near New Tripoli)

Spring Flights: Fair.

Autumn Flights: Excellent.

**Watch Site
Description:** Two rocky outcroppings on the crest of the Kittatinny Ridge. The North Lookout (used on westerly and northerly winds) is a small, level area atop a large boulder

The South Lookout, Bake Oven Knob, Pennsylvania.

pile. The South Lookout (used on easterly, southerly, and southwesterly winds) is an exposed rock outcropping terminated by a 1,000-foot drop to the forested slopes below.

Access: At the junction of U.S. Route 309 and State Route 143 at New Tripoli, drive north on U.S. 309 for 2 miles. Turn right (east) onto Mountain Road and continue for another 2 miles. Then turn left onto Ulrich Road, running between white buildings and a house. Continue on this road for about 0.25 mile. Do not turn when the paved road turns sharply right. Instead, drive straight ahead on an unpaved road and follow it to the top of the mountain. Park in one of two lots, then walk northeast on the Appalachian Trail (entered at the southeastern corner of the eastern parking lot) for about 0.3 mile to the summit of the knob. Shortly after crossing a large boulder field and climbing a steep incline, look for an old concrete foundation on the north side of the trail. The South Lookout is located about 150 feet east of this spot, and it's usually possible to see people on the lookout. The North

Lookout is reached by continuing to walk northeastward on the Appalachian Trail for about 0.25 mile. After passing a small campsite, walk along the north side of a large boulder pile for about 100 feet. Then climb to the top of the boulders; this is now the North Lookout.

References: *Cassinia*, 1969: 11–32; *Autumn Hawk Flights: The Migrations in Eastern North America* (Rutgers University Press, 1975); *A Guide to Hawk Watching in North America* (Pennsylvania State University Press, 1979); *The Migrations of Hawks* (Indiana University Press, 1986); *Bake Oven Knob Autumn Hawk Count Manual* (Wildlife Information Center, Inc. 2002).

Bear Rocks (near New Tripoli)

Spring Flights: Fair.

Autumn Flights: Excellent.

View of Bear Rocks looking upridge (northeast) with Bake Oven Knob in the background.

**Watch Site
Description:** A large outcropping of huge boulders on the crest of the Kittatinny Ridge approximately 1.5 miles southwest of Bake Oven Knob.

Access: Drive to the parking lots at Bake Oven Knob (see above). Then walk southwest (in the opposite direction for visiting the knob) on the Appalachian Trail to a grove of hemlocks and other trees through which you can see the boulder pile to the right about 200 feet north of the trail. Climb to the top of the boulder pile and select a spot for viewing.

Reference: *A Guide to Hawk Watching in North America* (Pennsylvania State University Press, 1979).

Brady's Bend Hawk Watch (near East Brady)

Spring Flights: Information unavailable.

Autumn Flights: Poor to fair.

View toward the northeast from Brady's Bend, Pennsylvania. Photo by Mark A. McConaughy.

Watch Site

Description: A scenic roadside pullover atop a high bluff overlooking a spectacular bend in the Allegheny River. There are excellent views toward the northwest, north, and east, but somewhat limited views toward the southeast, south, and southwest.

Access: From the bridge crossing the Allegheny River in East Brady in southwestern Armstrong County, drive east on State Route 68 for 2.7 miles to a marked roadside pullover with protective railings. There is convenient parking at the pullover, and a cafe is nearby.

References: *Pennsylvania Birds*, 2000, 14 (4): 210–216; *HMANA Hawk Migration Studies*, 2001, 27 (1): 169–170; 2002, 28 (1): 56.

Chickies Rock (near Marietta)

Spring Flights: Fair.

Autumn Flights: Fair.

Watch Site

Description: A 300-foot-high cliff on top of a towering hill overlooking the Susquehanna River. Observers have unrestricted views across the river, upriver, and partly downriver.

Access: From U.S. Route 30 at Columbia, drive 1.1 miles north (toward Marietta) on State Route 441. Park in a large area on the west side of the road just before entering a deep, rocky road cut. Walk west for less than 0.5 mile following a single-pole power line to a split in the trail. Follow the left fork for another 300 feet to the watch site.

References: *Hawk Mountain News*, 1978, 50: 26; *A Guide to Hawk Watching in North America* (Pennsylvania State University Press, 1979).

Chickies Rock, Pennsylvania.

College Hill Hawk Watch (in Easton)

Spring Flights: Poor to fair.

Autumn Flights: Good to excellent.

Watch Site Description: During autumn, the upper level of the Markle Parking Deck behind Markle Hall on the Lafayette College campus, with good views toward the north and east. In spring hawk watchers use a clearing on College Hill about 0.5 mile north of the college campus.

Access: From U.S. Route 22 in Easton, follow directional signs to Lafayette College. When on campus, seek directions to the parking deck between Markle Hall (the administration building) and the football field; hawk watching is done here in autumn. If necessary, park in a visitor area on campus and walk to the parking deck. During spring, explore high areas north of the college campus with wide views toward the south.

References: *Auk*, 1927, 44: 410; *The Migrations of Hawks* (Indiana University Press, 1986); *Hawk Watching in the Americas* (Hawk Migration Association of North America, 2001: 53–57).

Council Cup Hawk Watch (near Wapwallopen)

Spring Flights: None.

Autumn Flights: Fair.

Watch Site Description: The primary raptor migration watch site is on a rock shelf atop a 500-foot cliff that looks out over the north branch of the Susquehanna River; looks down upon Wapwallopen (a small village), across the river from PPL Inc.'s nuclear power plant; and offers excellent views toward the north, northeast, south, and southwest. A secondary watch site is an exposed spot on PPL property, used on very windy days in late October and early November, located about 150 feet uphill from the primary watch site.

Access: From the junction of State Routes 93 and 239 near Nescopeck, turn right (north) on Route 239 and continue past various farms toward the Susquehanna River. At the junction of Route 239 and the Nescopeck/Berwick Road near the river, turn right and continue for about 0.25 mile, then turn very sharply left and drive uphill for about a mile. After passing under an electric power line and following the road toward the right for about 0.5 mile, you will arrive at the gravel Council Cup entrance road. There are signs marking the route to the entrance to Council Cup, and marking the parking lot as well.

It is a ten-minute walk from the parking lot to the primary raptor migration watch site. The secondary watch site is reached via a small path beginning at the end of a chain-link fence; you will walk past this spot as you walk to the well-exposed primary site.

References: *Pennsylvania Birds*, 1990, 4 (4): 176; 1991, 5 (4): 188; 1992, 6 (2): 183; *Raptor Watch* (BirdLife International and Hawk Mountain Sanctuary, 2000).

Hawk Mountain Sanctuary (near Kempton)

Spring Flights: Poor.

Autumn Flights: Excellent.

Watch Site Description: Two rocky outcroppings on the crest of the Kittatinny Ridge. The North Lookout (used regardless of wind direction, and especially when westerly and northerly winds prevail) is atop the main fold of the ridge. The wheelchair-accessible South Lookout (especially useful to folks with limited walking or hiking ability, and when easterly or southerly winds prevail) is about 500 feet behind the entrance gate on a secondary escarpment. The visitor center, near the parking lots, is the gateway to the sanctuary's watch sites. It includes a gift shop, raptor-related educational exhibits, and restrooms.

The Acopian Center for Conservation Learning is Hawk Mountain's biological field station. It is not open to casual visitors. To make arrangements to visit this facility, contact Dr. Keith L. Bildstein by telephone at (570) 943–3411, ext. 108, or e-mail him at bildstein@hawkmtn.org. The postal mailing address is: Acopian Center for Conservation Learning, Hawk Mountain Sanctuary, 410 Summer Valley Road, Orwigsburg, PA 17961. Directions to the Acopian Center will be provided when arrangements are made for a visit.

Access: From Allentown or the Northeast Extension of the Pennsylvania Turnpike, drive west on U.S. Route 22/Interstate 78 for a number of miles to the junction with State Route 143 at Lenhartsville. Turn north onto Route 143 and drive for 4 miles to a crossroad where directional signs point to Hawk Mountain. Turn left onto Hawk Mountain Road and follow the signs along this paved road to Hawk Mountain. Near the top of the mountain, turn left into the parking lots, then stop at the visitor center before walking to the sanctuary's watch sites. An entrance fee is charged for nonmembers; members must show their membership cards before walking to the watch sites.

From Hamburg and points toward the west, follow I–78 east to the junction with State Route 61 at Hamburg. Turn north onto Route 61 and continue for 4 miles to the junction with State Route 895. Turn right (east) onto

North Lookout, Hawk Mountain Sanctuary, Pennsylvania.

The visitor center at Hawk Mountain Sanctuary, Pennsylvania.

Route 895 and continue another 2.5 miles to signs pointing to Drehersville and Hawk Mountain. Turn right, cross
a bridge over a small river, and continue up the mountain
to the Hawk Mountain entrance, parking lots, and visitor
center. Park in the areas provided, stop at the visitor center for additional information, pay the entrance fee (for
nonmembers), and walk along the trail to the South
Lookout and North Lookout.

References: *Hawks Aloft: The Story of Hawk Mountain* (Dodd, Mead,
1949); *A Guide to Hawk Watching in North America*
(Pennsylvania State University Press, 1979); *The Mountain and the Migration: A Guide to Hawk Mountain* (Cor-
nell University Press, 1991); *Pennsylvania Birds*, 1999, 13
(1): 11–15; *Hawk Mountain Sanctuary Migration Count
Manual* (Hawk Mountain Sanctuary, 2001).

Jack's Mountain (near Belleville)

Spring Flights: Fair.

Autumn Flights: Fair.

**Watch Site
Description:** During spring, a parking lot at the top of Jack's Mountain
on the east side of the Jack's Mountain Road is used as the
watch site. During autumn, observation shifts to a small
hill with a cross on top; this is found a short distance west
of the western parking lot at the top of Jack's Mountain.

Access: From Belleville, drive south on State Route 655 to a
church just south of town, then turn left onto Jack's
Mountain Road. Continue on this road for about 4.5
miles to the top of Jack's Mountain. There are two parking lots, one on each side of the road. Park in the eastern
parking lot and watch from there during spring. In
autumn park in the western lot, then walk the short distance to the top of the small hill with a cross on top.

References: *Pennsylvania Birds*, 1997, 11 (4): 210–223; 1998, 12 (4):
170–175; *HMANA Hawk Migration Studies*, 2001, 27 (1):
174–175; 2002, 28 (1): 62–63.

Lehigh Furnace Gap (near Slatedale)

Spring Flights: Fair.

Autumn Flights: Good to excellent.

Watch Site Description: Rocky outcroppings along a power-line right-of-way (used on southerly or easterly winds) or rocky outcroppings on the crest of the Kittatinny Ridge (used on northerly or westerly winds).

Access: From the junction of U.S. Route 309 and State Route 143 at New Tripoli, drive north on U.S. 309 for 2 miles. Turn right onto Mountain Road and continue ahead for another 5.2 miles to a crossroad. Turn left (north) onto another paved road (which eventually becomes gravel) and follow it to the top of the mountain. Park near the communications tower or along the power line (just over the top of the mountain on the north side). Then walk along the power-line right-of-way to a high vantage point on the south side of the ridge, or walk east or west along the right-of-way on the north side of the mountain to the highest point; here you can look down on the north side of the mountain. Other convenient rocky outcroppings can also be used, depending on wind direction and which side of the mountain hawks are migrating along.

References: *A Guide to Hawk Watching in North America* (Pennsylvania State University Press, 1979); *American Hawkwatcher*, 2000, 26: 23.

Lehigh Gap—East-Side Parking Lot (near Slatington)

Spring Flights: Poor to fair (occasionally good).

Autumn Flights: Poor to fair.

Watch Site Description: A large, unpaved parking lot on the east side of Lehigh Gap overlooking the Lehigh River, Lehigh Gap, and the landscape south of the Kittatinny Ridge. During spring, look for the largest hawk flights on days with prevailing southerly winds.

Access: From the traffic light at the junction of State Routes 498 and 946 near Slatington, drive east (toward Cherryville) on Route 946 for less than 0.1 mile to an easily missed small, rough, unpaved uphill entrance road cutting through woodland. Turn left onto this obscure road and continue ahead very slowly for about 100 feet to a large, flat, unpaved parking lot. Drive to the far end of the lot, park, and watch for migrating hawks approaching you from the south side of the Kittatinny Ridge across the Lehigh River. Alternatively, from the parking lot, follow the white blazes (patches of white paint) marking the Appalachian Trail up the very steep side of Lehigh Gap behind you and hike to a higher spot providing an even better view over the gap and adjacent landscape.

References: *Proceedings Hawk Migration Conference IV*, 1985: 1–11; *American Hawkwatcher*, 2000, 26: 23; 2001, 27: 20; 2002, 28: 20.

Lehigh Gap—West Side at Osprey House (near Slatington)

Spring Flights: Fair to good.

Autumn Flights: Poor to fair.

Watch Site Description: The outdoor, east-facing deck on Osprey House (headquarters of the Wildlife Information Center, Inc.) within Lehigh Gap on its west side—a water gap where the Lehigh River cuts through the Kittatinny Ridge—or the area adjacent to the building. During spring, look for the largest hawk flights on days with prevailing southerly winds. In autumn the largest hawk flights occur on days with prevailing easterly and/or southern winds. Because Osprey House is located within Lehigh Gap, rather than on the crest of the Kittatinny Ridge, many hawks will be overlooked during autumn on days with prevailing westerly and northerly winds.

Access: From the junction of State Routes 248 and 873 on the north side of the Lehigh River near Slatington, turn west onto Route 873 and drive across the long bridge over the river. Bear left (do *not* continue straight ahead and uphill on Mountain Road) and continue a short distance to Paint Mill Road on the left. Turn left onto Paint Mill

The Osprey House headquarters of the Wildlife Information Center, Inc., and west side of Lehigh Gap, Pennsylvania.

Road (which becomes unpaved) and continue straight ahead (*under* the bridge you just crossed) to a small, two-story stone building. Bear left and slightly uphill for about 50 feet, then bear right for approximately 100 feet to the small parking area across from Osprey House. Park there, then walk to the east-facing deck of Osprey House—or the area near the house—from which hawk watching can be done.

References: *Proceedings Hawk Migration Conference IV*, 1985: 1–11; *American Hawkwatcher*, 2000, 26: 23; 2001, 27: 20; 2002, 28: 20.

Little Gap (near Danielsville)

Spring Flights: Fair.

Autumn Flights: Fair to good.

View looking north from the pipeline cut atop the Kittatinny Ridge at Little Gap, Pennsylvania.

Watch Site Description: Several outcroppings of boulders on top of the Kittatinny Ridge from which observers can see hawks approaching or flying past. Alternatively, you can watch from the side of the main road crossing the mountain near the point where the Appalachian Trail crosses (marked by a sign), or along a pipeline cut just west of the road crossing the mountain and north of the Appalachian Trail (on north or west winds) or south of the Appalachian Trail (on east or south winds).

Access: At Danielsville (Northampton County), follow the paved road north to the top of the Kittatinny Ridge (Blue Mountain). Park in a lot on the left (west) side of the road near the top of the mountain, across from a boulder field called the "Devil's Potato Patch," then walk to any of the observation sites described above.

References: *A Guide to Hawk Watching in North America* (Pennsylvania State University Press, 1979); *The Migrations of Hawks*

(Indiana University Press, 1986); *HMANA Hawk Migration Studies*, 2001, 27 (1): 170–172; 2002, 28 (1): 65–66.

Militia Hill Hawk Watch (near Fort Washington)

Spring Flights: Fair.

Autumn Flights: Excellent.

Watch Site Description: An observation deck/platform in Fort Washington State Park overlooking a lawn and the surrounding landscape.

Access: From U.S. Route 309 near Fort Washington, take the Fort Washington exit and drive north on Pennsylvania Avenue to the Bethlehem Pike. Turn left onto the Bethlehem Pike and continue south to the first traffic light at State Route 73 (Skippack Pike). Turn right onto the Skippack Pike and proceed northwest to Militia Road (the first road on the left). Turn left onto Militia Road into Fort Washington State Park, continue to the top of the hill

Hawk watchers on the observation platform at Militia Hill Hawk Watch Site, Fort Washington, Pennsylvania.

(the observation deck/platform will be on your left), and turn right into the parking lot. Park, then walk back across the road to the observation deck/platform from which hawk watching is done. Picnic tables are available nearby.

If you are coming from the Pennsylvania Turnpike, take exit 26 (Fort Washington exit), drive north on Pennsylvania Avenue to Bethlehem Pike, then follow the remaining directions as provided above.

References: *HMANA Newsletter*, 1978, 3 (2): 22–25; 1979, 4 (2): 29–33; 1982, 7 (1): 17; *The Migrations of Hawks* (Indiana University Press, 1986); *Pennsylvania Birds*, 1989, 3 (4): 130; 1990, 4 (4): 177; *HMANA Hawk Migration Studies*, 2001, 27 (1): 165–166; 2002, 28 (1): 54–55.

Presque Isle State Park (near Erie)

Spring Flights: Fair.

Autumn Flights: Poor.

Watch Site Description: The parking lot of Beach 10 and the shoreline of Lake Erie east of the parking lot. Alternatively, you can observe from the trail, starting at the Thompson Bay traffic circle and leading west along Long Ridge. Fair hawk flights are also known to occur at Gull Point.

Access: From Interstate 90, drive north on State Route 832 to the park entrance near Erie. Secure park maps and other information at the park administration building about a mile inside the park. Then continue to the watch site areas.

References: *Annals of Carnegie Museum*, 1904, 2: 481–613; *A Guide to Hawk Watching in North America* (Pennsylvania State University Press, 1979).

Rocky Ridge County Park (near York)

Spring Flights: Fair.

Autumn Flights: Fair.

Watch Site
Description: A county park on a ridge. Observation decks are available on the north and south sides of the park. The north deck provides panoramic views of the Susquehanna River Valley and is used with prevailing northerly and easterly winds. The south deck on the south side of the park provides views of the York Valley and can also be used with prevailing southerly winds.

Access: From the junction of U.S. Route 30 and State Route 24 (Mount Zion Road), drive north on Route 24 for a mile to the junction with Deininger Road. Turn right onto Deininger Road and continue to the park.

References: *Pennsylvania Birds*, 1997, 11 (1): 8–13; *Raptor Watch* (BirdLife International and Hawk Mountain Sanctuary, 2000); *HMANA Hawk Migration Studies*, 2002, 28 (1): 110–111.

Rose Tree Park Hawk Watch (near Media)

Spring Flights: Poor.

Autumn Flights: Excellent.

Watch Site
Description: A county park west of Philadelphia with expanses of mowed lawn mixed with deciduous strips of deciduous woodland adjacent to watersheds. During spring, the watch site is positioned at the north edge of the eastern parking lot. During autumn, however, the watch site is moved to open lawn north of the gazebo between the park's two lots.

Access: From the junction of Interstate 476 (exit 5) and U.S. Route 1 near Media, drive west on U.S. 1 for 1.5 miles to State Route 252, then continue north on Route 252 for 0.25 mile to the entrance to Rose Tree Park on the right. Enter the park and continue to the east parking lot. From there, walk to the spring or autumn watch site.

References: *HMANA Hawk Migration Studies*, 2001, 27 (1): 166–167; 2002, 27 (2): 113–114; 2002, 28 (1): 53–54; *Rose Tree Park HawkWatch Site Manual* (Rose Tree Park Hawk-Watch, 2003).

Route 183 (near Strausstown)

Spring Flights: Poor.

Autumn Flights: Fair.

Watch Site Description: A large, open field with good views toward the north and northeast, but somewhat restricted views in other directions. The best hawk flights are seen here on prevailing north or northwest winds.

Access: From the junction of State Route 183 and Interstate 78 near Strausstown, drive north on Route 183 past the junction with State Route 419 to the top of the Kittatinny Ridge (Blue Mountain). Just before the highway descends the north side of the mountain, park on the opposite (west) side a safe distance off the road. Walk on the trail for a short distance west, then north, to the spot where hawk watchers gather.

References: *A Guide to Hawk Watching in North America* (Pennsylvania State University Press, 1979); *Pennsylvania Birds,* 1989, 3 (4): 131, 159; 1990, 4 (4): 176.

Hawk watchers at Route 183 near Strausstown, Pennsylvania.

Route 309 (near New Tripoli)

Spring Flights: Information unavailable.

Autumn Flights: Fair.

Watch Site Description: The large, private parking lot of the Blue Ridge Summit Bed and Breakfast at the top of the Kittatinny Ridge (Blue Mountain) on the border between Lehigh and Schuylkill Counties.

On southerly winds position yourself between the highway and a small building in the parking lot with a communications tower, looking upridge and also southward for approaching hawks. On westerly and northerly winds, park somewhere near the back (west edge) of the parking lot (behind the small building), away from the area near the restaurant used by customers, and look upridge and toward the northwest for approaching hawks. Either sit in your vehicle to look for migrating hawks, or use a folding chair and sit in the parking lot.

When possible, please patronize the restaurant and bed-and-breakfast for lunch or supper, or even an overnight stay. The restaurant is open Thursday through Saturday, 11:00 A.M. to 9:00 P.M.; Sunday, 11:00 A.M. to 8:00 P.M.

Access: From the junction of U.S. Route 309 and State Route 143 at New Tripoli, drive north on U.S. 309 for 4.9 miles to the top of the Kittatinny Ridge. The large parking lot from which hawk watching is done is on the left (west) side of the road. Pull into the parking lot and observe from the locations already indicated.

References: *American Hawkwatcher*, 1997, 23: 11; www.bluemountainsummit.com.

Second Mountain Hawk Watch (near Fort Indiantown Gap)

Spring Flights: Information unavailable.

Autumn Flights: Fair.

Watch Site Description: The parking area on top of Second Mountain north of the Kittatinny Ridge. There are wide views toward the east and poorer views toward the north.

Access: From the junction of Interstate 81 and State Route 934 (exit 85) at Fort Indiantown Gap Military Reservation, north of Annville, drive north on Route 934 for 2.5 miles to the junction with State Route 443. Turn left (west) onto Route 443 and continue to Tomstown Road. Turn left onto Tomstown Road and continue several miles to a T intersection (usually with a HAWK WATCH sign). Turn right and follow this road (which eventually is unpaved) to the top of Second Mountain and the parking lot and watch site.

References: *Pennsylvania Birds*, 1992, 6 (2): 182; *Raptor Watch* (BirdLife International and Hawk Mountain Sanctuary, 2000); *HMANA Hawk Migration Studies*, 2001, 27 (1): 175–177; 2002, 28 (1): 60–62.

State Hill Hawk Watch (near Reading)

Spring Flights: Information unavailable.

Autumn Flights: Fair to good.

Watch Site Description: An overlook above the State Hill Boat Ramp on the south side of Blue Marsh Lake overlooking the lake and the landscape toward the north, including the Kittatinny Ridge in the distance. Moderate numbers of Bald Eagles are attracted to the lake and are seen from the State Hill Hawk Watch.

Access: From the junction of U.S. Route 222 and State Route 183, drive north on Route 183 for a few miles to Paradise Drive. Turn left onto Paradise Drive and continue a few miles to Rebers Bridge Road. Turn right onto Rebers Bridge Road (which eventually becomes Brownsville Road) and continue to the State Hill Boat Ramp on the right. Turn into the boat-ramp entrance and drive a short distance to the parking area at the overlook. Leave your vehicle here and walk a few feet to the overlook.

Reference: *International Hawkwatcher*, 2000, 1: 13–14.

Sterrett's Gap (near Carlisle Springs)

Spring Flights: Poor.

Autumn Flights: Good.

Watch Site Description: A power-line right-of-way on top of the Kittatinny Ridge, or the same right-of-way beside a paved road on the north slope of the mountain.

Access: From the junction of State Routes 34 and 944 at Carlisle Springs, drive north for several miles on Route 34 to Sterrett's Gap. At the top of the mountain, turn right (east) onto Mountain Road (located at a service station) and continue for 0.3 mile to the power-line right-of-way. Park at a suitable spot. Then hike uphill along the power line for a relatively short distance to the ridge crest and observe from there. Alternatively, observe from the power line in the vicinity of the spot where it crosses Mountain Road.

References: *Auk*, 1940, 57: 247–250; *A Guide to Hawk Watching in North America* (Pennsylvania State University Press, 1979).

Stone Mountain (near Ennisville)

Spring Flights: Information unavailable.

Autumn Flights: Fair.

Watch Site Description: A platform on a rocky point atop Stone Mountain providing views over the surrounding landscape.

Access: From Ennisville, drive south on State Route 26 for about 3 miles to the hamlet of Jacks Corner. From there, turn left, cross a creek, and continue on East Branch Road for about 1.5 miles to the first public road on the right. Turn right onto Allensville Road and continue for 3 miles to the top of Stone Mountain. Park at the top of the mountain, then walk left (northeast) on a trail (which later has orange blazes over a rock field) for about 0.3 mile to the hawk watching platform, which is clearly visible.

References: *Pennsylvania Birds*, 1997, 11 (1): 8–13; 1998, 12 (4): 170–175; 1999, 13 (4): 190–196; 2000, 14 (4): 210–216; *HMANA Hawk Migration Studies*, 2001, 27 (1): 177–178.

Tuscarora Mountain (near Chambersburg)

Spring Flights: Fair.

Autumn Flights: Fair.

Watch Site Description: A flat, exposed area on top of a large pile of rocks known locally as The Pulpit.

Access: From Chambersburg, drive west on U.S. Route 30 toward McConnellsburg. At the top of Tuscarora Mountain, park beside an inn and walk along the path (marked by a sign) leading to The Pulpit.

References: *A Guide to Hawk Watching in North America* (Pennsylvania State University Press, 1979); *Pennsylvania Birds*, 1992, 6 (2): 181; *HMANA Hawk Migration Studies*, 2001, 27 (1): 178–179; 2002, 27 (2): 112–113; 2002, 28 (1): 111–112.

The Pulpit, Tuscarora Mountain, Pennsylvania.

Tussey Mountain Hawk Watch (near State College)

Spring Flights: Fair (excellent for Golden Eagles).

Autumn Flights: Information unavailable.

**Watch Site
Description:** A power line crossing forested Tussey Mountain. This site is noted for the large numbers of Golden Eagles seen during spring (especially March), with other raptor migrations continuing through April. In 2001 a spring count of 166 Golden Eagles was reported at Tussey Mountain.

Access: From State College, drive south on State Route 26 for about 7 miles to the top of Tussey Mountain (known locally as Pine Grove Mountain). Park in a large unpaved lot on the right side of the highway, close to the Jo Hays Vista, and walk southwest for about 0.7 mile on the Mid-State Trail to the power line from which hawk watching is done. Dress warmly for this exposed, windy site.

References: *Pennsylvania Birds*, 1997, 11 (1): 8–13; 2000, 14 (2): 94–96; 2001, 15 (2): 53–56; *HMANA Hawk Migration Studies*, 2002, 27 (2): 123–124; www.users.fast.net/~aquilac/tussey/.

Waggoner's Gap (near Carlisle)

Spring Flights: Information unavailable.

Autumn Flights: Good to excellent.

**Watch Site
Description:** An exposed boulder pile on the crest of the Kittatinny Ridge.

Access: From Carlisle, drive north on State Route 74 to the top of the Kittatinny Ridge, continue a short distance down the north side of the mountain, and leave your vehicle in the designated parking area. Follow the path from the parking area to the watch site on the crest of the ridge.

References: *Atlantic Naturalist*, 1966, 21: 161–168; *Autumn Hawk Flights: The Migrations in Eastern North America* (Rutgers University Press, 1975); *A Guide to Hawk Watching in North America* (Pennsylvania State University Press, 1979); *HMANA Hawk Migration Studies*, 2001, 27 (1): 179–182; 2002, 28 (1): 50–52.

Hawk watchers at Waggoner's Gap, Pennsylvania.

West Lake Middle School (in Erie)

Spring Flights: Good.

Autumn Flights: None.

Watch Site Description: A grass slope at the rear (northwest corner) of the school. The site overlooks an expanse of land between the school and the shoreline of Lake Erie.

Access: The school is located at 4330 West Lake Road (State Route 5A) in Erie. From the junction of State Routes 5A and 832, drive west on Route 5A for about 2 miles to the school on the north side of the highway.

Reference: *A Guide to Hawk Watching in North America* (Pennsylvania State University Press, 1979).

White Deer Ridge Hawk Watch (near South Williamsport)

Spring Flights: Fair.

Autumn Flights: Information unavailable.

Watch Site Description: The vicinity of a power-line cut, with two utility towers on the top of a mountain providing good views toward the north and south. Observe from the vicinity of the towers. On days with southerly winds, follow a trail leading down the south side to a spot with better views. Golden Eagles are among the raptors observed at White Deer Ridge.

Access: Follow State Route 554 (Sulphur Springs Road) out of South Williamsport to the top of North White Deer Ridge. Park in a small area near a large yellow gate (do not block entrance to the gate) at a paved entrance road and walk for about 0.25 mile on a paved trail to the two large utility towers.

References: *Pennsylvania Birds*, 2000, 14 (2): 94–96; 2001, 15 (2): 53–56; *HMANA Hawk Migration Studies*, 2002, 27 (2): 110–111.

Rhode Island

Napatree Point (near Watch Hill)

Spring Flights: Information unavailable.

Autumn Flights: Good.

**Watch Site
Description:** A barrier beach along Block Island Sound at the extreme southwestern corner of Rhode Island. Here hawk watchers observe migrating raptors—especially Ospreys, Sharp-shinned Hawks, American Kestrels, Merlins, and Peregrine Falcons—flying south along the seaside dunes.

Access: Park in a suitable area in the small village of Watch Hill, located south of Westerly, then walk along Fort Road for about a mile to Napatree Point. Hawk watching is done along the ocean side of the point.

References: *Narragansett Naturalist*, 1958, 1 (4): 118–119; *The Migrations of Hawks* (Indiana University Press, 1986).

South Carolina

Caesars Head State Park (near Cleveland)

Spring Flights: Information unavailable.

Autumn Flights: Good.

**Watch Site
Description:** A rocky outcropping, elevation 3,208 feet, on the summit of a mountain in a state park on the Blue Ridge Escarpment with superb views over the adjacent landscape.

Access: From Cleveland, drive north on U.S. Route 276 to the park entrance near Caesars Head. Enter the park and continue to the summit of the mountain, from which hawk watching is done.

Reference: *Guide to Birdwatching Sites/Eastern U.S.* (National Geographic Society, 1999).

Hilton Head Island

Spring Flights: Information unavailable.

Autumn Flights: Fair.

**Watch Site
Description:** Any exposed, publicly accessible area on the island or along the ocean beach.

Access: From the junction on Interstate 95 (exit 8) and U.S. Route 278 north of Hardeeville, drive east on U.S. 278 to Hilton Head Island and continue south on the island to Forest Beach. Locate any area along the ocean beach that is accessible to the public and watch from there. Some exploratory hawk watching is necessary on this island to locate the best publicly accessible sites.

Reference: *Raptor Watch* (BirdLife International and Hawk Mountain Sanctuary, 2000).

Sullivans Island (near Mount Pleasant)

Spring Flights: Information unavailable.

Autumn Flights: Poor.

**Watch Site
Description:** Any exposed area in the vicinity of Sullivans Island.

Access: From Mount Pleasant, drive east on the road leading to Sullivans Island. Some exploratory hawk watching is necessary to locate the best publicly accessible sites with adequate views.

Reference: *Raptor Watch* (BirdLife International and Hawk Mountain Sanctuary, 2000).

Tennessee

Dunlap Fire Tower (near Chattanooga)

Spring Flights: Information unavailable.

Autumn Flights: Fair.

Description: A fire tower on Walden Ridge where U.S. Route 127 crosses the time-zone boundary.

Access: From Chattanooga, drive north on U.S. Route 127 to Walden Ridge. The fire tower is located beside the highway and is readily accessible.

Reference: *A Guide to Hawk Watching in North America* (Pennsylvania State University Press, 1979).

Fall Creek Falls State Park (near Spencer)

Spring Flights: Information unavailable.

Autumn Flights: Fair.

**Watch Site
Description:** A fire tower in the state park, on the Cumberland Plateau.

Access: From Pikeville, drive northwest on State Route 30 for several miles to Fall Creek Falls State Park. Continue to the fire tower from which hawk watching is done.

References: *Migrant*, 1949, 20 (1): 16; A *Guide to Hawk Watching in North America* (Pennsylvania State University Press, 1979).

Rogersville–Kyles Ford Fire Tower (near Edison)

Spring Flights: Information unavailable.

Autumn Flights: Good.

**Watch Site
Description:** A fire tower on the crest of Clinch Mountain.

Access: From Rogersville, drive north on State Route 70 to the summit of Clinch Mountain. The fire tower, which can be seen from the road, is located on the ridge east of the highway. Park along the side of the highway, then hike for about ten minutes until you reach the tower.

Reference: *A Guide to Hawk Watching in North America* (Pennsylvania State University Press, 1979).

Texas

Aransas and Copano Bay Area (near Rockport)

Spring Flights: Excellent.

Autumn Flights: Information unavailable.

Watch Site Description: A suitable, exposed area on the north side of Aransas and Copano Bays at the narrowest point near the Copano Bay Bridge. Mid- to late April is a particularly productive hawk watching period.

Access: Full details are unavailable for this site, but from Rockport drive north on State Route 35 to the Copano Bay Bridge. Cross the bridge, then seek directions or locate the narrowest north-to-south point between the bays just west of the Copano causeway.

Reference: *A Guide to Hawk Watching in North America* (Pennsylvania State University Press, 1979).

Bentsen–Rio Grande Valley State Park (near Mission)

Spring Flights: Excellent.

Autumn Flights: Information unavailable.

Watch Site Description: Open areas on paved roads in the southwestern section of the park adjacent to moist woodlands and dry chaparral. Migrating hawks frequently roost in the park's woodland, and are especially visible in the early morning and evening when taking off or landing. Peak spring hawk flights occur from late March to late April.

Access: From the Inspiration Road exit off U.S. Business Route 83, west of Mission, drive south on Farm-to-Market (FM) Road 2062 for 3 miles to the entrance to the park. Enter, park at appropriate locations, and explore the area for raptors and other birds.

References: *A Guide to Hawk Watching in North America* (Pennsylvania State University Press, 1979); *Birding*, 1992, 24 (1):

10–17; *Birding Texas* (Falcon/Globe Pequot Press, 1998); *Raptor Watch* (BirdLife International and Hawk Mountain Sanctuary, 2000); *HMANA Hawk Migration Studies*, 2003, 28 (2): 42–44.

Daingerfield State Park (near Daingerfield)

Spring Flights: Information unavailable.

Autumn Flights: Good.

Watch Site Description: A small, 551-acre park with fields, agricultural fields, woodland, riparian areas, Lake Daingerfield, and creeks. Autumn raptor migrations are monitored during the last two weeks in September. Broad-winged Hawks are most abundant, but other raptors are also seen, including Ospreys, Sharp-shinned Hawks, Cooper's Hawks, Red-shouldered Hawks, Red-tailed Hawks, and American Kestrels. Occasionally a few Merlins and Peregrine Falcons are also counted.

Access: From Daingerfield, follow State Route 49 for 3 miles to Park Route 17 and the park's entrance. Secure details about the best spot to watch migrating hawks from the park's superintendent at Daingerfield State Park, Route 1, Box 186B, Daingerfield, TX 75638; (903) 645–2921.

Reference: *Birding Texas* (Falcon/Globe Pequot Press, 1998).

Hazel Bazemore County Park Hawk Watch (near Corpus Christi)

Spring Flights: Excellent.

Autumn Flights: World class.

Watch Site Description: Trees beside a golf course in a seventy-eight-acre county park on the south bank of the Nueces River with good views of the surrounding landscape from the northeast to the west, but somewhat restricted views toward the east. This watch site reports the largest autumn raptor migrations in North America (between half a million and nearly one million birds each autumn).

Access: From the junction of Interstate 37 and U.S. Route 77 near Corpus Christi, drive south on U.S. 77 for 0.5 mile and exit onto Farm-to-Market (FM) Road 624. Drive west on FM 624 for 0.7 mile to the park entrance on the right. Enter the park, cross a speed bump, then turn left and follow the winding road past visitor facilities and over the top of a hill to the point where the road turns left. Hawk watchers park at this spot and watch hawk migrations from some trees adjacent to the seventeenth tee of a golf course. Bring your own folding chair, food and beverage, a hat, sunscreen, and other hawk watching equipment.

References: *Raptor Watch* (BirdLife International and Hawk Mountain Sanctuary, 2000); *HMANA Hawk Migration Studies*, 2001, 26 (2): 45; 2001, 27 (1): 203–212, 219–221; 2002, 28 (1): 10, 134–136; *Hawkwatching in the Americas* (Hawk Migration Association of North America, 2001): 67–91; HMANA Web site at www.hmana.org.

Hornsby Bend Hawk Watch (in Austin)

Spring Flights: Information unavailable.

Autumn Flights: Excellent.

Watch Site Description: An observation area on the edge of Pond 1 East in the 700-acre Hornsby Bend Biosolids Management Facility along the Colorado River in Austin.

Access: From the junction of Interstate 36 and U.S. Route 290, drive east on U.S. 290 to the junction with Farm-to-Market (FM) Road 973. Turn south onto FM 973 and continue to the entrance to the Hornsby Bend Biosolids Management Facility. Enter and continue to the Hornsby Bend Hawk Watch at the northwest corner of Pond 1 East.

Reference: Hornsby Bend Bird Observatory at www.hornsbybend.org.

Robstown

Spring Flights: Information unavailable.

Autumn Flights: Excellent.

Watch Site Description: Complete details about this site are unavailable, but presumably observers can see impressive flights of migrating hawks from an exposed area along County Route 75.

Access: Full details are unavailable. However, from Robstown drive to the junction of U.S. Route 77 and County Route 75. Turn west onto Route 75 and continue for 4.7 miles to a point about 1.5 miles south of the Nueces River. Observe from there.

Reference: *A Guide to Hawk Watching in North America* (Pennsylvania State University Press, 1979).

Santa Ana National Wildlife Refuge (near McAllen)

Spring Flights: Excellent.

Autumn Flights: Information unavailable.

Watch Site Description: The top of a 15-foot-high levee, providing unrestricted views over the northern portion of the refuge. Large flights of Broad-winged Hawks and Swainson's Hawks (up to 100,000) sometimes occur here in late March and early April. The best time to observe the raptors is early morning or evening, when they are taking off or landing at roosts. However, other periods throughout the day should not be overlooked.

Access: From McAllen, drive south on 10th Street (which becomes State Route 336) for about 6 miles to the junction with U.S. Route 281 (Old Military Road). Turn left (east) onto U.S. 281 and continue for another 10 miles toward Brownsville. Then look for the refuge sign along the right side of the highway. Turn right and drive for about 0.25 mile from a spot on the levee about 100 yards to the right. However, anywhere along the levee is suitable for observing hawk migrations.

References: *A Guide to Hawk Watching in North America* (Pennsylvania State University Press, 1979); *Birding*, 1992, 24 (1): 10–17; *Raptor Watch* (BirdLife International and Hawk Mountain Sanctuary, 2000); *HMANA Hawk Migration Studies*, 2002, 27 (2): 127; 2003, 28 (2): 42–44.

Smith Point Hawk Watch (near Houston)

Spring Flights: Information unavailable.

Autumn Flights: Excellent.

Watch Site Description: A three-level platform 30 feet high beside East Bay in the Candy Abshier Wildlife Management Area northeast of Galveston Bay.

Access: From Houston, drive east on Interstate 10 to the junction with State Route 61, then continue south on Route 61 to a four-way stop sign. Continue ahead when the road becomes Farm-to-Market (FM) Road 562. Drive south on FM 562 to a fork in the road. Take the right fork, and continue for approximately 14 miles to the village of Smith Point. Continue ahead, following signs for the hawk watch in the Candy Abshier Wildlife Management Area on the east side of FM 562. Drive to the parking area and hawk watching tower overlooking the coastal marsh and part of Galveston Bay. Observe from there.

References: *Raptor Watch* (BirdLife International and Hawk Mountain Sanctuary, 2000); *Hawkwatching in the Americas* (Hawk Migration Association of North America, 2001): 67–91; *HMANA Hawk Migration Studies*, 2001, 27 (1): 212–219, 222–224; 28 (1): 120–127, 136–138; Gulf Coast Bird Observatory at www.gcbo.org/research/sphawk.htm.

Utah

Gunsight Peak (near Clarkston)

Spring Flights: Information unavailable.

Autumn Flights: Fair.

Watch Site

Description: An 8,244-foot-high peak at the southwestern corner of the Clarkston mountain range. Visibility is restricted, but some migrating raptors can be seen.

Access: From Logan, drive north on U.S. Route 91 to Smithfield. Turn left at the traffic light and drive about 15 miles to the town of Clarkston. At the northwest corner of town, take a road (perhaps still unpaved) north out of town. Drive for several miles, then turn left at the fork and head westward toward the Clarkston range. Park at the end of the road and hike up Winter Canyon to the top of the ridge. Gunsight Peak is located at the extreme western end of the range. The 4 miles of hiking is rigorous and requires at least two and a half hours.

Reference: *A Guide to Hawk Watching in North America* (Pennsylvania State University Press, 1979).

Hyde Park Knoll (near Hyde Park)

Spring Flights: Fair.

Autumn Flights: Fair.

Watch Site

Description: An exposed area at an elevation of 7,100 feet on the western slope of the Bear River range. The watch site is most productive for accipiters and American Kestrels in September.

Access: From Logan, drive north on 800 East Street for about 2 miles to the town of Hyde Park. At the first intersection turn right (east) and continue on the paved road, which may become unpaved after about 0.5 mile. Remain on the main (possibly unpaved) road until you arrive at the mouth of a canyon (about 2 miles). Park here and walk to the top of the knoll north of the canyon. It is about 0.75 mile and some 1,500 vertical feet to the top. Most hawks pass high overhead and to the east farther up the mountain face.

Reference: *A Guide to Hawk Watching in North America* (Pennsylvania State University Press, 1979).

Jordanelle Hawk Watch (near Salt Lake City)

Spring Flights: Poor.

Autumn Flights: Information unavailable.

Watch Site Description: An elevated site with views of the adjacent landscape.

Access: From Salt Lake City, drive east on Interstate 80 to the junction with U.S. Route 40 at Silver Creek Junction. Turn right (south) onto U.S. 40 and proceed for 11 miles to the Jordanelle Reservoir on the left. Watch carefully for mile marker 11, just beyond which is a roadside pullover and parking area for a jeep trail. Park in this pullover area as far off the highway shoulder as possible. Then walk north-northwest for about 800 feet on the jeep trail (which runs parallel to the highway), following blazes and obvious use, to an elevated spot from which hawk watching is done.

References: *Raptor Watch* (BirdLife International and Hawk Mountain Sanctuary, 2000); *HMANA Hawk Migration Studies*, 2002, 27 (2): 36–38, 53–55; 2003, 28 (2): 61; HMANA Web site at www.hmana.org.

Utah Valley Hawk Migration Lookouts (near Orem)

Spring Flights: Information unavailable.

Autumn Flights: Fair.

Watch Site Description: A scenic overlook or parking area, and a knoll, with views over a nearby valley and mountain range.

Access: From Interstate 15 at Orem, take the northernmost Orem exit, marked STATE ROUTE 52. Drive east on Route 52 (8th North) for 3.6 miles to the junction with U.S. Route 189. Turn left onto U.S. 189 and drive north for 2 miles to the Squaw Peak Trail. Follow the trail for 4.1 miles to where the road forms a T intersection. Take a right-hand turn at the T and continue for a short distance to the scenic overlook or parking area, from which migrating hawks can be seen.

Alternatively, turn left at the T intersection and drive for 1.9 miles—the paved road ends just past the Hope Picnic Area—to a turnout and gravel parking area on the right side of the road. Park here and hike along the contours on the northeast to a knoll overlooking the valley. Birds approach from the north-northeast above and below the vantage points. West winds produce the largest flights, which seem to appear in peak numbers during the second and third weeks of September.

Reference: *A Guide to Hawk Watching in North America* (Pennsylvania State University Press, 1979).

Wellsville Mountain Hawk Lookout (near Wellsville)

Spring Flights: Poor.

Autumn Flights: Good.

Watch Site Description: A knoll (elevation more than 8,500 feet) on top of the northern end of the Wellsville mountain range from which observers enjoy splendid panoramic views of Cache Valley and the Wasatch Mountains to the east and the Promontory Mountains and Great Salt Lake to the west. Hawks usually fly along the west side of the range at eye level or slightly below. Most migrants are seen in September and October.

Access: From Wellsville, follow U.S. Routes 89/91 to the junction with State Route 23, then turn north onto Route 23 and continue for 7 miles to Mendon. In Mendon drive west on 3rd North Street for about 2.5 miles to the end of the road at a trailhead. Park here and look for a sign pointing to Deep Canyon Trail to the left. Hike the trail for about 3.5 miles to the ridge crest, then turn right (north) and follow it for another 0.5 to 0.7 mile to the hawk migration watch site, located at the highest point on the ridge.

References: *Southwest Hawk Watch Newsletter*, 1978, 2 (1): 2–3; *A Guide to Hawk Watching in North America* (Pennsylvania State University Press, 1979); *HMANA Hawk Migration Studies*, 2001, 27 (1): 43; 2002, 28 (1): 197–198.

Vermont

Camel's Hump (near Waterbury)

Spring Flights: Information unavailable.

Autumn Flights: Good.

Watch Site Description: An exposed ledge with views over a broad valley.

Access: From Waterbury, drive west on U.S. Route 2 to Jonesville, cross the Winooski River, then follow the first left turn onto a minor road for 2.5 miles to the BAMFORTH RIDGE TRAIL sign on the right. Walk along this trail for about 2 miles to a point where it tops out on the first spruce ridge. The exposed ledge is located nearby.

Reference: *A Guide to Hawk Watching in North America* (Pennsylvania State University Press, 1979).

Glebe Mountain (near Londonderry)

Spring Flights: Poor.

Autumn Flights: Fair.

Watch Site Description: A boulder-strewn slope at the top of Glebe Mountain from which observers enjoy good views from the southwest through the northeast.

Access: From Londonderry, drive east on State Route 11 for about 2 miles and follow signs to the Magic Mountain Ski Area base lodge. Park here, then begin a long and sometimes strenuous hike up the trail under the ski lift in front (and to the right) of the lodge. When you reach midstation, follow the trail leading to the right, then a maintenance road that gradually climbs the ridge. Hawk watching is done from the top of the steep boulder-strewn slope overlooking the road.

Reference: *A Guide to Hawk Watching in North America* (Pennsylvania State University Press, 1979).

Hogback Mountain (between Bennington and Brattleboro)

Spring Flights: Information unavailable.

Autumn Flights: Fair.

Watch Site Description: An overview beside the road with excellent views toward the south.

Access: From Bennington, drive east on State Route 9; from Brattleboro, head west. The highway crosses Hogback Mountain, and the overview beside the road is obvious.

Reference: *A Guide to Hawk Watching in North America* (Pennsylvania State University Press, 1979).

Merck Forest & Farmland Center (near East Rupert)

Spring Flights: Information unavailable.

Autumn Flights: Fair.

Watch Site Description: Exposed views looking toward the northwest from the entrance road can be used for autumn hawk watching.

Access: From East Rupert, drive west on State Route 315 for 2.6 miles to the entrance to the Merck Forest & Farmland Center. Turn left onto the entrance road and continue for 0.5 mile to the parking lot. Secure updated information at the center's headquarters. Donations are accepted to help maintain the center.

Reference: *Birdwatching in Vermont* (University Press of New England, 2002).

Mount Ascutney (near Ascutney)

Spring Flights: Information unavailable.

Autumn Flights: Fair.

Watch Site Description: The summit of a mountain (elevation 3,144 feet) with exposed views and a fire tower from which hawk watching can be done.

Access: From the junction of exit 8 off Interstate 91 and State Route 131, drive 0.5 mile to the junction with U.S. Route 5. Turn north on U.S. 5 and continue for 1.1 miles to the junction with State Route 44A. Turn left onto Route 44A and continue for 1.1 miles to the entrance to Ascutney State Park and the summit of Mount Ascutney. Turn into the park, pay any fee required, and continue on the park road to a parking lot in a saddle. Park here, then walk for about 0.8 mile on the trail to the summit of Mount Ascutney. Hawk watching is done from exposed areas or the fire tower. The park road is open mid-May until mid-October, 10:00 A.M. to thirty minutes before dark.

Reference: *Birdwatching in Vermont* (University Press of New England, 2002).

Mount Philo State Park (near Charlotte)

Spring Flights: Information unavailable.

Autumn Flights: Fair to good.

Watch Site Description: A rock outcrop with a protective railing at the southwest corner of the mountain's summit, providing a superb view of the Champlain Valley and Adirondack Mountains in the distance.

Access: From the junction of U.S. Route 7 and State Park Road a few miles south of Charlotte, turn onto State Park Road and continue for 0.6 mile to the entrance to the park. Pay an entrance fee and drive for about a mile on the steep road to the summit of the mountain. Park and walk to the southwest corner with the protective railing. The park road is open mid-May until mid-October, 10:00 A.M. to sunset.

Reference: *Birdwatching in Vermont* (University Press of New England, 2002).

Putney Mountain (near Putney)

Spring Flights: Information unavailable.

Autumn Flights: Fair to good.

Watch Site Description: The exposed summit of a mountain, providing excellent views of the adjacent landscape. This is one of Vermont's best autumn hawk watching locations.

Access: Take exit 4 off Interstate 91 near Putney, and drive about 0.2 mile to U.S. Route 5. Turn right onto U.S. 5 and continue for about 0.5 mile to the center of the town of Putney. From there, turn left (uphill) onto *unmarked* Westminster West Road and continue for 1.1 miles to the junction with West Hill Road. Turn left onto West Hill Road and continue for 2.5 miles to the junction with Putney Mountain Road. Turn right onto Putney Mountain Road and drive another 3.3 miles to the summit of Putney Mountain. Turn into the parking lot on the right, park your vehicle, then walk north on the so-called Main Trail (located behind the parking area) running along the ridge for about 0.6 mile to the summit of the mountain.

Reference: *Birdwatching in Vermont* (University Press of New England, 2002).

Smugglers Notch State Park (near Stowe)

Spring Flights: Information unavailable.

Autumn Flights: Fair.

Watch Site Description: The summit of Mount Mansfield, providing views of the surrounding landscape.

Access: From the junction of State Routes 100 and 108 in Stowe, drive north on Route 108 for 6.2 miles, pass through the Notch Passageway, and continue another 3 miles to Smugglers Notch State Park. Then take the toll road to the summit of Mount Mansfield.

Reference: *Vermont Wildlife Viewing Guide* (Falcon Press Publishing, 1994).

Virginia

Hawk watchers in Virginia long have enjoyed watching migrating raptors during autumn from coastal sites and inland mountain vistas, including various overlooks along the Skyline Drive in Shenandoah National Park, as well as the Blue Ridge Parkway. However, much remains to be learned about spring and autumn raptor migrations in the southern Appalachian Mountains. Hopefully, this book will induce hawk watchers to fill in some of the gaps in our knowledge about raptor migrations in Virginia's part of the southern Appalachians.

Big Schloss (near Luray)

Spring Flights: Information unavailable.

Autumn Flights: Good.

Watch Site Description: A prominent rocky outcropping from which observers have 330 degrees of unrestricted visibility.

Access: From Luray, follow State Route 675 northwest for about 25 miles to the Wolf Gap Recreation Park. Alternatively, from Wardensville, West Virginia, drive west on State Route 55 to the junction with State Route 259. Turn south on Route 259 and continue for some 13 or 14 miles into Wolf Gap. Park in a suitable location, then walk up the Blue Trail for about 2 miles to the lookout on top of Big Schloss.

References: *A Guide to Hawk Watching in North America* (Pennsylvania State University Press, 1979); *The Migrations of Hawks* (Indiana University Press, 1986).

Blue Ridge Parkway

In addition to established raptor migration watch sites along the Blue Ridge Parkway in Virginia, other selected roadside overlooks are also potentially useful hawk watching and raptor migration study sites. Some of the latter are included here as *experimental* sites. I encourage hawk watchers to evaluate these overlooks to determine their value for hawk watching and raptor migration monitoring.

Blue Ridge Parkway overlooks, and other sites along this spectacular road, are presented from north to south to correspond with maps provided by the National Park Service, as well as the two-volume *Blue Ridge Parkway Guide* (Menasha Ridge Press, 2002). Virginia's 216.9-mile-long part of the Blue Ridge Parkway begins at milepost 0 at Rockfish Gap, where it connects with the southern end of the Skyline Drive in Shenandoah National Park, near Waynesboro, and continues south to milepost 216.9, where it ends at the North Carolina–Virginia state line.

Rockfish Gap (near Waynesboro)

Spring Flights: Information unavailable.

Autumn Flights: Fair.

Watch Site Description: This watch site, elevation 1,909 feet, is sometimes called Afton Mountain in older hawk migration literature, and is the parking lot of a motel at the junction where milepost 105.4 on the Skyline Drive in Shenandoah National Park, milepost 0 on the Blue Ridge Parkway, U.S. Route 250, and Interstate 64 meet at Rockfish Gap.

Access: From Waynesboro, drive south on U.S. Route 250 for a few miles to the motel parking lot at the Rockfish Gap junction mentioned above. Observe from the parking lot.

References: *Redstart*, 1953, 20 (3): 39–54; *A Guide to Hawk Watching in North America* (Pennsylvania State University Press, 1979); *The Migrations of Hawks* (Indiana University Press, 1986); *Birds of the Blue Ridge Mountains* (University of North Carolina Press, 1992); *John Anthony Alderman Guide to Hawk Watching on the Blue River Parkway* (Hawk Migration Association of North America, no date); *HMANA Hawk Migration Studies*, 2001, 27 (1): 193–194.

Apple Orchard Mountain Overlook (near Big Island)

Spring Flights: Experimental (not evaluated).

Autumn Flights: Experimental (not evaluated).

**Watch Site
Description:** An east-facing overlook, elevation 3,950 feet (the highest on the Blue Ridge Parkway in Virginia), providing excellent views of ridges and valleys toward the east. Migrating hawks are reported from this site, but based only on very limited observations. Apple Orchard Mountain Overlook is probably best used on days with prevailing southerly (and perhaps easterly) winds and provides hawk watchers with opportunities to look for migrating hawks from an unusually high-elevation Virginia location.

Access: From Big Island, drive west on U.S. Route 501 to the Blue Ridge Parkway, then head south on the parkway to the Apple Orchard Mountain Overlook at milepost 76.3.

Reference: *The Migrations of Hawks* (Indiana University Press, 1986).

View from Apple Orchard Mountain Overlook at milepost 76.3 on the Blue Ridge Parkway, Virginia.

Purgatory Mountain Overlook (near Buchanan)

Spring Flights: Poor.

Autumn Flights: Excellent.

Watch Site Description: A parkway overlook, elevation 2,415 feet, with excellent views of valleys and ridges (including Purgatory Mountain) toward the west. This site is used during autumn with prevailing westerly and northwesterly winds.

Access: From Buchanan, drive east on State Route 43 to the Blue Ridge Parkway, then continue south on the parkway to the Purgatory Mountain Overlook at milepost 92.2.

References: *Virginia Society of Ornithology Newsletter*, 1972, 18 (5): 2–3; *A Guide to Hawk Watching in North America* (Pennsylvania State University Press, 1979); *The Migrations of Hawks* (Indiana University Press, 1986); *Birds of the Blue Ridge Mountains* (University of North Carolina Press, 1992); *John Anthony Alderman Guide to Hawk Watching on the Blue River Parkway* (Hawk Migration Association of North America, no date).

Purgatory Mountain Overlook at milepost 92.2 on the Blue Ridge Parkway, Virginia.

Pine Tree Overlook (near Buchanan)

Spring Flights: Experimental (not evaluated).

Autumn Flights: Experimental (not evaluated).

Watch Site Description: An east-facing overlook, elevation 2,490 feet, diagonally across from the Harvey's Knob Overlook. It can be used in combination with the Harvey's Knob Overlook to see migrating hawks flying along the east side of the mountain with prevailing easterly and southerly winds.

Access: From Buchanan, drive southeast on State Route 43 to its junction with the Blue Ridge Parkway, then continue south on the parkway to milepost 95.2 and the Pine Tree Overlook (ample parking is available in the nearby Harvey's Knob Overlook at milepost 95.3; see below).

References: None.

Harvey's Knob Overlook (near Buchanan)

Spring Flights: Poor.

Autumn Flights: Excellent.

Watch Site Description: An overlook and large parking lot, elevation 2,524 feet, along the Blue Ridge Parkway with excellent views of the surrounding Great Valley from the west through the northwest. This is one of the best autumn hawk watching locations along the parkway, and is used regularly by local hawk watchers when westerly and northwesterly winds prevail.

Access: From Buchanan, drive southeast on State Route 43 to its junction with the Blue Ridge Parkway, then continue south on the parkway to milepost 95.4 and the Harvey's Knob Overlook. Ample parking is available at this location.

References: *A Guide to Hawk Watching in North America* (Pennsylvania State University Press, 1979); *The Migrations of Hawks* (Indiana University Press, 1986); *Birds of the Blue Ridge Mountains* (University of North Carolina Press, 1992);

Harvey's Knob Overlook at milepost 95.4 on the Blue Ridge Parkway, Virginia.

John Anthony Alderman Guide to Hawk Watching on the Blue River Parkway (Hawk Migration Association of North America, no date); *HMANA Hawk Migration Studies*, 2001, 27 (1): 192–193.

Great Valley Overlook (near Roanoke)

Spring Flights: Information unavailable.

Autumn Flights: Excellent.

Watch Site Description: A west-facing overlook, elevation 2,493 feet, providing views of part of the Great Valley. This site is best used during autumn on days with prevailing west and northwest winds.

Access: From Roanoke, drive north on U.S. Routes 221/460 to the Blue Ridge Parkway, then continue north on the parkway to the Great Valley Overlook at milepost 99.6.

References: *The Migrations of Hawks* (Indiana University Press, 1986); *Birds of the Blue Ridge Mountains* (University of North Carolina Press, 1992); *John Anthony Alderman Guide to Hawk Watching on the Blue River Parkway* (Hawk Migration Association of North America, no date).

Devil's Backbone Overlook (near Ferrum)

Spring Flights: Poor.

Autumn Flights: Good.

Watch Site Description: A northeast-facing overlook, providing views of nearby Devil's Backbone. This site is best used during autumn on days with prevailing southerly winds.

Access: From Ferrum, drive west on State Route 602 to the junction with State Route 640, then continue south on Route 640 to its junction with the Blue Ridge Parkway. Turn north onto the parkway and drive to Devil's Backbone Overlook at milepost 143.9.

Reference: *The Migrations of Hawks* (Indiana University Press, 1986).

Chincoteague National Wildlife Refuge (near Chincoteague)

Spring Flights: Information unavailable.

Autumn Flights: Fair.

Watch Site Description: A barrier beach island along which migrating falcons and other raptors appear. Observations are made from the vicinity of two observation blinds on opposite sides of a freshwater pond along Wildlife Drive, or from the barrier beach where Peregrine Falcons sometimes appear.

Access: From Pocomoke City, Maryland, drive south on U.S. Route 13 to Oak Hall, Virginia. Turn east onto Virginia State Route 175 and drive to the town of Chincoteague.

When entering the town on Route 175, turn left onto Main Street and continue for 7 blocks. Then turn right onto Maddox Boulevard and follow it to the refuge headquarters or information center located 0.5 mile beyond the Assateague Channel bridge. The refuge's Wildlife Drive is open from 6:00 A.M. to 3:00 P.M. for hiking and biking, and from 3:00 P.M. to sunset for auto traffic.

Reference: *A Guide to Hawk Watching in North America* (Pennsylvania State University Press, 1979).

High Knob (near Norton)

Spring Flights: Information unavailable.

Autumn Flights: Fair.

Watch Site Description: An observation tower on the summit of a 4,160-foot mountain providing excellent views of the surrounding landscape. Broad-winged Hawks and various other raptors migrate past this site during autumn.

Access: From Norton, drive south on State Route 619 for 3.7 miles up the mountain to the junction with Forest Service Road 238. Turn left (east) onto FR 238 and continue for 0.3 mile to the tower entrance on the right side of the road. Park and walk for 0.25 mile to the observation tower.

Reference: *Virginia Wildlife Viewing Guide* (Falcon Press Publishing, 1994).

Kennedy Peak (near Luray)

Spring Flights: Information unavailable.

Autumn Flights: Excellent.

Watch Site Description: A low tower-shelter on the peak of Mount Kennedy with good visibility from the north through the southwest but restricted visibility to the west and northwest.

Access: From Luray, drive west on U.S. Route 211. After passing a Holiday Inn, continue for about 1.5 miles to the off-ramp leading to U.S. Route 340 south. Take this exit. Turn left at the bottom of the ramp, continue for 0.3 mile on U.S. 340, then turn right onto State Route 675. Follow Route 675 for about 7 miles, crossing the south fork of the Shenandoah River. At the end of the bridge, turn left, continue for 0.3 mile, then turn right. Drive about 2.5 miles to the Kennedy Peak parking area. Park, then walk on the trail leading off the right side of the road following the signs for Kennedy Peak (2 miles). Walk 1.8 miles, then turn right where the trail begins a long descent slightly to the left, at a wooden marker. Continue up a steep incline to the peak some 300 yards away.

Reference: *A Guide to Hawk Watching in North America* (Pennsylvania State University Press, 1979).

Kiptopeke State Park (near Cape Charles)

Spring Flights: None.

Autumn Flights: Excellent.

Watch Site Description: An observation platform in a state park at the tip of the Delmarva Peninsula about a mile south of the town of Kiptopeke. An annual Fall Birding Festival also is held each October in the park.

Access: From Norfolk to the south, or more northern points on the Delmarva Peninsula, follow U.S. Route 13 to the southern end of the peninsula and look for local directional signs pointing to Kiptopeke State Park at 3540 Kiptopeke Drive in Cape Charles.

References: *Autumn Hawk Flights: The Migrations in Eastern North America* (Rutgers University Press, 1975); *A Guide to Hawk Watching in North America* (Pennsylvania State University Press, 1979); *Living Bird*, 1999, 18 (4): 16–20; *HMANA Hawk Migration Studies*, 2001, 27 (1): 187–188; 2002, 28 (1): 42–44.

Mendota Fire Tower (near Hansonville)

Spring Flights: None.

Autumn Flights: Excellent.

Watch Site Description: A fire tower providing exposed views from the summit of Clinch Mountain. This is traditionally considered a Tennessee hawk watching location despite being in Virginia near the Tennessee border.

Access: From Abingdon, drive north on U.S. Route 19 (Alternate U.S. Route 58) to Hansonville, then follow State Route 802 to State Route 614 and continue to the top of the mountain. Park in the saddle at the top, and hike on the trail on the right for about fifteen minutes until you reach the fire tower.

References: *A Guide to Hawk Watching in North America* (Pennsylvania State University Press, 1979); *HMANA Hawk Migration Studies*, 2001, 27 (1): 195.

Skyline Drive (in Shenandoah National Park)

Skyline Drive is a scenic road extending for 105.4 miles along the crest of the Appalachian Mountains in Shenandoah National Park between its beginning at milepost 0 at Front Royal and its terminus at milepost 105.4 at Rockfish Gap. Numerous roadside overlooks allow visitors to enjoy views over adjacent valleys and mountains. Some of these overlooks are established raptor migration observation sites, and are discussed here, whereas others are selected experimental raptor migration monitoring sites needing evaluation to determine their importance for hawk watching purposes.

Dickey Ridge Visitor Center (near Front Royal)

Spring Flights: Experimental (not evaluated).

Autumn Flights: Experimental (not evaluated).

Watch Site Description: A west-facing observation point near the Dickey Ridge Visitor Center, elevation 1,940 feet, providing sweeping views toward the west and northwest. The site is best used during autumn with prevailing westerly and northwesterly winds.

Access: From the north entrance to Shenandoah National Park at Front Royal, drive south on the Skyline Drive for 4.6 miles to the Dickey Ridge Visitor Center. Park in the lot and walk to the visitor center to enjoy exhibits, secure information, use restrooms, and perhaps purchase books or other souvenirs. To reach the hawk watching site, walk a few hundred feet along the footpath extending from the parking lot to the west-facing vista. Several benches are provided for the comfort of visitors.

References: None.

Gooney Run and Gooney Manor Overlooks (near Front Royal)

Spring Flights: Experimental (not evaluated).

Autumn Flights: Experimental (not evaluated).

Watch Site Description: Gooney Run is a west-facing roadside overlook, elevation 2,085 feet, providing views toward the west and north-

View from Gooney Run Overlook at milepost 6.9 on the Skyline Drive, Shenandoah National Park, Virginia.

west; it best used during autumn with prevailing westerly and northwesterly winds. The nearby Gooney Manor Overlook, at approximately milepost 7.1, provides views somewhat similar to those at the Gooney Run Overlook and is used when similar wind conditions prevail.

Access: From the north entrance to Shenandoah National Park at Front Royal, drive south on the Skyline Drive for approximately 6.9 miles to the Gooney Run Overlook, or continue farther to the Gooney Manor Overlook approximately at milepost 7.1; hawk watching can also be done here.

References: None.

Hogwallow Flats Overlook (near Front Royal)

Spring Flights: Experimental (not evaluated).

Autumn Flights: Experimental (not evaluated).

Watch Site Description: An east-facing roadside overlook, elevation 2,665 feet, providing sweeping views from the southeast toward the

View from Hogwallow Flats Overlook at milepost 13.9 on the Skyline Drive, Shenandoah National Park, Virginia.

southwest. This overlook is best used during spring, or autumn, with prevailing southerly winds.

Access: From the north entrance to Shenandoah National Park at Front Royal, drive south on the Skyline Drive for approximately 13.9 miles to the Hogwallow Flats Overlook.

References: None.

Browntown Valley Overlook (near Front Royal)

Spring Flights: Experimental (not evaluated).

Autumn Flights: Experimental (not evaluated).

Watch Site Description: A west-facing roadside overlook at milepost 15, providing sweeping views toward the west and northwest. The site is best used during autumn with prevailing westerly and northwesterly winds.

Access: From the north entrance to Shenandoah National Park at Front Royal, drive south on the Skyline Drive for 15 miles to the Browntown Valley Overlook.

References: None.

Browntown Valley Overlook at milepost 15 on the Skyline Drive, Shenandoah National Park, Virginia.

View from the Range View Overlook at milepost 17.4 on the Skyline Drive, Shenandoah National Park, Virginia.

Range View Overlook (near Front Royal)

Spring Flights: Experimental (not evaluated).

Autumn Flights: Experimental (not evaluated).

Watch Site Description: A southeast-facing roadside overlook, elevation 2,810 feet, providing excellent southerly views. The site is best used during spring, or on autumn days with prevailing southerly winds.

Access: From the north entrance to Shenandoah National Park at Front Royal, drive south on the Skyline Drive for approximately 17.4 miles to the Range View Overlook.

References: None.

Hogback Overlook (near Front Royal)

Spring Flights: Experimental (not evaluated).

Autumn Flights: Experimental (not evaluated).

Watch Site Description: A west- and northwest-facing roadside overlook, elevation 3,385 feet, providing excellent views over the adjacent landscape.

Access: From the north entrance to Shenandoah National Park at Front Royal, drive south on the Skyline Drive for 20 miles to the Hogback Overlook.

Reference: *Birds of the Blue Ridge Mountains* (University of North Carolina Press, 1992).

Tunnel Parking Overlook (near Luray)

Spring Flights: Experimental (not evaluated).

Autumn Flights: Experimental (not evaluated).

Watch Site Description: A southeast-facing roadside overlook, elevation 2,510 feet, providing excellent southerly views. The site is best used

View from Tunnel Parking Overlook, Skyline Drive, Shenandoah National Park, Virginia.

during spring, or on autumn days with prevailing southerly winds.

Access: From the junction of U.S. Route 211 and the Skyline Drive at the Thornton Gap Entrance Station to Shenandoah National Park a few miles east of Luray, drive south a short distance on the Skyline Drive to the Tunnel Parking Overlook.

References: None.

Jewell Hollow Overlook (near Luray)

Spring Flights: Experimental (not evaluated).

Autumn Flights: Experimental (not evaluated).

Watch Site Description: A west-facing roadside overlook, elevation 3,320 feet, providing excellent views toward the west and northwest. The site is best used during autumn on days with prevailing west or northwest winds.

Access: From the junction of U.S. Route 211 and the Skyline Drive at the Thornton Gap Entrance Station to Shenan-

View from Jewell Hollow Overlook at milepost 35.2 on the Skyline Drive, Shenandoah National Park, Virginia.

doah National Park a few miles east of Luray, drive south on the Skyline Drive to the Jewell Hollow Overlook at approximately milepost 35.2.

References: None.

Stony Man Overlook (near Luray)

Spring Flights: Experimental (not evaluated).

Autumn Flights: Experimental (not evaluated).

Watch Site Description: A west-facing roadside overlook, elevation 3,100 feet, providing excellent views toward the west and northwest. Some migrating hawks passing the summit of Stony Man Mountain might drift toward the Stony Man Overlook and also be visible from this overlook.

Access: From the junction of U.S. Route 211 and the Skyline Drive at the Thornton Gap Entrance Station to Shenandoah National Park a few miles east of Luray, drive south on the Skyline Drive to the Stony Man Overlook at approximately milepost 38.6. Alternatively, hike to the

View from Stony Man Overlook at milepost 38.6 on the Skyline Drive, Shenandoah National Park, Virginia.

summit of Stony Man Mountain (see below) and observe from there. A coordinated, comparative hawk watch at both sites might be very interesting in understanding the local movements of migrant raptors in the Stony Man Mountain area.

Reference: *Birds of the Blue Ridge Mountains* (University of North Carolina Press, 1992).

Stony Man Mountain (near Luray)

Spring Flights: Poor.

Autumn Flights: Fair.

Watch Site Description: An exposed, rocky mountain summit (elevation 4,011 feet), providing excellent views of the surrounding landscape. Large cliffs below the summit on the western side of the mountain might provide deflective updrafts, or perhaps even thermals, useful for migrating raptors such as Sharp-shinned Hawks and Red-tailed Hawks.

Access: From the junction of U.S. Route 211 and the Skyline Drive at the Thornton Gap Entrance Station to Shenandoah National Park a few miles east of Luray, drive south on the Skyline Drive to the Stony Man Overlook at approximately milepost 38.6 to enjoy the view. Then continue about 0.4 mile farther to the Little Stony Man parking area on the right (north), park here, and follow the Appalachian Trail (marked with white blazes on trees) for about 1.5 miles to the summit of Stony Man Mountain. As you approach within about 0.2 mile of the summit, look for a concrete trail marker at an intersection. Follow the branch trail (to the right) for about 0.2 mile to the summit of Stony Man Mountain, where hawk watching is done.

References: *The Migrations of Hawks* (Indiana University Press, 1986); *Birds of the Blue Ridge Mountains* (University of North Carolina Press, 1992).

View from Timber Hollow Overlook at milepost 43.7 on the Skyline Drive, Shenandoah National Park, Virginia.

Timber Hollow Overlook (near Luray)

Spring Flights: Experimental (not evaluated).

Autumn Flights: Experimental (not evaluated).

Watch Site Description: A west-facing roadside overlook, elevation 3,360 feet, providing excellent views toward the west and northwest. The site is best used during autumn on days with prevailing west or northwest winds.

Access: From the junction of U.S. Route 211 and the Skyline Drive at the Thornton Gap Entrance Station to Shenandoah National Park a few miles east of Luray, drive south on the Skyline Drive to the Timber Hollow Overlook at approximately milepost 43.7.

References: None.

Crescent Rock Overlook (near Luray)

Spring Flights: Experimental (not evaluated).

Autumn Flights: Experimental (not evaluated).

Watch Site Description: A west-facing roadside overlook, elevation 3,550 feet, providing excellent views toward the west and northwest. The site is best used during autumn on days with prevailing west or northwest winds.

Access: From the junction of U.S. Route 211 and the Skyline Drive at the Thornton Gap Entrance Station to Shenandoah National Park a few miles east of Luray, drive south on the Skyline Drive to the Crescent Rock Overlook at approximately milepost 44.7.

References: None.

View from Crescent Rock Overlook at mile post 44.7 on the Skyline Drive, Shenandoah National Park, Virginia.

Hawksbill Mountain (near Luray)

Spring Flights: Information unavailable.

Autumn Flights: Good.

Watch Site Description: An exposed, rocky mountain summit (elevation 4,051 feet, the highest in Shenandoah National Park), providing excellent views from the west toward the east. A stone wall at the peak prevents visitors from falling off; picnic tables and a three-sided stone shelter along the trail below the summit are also provided for the use of hikers and other visitors. Hawksbill Mountain is one of the better autumn hawk watching sites in Shenandoah National Park.

Access: From the junction of U.S. Route 211 and the Skyline Drive at the Thornton Gap Entrance Station to Shenandoah National Park a few miles east of Luray, drive south on the Skyline Drive to the Hawksbill Gap parking area at milepost 46.7. Park here and follow the clearly marked (with white blazes) Appalachian Trail for about 1.5 miles to the summit of Hawksbill Mountain.

References: *The Migrations of Hawks* (Indiana University Press, 1986); *Birds of the Blue Ridge Mountains* (University of North Carolina Press, 1992).

Franklin Cliffs Overlook (near Luray)

Spring Flights: Experimental (not evaluated).

Autumn Flights: Experimental (not evaluated).

Watch Site Description: A west-facing roadside overlook, elevation 3,140 feet, providing excellent views toward the west and northwest. The site is best used during autumn on days with prevailing west or northwest winds.

Access: From the junction of U.S. Route 211 and the Skyline Drive at the Thornton Gap Entrance Station to Shenandoah National Park a few miles east of Luray, drive south on the Skyline Drive to the Franklin Cliffs Overlook at approximately milepost 48.1.

References: None.

Franklin Cliffs Overlook at milepost 48.1 on the Skyline Drive, Shenandoah National Park, Virginia.

Bacon Hollow Overlook (near Elkton)

Spring Flights: Experimental (not evaluated).

Autumn Flights: Experimental (not evaluated).

Watch Site Description: A southwest-facing roadside overlook, elevation 2,450 feet, providing views toward the south. The site is best used during spring, or on autumn days with prevailing south winds.

Access: From the junction of U.S. Route 33 and the Skyline Drive at the Swift Run Gap Entrance Station to Shenandoah National Park a few miles east of Elkton, drive south on the Skyline Drive to the Bacon Hollow Overlook at approximately milepost 70.4.

References: None.

Bacon Hollow Overlook at milepost 70.4 on the Skyline Drive, Shenandoah National Park, Virginia.

Eaton Hollow Overlook (near Elkton)

Spring Flights: Experimental (not evaluated).

Autumn Flights: Experimental (not evaluated).

Watch Site Description: A west-facing roadside overlook, elevation 2,490 feet, providing views toward the west and northwest. The site is best used during autumn on days with prevailing west or northwest winds.

Access: From the junction of U.S. Route 33 and the Skyline Drive at the Swift Run Gap Entrance Station to Shenandoah National Park a few miles east of Elkton, drive south on the Skyline Drive to the Eaton Hollow Overlook at approximately milepost 71.5.

References: None.

Ivy Creek Overlook (near Elton)

Spring Flights: Experimental (not evaluated).

Autumn Flights: Experimental (not evaluated).

Watch Site Description: An east-facing roadside overlook, elevation 2,885 feet, providing views toward the south. The site is best used during spring, or on autumn days with prevailing south winds.

Access: From the junction of U.S. Route 33 and the Skyline Drive at the Swift Run Gap Entrance Station to Shenandoah National Park a few miles east of Elkton, drive south on the Skyline Drive to the Ivy Creek Overlook at milepost 77.

References: None.

Ivy Creek Overlook at milepost 77 on the Skyline Drive, Shenandoah National Park, Virginia.

Snicker's Gap Hawk Watch (near Bluemont and Round Hill)

Spring Flights: Information unavailable.

Autumn Flights: Fair.

Watch Site Description: A large commuter parking lot atop 1,100-foot-high Snicker's Gap, providing excellent views of the sky.

Access: This watch site is in northern Virginia (north-northeast of Shenandoah National Park) near the West Virginia border. From the junction of State Routes 7 and 601 a mile past the Bluemont exit, turn left onto Route 601, then turn left into a large commuter parking lot on the south side of the highway at the top of the mountain. Park here, joining other hawk watchers in the same lot.

References: *Raptor Watch* (BirdLife International and Hawk Mountain Sanctuary, 2000); *HMANA Hawk Migration Studies*, 2001, 27 (1): 189–191; HMANA Web site at www.hmana.org.

Turkey Mountain (near Amherst)

Spring Flights: Information unavailable.

Autumn Flights: Excellent.

Watch Site Description: The side of a dead-end road overlooking pastures and farmland on Turkey Mountain. Hawks approach from the north and pass over the watch site or to one side of it.

Access: From Lynchburg, drive north on U.S. Route 29 for about 15 miles to the junction with State Route 151. Turn left onto Route 151 and continue for about 2 miles to State Route 610. Turn left onto Route 610 and continue for about 1 mile to State Route 738 on the right. Turn right and follow Route 738 for a few hundred feet until you reach the spot with a view of Turkey Mountain on the right. Park and observe from the side of the road.

Reference: *A Guide to Hawk Watching in North America* (Pennsylvania State University Press, 1979).

Virginia Coast Reserve

Spring Flights: Information unavailable.

Autumn Flights: Good.

Watch Site Description: A chain of nine undisturbed barrier beach islands and four interior islands extending along the Delmarva Peninsula from the Virginia–Maryland border southward to the mouth of the Chesapeake Bay. Parramore, Revel's, and Ship Shoal Islands are closed to public use except by special permission. Day use is permitted, however, on Metomkin, Cedar, Sandy, Hog, Rogue, Cobb, Godwin, Myrtle, Mink, and Smith Islands. The best raptor viewing area on each island is usually at the southern tip of the beach. Accipiters and falcons are the most common autumn migrants. About ten species of hawks also winter on the islands.

Access: The islands of the reserve can be reached only by boat. Since the channels around them are frequently dangerous, people wishing to visit the reserve are encouraged to contact the reserve manager (c/o The Nature Conservancy, Brownsville, Nassawadox, VA 23413) for full details concerning the best navigation routes to follow to the islands, information on possible guide services, and limitations concerning island use.

References: *Virginia Coast Reserve Study* (The Nature Conservancy, 1976); *A Guide to Hawk Watching in North America* (Pennsylvania State University Press, 1979).

Virginia National Wildlife Refuge (near Cape Charles)

Spring Flights: Information unavailable.

Autumn Flights: Good.

Watch Site Description: An elevated viewing platform near the refuge headquarters from which migrating Sharp-shinned Hawks, American Kestrels, Merlins, and sometimes other raptors can be observed.

Access: From the town of Cape Charles at the southern tip of the Delmarva Peninsula, drive south on U.S. Route 13 for 10

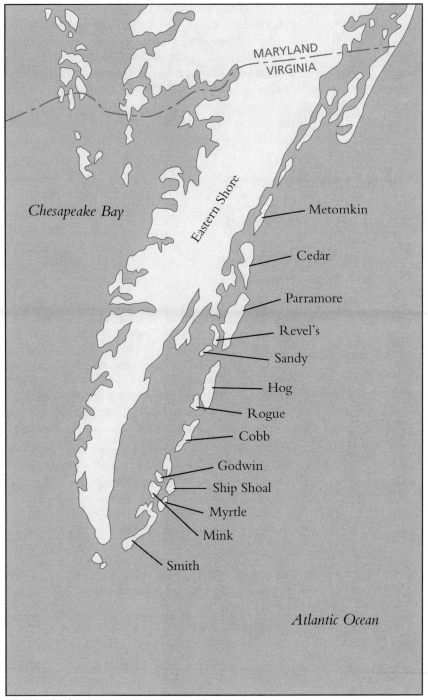

The islands of the Virginia Coast Reserve, Virginia.

Map courtesy of The Nature Conservancy.

miles to the junction with Seaside Road (the last exit before the Bay Bridge Tunnel). Turn left onto Seaside Road and drive for 0.25 mile to the refuge entrance; continue to the headquarters and visitor center to secure literature and maps of the refuge. The elevated viewing platform is located near the refuge headquarters.

Reference: *Virginia Wildlife Viewing Guide* (Falcon Press Publishing, 1994).

Washington

Chelan Ridge (near Pateros)

Spring Flights: Information unavailable.

Autumn Flights: Poor to fair.

Watch Site Description: The top of a ridge, providing a panoramic view over the surrounding wilderness landscape. A cliff forms the southwest side of the watch site, produces deflective updrafts used by migrating raptors, and sometimes allows the birds to be seen at close range. Sharp-shinned Hawks, Cooper's Hawks, and Red-tailed Hawks are seen most frequently, but Northern Goshawks, Golden Eagles, and Merlins also occur in smaller numbers, as do occasional other raptors.

Access: From the junction of U.S. Route 97 and State Route 153 at Pateros, drive north on Route 153 for approximately 7 miles to the junction with Forest Service Road 4010. Turn left onto FR 4010 and continue for 9 miles to the junction with Forest Service Road 8020. Turn left onto FR 8020 and continue for approximately 3.5 miles to the small parking area for the Chelan Ridge hawk watching site. Park and walk to the nearby watch site. This small site, designated an Important Bird Area by Audubon Washington, can accommodate about fifty people per day.

Reference: *Important Bird Areas of Washington* (Audubon Washington, 2001).

Salt Creek Recreation Area County Park (near Port Angeles)

Spring Flights: Information unavailable.

Autumn Flights: Poor.

**Watch Site
Description:** A recreation area on a coastal plain of the Olympic Penin-sula in northwestern Washington. Monitoring Turkey Vul-tures migrating across the Strait of Juan de Fuca from Vancouver Island, British Columbia, to the Olympic Peninsula in the state of Washington is the primary activ-ity at this watch site, but additional raptor species are also seen.

Access: From Port Angeles, drive west on U.S. Route 101 to the junction with U.S. 101 and State Route 112, then turn right onto Route 112 and continue for 13.7 miles to Camp Hayden Road. Follow Camp Hayden Road for 4.2 miles to the Salt Creek Recreation Area campground. Drive through the campground to the road's end at Tongue Point. Park at a suitable spot, then walk on the last paved pathway leading north to the strait, from which vulture and raptor watching is done. The path and watch site are accessible for wheelchairs. Salt Creek Recreation Area County Park is located at 3506 Camp Hayden Road, Port Angeles, WA 98363.

References: *Raptor Watch* (BirdLife International and Hawk Mountain Sanctuary, 2000); HMANA Web site at www.hmana.org.

West Virginia

Backbone Mountain (near Thomas)

Spring Flights: Information unavailable.

Autumn Flights: Fair.

**Watch Site
Description:** A scenic roadside overlook (elevation about 3,000 feet) on Backbone Mountain at Centennial Park.

Access: From Thomas, drive north on U.S. Route 219 for 4.2 miles to the overlook beside the road. Observe from there.

References: *Redstart*, 1953, 20 (3): 39–54; 1976, 43 (3): 116; *A Guide to Hawk Watching in North America* (Pennsylvania State University Press, 1979).

Bear Rocks (in Monongahela National Forest)

Spring Flights: Information unavailable.

Autumn Flights: Good.

Watch Site Description: A rocky outcropping on the Allegheny Front overlooking the Dolly Sods Scenic Area. Easterly and southerly winds are most productive for hawk watching.

Access: From the Dolly Sods Picnic Area in Monongahela National Forest, drive north on Forest Service Road 75 past the Red Creek Camp Ground to the parking area for Bear Rocks. Park here and walk on the path for a short distance to the watch site rocks.

References: *Redstart*, 1974, 41 (4): 119–120; *A Guide to Hawk Watching in North America* (Pennsylvania State University Press, 1979).

Bear Rocks, West Virginia.

Cheat Mountain (near Mace)

Spring Flights: Information unavailable.

Autumn Flights: Fair.

Watch Site
Description: Two roadside areas overlooking adjacent valleys. One area is located north of Mace, the other south.

Access: From Mace, drive north or south on U.S. Route 219 for about a mile in either direction to the respective roadside recreation sites. Observe from either watch site.

References: *Redstart*, 1953, 20 (3): 39–54; *A Guide to Hawk Watching in North America* (Pennsylvania State University Press, 1979).

Cold Knob Scenic Area (near Frankford)

Spring Flights: Information unavailable.

Autumn Flights: Good.

Watch Site
Description: Boulder outcroppings and impressive vistas from the summit of 4,200-foot-high Cold Knob.

Access: From the junction of U.S. Route 219 and County Route 17 (Williamsburg Road) at Frankford, turn west onto Route 17 and continue for 8.4 miles to the junction of County Route 9 at Williamsburg. Turn north onto Route 9 and continue for 3.2 miles to the junction with County Route 10 (Trout Road). Turn left onto Route 10 and continue for 5.9 miles to the sign on the right for the Cold Knob Scenic Area. Turn right and continue for 0.1 mile to the parking area. Follow trail signs to the summit, where hawk watching can be done. There are no visitor facilities in the Cold Knob Scenic Area.

Reference: *West Virginia Wildlife Viewing Guide* (Falcon Publishing, 1999).

Hanging Rock Raptor Observatory (near Waiteville)

Spring Flights: None.

Autumn Flights: Excellent.

Watch Site Description: A rebuilt 14-by-14-foot fire tower with an outside catwalk placed on a rocky outcropping at an elevation of 3,812 feet on the crest of Peters Mountain. This is one of West Virginia's best-known autumn hawk watching locations.

Access: From Roanoke, Virginia, follow Virginia State Route 311 to Paint Bank and the junction of Route 311 and Virginia State Route 600. Turn left onto Route 600 and continue into West Virginia, where the road becomes West Virginia State Route 17. Continue on Route 17 toward Waiteville. At the junction of State Routes 17 and 15, turn right onto Route 15 and follow it to the top of Peters Mountain.

If you are coming from Gap Mills, West Virginia, follow State Route 3 to its junction with State Route 15 and follow Route 15 to the top of Peters Mountain.

Park near the trailhead at the top of the mountain, then hike on the moderately difficult trail for about twenty minutes to the reconstructed former fire tower perched on a rocky outcropping.

References: *A Guide to Hawk Watching in North America* (Pennsylvania State University Press, 1979); Hanging Rock Raptor Observatory Web site at www.hangingrocktower.org/index.html; George Washington & Jefferson National Forests Web site at http://www.southernregion.fs.fed.us/gwj.

Pipestem State Park (near Pipestem)

Spring Flights: Information unavailable.

Autumn Flights: Fair.

Watch Site Description: An observation tower overlooking forests, old fields, wetlands, and a lake. Broad-winged Hawks represent many of the migrant raptors during September, but sometimes

The Hanging Rock Raptor Observatory, West Virginia. Photo by Rodney Davis.

other raptors and Turkey Vultures are also observed. Occasionally Bald Eagles, and rarely Golden Eagles, are seen during winter.

Access: From the junction of Interstate 77 (exit 14) and County Route 7 near Athens, turn east onto Route 7 and continue to the junction of State Route 20. Continue north on Route 20 for 10 miles to the entrance to the park on the left. Enter the park and stop at the park office to secure current hawk watching information and directions to the observation tower.

Reference: *West Virginia Wildlife Viewing Guide* (Falcon Publishing, 1999).

Wisconsin

Bark Point (near Herbster)

Spring Flights: Fair.

Autumn Flights: Information unavailable.

Watch Site Description: A peninsula in extreme northern Wisconsin extending northeastward into Lake Superior. Select an exposed spot near the tip of the point for hawk watching.

Access: From Herbster, drive east on State Route 13 for several miles, then look for any connecting roads leading to Bark Point.

References: *HMANA Newsletter*, 1983, 8 (1): 18–20; *The Migrations of Hawks* (Indiana University Press, 1986).

Cedar Grove Ornithological Station (near Cedar Grove)

Spring Flights: Fair.

Autumn Flights: Good.

Watch Site Description: A high bluff near Lake Michigan—or any spot near the lake shoreline with an unrestricted view.

Access: Drive east on U.S. Route 141 to the junction of State Route 42 near Cedar Grove. Continue east on U.S. 141 for 0.5 mile to the point where the highway turns north. Turn onto a gravel road and continue eastward 0.25 mile toward Lake Michigan, then turn sharply north onto the first road on the left. Continue for 0.5 mile. Cross Bahr Creek and park near the sanctuary. Presumably hawk watchers are not welcome at the research station, where they can cause undesirable disturbance, but it may be possible to watch migrating hawks from the vicinity of the sanctuary.

References: *Wilson Bulletin*, 1961: 171–192; *A Guide to Hawk Watching in North America* (Pennsylvania State University Press, 1979); *Raptor Watch* (BirdLife International and Hawk Mountain Sanctuary, 2000).

Chequamegon Bay Hawk Watch (near Ashland)

Spring Flights: Good to excellent.

Autumn Flights: None.

The Northern Great Lakes Visitor Center used for hawk watching at the Chequamegon Bay Hawk Watch, Wisconsin. Photo by Ryan Brady.

Watch Site
Description: A 58-foot-high observation tower at the Northern Great Lakes Visitor Center overlooking the surrounding Fish Creek Valley and the southern end of Chequamegon Bay on Lake Superior. Bald Eagles are especially notable migrants at this watch site.

Access: From Ashland, drive west on U.S. Route 2 for about 2.5 miles to the junction with Bayfield County Highway G. The driveway to the visitor center is about 200 feet west of the junction of U.S. 2 and Highway G. Follow the directional signs to the observation tower, which is visible from a distance. Observe from atop the tower.

References: *Passenger Pigeon*, 1999, 61 (4): 389–394; 62 (3–4): 239–250; *HMANA Hawk Migration Studies*, 2002, 27 (2): 63–64, 73–75; 2003, 28 (2): 46.

Concordia University (in Mequon)

Spring Flights: Information unavailable.

Autumn Flights: Good to excellent.

Watch Site
Description: A campus parking lot near bluffs along the south shoreline of Lake Michigan. The site is especially productive for migrating Sharp-shinned Hawks, Merlins, and Peregrine Falcons in spring.

Access: Concordia University is located at 12800 North Lake Shore Drive, Mequon, WI 53097. From the junction of Lake Shore Drive and Highland Road in Mequon, drive east for a short distance on Highland Road to the main entrance to Concordia University. Turn left (north) onto the university campus and continue to the parking lot on the right overlooking Lake Michigan.

References: *Raptor Watch* (BirdLife International and Hawk Mountain Sanctuary, 2000); *HMANA Hawk Migration Studies*, 2001, 27 (1): 82–83; 2002, 28 (1): 156–158.

Eagle Valley Nature Preserve (near Cassville)

Spring Flights: Good.

Autumn Flights: Good to excellent.

Watch Site Description: A five-acre prairie on top of a 300-foot-high bluff overlooking the Mississippi River. The watch site is part of the 1,400-acre preserve. Large numbers of migrating Bald Eagles are seen in late November and early December, and again in February and early March.

Access: From Cassville, follow County Route VV north for about 7 miles, passing Nelson Dewey State Park. Continue driving for another 0.5 mile past the Charlotte cemetery to Duncan Road (perhaps unpaved), then turn left and follow Duncan Road for about a mile to the nature preserve entrance on the left in the valley. For additional details, contact Eagle Valley Environmentalists, Inc., P.O. Box 155, Apple River, IL 61001.

References: *Eagle Valley News*, 1976, 5 (3): 27–28; 1976, 5 (4): 6; *A Guide to Hawk Watching in North America* (Pennsylvania State University Press, 1979); *HMANA Hawk Migration Studies*, 2001, 27 (1): 82.

Harrington Beach State Park (near Port Washington)

Spring Flights: Information unavailable.

Autumn Flights: Good.

Watch Site Description: An exposed vantage point along Lake Michigan at the northern end of the park.

Access: From Port Washington, drive north on U.S. Route 141 for 5.5 miles to the village of Lake Church. Here turn east onto County Route D and continue to the parking area. Then walk to the lakeshore, from which hawk watching is done.

Reference: *A Guide to Hawk Watching in North America* (Pennsylvania State University Press, 1979).

Schlitz Audubon Center (near Milwaukee)

Spring Flights: Information unavailable.

Autumn Flights: Fair.

Watch Site Description: Open fields near the shoreline of Lake Michigan.

Access: In Milwaukee drive north on U.S. Route 141 to State Route 100 (Brown Deer Road). Exit and drive east to the corner of North Lake Drive. The entrance to the center is on the right side of Brown Deer Road just east of North Lake Drive. Enter and continue to the headquarters. Park and ask about the best location for watching hawks in the sanctuary. The center is open Tuesday through Saturday.

Reference: *A Guide to Hawk Watching in North America* (Pennsylvania State University Press, 1979).

Wyoming

Indian Medicine Wheel (near Lovell)

Spring Flights: Information unavailable.

Autumn Flights: Good.

Watch Site Description: A rounded knob on the eastern edge of the Bighorn National Forest, providing observers with views over the Bighorn Basin and the northern portion of the Bighorn Mountains. Late August to mid-September is the best period to see migrating hawks.

Access: From Lovell, drive east on Alternate U.S. Route 14 for about 30 miles to the Indian Medicine Wheel (marked as a "point of interest" on state highway maps). Observers can drive within approximately 600 feet of the summit of the knob, then make an easy hike to the top.

Reference: *A Guide to Hawk Watching in North America* (Pennsylvania State University Press, 1979).

Canadian Hawk Migration Watch Sites

Alberta

Canmore Collegiate High School (in Canmore)

Spring Flights: Information unavailable.

Autumn Flights: Excellent.

Watch Site Description: An exposed watch site on the campus of a high school in the Kananaskis Valley with panoramic views in all directions, including the Front Range and Rocky Mountains. Excellent Golden Eagle migrations occur on northwest winds during autumn at this watch site.

Access: Canmore is located along Trans-Canada Highway 1 in southern Alberta. The Canmore Collegiate High School is in Canmore at 1800 8th Avenue.

Reference: *Raptor Watch* (BirdLife International and Hawk Mountain Sanctuary, 2000).

British Columbia

Becher Bay Headlands (near Victoria)

Spring Flights: Information unavailable.

Autumn Flights: Good.

Watch Site Description: This coastal plain watch site is used mostly for monitoring migrating Turkey Vultures. However, very small numbers of raptors also appear on west winds during September and October.

Access: The Becher Bay Headlands site is on the coastal plain at the far southeastern point on Vancouver Island. Additional directions can be secured in Victoria.

Reference: *Raptor Watch* (BirdLife International and Hawk Mountain Sanctuary, 2000).

Manitoba

Patricia Beach Provincial Park (near Grand Beach)

Spring Flights: Information unavailable.

Autumn Flights: Fair.

Watch Site Description: Patricia Beach Provincial Park is a sandy peninsula extending into the south end of Lake Winnipeg. Migrating Bald Eagles cross the site during late October and early November. Hawk watching is done from the beach near a wooded ridge.

Access: From the junction of Trans-Canada Highway 1 and Provincial Route 59 on the north side of Winnipeg, drive north on Route 59 for about 39 miles to its junction with Provincial Route 319. Look for signs there directing visitors to Patricia Beach Provincial Park. Turn left onto Route 319 (an unpaved, gravel road) and continue for 3.1 miles to some houses and cottages. Look there for a sign pointing right to the park. Turn right and continue a short distance to the park entrance (a small entrance fee is collected from June through September). Enter the park and continue to the beach near a wooded ridge.

Reference: *Raptor Watch* (BirdLife International and Hawk Mountain Sanctuary, 2000).

Pembina Valley Wildlife Management Area (near Windygates)

Spring Flights: Fair to good.

Autumn Flights: Information unavailable.

**Watch Site
Description:** The rim of a canyon of the Pembina River, from which hawk watchers have views of the surrounding landscape. South winds produce the largest hawk flights during spring. The watch site is also known as Brown's Hill and Pembina Valley.

Access: The Pembina Valley Wildlife Management Area is located about 6.2 miles northeast of Windygates on the U.S.–Canada border. Secure more detailed access directions in Windygates.

References: *Raptor Watch* (BirdLife International and Hawk Mountain Sanctuary, 2000).

St. Adolphe Bridge (near Winnipeg)

Spring Flights: Fair.

Autumn Flights: Information unavailable.

**Watch Site
Description:** An abutment of the St. Adolphe Bridge crossing the Red River south of Winnipeg. Hawk watchers enjoy a panoramic view of the surrounding landscape.

Access: From Winnipeg, drive south a few miles on Provincial Route 59 to the St. Adolphe Bridge across the Red River. Find a suitable parking spot and watch from the vicinity of the bridge abutments.

Reference: *The Migrations of Hawks* (Indiana University Press, 1986); *Raptor Watch* (BirdLife International and Hawk Mountain Sanctuary, 2000).

New Brunswick

Fundy National Park (near Penobsquis)

Spring Flights: Poor to fair.

Autumn Flights: Poor.

**Watch Site
Description:** Any exposed area with views of the surrounding landscape near the park's headquarters.

Access: From the junction of Provincial Routes 1 and 114 at Penobsquis, drive southeast on Route 114 for about 44 miles to Fundy National Park along Chignecto Bay. Enter the park and continue to the park headquarters, from whose vicinity spring and autumn hawk migrations sometimes are seen.

References: *Atlantic Canada News*, 1981, 1: 2–10; *HMANA Newsletter*, 1981, 6 (2): 11; *The Migrations of Hawks* (Indiana University Press, 1986).

Grand Manan

Spring Flights: Poor.

Autumn Flights: Poor.

Watch Site Description: This New Brunswick island is located near the mouth of the Bay of Fundy east of Lubec, Maine. Some exploratory hawk watching will be necessary to locate the best spring and autumn raptor migration watch sites, but the area around Long Eddy Point at the northern end of the island may be suitable during spring, and Southwest Head at the southern end of the island may be productive during autumn. Spring hawk flights tend to include Sharp-shinned Hawks and American Kestrels. Available data demonstrate that worthwhile autumn flights of Sharp-shinned Hawks, American Kestrels, and Merlins are reported from the island.

Access: Grand Manan Island is reached only via daily (except December 25 and January 1) ferry departing from Blacks Harbour, New Brunswick, and docking at North Head, Grand Manan; advance tickets are strongly recommended—especially during July and August. Air service is also available to the island. Consult your travel agent for current details.

References: *American Birds*, 1973, 27 (1): 24–30; *Atlantic Canada News*, 1981, 1: 2–10; *The Migrations of Hawks* (Indiana University Press, 1986).

St. Andrews (near Calais, Maine)

Spring Flights: Fair.

Autumn Flights: Information unavailable.

**Watch Site
Description:** Exposed areas along the tidal inlet at the federal fisheries and ocean research station at the western end of town. Migrating Bald Eagles appear here, and a population of nesting Ospreys is also present.

Access: From Calais, Maine, on the U.S.–Canada border, drive east into New Brunswick on Highway 1 and continue for a few miles to the junction with Provincial Route 127. Turn right (south) onto Route 127 and follow it to St. Andrews, where directions can be secured for reaching the research station and tidal inlet.

Reference: *A Guide to Hawk Watching in North America* (Pennsylvania State University Press, 1979).

Nova Scotia

Brier Island (near Digby)

Spring Flights: Poor to fair.

Autumn Flights: Good to excellent.

**Watch Site
Description:** Open areas around either of two lighthouses. The North Point Light, in whose vicinity most hawk migration observations are made, is on a rocky point 50 feet above sea level. An open area covered with heath-type vegetation surrounds the light. The vicinity of the South Light is sometimes more productive for hawk watching when weather changes force hawks to stop over on the island.

Access: From Digby, drive on Provincial Route 217 for about 30 miles to East Ferry. Board a car ferry here (operating hourly) and cross to Long Island and the village of Tiverton. Continue on Route 217 for about 11 miles to

Freeport. Here board another car ferry and cross to West-port—the only village on Brier Island. From Westport, continue to the appropriate lighthouse. A good road runs from one end of the island to the other.

References: *The Birds of Nova Scotia* (Nova Scotia Museum, 1962); *A Guide to Hawk Watching in North America* (Pennsylvania State University Press, 1979); *The Migrations of Hawks* (Indiana University Press, 1986).

Ontario

Amherstburg (south of Windsor)

Spring Flights: Information unavailable.

Autumn Flights: Good to excellent.

Watch Site Description: Any publicly accessible site providing open views of the surrounding landscape in the vicinity of the Malden Central Public School. Large flights of migrating Broad-winged Hawks, and lesser numbers of other migrant raptors, were reported from Amherstburg in the mid-twentieth century.

Access: In Amherstburg seek local directions to the Malden Central Public School located at 5620 County Road 20 (formerly Highway 18). Select a publicly accessible site with open views of the surrounding landscape from which to watch for migrating hawks.

Reference: *The Migrations of Hawks* (Indiana University Press, 1986).

Cobourg

Spring Flights: Information unavailable.

Autumn Flights: Good.

Watch Site Description: Full details are unavailable, but exposed areas along the Lake Ontario shoreline are probably suitable observation points. Hawk flights are known to occur from Cobourg westward along Lake Ontario.

Access: From Toronto, drive east on Provincial Route 401 to the exit for the town of Cobourg. Leave the main highway here and drive into town. Ask for directions to suitable exposed areas along the Lake Ontario shoreline where hawk watching can be done. Some exploration of the area will be necessary to locate productive spots, which may change from day to day.

References: *Audubon Magazine*, 1962, 64 (1): 44–45, 49; *A Guide to Hawk Watching in North America* (Pennsylvania State University Press, 1979).

Cranberry Marsh Raptor Watch (near Whitby)

Spring Flights: Information unavailable.

Autumn Flights: Excellent.

Watch Site Description: An observation platform placed in the southwest corner of a flat area provides a panoramic view of the surrounding landscape.

Access: In Whitby at the intersection of Lake Ridge Road and Hall's Road, drive south on Hall's Road for about 0.9 mile toward Lake Ontario and leave your vehicle in a roadside parking area. Then walk toward the east on a paved path to the platform from which hawk watching is done.

References: *OFO News*, 1999, 17 (3): 1–8; *Raptor Watch* (BirdLife International and Hawk Mountain Sanctuary, 2000); *HMANA Hawk Migration Studies*, 2001, 27 (1): 85–86, 105–107; 2002, 27 (2): 14; 2002, 28 (1): 150–151.

Hamilton Area

Spring Flights: Poor.

Autumn Flights: Excellent.

Watch Site Description: Excellent September migrations of Broad-winged Hawks, and lesser numbers of other migrant raptors, are reported from the Hamilton area. However, exploratory hawk watching is necessary because no specific sites are identified in the hawk migration literature.

Access: Any publicly owned park or other area along the southwestern end of Lake Ontario with good views of the adjacent landscape can be used for autumn hawk watching purposes.

Reference: *The Migrations of Hawks* (Indiana University Press, 1986).

Hawk Cliff (near Port Stanley)

Spring Flights: None.

Autumn Flights: Excellent.

Watch Site Description: Fields near the edge of a 100-foot-high cliff at the edge of the north shore of Lake Erie, or a wooded ravine inland about 0.25 mile from the lake.

Access: At the junction of Provincial Route 4 (Main Street) and Joseph Street in Port Stanley, drive uphill on Joseph Street for about 1 mile to the junction with County Route 24 on the right. Turn east onto Route 24 and continue for approximately 1.9 miles to the road to Hawk Cliff on the south opposite the junction with County Route 22 going to the north. Follow the road to the cliffs overlooking Lake Erie.

References: *Search*, 1972, 2 (16): 1–60; *Autumn Hawk Flights: The Migrations in Eastern North America* (Rutgers University Press, 1975); *A Guide to Hawk Watching in North America* (Pennsylvania State University Press, 1979); *A Bird-Finding Guide to Ontario* (University of Toronto Press, 1982); *HMANA Hawk Migration Studies*, 2001, 27 (1): 94–95; 2002, 28 (1): 152.

High Park (in Toronto)

Spring Flights: Information unavailable.

Autumn Flights: Good to excellent.

Watch Site
Description: A hill ("Hawk Hill") adjacent to the Grenadier Restaurant's parking lot in the center of High Park near downtown Toronto.

Access: From the Gardiner Expressway running along the southern side of Toronto, take exit 145 (the Lakeshore Boulevard exit *after* the Park Lawn Drive exit) onto Parkside Drive and continue for about 1.25 miles to Bloor Street. Turn left onto Bloor Street and continue for about 0.25 mile to the High Park entrance on the left. Turn into the park and continue for about 0.6 mile to the restaurant parking lot on the left. Park and walk to "Hawk Hill" on the north side of the parking lot.

References: *OFO News*, 1999, 17 (3): 1–8; *Raptor Watch* (BirdLife International and Hawk Mountain Sanctuary, 2000); *HMANA Hawk Migration Studies*, 2001, 27 (1): 85, 97–98; 2002, 28 (1): 152–154.

Holiday Beach Migration Observatory (near Windsor)

Spring Flights: Information unavailable.

Autumn Flights: Excellent.

Watch Site
Description: An observation tower overlooking the surrounding landscape from which hawk watching is done. The tower is located in the Holiday Beach Conservation Area near the Detroit River on the northern shore of Lake Erie at the southwestern tip of southern Ontario. During some autumns more than 140,000 migrating raptors are counted at this watch site.

Access: From Windsor, follow Provincial Route 18 through Amherstburg. After crossing Big Creek, continue for about 2 miles to the intersection of Provincial Route 18A. Turn right and continue for about 3 miles to the park entrance on the right. Enter, pay a small fee, and follow the signs to the observation tower within the park. Observe from the tower or its immediate vicinity.

References: *OFO News*, 1999, 17 (3): 1–8; *Hawks of Holiday Beach* (Holiday Beach Migration Observatory, 2002); *HMANA Hawk Migration Studies*, 2001, 27 (1): 86, 101–102; 2002, 28 (1): 154–156.

The tower used by hawk watchers at the Holiday Beach Conservation Area, Ontario.
Photo by Betty Leamouth.

Killarney Provincial Park (near Killarney)

Spring Flights: Information unavailable.

Autumn Flights: Good.

Watch Site Description: Any exposed summit of ridge crests. Hawks generally follow a westward flight-line, but Turkey Vultures appear to fly eastward.

Access: From Sudbury, drive south on Canadian Route 69 for about 20 miles to Provincial Route 637. Turn west onto Route 637 and continue for about 44 miles to the park entrance. Hiking trails and canoe routes run throughout the park and can be used to reach suitable hawk watching sites such as those previously described. Exploratory hawk watching is needed in this park.

Reference: *A Guide to Hawk Watching in North America* (Pennsylvania State University Press, 1979).

Niagara Peninsula Hawk Watch (near Grimsby)

Spring Flights: Good to excellent.

Autumn Flights: Information unavailable.

Watch Site Description: The tip of Beamer Point in the Beamer Memorial Conservation Area in Grimsby.

Access: Take exit 71 off the Queen Elizabeth Way at Grimsby, follow Christie Street South to Mountain Avenue, and continue to the top of the escarpment. Turn right (west) opposite a church onto Ridge Road (Regional Road 89) and continue for 0.9 mile to Quarry Road. Turn right onto Quarry Road and continue for 300 feet to the entrance to the Beamer Memorial Conservation Area. Park inside the conservation area near the entrance and walk to the hawk watch at the end of Beamer Point. *Do not leave valuable items in your car.*

References: *Newsletter Hawk Migration Association of North America,* 1978, 3 (1): 10–13; *A Guide to Hawk Watching in North America* (Pennsylvania State University Press, 1979); *A*

Bird-Finding Guide to Ontario (University of Toronto Press, 1982); *HMANA Hawk Migration Studies*, 2002, 27 (2): 65–66, 78–80; 2003, 28 (2): 46.

Port Burwell Provincial Park (near Tillsonburg)

Spring Flights: None.

Autumn Flights: Excellent.

Watch Site Description: A parking lot at the westernmost day-use area of the park, or flats along the mouth of Otter Creek with excellent views toward the west, north, and east. This watch site is now used instead of Hawk Cliff because of increasingly restricted views of migrating raptors at Hawk Cliff.

Access: From Provincial Route 401 at Ingersoll, turn south onto Provincial Route 19 and continue past Tillsonburg to Port Burwell Provincial Park. Pay the entrance fee, then drive to the parking lot at the westernmost day-use area. Park and watch for migrating hawks from here, or go to parking areas near flats along the mouth of Otter Creek.

Reference: *OFO News*, 1999, 17 (3): 1–8.

Port Credit

Spring Flights: None.

Autumn Flights: Good.

Watch Site Description: The vicinity of the Route 10 bridge over the Queensway.

Access: Drive about 15 miles southwest of Toronto on the Queen Elizabeth Way. At the junction of Provincial Route 10, turn onto it and continue to the bridge crossing the Queensway. Observe from this general area.

References: *Audubon Magazine*, 1962, 64 (1): 44–45, 49; *A Guide to Hawk Watching in North America* (Pennsylvania State University Press, 1979).

Point Pelee National Park (near Leamington)

Spring Flights: None.

Autumn Flights: Excellent.

Watch Site Description: The forest or open beach at the tip of the point, the parking lot at the park's interpretive center, and the parking lot for the Delaurier Trail.

Access: From Leamington, drive south for about 6 miles into the park. An entrance fee is charged.

References: *Wilson Bulletin*, 1966: 122; *A Guide to Hawk Watching in North America* (Pennsylvania State University Press, 1979); *OFO News*, 1999, 17 (3): 1–8.

Rondeau Provincial Park (near Blenheim)

Spring Flights: None.

Autumn Flights: Excellent.

Watch Site Description: Exposed areas on the park's south beach along Lake Erie. The site is particularly good for observing Sharp-shinned Hawks and Broad-winged Hawks.

Access: From Blenheim, drive east on Provincial Route 3 for a few miles to a road (perhaps unmarked) leading south into Rondeau Provincial Park. Upon entering the park, drive about 6 miles to the southern end, where a beach along Lake Erie is located. Hawk watching is done from here. Some exploratory hawk watching is needed in this park.

Reference: *A Guide to Hawk Watching in North America* (Pennsylvania State University Press, 1979).

Tobermory (and nearby Cove Island)

Spring Flights: Excellent.

Autumn Flights: Information unavailable.

**Watch Site
Description:** The vicinity of the ferry terminal (on the "Big Tub") in the village of Tobermory on the Bruce Peninsula extending into Lake Huron. The first two weeks in May are particularly good for hawk watching at this site.

Access: From Owen Sound, drive west on Provincial Route 21 for about 11 miles to the junction with Provincial Route 6. Turn north onto Route 6 and follow it for about 61 miles to the village of Tobermory. Continue to the vicinity of the ferry terminal, where hawk watching is done. You can also observe from the base of the lighthouse on the northeast shore of nearby Cove Island (part of Fathom Five National Marine Park), reached by ferry from Tobermory.

References: *A Guide to Hawk Watching in North America* (Pennsylvania State University Press, 1979); *The Migrations of Hawks* (Indiana University Press, 1986); *Raptor Watch* (BirdLife International and Hawk Mountain Sanctuary, 2000).

Quebec

Ile Perrot (near Montreal)

Spring Flights: Fair.

Autumn Flights: Fair.

**Watch Site
Description:** An exposed area on the south side of Don Quichotte Road overlooking fields just east or west of a small wooded plateau. Occasionally hawk watching also is done at other points along Don Quichotte Road.

Access: From the western end of Montreal, follow Canadian Route 20 onto Ile Perrot. Take exit 38 onto Boul Perrot and follow it southeast to the junction with Boul St. Joseph. Turn south onto Boul St. Joseph and continue to Don Quichotte Road. Turn east onto Don Quichotte Road and continue for about 2 or 3 miles toward Windmill Point. After crossing a small wooded plateau about 100 feet in elevation, look for fields at the eastern side of the plateau. Observe from the south side of the road, looking north across the road and fields.

References: *American Birds*, 1976, 30 (1): 37; *A Guide to Hawk Watching in North America* (Pennsylvania State University Press, 1979).

Morgan Arboretum (west end of Montreal)

Spring Flights: Fair.

Autumn Flights: Good.

Watch Site Description: A ridge at the top of Montreal Island along Canadian Route 40 near the Ste. Anne de Bellevue exit at the west end of Montreal. Observers on the ridge have good views north and south.

Access: From Canadian Route 40, take exit 41 at Ste. Anne de Bellevue at the west end of Montreal and follow road signs for Chemin Ste. Marie. When you arrive at a stop sign at the top of the hill, turn left onto Chemin des Pins and follow road signs for the Pines office in the arboretum. Leave your vehicle in the parking area, pay the entrance fee, and walk to the south end of the arboretum, from which hawk watching is done. Secure detailed directions at the arboretum for walking to the hawk migration watch site. Morgan Arboretum is open daily from 9:00 A.M. to 4:00 P.M.

References: *Birding News Survey*, 1978, 1 (1): 13–14; *A Guide to Hawk Watching in North America* (Pennsylvania State University Press, 1979); *The Migrations of Hawks* (Indiana University Press, 1986); *Raptor Watch* (BirdLife International and Hawk Mountain Sanctuary, 2000).

Mount Royal (in Montreal)

Spring Flights: Fair.

Autumn Flights: Fair.

Watch Site Description: Two exposed areas, one a park and the other a cemetery, on a mountaintop within Montreal with exposed views in various directions.

- Mount Royal Park and its 1.5-mile trail around the top of the mountain within the park.

- Mount Royal Cemetery offers good panoramic views over the adjacent city and landscape.

Access: From the junction of Canadian Route 40 (Autoroute Metropolitaine) and Canadian Route 15 (Autoroute Decarie) in metropolitan Montreal, drive south on Route 15 to exit 69. Leave Route 15 at exit 69 and drive east on Rue Jean-Talon to Chemin de la Cote-des-Neiges. Turn south onto Chemin de la Cote-des-Neiges and continue for several miles to Chemin Remembrance (Remembrance Road). Turn east onto Chemin Remembrance and follow signs for Mount Royal Park—Beaver Lake and the Lookout to the top of Mount Royal Park. Leave your vehicle in the parking lot, then follow signs pointing to the Lookout and walk there—a distance of about 0.3 mile. The trail continues around the top of the mountain— about 1.5 miles—and offers various potential hawk watching opportunities. Pick the side of the mountain from which the wind is blowing as a likely place for hawk watching.

The top of the Mount Royal Cemetery also can be used for hawk watching and is reached by walking or driving about 600 feet to the cemetery's entrance gate on Camillien Houde Drive, located across from the top of the Mount Royal Park parking lot. Continue to any spot with a panoramic view over the adjacent city and landscape.

References: *Birding News Survey*, 1978, 1 (1): 13–14; *A Guide to Hawk Watching in North America* (Pennsylvania State University Press, 1979); *HMANA Hawk Migration Studies*, 2001, 27 (1): 87.

Salaberry-de-Valleyfield

Spring Flights: Poor.

Autumn Flights: Information unavailable.

Watch Site Description: A small site at the western end of a bridge just west of Salaberry-de-Valleyfield at the eastern end of Lake St. Francis.

Access: From Salaberry-de-Valleyfield (about 60 miles southwest of Montreal), drive west on Provincial Route 132 to the seaway lift bridge. Continue to the western end of the bridge; a small hawk watching site is located at the junction of the seaway road. Observe from there.

References: *Birding News Survey*, 1978, 1 (1): 13–14; *A Guide to Hawk Watching in North America* (Pennsylvania State University Press, 1979); *HMANA Hawk Migration Studies*, 2002, 27 (2): 69–71, 88–90; 2003, 28 (2): 46.

Bald Eagle Viewing Areas

Bald Eagles are spectacular birds of prey worth watching at various concentration areas in the United States and Canada in winter, during migration, and during the breeding season. As populations of these birds continue to increase, even more eagle watching opportunities will become available in various parts of North America.

Bald Eagle watching is possible at many locations in the United States and Canada. However, it is very important that birders and photographers adhere to correct eagle watching etiquette to avoid disturbing these birds. Photo courtesy of Glacier National Park.

Eagle Watching Etiquette

Bald Eagles are very sensitive to close human disturbance. Their safety and conservation always must take precedence over recreational eagle watching. Therefore, when visiting some of the sites discussed in the following pages, please follow the general eagle watching etiquette recommendations provided here so you will not disturb these birds. At a few locations, such as several places in Alaska, variations on these general eagle watching etiquette recommendations are used.

- Bald Eagles are most active early in the morning (sunrise to 11:00 A.M.) and late in the afternoon, so plan your eagle watching field trips during these time periods.

- Patience is often necessary for successful Bald Eagle watching.

- Whenever possible, remain in your vehicle and use it as an observation blind to enjoy Bald Eagle viewing. If eagles flush, back away to a safer distance. Never approach perched, feeding, roosting, or nesting Bald Eagles closer than about 3,000 feet, and do not try to make perched eagles fly. There are severe federal penalties (up to $50,000 and/or a year imprisonment for the first offense) for doing so.

- Winter Bald Eagle viewing can be very cold, so dress very warmly and have hot beverages with you to avoid hypothermia.

- Use binoculars and/or telescopes to see Bald Eagles more clearly. Window mounts for telescopes work well.

- Some of the photographic equipment recommendations listed for Bald Eagle photography at the Alaska Chilkat Bald Eagle Preserve write-up also apply elsewhere when eagle photography is desired.

- Be as quiet as possible when watching Bald Eagles. Always avoid slamming vehicle doors, using vehicle horns, playing loud music, and yelling.

- Do not trespass on private property or other areas closed to pubic entry to get closer views of Bald Eagles.

- When parking on the shoulder of a road, be certain to completely pull off the road to avoid becoming a traffic hazard.

- Use designated parking areas, and viewing areas, provided at some Bald Eagle viewing locations.

- Take advantage of available handout information, and/or volunteers, at some eagle viewing locations.

- To receive maximum enjoyment from Bald Eagle watching, read books and/or other information, and watch videos about Bald Eagles, before taking eagle watching field trips.

Alaska

Berners Bay (near Juneau)

Raptors: Bald Eagles feeding on smelt runs.

Viewing Season: Early to mid-May.

**Watch Site
Description:** The shorelines of rivers running into Berners Bay in which smelt provide abundant food for the eagles.

Access: From Juneau, you can arrange a short charter flight to visit Berners Bay and the rivers entering it along which eagles feed.

References: *Bald Eagles in Alaska* (U.S. Department of the Interior and Agriculture, no date); *A Guide to Hawk Watching in North America* (Pennsylvania State University Press, 1979).

Alaska Chilkat Bald Eagle Preserve (near Haines)

Raptors: Large concentrations of Bald Eagles (maximum 3,000 per day) feeding on the carcasses of five species of salmon that spawn in river waters in the eagle preserve.

Viewing Season: Late October through early February, with maximum eagle concentrations in mid-November.

**Watch Site
Description:** A 48,000-acre Bald Eagle preserve consisting of river bottomland in the Chilkat, Chilkoot, Klehini, and Tsirku Rivers. The primary Bald Eagle viewing areas are along the Chilkat River flats—a shallow river, river shoreline, and edges of dense surrounding forest—between miles 18 and 21.5 along the Haines Highway. Four parking areas are available, two of which have interpretive displays; one has restroom facilities. There also is a 4,000-square-foot elevated platform for use by eagle watchers and photographers. An annual Alaska Bald Eagle Festival is held in mid-November.

Bald Eagle watching etiquette appropriate for those attending the Alaska Bald Eagle Festival includes the following recommendations:

- Do not walk onto the flats along the river.
- View Bald Eagles from areas between the Haines Highway and the Chilkat River.
- Do not disturb or move the fish in any way.
- Use binoculars and/or a telescope to watch eagles from a distance. If eagles flush, back away to a safer distance.

- Do not set up tripods on the road.
- Use bus transportation from Haines to the eagle viewing sites. Naturalists are part of these organized bus trips to provide information and answer questions.
- If driving to the designated eagle viewing sites by private vehicle, park *only* in designated pullovers along the road.

Excellent Bald Eagle photographic opportunities exist along the Haines Highway and the Chilkat River. The following is recommended photographic equipment:

- Use a 35mm single-lens reflex camera.
- Use a very good-quality tripod *without* plastic parts. Also, wrap water pipe insulation foam around the upper legs to prevent your bare hands from freezing to the metal.
- Use a 28 to 50mm lens for photographing landscapes and scenery.
- Use a 200mm lens for photographing eagles perched in trees or on the river edge.
- Use a 300mm lens for photographing eagles filling about one-quarter of the frame.
- Use a 400mm lens for photographing small groups of eagles or individual birds filling about one-half of the frame.

- Use a 500mm lens for photographing individual eagles filling about three-quarters of the frame.
- Alternatively, use a 175 to 500mm zoom lens if you prefer not to carry a large assortment of lenses.
- Take at least six rolls of ISO 100- to 200-speed film with you each day, and at least double that number if you are a serious bird photographer.
- Take plenty of extra camera batteries—they quickly lose power in cold weather.
- Take waterproof gear for yourself and your photographic equipment, including a collapsible umbrella and some plastic bags.

Access: From Haines, drive north on State Route 7 (Haines Highway) to mile markers 18 to 21.5, where large numbers of Bald Eagles can be seen along the river from the road. Limited parking is available at designated locations, but Bald Eagle watching bus trips are scheduled daily during the annual Alaska Bald Eagle Festival in mid-November. For additional details, refer to www.baldeaglefest.org or write to the Haines Chamber of Commerce, P.O. Box 1449, Haines, AK 99827.

References: *Bald Eagles in Alaska* (U.S. Department of the Interior and Agriculture, no date); *A Guide to Hawk Watching in North America* (Pennsylvania State University Press, 1979); *The Bald Eagle of Alaska, BC and Washington* (Hancock House Publishers, 2003); *9th Annual Alaska Bald Eagle Festival, November 12–16, 2003* (Haines Chamber of Commerce, 2003).

Cook Inlet (near Anchorage)

Raptors: Bald Eagles.

Viewing Season: Year-round, with largest numbers appearing in mid-April.

Watch Site Description: The shorelines and edges of forests bordering rivers that enter Cook Inlet from the Kenai Peninsula south of Anchorage.

Access: By private airplane flights to various small towns and villages along Cook Inlet, or by boat.

References: *Bald Eagles in Alaska* (U.S. Department of the Interior and Agriculture, no date); *A Guide to Hawk Watching in North America* (Pennsylvania State University Press, 1979).

Glacier Bay National Monument

Raptors: Bald Eagles (more than a hundred active eagle nests around Glacier Bay, and others elsewhere within the national monument boundaries).

Viewing Season: All year.

**Watch Site
Description:** An outstanding Bald Eagle viewing area set against a kalei-doscope of glaciers, sea, forests, muskegs, and high mountains. Eagle watching can be done from cruise ships, from tour boats, or from the visitor facilities at the headquarters in Bartlett Cove.

Access: Glacier Bay is located 100 miles northwest of Juneau. It is reached by commercial airlines, private plane charters, summer cruise ships, and private boats.

Reference: *A Guide to Hawk Watching in North America* (Pennsylvania State University Press, 1979).

Katmai National Park and Preserve

Raptors: Bald Eagles.

Viewing Season: Summer.

**Watch Site
Description:** The park's coast, bordering the Shelikof Strait.

Access: The summer headquarters of Katmai National Monument are located at Brooks Camp about 406 miles southwest of Anchorage. No visitor facilities are available. The area is accessible only by private or charter airplanes.

Reference: *A Guide to Hawk Watching in North America* (Pennsylvania State University Press, 1979).

Kenai Peninsula (south of Anchorage)

Raptors: Bald Eagles.

Viewing Season: Year-round.

**Watch Site
Description:** Bald Eagles can be seen just about anywhere on the Kenai Peninsula, but the following sites are especially worthwhile eagle watching locations:

- *Deep Creek State Recreation Area.* The mouth of the creek flowing into Cook Inlet at the Deep Creek State Recreation Area's campground just south of Ninilchik on State Route 1 (Sterling Highway). Many Bald Eagles feed on fish scraps washing onto the beach.

- *Homer.* This town is located at the end of State Route 1 (Sterling Highway) on the Kenai Peninsula. During summer numerous Bald Eagles can be seen in and around the town's harbor, campground, and the Homer Spit. Eagles also occur in and around Homer year-round.

- *Interior of the Peninsula.* Bald Eagles can be seen in the peninsula's interior such as around Kenai Lake, and on sandbars, gravel shoals, and trees in the Cooper Landing section of the Kenai River.

- *Kenai River and Flats.* Bald Eagles commonly are seen along the Kenai River below Skilak Lake; at flats at the river's mouth, eagles feed on weak and dead waterfowl and migrating Hooligan (small smelt).

- *Seward Area.* Bald Eagles can be seen anywhere in the Seward area—especially along the town waterfront and harbor, and at the mouth of the Resurrection River.

- *Soldotna-to-Homer Area.* Good eagle viewing also can be enjoyed along State Route 1 (Sterling Highway) between the towns of Soldotna and Homer—especially on beaches, the sides of bluffs, aloft over streams draining into Cook Inlet, and at the village of Ninilchik north of Homer.

Access: The Kenai Peninsula and its various eagle watching sites are reached by driving south from Anchorage on State Route 1 (Sterling Highway) to the peninsula, then continuing via Route 1 to the above-mentioned locations. The exception is Seward, which is reached via State Route 9, which branches off Route 1 farther north on the Kenai Peninsula. Ferry and airplane services also connect Homer and Seward with various points elsewhere in Alaska.

Reference: Alaska Outdoors at www.alaskaoutdoorjournal.com.

Klondike Gold Rush National Historical Park (near Skagway)

Raptors: Bald Eagles.

Viewing Season: Year-round.

Watch Site
Description: Areas along the Taiya River and its delta between April and May, when dozens of Bald Eagles feed on spring runs of Eulachon (anadromous smelt). During summer approximately six Bald Eagle nesting territories are found in the Skagway area, including three within the park. During September and October dozens of Bald Eagles feed on salmon runs in the Skagway and Taiya Rivers. In the Dyea section of the park, especially good months for viewing Bald Eagles are September and October, when the raptors congregate and feed on autumn Coho Salmon runs in the Taiya River.

Access: Skagway is located in southeastern Alaska and is reached by commercial airlines, summer cruise ships, and the Alaska Marine Highway (Ferry) System. Skagway is also located 110 miles south of the Alaska Highway and is connected to that road by the South Klondike Highway (State Route 2). Details on reaching the Taiya River and other park areas are available at the national park headquarters in Skagway.

Reference: *A Guide to Hawk Watching in North America* (Pennsylvania State University Press, 1979).

Kodiak National Wildlife Refuge

Raptors: Bald Eagles.

Viewing Season: All year.

Watch Site
Description: The shorelines of various rivers and bays around Kodiak Island.

Access: By ferry (from Homer or Anchorage) or airplane. There are no roads on the island. Additional information is available by writing to the Refuge Manager, Kodiak National Wildlife Refuge, 1390 Buskin River Road, Kodiak, AK 99615.

References: *Bald Eagles in Alaska* (U.S. Department of the Interior and Agriculture, no date); *A Guide to Hawk Watching in North America* (Pennsylvania State University Press, 1979).

Paxson Alpine Tours and Denali Highway Cabins

Raptors: Bald Eagles and Merlins.

Viewing Season: August through early September.

Watch Site Description: Evening nonwhitewater float trips lasting three hours on the upper Gulkana River through the Paxson Wildlife Reserve from the Denali Highway south to Paxson Lake. Numerous Bald Eagles are observed in flight and feeding on salmon. The float trips are arranged on even-numbered days by Paxson Alpine Tours and Denali Highway Cabins. Merlins also nest in season (June and July) at Paxson Tours and Cabins and are very habituated to close human presence, which allows exceptionally good viewing opportunities.

Access: At the junction of State Route 4 (the Richardson Highway) and State Route 8 (the Denali Highway) at Paxson (a very tiny hamlet with a gas station, snowplow site, one house, and the Paxson Alpine Tours compound), there is one entrance to the Paxson compound about 250 yards west on Route 8 and another entrance 250 yards north on Route 4.

References: *A Birder's Guide to Alaska* (American Birding Association, 2002); Paxson Alpine Tours and Denali Highway Cabins, HC72, Box 7292, Paxson, AK 99739; www.denalihwy.com.

Richardson Highway (State Route 4)

Raptors: Bald Eagles.

Viewing Season: August and early September.

Watch Site Description: The Richardson Highway is a major road where Bald Eagles can be seen between mileposts 185 (at the junction with State Route 8, the Denali Highway, at Paxson) and 191 at Summit Lake.

Access: From the junction of State Routes 4 and 8 (the Rich–Denali Highways at Paxson), drive north on Route 4 (the Richardson Highway) from milepost 185 to milepost 191 at Summit Lake and watch for Bald Eagles along this stretch of road.

References: *A Birder's Guide to Alaska* (American Birding Association, 2002); Paxson Alpine Tours and Denali Highway Cabins, HC72, Box 7292, Paxson, AK 99739; www.denalihwy.com.

Prince William Sound (near Anchorage)

Raptors: Bald Eagles.

Viewing Season: Year-round, with largest numbers appearing in mid-April.

Watch Site
Description: The shorelines and edges of forests bordering rivers that enter Prince William Sound.

Access: By private airplane flights to various small towns and villages along the sound, or by boat.

References: *Bald Eagles in Alaska* (U.S. Department of the Interior and Agriculture, no date); *A Guide to Hawk Watching in North America* (Pennsylvania State University Press, 1979).

Seymour Eagle Management Area (on Admiralty Island)

Raptors: Nesting Bald Eagles (two nests per mile).

Viewing Season: April through August.

Watch Site
Description: The shorelines of several small islands in Seymour Canal, on Admiralty Island in the Tongass National Forest, and nearby shorelines of the Glass Peninsula bordering the Seymour Canal and other shoreline areas west of the canal.

Access: From Juneau or Sitka, take a short charter flight to Admiralty Island.

References: *Bald Eagles in Alaska* (U.S. Department of the Interior and Agriculture, no date); *A Guide to Hawk Watching in North America* (Pennsylvania State University Press, 1979).

Sitka National Historical Park

Raptors: Bald Eagles.

Viewing Season: All year.

Watch Site Description: The harbor, park, and areas near the park, including the old Russian settlement.

Access: Sitka is located on Baranof Island in southeastern Alaska and is reached by commercial airlines, summer cruise ships, and the Alaska Marine Highway (Ferry) System.

Reference: *A Guide to Hawk Watching in North America* (Pennsylvania State University Press, 1979).

Stikine River (near Wrangell)

Raptors: Bald Eagles feeding on smelt runs.

Viewing Season: Mid-April.

Watch Site Description: The shorelines of the Stikine River, in which smelt runs provide abundant food for eagles.

Access: The Stikine River can be reached through Wrangell or Petersburg via the Alaska Marine Highway (Ferry) System.

References: *Bald Eagles in Alaska* (U.S. Department of the Interior and Agriculture, no date); *A Guide to Hawk Watching in North America* (Pennsylvania State University Press, 1979).

California

Klamath Basin National Wildlife Refuges (south of Klamath Falls, Oregon)

Raptors: Bald Eagles, Rough-legged Hawks, and Golden Eagles.

Viewing Season: December through February.

Watch Site Description: Three wildlife refuges in the Klamath Basin area are in California (three more are north of the California border in Oregon), providing freshwater marshes, lakes, and adjacent upland areas. The two most important California refuges for Bald Eagle viewing are discussed here:

- Lower Klamath National Wildlife Refuge provides major winter habitat and waterfowl food resources for Bald Eagles.

- Tule Lake National Wildlife Refuge also provides major winter habitat and waterfowl food resources for Bald Eagles.

Access: From the junction of U.S. Route 97 and State Route 161 north of the town of Doris, drive east for 10 miles on Route 161 to the point where the auto tour route for the Lower Klamath National Wildlife Refuge begins. Follow the auto tour route through the refuge, looking for Bald Eagles. The refuge headquarters and visitor center is reached by returning to Route 161 and continuing east on this road for approximately 7.5 miles to the junction with Hill Road. Turn south on Hill Road and continue for another 2.9 miles to the visitor center and headquarters.

To visit Tule Lake National Wildlife Refuge from the town of Tulelake, drive west on State Route 139 to the junction with the East-West Road and continue for approximately 4.8 miles to Hill Road. Turn south on Hill Road and continue for 0.5 mile to the visitor center. Stop for updated eagle viewing information, then continue south on Hill Road for 4.7 miles to the entrance to the auto tour route for the Tule Lake refuge. Follow the auto tour route around the refuge, looking for eagles as you progress.

Reference: *Birding Northern California* (Falcon/Globe Pequot Press, 1999).

Modoc National Wildlife Refuge (near Alturas)

Raptors: Bald Eagles and Northern Harriers.

Viewing Season: Winter.

Watch Site
Description: A 6,283-acre wildlife refuge containing lakes, ponds, islands, wetlands, Sagebrush uplands, and cottonwood trees.

Access: From the junction of U.S. Route 395 and State Route 299 near Alturas, drive south for 1 mile on U.S. 395 to the junction with County Road 56. Turn east onto Road 56 and continue for 0.6 mile to the junction with County Road 115. Turn south onto Road 115 and continue for 1.5 miles to the entrance to the refuge. Enter and explore the refuge for Bald Eagles and other birds.

Reference: *Birding Northern California* (Falcon/Globe Pequot Press, 1999).

Colorado

Monte Vista National Wildlife Refuge (near Monte Vista)

Raptors: Bald Eagles (maximum forty per day).

Viewing Season: Mid-December through February.

Watch Site
Description: Waterfowl ponds along the refuge's tour route; a marsh along the north side of County Road 7 Miles South; cottonwood trees along the southwestern corner of the refuge within sight of County Road 8 Miles South; and cottonwood trees along the east side of State Route 15 a short distance north of the refuge headquarters.

Access: From Monte Vista, drive south on State Route 15 for about 5 miles to the refuge. Stop at the headquarters just off the highway and secure a visitor map of the area and perhaps more details on the best spots for eagle viewing.

References: *Wintering of the Migrant Bald Eagle in the Lower 48 States* (National Agricultural Chemicals Association, 1976); *A Guide to Hawk Watching in North America* (Pennsylvania State University Press, 1979).

Connecticut

Connecticut River Eagle Festival (in Essex)

Raptors: Bald Eagles.

Viewing Season: January through March. The annual Connecticut River Eagle Festival (organized and hosted by the Connecticut Audubon Society) is held in mid-February on Presidents' Day weekend.

Watch Site Description: The lower Connecticut River at Essex, where open waters allow Bald Eagles to feed. Guided eagle viewing boat trips are provided on the Connecticut River on heated boats; there is a charge, and reservations are required. Additional eagle-related activities, lectures, exhibits, and music are provided on Main Street and elsewhere in Essex during the festival weekend.

Access: From the junction of Interstate 95 and State Route 9, drive north on Route 9 for about 3 miles to Essex. The Connecticut River Eagle Festival is well promoted, and a wide range of additional information, programs, and activities are also available. Free shuttle buses are provided to Bald Eagle viewing sites along the shoreline of the Connecticut River, and to other festival activities.

Reference: Connecticut Audubon Society at www.ctaudubon.org/eaglemore.htm.

Shepaug Eagle Observation Area (near Southbury)

Raptors: Concentrations of Bald Eagles. Other raptors also seen at this site include Sharp-shinned Hawks, Northern Goshawks, and Red-tailed Hawks. A range of waterfowl and Great Blue Herons also can be seen here.

Viewing Season: Late December through March.

Watch Site Description: The interior of a building from which eagle watchers overlook open water with Bald Eagles near a hydroelectric station on the Housatonic River, and nearby trees on which eagles sometimes perch. The observation area is open to the public Wednesday and Sunday from early December through mid-March. Admission is free, but it is necessary to make reservations by telephoning (800) 368–8954. An information packet and admittance letter will be mailed to you.

Access: From the junction of Interstate 84 and U.S. Route 6 just south of Southbury, leave I-84 at exit 15 and drive north on U.S. 6 for a short distance into Southbury. Seek local directions to the nearby Shepaug Eagle Observation Area along the Housatonic River.

Reference: Northeast Utilities at www.nu.com/environmental/ steward/shepaug.asp.

Delaware

Bombay Hook National Wildlife Refuge (near Smyrna)

Raptors: Bald Eagles, Northern Harriers, Red-shouldered Hawks, Rough-legged Hawks, and American Kestrels.

Viewing Season: December through May.

Watch Site Description: Trees and snags along the west side of Shearness Pool, with viewing points available at safe distances along Whitehall Neck Road and the refuge tour route passing along the eastern side of Shearness Pond.

Access: From Smyrna, drive south on U.S. Route 13 to the southern edge of town, then turn left at a well-marked sign pointing to Bombay Hook National Wildlife Refuge. Follow the signs for about 6 miles to the refuge. Stop at the headquarters to secure current information and restrictions on eagle viewing. Never attempt to walk close to eagle nests.

Reference: *A Guide to Hawk Watching in North America* (Pennsylvania State University Press, 1979).

Florida

Charlotte Harbor Environmental Center/Alligator Creek Site (near Punta Gorda)

Raptors: Bald Eagles.

Viewing Season: December through April.

Watch Site Description: A 3,000-acre tract containing freshwater and saltwater marshes, mangrove swamp, Cabbage Palm and oak hammock, and pine flatwoods. A visitor center and museum is also open to the public. Ask naturalists at the visitor center for current eagle viewing information.

Access: From the junction of U.S. Route 41 and County Route 765 near Punta Gorda, drive south on Route 765 (Burnt Store Road) for 1 mile to the entrance to the environmental center on the west side of the road.

Reference: www.floridaconservation.org.

Emeralda Marsh Conservation Area

Raptors: Bald Eagles.

Viewing Season: Year-round (especially winter and spring).

Watch Site Description: Saw grass and wet prairie marshes, hammocks, pastures, and levees near the headwaters of the Ocklawaha River.

Access: From Leesburg, drive south on U.S. Route 441 for 2 miles to County Route 44. Follow Route 44 to Emeralda Avenue, then turn left (north) onto Emeralda Island Road northwest. Entrances to the conservation area are located on both sides of the road.

Reference: www.floridaconservation.org.

Lake Kissimmee State Park

Raptors: Bald Eagles and Snail Kites.

Viewing Season: Winter and spring.

Watch Site
Description: Lake Kissimmee and other habitats, including natural lakes, flowering wet prairies, scrub, and pine flatwoods. Canoes can be used on the lakes, and hiking trails and an observation tower also are available. This park is noted as an excellent place to see Bald Eagles; look for nesting Snail Kites at the southern end of Lake Kissimmee.

Access: From the junction of State Routes 17 and 60 at Lake Wales, drive east on Route 60 for 10 miles to Boy Scout Road. Turn left onto Boy Scout Road and continue 3.7 miles to Camp Mack Road. Turn right onto Camp Mack Road and continue for 5.6 miles to the park entrance. Go into the park and seek current eagle and kite watching information from park officials.

Reference: www.floridaconservation.org.

Lower Suwannee National Wildlife Refuge

Raptors: Bald Eagles, Swallow-tailed Kites (spring and summer), Red-shouldered Hawks, Black Vultures, and Turkey Vultures.

Viewing Season: Year-round.

Watch Site
Description: A large wildlife refuge along the lower Suwannee River and part of the Gulf of Mexico, with a range of habitats including offshore islands, tidal marshes, coastal pine flatwoods, cypress swamps, and hardwood forests.

Access: From Chiefland, drive south on County Route 347 for 15 miles; north of the river, County Route 349 leads to additional roads and observation platforms in the refuge.

Reference: www.floridaconservation.org.

St. Marks National Wildlife Refuge (near Tallahassee)

Raptors: Bald Eagles.

Viewing Season: Winter.

Watch Site
Description: A wildlife rich area with pine flatwoods, pine-oak uplands adjacent to Apalachee Bay, impoundments, salt marshes,

and hardwood swamps. Bald Eagles often are seen perched on dead tree snags.

Access: From Tallahassee, drive south on State Route 363 to the junction with State Route 267 near Wakulla. Turn left onto Route 267 and continue for 3.5 miles to U.S. Route 98. Turn left onto U.S. 98 and continue for 0.5 mile, then turn south onto County Route 59 and continue to the refuge entrance. Enter, and secure current eagle watching information at the refuge office.

Reference: www.floridaconservation.org.

St. Vincent Island National Wildlife Refuge (near Apalachicola)

Raptors: Bald Eagles, Ospreys, and other hawks and falcons.

Viewing Season: Winter for Bald Eagles.

Watch Site Description: An undeveloped barrier beach island with dunes, tidal marshes, freshwater sloughs and lakes, and upland Slash Pine woodland. Bald Eagles nest on the island in winter. Ospreys also nest there in summer, and hawks and falcons migrate past the island during autumn.

Access: Accessible by boat. From Apalachicola, drive west on U.S. Route 98 for 8 miles to the junction with County Route 30A. Turn left onto Route 30A and continue for 10 miles to County Route 30B. Turn onto Route 30B and continue to the boat ramp at the end of the road; from here, boats can be launched to go to the island. The visitor center and refuge office is located in the Harbor Master Building on Main Street in Apalachicola.

Reference: www.floridaconservation.org.

Three Lakes Wildlife Management Area/Prairie Lakes Unit (near Kenansville)

Raptors: Bald Eagles, Red-shouldered Hawks, Crested Caracaras, and Burrowing Owls.

Viewing Season: Year-round.

Watch Site

Description: Former ranchland with a diversity of habitats, including several lakes, freshwater marsh, wet prairie, dry prairie, and pine flatwoods. A high concentration of nesting Bald Eagles is present in the area. Various trails and roads are present on the site. Part of the Florida National Scenic Trail also crosses the site.

Access: From the junction of U.S. Route 441 and State Route 523 at Kenansville, drive northwest on Route 523 (Canoe Creek Road) for 9 miles to the entrance to the management area on the left (west). Enter and explore the area, looking for Bald Eagles and other raptors. *Warning:* Do not approach closely or disturb active Bald Eagle nests. There are severe federal and state penalties for doing so.

Reference: www.floridaconservation.org.

Vera Carter Environmental Center (at Lake Tibet-Butler)

Raptors: Bald Eagles, Ospreys, Swallow-tailed Kites (spring and summer), and Red-tailed Hawks.

Viewing Season: Year-round.

Watch Site

Description: Trails and boardwalks along the southwest shore of Lake Tibet-Butler, providing access to cypress swamps, freshwater marshes, and pine and scrub woodland.

Access: From the junction of Interstate 4 and County Route 535 (Winter Garden–Vineland Road) at Lake Buena Vista, take exit 68 off I–4 onto Route 535 and continue north for about 5 miles to the entrance to the Tibet-Butler Preserve and Vera Carter Environmental Center on the right (east) side of the road. Enter and drive to the environmental center. Ask naturalists at the center about current Bald Eagle viewing opportunities.

Reference: www.floridaconservation.org.

Idaho

Minidoka National Wildlife Refuge (near Rupert)

Raptors: Wintering Bald Eagles and Golden Eagles.

Viewing Season: November through March.

Watch Site Description: Cottonwood trees adjacent to Lake Walcot at the refuge headquarters.

Access: From Rupert, drive northeast on State Route 24 for 6 miles, then turn east onto County Route 400 north (marked by a refuge sign) and continue another 6 miles to the refuge headquarters.

References: *Wintering of the Migrant Bald Eagle in the Lower 48 States* (National Agricultural Chemicals Association, 1976); *A Guide to Hawk Watching in North America* (Pennsylvania State University Press, 1979).

Illinois

Crab Orchard National Wildlife Refuge (near Marion)

Raptors: Concentrations of Bald Eagles.

Viewing Season: October through March, with peak numbers appearing in late January and early February when Crab Orchard Lake is frozen.

Watch Site Description: Trees near the shoreline of Crab Orchard Lake, open water near the refuge's water plant, and frozen sections of the lake, where dead geese provide food for eagles.

Access: From the junction of Interstate 57 and U.S. Route 13 near Marion, drive west on U.S. 13 for about 5 miles to Wolf Creek Road. Turn left (south) onto Wolf Creek Road and continue for about 2 miles to the refuge water plant. Observe from a spot about 0.13 mile southeast of the water plant.

References: *Wintering of the Migrant Bald Eagle in the Lower 48 States* (National Agricultural Chemicals Association, 1976); *A*

Guide to Hawk Watching in North America (Pennsylvania State University Press, 1979).

Fort Edwards (Warsaw)

Raptors: Concentrations of Bald Eagles.

Viewing Season: November to mid-March.

Watch Site Description: Open areas along Great River Road between Warsaw and Hamilton, which provide views over the Mississippi River toward Missouri and upriver toward the islands and mouth of the Des Moines River. Sometimes dozens of eagles soar above the river on clear, mild winter days. Best viewing times are from late morning to early afternoon.

Access: From Hamilton, ask directions to Great River Road and follow it southwestward to Warsaw and Fort Edwards.

Reference: *A Guide to Hawk Watching in North America* (Pennsylvania State University Press, 1979).

Fulton Bald Eagle Watch (in Fulton)

Raptors: Bald Eagles.

Viewing Season: November through February.

Watch Site Description: An observation area providing views over Mississippi Lock & Dam No. 13 and the unfrozen water of the Mississippi River where Bald Eagles feed on fish and roost in nearby trees. *Warning:* Do not disturb feeding or roosting eagles by approaching them closely.

Access: From Fulton, drive north on State Route 84 for a few miles to the overlook building at Mississippi Lock & Dam No. 13. Bald Eagles can also be observed roosting on trees downriver from the dam and lock, and from the Albany Landing in Albany, Illinois, along Route 84.

References: *Birding Illinois* (Falcon Publishing, 2000); city of Fulton Web site at www.cityoffulton.us/events.html.

Horseshoe Lake Conservation Area (near Olive Branch)

Raptors: Bald Eagles.

Viewing Season: Winter.

Watch Site Description: A 1,200-acre lake surrounded by fields and wooded areas.

Access: From Olive Branch, a small town in extreme southwestern Illinois, drive southeast on State Route 3 for about 2 miles to the sign marking the entrance road to the conservation area. Turn and follow the road to the lakeshore.

References: *A Guide to Bird Finding East of the Mississippi* (Oxford University Press, 1977); *A Guide to Hawk Watching in North America* (Pennsylvania State University Press, 1979); *Birding Illinois* (Falcon Publishing, 2000).

Lake Chautauqua National Wildlife Refuge (near Havana)

Raptors: Bald Eagles.

Viewing Season: Winter.

Watch Site Description: A 4,488-acre wildlife refuge containing open water, floodplain forest, and upland habitats adjacent to the Illinois River.

Access: From Havana, drive east on U.S. Route 136 for about 5 miles to the junction with County Route 2130E. Turn onto Route 2130E and continue for about 4 miles to the junction with County Route 2000N, turn north, and continue for about 2 miles to the junction with County Route 1950E. Turn north onto Route 1950E and continue for about a mile to the refuge entrance sign. Enter, stop at the headquarters to secure a refuge map and current Bald Eagle viewing opportunities, and explore the refuge looking for eagles.

Reference: *Birding Illinois* (Falcon Publishing, 2000).

Mississippi Lock & Dam No. 14 (near East Moline)

Raptors: Concentrations of Bald Eagles.

Viewing Season: Early winter.

Watch Site Description: A public-use area providing a view of the Mississippi River and a dam below which eagles gather.

Access: From the north side of East Moline, drive north on State Route 84 for 2.9 miles to the public-use area. Leave your vehicle in the parking lot and look over the river for eagles.

References: *American Birds*, 1966, 140: 32–34; *A Guide to Hawk Watching in North America* (Pennsylvania State University Press, 1979).

Mississippi Lock & Dam No. 16 (near Illinois City)

Raptors: Concentrations of Bald Eagles.

Viewing Season: Winter.

Watch Site Description: A gravel dike road running along the Mississippi River for almost 5 miles past the locks. Good views over the river are enjoyed, and eagles in the area can be easily seen.

Access: From the fire station in Illinois City, follow State Route 92 toward the Mississippi River for 7.8 miles. Then turn right onto a gravel road near the approach to the bridge crossing the river. Follow this dike road (in good weather) for about 4.4 miles while keeping watch over the river for eagles.

References: *American Birds*, 1966, 140: 32–34; *A Guide to Hawk Watching in North America* (Pennsylvania State University Press, 1979).

Mississippi Lock & Dam No. 17 (near New Boston)

Raptors: Concentrations of Bald Eagles.

Viewing Season: Winter.

Watch Site
Description: An exposed area alongside the Mississippi River upstream from New Boston, or the riverfront at New Boston.

Access: In New Boston, drive to the riverfront; eagles sometimes can be seen here. Alternatively, drive upstream on State Route 17 from the New Boston Post Office to the edge of town. At a roadside park, turn right from Route 17 onto County Road and drive 2.1 miles to the turnoff for the river. Turn onto the road leading to the river and continue another 1.5 miles to the river, where eagles can frequently be seen.

References: *American Birds*, 1966, 140: 32–34; *A Guide to Hawk Watching in North America* (Pennsylvania State University Press, 1979).

Mississippi Palisades State Park (near Savanna)

Raptors: Bald Eagles and a few Golden Eagles.

Viewing Season: Winter.

Watch Site
Description: Several park overlooks along the Mississippi River from which Bald Eagles can be seen on the river.

Access: From Savanna, drive north on State Route 84 to either of two park entrances, north and south.

Reference: *Birding Illinois* (Falcon Publishing, 2000).

Montebello Conservation Area (near Hamilton)

Raptors: Concentrations of feeding Bald Eagles.

Viewing Season: November to mid-March, with peak numbers of birds frequently appearing in January during very cold weather.

Watch Site
Description: Open areas of water in the Mississippi River just below Lock & Dam No. 19 south of the Hamilton–Keokuk Bridge. The best viewing time is between half an hour and two hours after sunrise.

Access: The Montebello Conservation Area is located west of Hamilton and just upriver from the bridge. From Hamilton, drive west on U.S. Route 136 for a short distance. The park is located to the right of the highway as you approach the bridge.

References: *A Guide to Bird Finding East of the Mississippi* (Oxford University Press, 1977); *A Guide to Hawk Watching in North America* (Pennsylvania State University Press, 1979).

Pere Marquette State Park (near Grafton)

Raptors: Bald Eagles.

Viewing Season: December through March.

Watch Site Description: Bald Eagles perched on trees along the Illinois River. Bald Eagle watching drives are organized by the park's interpreter, and depart from the park's visitor center at 8:30 A.M. Call the center at (618) 786–3323 for current information and reservations, or write to Pere Marquette State Park, P.O. Box 158, Grafton, IL 62037.

Access: From Grafton, drive north (west) on State Route 100 to the entrance to Pere Marquette State Park. Enter the park and continue to the visitor center, where current information about eagle watching can be secured.

References: *Birding Illinois* (Falcon Publishing, 2000); Illinois Department of Natural Resources at www.dnr.state.il.us.

Iowa

Bellevue

Raptors: Bald Eagles.

Viewing Season: Winter.

Watch Site Description: A public boat landing overlooking the Mississippi River.

Access: From Bellevue, drive south on U.S. Route 52 for about a mile to the public boat landing. Park there and look for eagles downstream or across the river.

References: *Winter Birding Along the Mississippi River* (Eagle Valley Environmentalists, no date); *A Guide to Hawk Watching in North America* (Pennsylvania State University Press, 1979).

Davenport Area

Raptors: Bald Eagles.

Viewing Season: Mid-January.

Watch Site Description: Several Bald Eagle viewing areas are available along the Mississippi River in the Davenport area. Bald Eagles gather in open water below Lock & Dam No.14 on the Mississippi River at LeClaire Park, and roost in trees in the Rock Island Arsenal on Rock Island in the Mississippi River between Davenport, Iowa, and Rock Island, Illinois.

Access: In Davenport, follow River Drive (U.S. Routes 61/67) along the Mississippi River for some eagle viewing opportunities.

References: None.

DeSoto National Wildlife Refuge (near Missouri Valley)

Raptors: Bald Eagles.

Viewing Season: December through March.

Watch Site Description: A former bend of the Missouri River that attracts waterfowl and Bald Eagles during winter. Eagle viewing is done from the visitor center and/or a wildlife observation platform in the refuge. Current eagle viewing information and refuge literature can be secured at the visitor center.

Access: From the junction of Interstate 29 (exit 75) and U.S. Route 30 at Missouri Valley, drive west on U.S. 30 for 5.7 miles to the refuge entrance on the left side of the highway. Enter and continue to the visitor center.

Reference: *Iowa Wildlife Viewing Guide* (Falcon Press Publishing, 1995).

Forney Lake Wildlife Area (near Thurman)

Raptors: Bald Eagles.

Viewing Season: March.

Watch Site Description: Large cottonwood trees on which Bald Eagles roost at the east end of a marsh. Do not approach roosting eagles closely. Use your vehicle as an observation blind to avoid disturbing the birds.

Access: From Interstate 29 at Bartlett, take exit 24 and continue east on County Line Road L31 for 0.1 mile, then head south on the same road for another 2.8 miles to the junction with a gravel road. Turn east on the gravel road and continue for 0.6 mile to the marsh located north of the road. Continue on the gravel road to the east end of the marsh and the cottonwood trees used as roosts by Bald Eagles. Park along the side of the road and watch the eagles from there.

Reference: *Iowa Wildlife Viewing Guide* (Falcon Publishing, 1995).

Heron Bend Conservation Area (near Montrose)

Raptors: Bald Eagles.

Viewing Season: Winter.

Watch Site Description: Scenic Pool 19 on the Mississippi River, which attracts numerous Bald Eagles during winter. Observe from the area around the pool.

Access: From the junction of U.S. Route 61 and State Route 404 at Montrose, drive north on U.S. 61 for 3.6 miles to the entrance on the right to the Heron Bend Conservation Area.

Reference: *Iowa Wildlife Viewing Guide* (Falcon Press Publishing, 1995).

Lake Manawa State Park (near Council Bluffs)

Raptors: Bald Eagles.

Viewing Season: March; November to freeze-up.

Watch Site Description: A boat ramp from which observers have excellent views of the south side of Lake Manawa.

Access: From the junction of exit 47 off Interstate 29 and U.S. Route 275/State Route 92 at Council Bluffs, drive west on U.S. 275/Route 92 for 1.5 miles to the junction with South 11th Street. Turn south onto South 11th Street and continue for 0.1 mile to the entrance to the park. Enter and follow Shore Drive and signs to the park office, where you can secure current Bald Eagle viewing information and a park map.

Reference: *Iowa Wildlife Viewing Guide* (Falcon Publishing, 1995).

Le Claire–Princeton Area

Raptors: Bald Eagles.

Viewing Season: Winter.

Watch Site Description: A highway paralleling the Mississippi River over which Bald Eagles are seen, and cottonwood trees along the river on which eagles sometimes roost.

Access: From Le Claire, drive north on U.S. Route 67 along the Mississippi River looking for eagles over the river or roosting in trees.

References: None.

Mississippi Lock & Dam No. 9 (McGregor)

Raptors: Bald Eagles.

Viewing Season: Winter.

Watch Site Description: Open water below a Mississippi River lock and dam where Bald Eagles gather to feed during winter.

Access: Begin by stopping at the Upper Mississippi River National Wildlife and Fish Refuge, located 0.2 mile north of McGregor on U.S. Route 18. Obtain literature and maps here. Then drive to Harper's Ferry to the junction of County Route B25 and County Route X52 (Great River Road), continue north on Route X52 for 2.6 miles, then turn east and follow a gravel road northeast for 0.5 mile to the end of the gravel. Then continue another 0.2 mile to a spot where, in the distance, it's possible to see Mississippi Lock & Dam No. 9 and the Bald Eagles gathering there.

Reference: *Iowa Wildlife Viewing Guide* (Falcon Press Publishing, 1995).

Mississippi Lock & Dam No. 10 (Guttenburg)

Raptors: Bald Eagles.

Viewing Season: Winter.

Watch Site Description: Open water between islands in the main river channel below the dam, and trees beside the main river channel.

Access: In Guttenburg, drive along U.S. Route 52 to a point in or near the town where the dam and river can be seen from the highway. Look for eagles from this spot. Alternatively, drive or hike to the top of the bluff at Guttenburg and look for eagles along the river or perched in trees beside it. An excellent view of the Eagle Valley Nature Preserve, located across the river, can also be enjoyed.

References: *Winter Birding Along the Mississippi River* (Eagle Valley Environmentalists, no date); *A Guide to Hawk Watching in North America* (Pennsylvania State University Press, 1979).

Mississippi Lock & Dam No. 11 (Dubuque)

Raptors: Bald Eagles.

Viewing Season: Winter.

Watch Site
Description: Open areas on the Mississippi River below Mississippi
Lock & Dam No. 11 near the Mathias Ham House
Museum north of U.S. Routes 61/151, areas along the
river south of U.S. Route 20 where it crosses the river, or
across the river from bluffs south of East Dubuque, Illinois.

Access: In Dubuque, from the junction of U.S. Route 52 and
22nd Street, follow 22nd Street east to Windsor Avenue,
turn right onto Windsor and continue a short distance to
Lincoln Avenue, then turn left onto Lincoln Avenue and
follow it to the Mathias Ham House Museum property.
Alternatively, locate any available parking area along the
Mississippi River near the spot where U.S. Route 20
crosses the river into Illinois.

References: *Winter Birding Along the Mississippi River* (Eagle Valley
Environmentalists, no date); *A Guide to Hawk Watching
in North America* (Pennsylvania State University Press,
1979).

Mississippi Lock & Dam No. 12 (Bellevue)

Raptors: Concentrations of Bald Eagles.

Viewing Season: Mid-February.

Watch Site
Description: Open areas of water along the Mississippi River below the
locks and dam.

Access: Various spots along U.S. Route 52 near Bellevue provide
views of the locks and a few eagles. A public boat landing
in Bellevue State Park about a mile south of Bellevue
along U.S. 52 is especially productive for eagle watching.

References: *American Birds*, 1966, 140: 32–34; *A Guide to Hawk
Watching in North America* (Pennsylvania State University
Press, 1979).

Mississippi Lock & Dam No. 14 (Le Claire)

Raptors: Bald Eagles.

Viewing Season: November through March, peaking December through February.

Watch Site Description: A boat launch along the Mississippi River near a lock and dam from which numerous Bald Eagles can be observed.

Access: From the intersection of 181st Street and 182nd Street in Le Claire, drive north on 182nd Street to the lock and dam recreation area on the right. Observe eagles from the boat launch.

Reference: *Iowa Wildlife Viewing Guide* (Falcon Press Publishing, 1995).

Mississippi Lock & Dam No. 15 (Davenport)

Raptors: Concentrations of Bald Eagles.

Viewing Season: Winter.

Watch Site Description: Cedar Island Park in the Mississippi River, providing views of the river and eagles that may be gathering in open water.

Access: From the junction of Interstate 280 and U.S. Route 61 in Davenport, leave I–280 at exit 6 and follow U.S. 61 east to the entrance road to Cedar Island Park, find a suitable place to park, then walk to the river and view from there. Alternatively, follow 18th Avenue to Rock Island, Illinois, to its west end and look over the river toward a small island beside Cedar Island, Iowa, where Bald Eagles often gather.

References: *American Birds*, 1966, 140: 32–34; *A Guide to Hawk Watching in North America* (Pennsylvania State University Press, 1979).

Mississippi Lock & Dam No. 19 (Keokuk)

Raptors: Bald Eagles.

Viewing Season: December through March.

Watch Site Description: A sidewalk near a power plant allowing views of the lock and dam, and along the nearby riverfront.

Access: In Keokuk, at the junction of U.S. Route 136 (7th Street) and U.S. Route 218 (Main Street), drive south on U.S. 218 for 5 blocks to 2nd Street (just before reaching a bridge across the Mississippi River). Turn right onto 2nd Street and continue for 3 blocks to Bank Street. Turn left onto Bank Street and continue to a T intersection beside the river. Turn north and continue for 0.3 mile to Mississippi Lock & Dam No. 19. Alternatively, drive south along the river to a public boat ramp at Hubinger Landing; good views of eagles on the river are also possible here.

Reference: *Iowa Wildlife Viewing Guide* (Falcon Press Publishing, 1995).

Rathbun Lake and Wildlife Area (near Centerville)

Raptors: Bald Eagles (November and December), Northern Harriers, Red-tailed Hawks, and Rough-legged Hawks.

Viewing Season: Winter.

Watch Site Description: A large reservoir surrounded by upland fields and forest. Secure current eagle and hawk viewing information at the visitor center.

Access: From the junction of State Routes 2 and 5 at Centerville, drive north on Route 5 for 3.7 miles to the junction with County Route J29. Turn west onto Route J29 and continue for 3.8 miles to a T intersection. Turn north and then immediately into the visitor center.

Reference: *Iowa Wildlife Viewing Guide* (Falcon Press Publishing, 1995).

Victory Park (in Keokuk)

Raptors: Concentrations of Bald Eagles.

Viewing Season: November to mid-March, with peak numbers of eagles frequently appearing in January during very cold weather.

Watch Site Description: A park overlooking the Mississippi River near Lock & Dam No. 19. Bald Eagles gather in open water to feed.

Access: From the center of Keokuk in extreme southeastern Iowa, drive east on Main Street for 8 blocks, then turn right into the park. Find a suitable place to park, and walk to the river.

References: *A Guide to Bird Finding East of the Mississippi* (Oxford University Press, 1977); A *Guide to Hawk Watching in North America* (Pennsylvania State University Press, 1979).

Wasp Environmental Center (near Dixon)

Raptors: Bald Eagles.

Viewing Season: Winter.

Watch Site Description: A large room in the Wasp Environmental Center, from which Bald Eagles are observed with telescopes.

Access: From Davenport, drive west on Interstate 80 to the junction of exit 284 and County Route Y40. Take exit 284 and drive north on Route Y40 to the town of Dixon. Secure directions for the nearby Wasp Environmental Center in town.

References: None.

Kansas

Quivira National Wildlife Refuge (near Great Bend)

Raptors: Concentrations of Bald Eagles.

Viewing Season: Early October to mid-March, with concentrations usually occurring from mid-December to mid-January.

Watch Site Description: A 21,820-acre refuge with a variety of habitats, including marshes, lakes, and rangeland. Eagle watching can be done with a telescope from the vicinity of the refuge office as the birds sit on ice.

Access: From Great Bend, drive south on U.S. Route 281 to the junction with State Route 19. Turn left (east) onto Route 19 and continue to the Quivira National Wildlife Refuge.

References: *Wintering of the Migrant Bald Eagle in the Lower 48 States* (National Agricultural Chemicals Association, 1976); *A Guide to Hawk Watching in North America* (Pennsylvania State University Press, 1979).

Kentucky

Lake Barkley State Resort Park and Land Between the Lakes Recreation Area (near Cadiz)

Raptors: Bald Eagles, Golden Eagles, Red-shouldered Hawks, Red-tailed Hawks, and Rough-legged Hawks.

Viewing Season: From mid-November to mid-March. The largest numbers of Bald Eagles are seen in January and February.

Watch Site Description: Lake Barkley State Resort Park, just east of Land Between the Lakes Recreation Area, annually holds an "Eagle Weekend" in February during which organized eagle viewing field trips and programs are provided to the public. Eagle viewing is done in the nearby 170,000-acre Land Between the Lakes Recreation Area, where eagles tend to gather along the wooded shorelines of the bays and inlets along the various lakes. The Honker Bay and Fulton Bay areas along Lake Barkley are perhaps the best locations for observing wintering Bald Eagles, but other areas also are productive.

Access: From Cadiz, drive west on U.S. Route 68/State Route 80 to the Lake Barkley State Resort Park, where naturalists can provide additional information on eagle watching. Alternatively, drive west on Routes 68/80 to the information station at the junction of Route 80 and State Route 453 (called The Trace), where information, maps, and other materials are also are available.

References: *Wintering of the Migrant Bald Eagle in the Lower 48 States* (National Agricultural Chemicals Association, 1976); *A Guide to Hawk Watching in North America* (Pennsylvania State University Press, 1979).

Maryland

Blackwater National Wildlife Refuge (near Cambridge)

Raptors: Bald Eagles (nesting); other eastern raptors.

Viewing Season: All year.

Watch Site Description: Dead snags along the edge of the marsh behind the refuge visitor center, or an observation tower along the road behind the public picnic area and restroom facilities. Observers enjoy excellent views of the marshes on which eagles are seen from this tower.

Access: From Cambridge, drive south on State Route 16 for 7 miles to the village of Church Creek. Turn left there onto State Route 335 and continue for 4 miles to the refuge sign. Turn left at the sign and continue another 2 miles to the refuge visitor center, where full information and restrictions on eagle viewing can be secured. Never attempt to approach eagle nests on foot. The visitor center is closed on Christmas Day.

References: *A Guide to Bird Finding East of the Mississippi* (Oxford University Press, 1977); *A Guide to Hawk Watching in North America* (Pennsylvania State University Press, 1979).

Massachusetts

Quabbin Reservoir (near Belchertown)

Raptors: Wintering Bald Eagles; occasionally Golden Eagles.

Viewing Season: January through March.

Watch Site Description: A high point at the south end of the reservoir known as the Enfield Lookout from which observers look over two valleys of the reservoir. Eagles can usually be seen feeding on the ice if you use a telescope or binoculars. *Warning:* Never leave the lookout and attempt to approach the birds on the ice.

Access: From exit 8 (Palmer) off the Massachusetts Turnpike (Interstate 90), drive north on State Route 32 for about 8 miles to its junction with State Route 9 in the town of Ware. Turn left onto Route 9 and continue for about 3 miles toward Belchertown, to a clearly visible QUABBIN RESERVOIR sign. Turn onto the road and follow the signs for about 1.25 miles to the well-marked Enfield Lookout. Observe from there.

References: *Wintering of the Migrant Bald Eagle in the Lower 48 States* (National Agricultural Chemicals Association, 1976); *A Guide to Hawk Watching in North America* (Pennsylvania State University Press, 1979).

Minnesota

Bear Head Lake State Park (near Ely)

Raptors: Bald Eagles.

Viewing Season: Summer.

Watch Site Description: Look for eagles from various lakes within the park.

Access: From Ely, drive southwest on State Routes 169/1 to the junction with County Route 128 between Robinson and Soudan. Turn left (south) onto Route 128 and continue to the state park. Enter and ask park naturalists or rangers for current information on eagle watching.

Reference: Minnesota Department of Natural Resources at
www.dnr.state.mn.us.

Camp Lacupolis to Read's Landing Area (near Wabasha)

Raptors: Bald Eagles.

Viewing Season: Winter.

**Watch Site
Description:** Three roadside pullovers between Camp Lacupolis and
Read's Landing, as well as areas along the Mississippi
River at Read's Landing, all along U.S. Route 61.

Access: From the junction of State Route 60 and U.S. Route 61
at Wabasha, drive north on U.S. 61 for a few miles to
Read's Landing, then continue north on U.S. 61 to three
roadside pullovers along the route just south of Camp
Lacupolis.

Reference: Minnesota Department of Natural Resources at
www.dnr.state.mn.us.

Chippewa National Forest Area (near Grand Rapids)

Raptors: Bald Eagles and Ospreys.

Viewing Season: Spring through autumn.

**Watch Site
Description:** A 1.6-million-acre forest containing more than 1,300
lakes, 923 rivers and streams, and 400,000 acres of wetlands. Look for Bald Eagles flying over roads, lakes, rivers,
and steams, or perched on trees along waterways.

Access: Various parts of the Chippewa National Forest offer
important eagle watching opportunities:

- National Forest Scenic Byway/Minnesota State Scenic
Byway 46 ("Avenue of the Pines") is a 46-mile-long
diagonal route through the Chippewa National Forest
linking Northome in the northwest with U.S. Route 2
at Ball Club in the southeast.

- State Route 38 ("Edge of the Wilderness Scenic Byway")
is very rustic and extends for 47 miles between Effie in
the north and Grand Rapids in the south.

- Federal Dam, Kabekona Narrows, Walker Bay, Stony Point, and Battle Pont at Leech Lake.
- Tamarack Point on the south side of, and Winnie Dam at the eastern end of, Lake Winnibigoshish.
- Cass Lake and Knutson Dam, and the lake's Norway Beach Campground, with wide views of the lake where eagles fish.
- The Cass Lake Wayside Rest along U.S. Route 2.
- The intersection of the Mississippi River with U.S. Route 2 about 8 miles west of Deer River.

References: *Birding Minnesota* (Falcon/Globe Pequot Press, 1996); Chippewa National Forest, 200 Ash Avenue, Cass Lake, MN 56633, (218) 335–8600; www.fs.fed.us/r9/chippewa/flyer/eagle.htm.

Cross Lake

Raptors: Bald Eagles.

Viewing Season: Summer.

Watch Site
Description: The west shore of Cross Lake some 150 yards north of the Ox Lake Tavern. The eagle nest can be seen from the nearby highway.

Access: From Cross Lake, drive north on County Route 6 for about 2.5 miles to the tavern, or a favorable spot along the highway, to see the eagle nest. Do *not* approach this nest.

Reference: Minnesota Department of Natural Resources at www.dnr.state.mn.us.

Mississippi Lock & Dam No. 2 (near Hastings)

Raptors: Bald Eagles.

Viewing Season: Winter.

Watch Site
Description: The bridge over which U.S. Routes 10/61 cross the Mississippi River.

Access: From Hastings, follow U.S. Routes 10/61 to the Mississippi River. Watch for eagles while crossing the bridge, or park at suitable places near the bridge and explore the nearby areas for eagles.

References: *Wintering of the Migrant Bald Eagle in the Lower 48 States* (National Agricultural Chemicals Association, 1976); *A Guide to Hawk Watching in North America* (Pennsylvania State University Press, 1979).

Read's Landing (near Lake City)

Raptors: Bald Eagles.

Viewing Season: February and March.

Watch Site Description: A highway beside a narrowing of the Mississippi River where eagles congregate during winter.

Access: From Lake City, drive east on U.S. Route 61 for about 10 miles to Read's Landing, located along U.S. 61 northwest of Wabasha. Observe eagles from the side of this road, or turn onto County Route 77, which leads into the landing area.

Reference: *Birding Minnesota* (Falcon/Globe Pequot Press, 1996).

Red Wing

Raptors: Bald Eagles.

Viewing Season: Winter.

Watch Site Description: Bald Eagle watching locations include Bay Point Park, Colvill Park, and the waterfront area in Red Wing between them.

Access: From U.S. Routes 61/63 in Red Wing, follow signs to the two parks along the waterfront.

References: *Wintering of the Migrant Bald Eagle in the Lower 48 States* (National Agricultural Chemicals Association, 1976); *A Guide to Hawk Watching in North America* (Pennsylvania State University Press, 1979); Minnesota Department of Natural Resources at www.dnr.state.mn.us.

Saint Croix National Scenic Riverway
(between Stillwater and Taylor's Falls)

Raptors: Bald Eagles.

Viewing Season: Summer.

Watch Site Description: Bald Eagles in flight, or perched, along the Saint Croix National Scenic Riverway.

Access: From Stillwater, east of St. Paul, drive north on State Route 95 to Taylor's Falls. The highway parallels the Saint Croix National Scenic Riverway.

Reference: Minnesota Department of Natural Resources at www.dnr.state.mn.us.

Sherburne National Wildlife Refuge (near Zimmerman)

Raptors: Bald Eagles, Northern Harriers, Red-tailed Hawks, and American Kestrels.

Viewing Season: Spring and summer.

Watch Site Description: A 30,000-acre area of wetlands, prairie, oak savanna, and oak woodland.

Access: From Zimmerman, drive north on U.S. Route 169 for about 4.5 miles, then continue west on County Route 9 for about 5 miles to the refuge headquarters. To reach the auto tour route, drive west from Zimmerman on County Route 4 to the junction with County Route 5. Turn north onto Route 5 and continue for a short distance to the entrance to the auto tour route. Ask at the refuge headquarters for information regarding the best current Bald Eagle viewing locations.

References: *Guide to the National Wildlife Refuges* (Anchor Press/Doubleday, 1979); *Birding Minnesota* (Falcon/Globe Pequot Press, 1996); Minnesota Department of Natural Resources at www.dnr.state.mn.us.

Tamarac National Wildlife Refuge (near Detroit Lakes)

Raptors: Bald Eagles.

Viewing Season: Spring through autumn.

Watch Site Description: A 43,000-acre area of wetlands, bogs, lakes, rivers, and deciduous forests. Look for Bald Eagles flying overhead, or perched on trees, while driving through the refuge.

Access: From Detroit Lakes, drive east on State Route 34 for 8 miles to the junction with County Route 29, then turn north onto Route 29 and continue for 10 miles to the refuge. Current eagle viewing conditions and information can be secured at the headquarters. Some parts of the refuge are closed during the Bald Eagle nesting season.

References: *Guide to the National Wildlife Refuges* (Anchor Press/Doubleday, 1979); *Birding Minnesota* (Falcon/Globe Pequot Press, 1996); Minnesota Department of Natural Resources at www.dnr.state.mn.us.

Wabasha EagleWatch (in Wabasha)

Raptors: Concentrations of Bald Eagles.

Viewing Season: November through March.

Watch Site Description: An observation deck and information center in downtown Wabasha along the Mississippi River.

Access: From the junction of U.S. Route 61 and State Route 60 at Wabasha, drive east on U.S. 61 (Pembroke Avenue) to its dead end at the EagleWatch Observation Deck and Information Center at Pembroke Avenue and Lawrence Boulevard in the downtown part of the city. Watch for Bald Eagles from the observation deck. The office of EagleWatch is located at 152 Main Street, about a block from the deck.

Reference: EagleWatch at www.eaglewatch.org.

Missouri

Lake Taneycomo (in Branson)

Raptors: Bald Eagles.

Viewing Season: November through February.

Watch Site Description: The shoreline of a lake in downtown Branson.

Access: In Branson, drive to the lakefront, park in an appropriate place, and look for eagles along the shoreline or aloft over the water. Do not closely approach perched eagles or cause them to fly.

Reference: Branson Connection at www.bransonconnection.com.

Mississippi Lock & Dam No. 24 (in Clarksville)

Raptors: Concentrations of Bald Eagles.

Viewing Season: Winter.

Watch Site Description: Exposed sections of the Mississippi River along the Clarksville business district or trees on nearby islands in midriver.

Access: From the junction of U.S. Route 54 and State Route 79 at Louisiana, drive south on Route 79 to Clarksville. Continue to the town's business district, park at any convenient location near the Mississippi River, and walk to the riverbank. Eagles often can be seen flying low over the water or perched in trees on nearby islands.

References: *American Birds*, 1966, 140: 32–34; *A Guide to Hawk Watching in North America* (Pennsylvania State University Press, 1979).

Squaw Creek National Wildlife Refuge (near Mound City)

Raptors: Large concentrations (maximum 263 per day) of wintering Bald Eagles.

Viewing Season: November through February. Peak numbers occur in January and February.

Watch Site
Description: Three areas of the refuge are frequented by eagles and can be studied from refuge roads and/or observation towers. An older stand of cottonwood forest near the southwestern end of the Northeast Pool is used as a night roost, and eagles can be seen flying into this area from the South Pool in early evening. During the day a smaller willow forest bordering the north edge of the South Pool is used as a loafing area by large numbers of eagles. Finally, eagles also use the South Pool as a hunting area.

Access: From Mound City, drive south for a few miles on Interstate 29 to the junction with U.S. Route 158, then continue west on U.S. 158 to the entrance to the refuge. Maps of the refuge are available at the headquarters building.

References: *Wintering of the Migrant Bald Eagle in the Lower 48 States* (National Agricultural Chemicals Association, 1976); *A Guide to Hawk Watching in North America* (Pennsylvania State University Press, 1979).

Swan Lake National Wildlife Refuge (near Sumner)

Raptors: Bald Eagles.

Viewing Season: Early October to late March, with peak numbers appearing in mid- to late December. Occasionally large numbers of eagles also appear in late February if a winter fish kill occurs.

Watch Site
Description: The levee road adjacent to the west side of Swan Lake connecting the refuge headquarters with State Route RA, or the high observation tower adjacent to the refuge headquarters. With the aid of binoculars or telescopes, you can see eagles feeding on the frozen lake. The best time to view the birds is morning.

Access: From Sumner, drive south on State Route RA for about 1 mile to the refuge sign and road leading to the refuge. Turn onto the entrance road and continue for about 1.5 miles to the headquarters building, watching along the way for eagles on Swan Lake. Ask at headquarters for current information on the status of Bald Eagles in the refuge.

References: *Wintering of the Migrant Bald Eagle in the Lower 48 States* (National Agricultural Chemicals Association, 1976); *A Guide to Hawk Watching in North America* (Pennsylvania State University Press, 1979).

Table Rock Lake (near Branson)

Raptors: Bald Eagles and Golden Eagles.

Viewing Season: November through February.

Watch Site
Description: Various campgrounds and other areas with views over an Army Corps of Engineers lake that attracts wintering Bald Eagles and some Golden Eagles.

Access: From Branson, drive west on many local roads—including Routes 13, 39, 76, 86, 165, and 265—that pass close to various parts of Table Rock Lake.

Reference: Branson Connection at www.bransonconnection.com.

Montana

Canyon Ferry Bald Eagle Watch (near Helena)

Raptors: Bald Eagles.

Viewing Season: October 30 through December 1.

Watch Site
Description: Bald Eagles feeding on spawning Kokanee Salmon along the shoreline of the Missouri River below the Canyon Ferry Dam. Stop at the Canyon Ferry Visitor Center and secure current information on approved eagle viewing areas. Use *only* those areas; do *not* enter closed areas along the riverbanks. Exhibits and information about Bald Eagle ecology also are available at the visitor center (open daily, 8:00 A.M. to 4:00 P.M., October 30 through December 1).

Access: From the junction of Interstate 15 and U.S. Routes 12/287 (exit 192) at Helena, drive east on U.S. 12/287 for 5.5 miles to its junction with State Route 284 (at a blinking light). Turn left (north) on Route 284 and continue past the Canyon Ferry Dam to the Canyon Ferry

Visitor Center (7661 Canyon Ferry Road, Helena, MT 59601), where current eagle watching information (and restrictions) can be secured.

Reference: Bureau of Land Management at www.mt.blm.gov.

Nebraska

Gavins Point Dam (near Crofton)

Raptors: Bald Eagles.

Viewing Season: March.

Watch Site Description: A visitor center at the Gavins Point Dam from which you can view Bald Eagles without disturbing them.

Access: From the junction of State Routes 12 and 121 near Crofton, drive north on Route 121 for approximately 9 miles to the Gavins Point Dam. Follow signs there to the visitor center.

Reference: *Nebraska Wildlife Viewing Guide* (Falcon Publishing, 1997).

Lake Ogallala (near Ogallala)

Raptors: Bald Eagles.

Viewing Season: Mid-December to late February or early March.

Watch Site Description: An eagle observation building overlooking the shoreline of Lake Ogallala and the Kingsley Dam. The observatory is open Saturday and Sunday (8:00 A.M. to 4:00 P.M.) and by appointment; call (308) 284–2332.

Access: From the junction of U.S. Route 26 and State Routes 61/92 north of Ogallala, drive north on Routes 61/92 for a few miles to Lake Ogallala and the Kingsley Dam and Bald Eagle viewing facility. An access road leads from Routes 61/92 to the Kingsley Bald Eagle Viewing Facility below the south end of the dam.

References: *Nebraska Wildlife Viewing Guide* (Falcon Publishing, 1997); Central Nebraska Public Power and Irrigation District at www.cnppid.com/eagle.html.

Ponca State Park (near Ponca)

Raptors: Bald Eagles and Turkey Vultures.

Viewing Season: Winter for Bald Eagles; summer for Turkey Vultures.

Watch Site Description: Forest overlooking a section of the Missouri River. Bald Eagles can be seen by looking overhead during winter, and Turkey Vultures are sometimes seen overhead during summer. Inquire at the park office for the best current opportunities and locations.

Access: From the junction of State Route 12 and Spur Route 26E at Ponca, drive north on Route 26E for about 2 miles to the park's entrance. Enter the park and drive to the park office, where you can secure current Bald Eagle viewing information along with park literature and trail maps.

Reference: *Nebraska Wildlife Viewing Guide* (Falcon Publishing, 1997).

Nevada

Stillwater Wildlife Management Area (near Fallon)

Raptors: Wintering Bald Eagles.

Viewing Season: December through February.

Watch Site Description: Large dead cottonwood trees near open water along Indian Lake.

Access: From Fallon, drive east on U.S. Route 50 to Stillwater Road, then continue on Stillwater Road following the signs to the refuge. Vehicles may not be allowed in the refuge, thus requiring exploration by foot.

References: *Wintering of the Migrant Bald Eagle in the Lower 48 States* (National Agricultural Chemicals Association, 1976); *A*

Guide to Hawk Watching in North America (Pennsylvania
State University Press, 1979); *Nevada Wildlife Viewing
Guide* (Falcon Press Publishing, 1993).

New Jersey

Kittatinny Point Visitor Center
(in Delaware Water Gap National Recreation Area)

Raptors: Bald Eagles.

Viewing Season: Winter.

**Watch Site
Description:** A visitor center along Interstate 80 in Delaware Water
Gap National Recreation Area.

Access: From Stroudsburg, Pennsylvania, drive east on Interstate
80 into nearby New Jersey and the Delaware Water Gap
National Recreation Areas. The visitor center is located
along I–80 as you drive through the water gap.

Reference: *Bald Eagles on the Upper Delaware* (Delaware Water Gap
National Recreation Area information sheet, 1998).

New Mexico

Caballo Lake State Park (near Truth or Consequences)

Raptors: Bald Eagles.

Viewing Season: October through February.

**Watch Site
Description:** A narrow Rio Grande reservoir with the Caballo Mountains on the east and the Chihuahuan Desert around the
park.

Access: From exit 59 of Interstate 25 approximately 16 miles
south of Truth or Consequences, leave I–25 and follow
directional signs to Caballo Lake State Park on the left.
Enter the park and explore the shoreline and waters of
Caballo Lake, looking for Bald Eagles.

Reference: *New Mexico Wildlife Viewing Guide* (Falcon Publishing, second edition, 2000).

Maxwell National Wildlife Refuge (near Maxwell)

Raptors: Bald Eagles.

Viewing Season: Winter.

Watch Site Description: Refuge areas that are open or exposed, such as grassland and old homesites, particularly west of Lake 14 and north of Lake 12.

Access: From the junction of Interstate 25 and State Route 505 at Maxwell, turn west onto Route 505 and continue for about 2 miles to a road leading to the refuge headquarters, where current eagle watching information can be secured.

References: *Wintering of the Migrant Bald Eagle in the Lower 48 States* (National Agricultural Chemicals Association, 1976); *A Guide to Hawk Watching in North America* (Pennsylvania State University Press, 1979).

Navajo Lake State Park—San Juan River Unit (near Aztec)

Raptors: Bald Eagles.

Viewing Season: Winter.

Watch Site Description: A section of the San Juan River flowing through a canyon with adjacent forested mesas.

Access: From Aztec, drive east on U.S. Route 550 to the junction with State Route 173. Turn right onto Route 173 (marked by a sign for Navajo Dam State Park). Continue for approximately 19 miles to the junction with State Route 511. Turn left at the T intersection onto Route 511 and continue for about 2 miles to a small adobe Catholic church. Turn left onto a paved road at the church and continue for 0.5 mile to the river. Look for wintering Bald Eagles there.

Reference: *New Mexico Wildlife Viewing Guide* (Falcon Publishing, second edition, 2000).

New York

Barryville

Raptors: Bald Eagles.

Viewing Season: Winter.

Watch Site Description: The public access area along the Delaware River at Barryville along State Route 97.

Access: At Barryville, drive to the public access area to the Delaware River and observe from there.

Reference: *Bald Eagles on the Upper Delaware* (Delaware Water Gap National Recreation Area information sheet, 1998).

Basherkill Marsh (near Westbrookville)

Raptors: Bald Eagles.

Viewing Season: Mid-March to mid-April.

Watch Site Description: An extensive freshwater marsh used regularly by eagles before their spring migrations begin.

Access: From Port Jervis, drive north on U.S. Route 209 for about 15 miles to the town of Westbrookville. Drive through the town and continue north on U.S. 209 for about 2 miles, then turn right onto an asphalt road that takes you to the marsh.

Alternatively, from exit 113 off State Route 17 near the village of Wurtsboro, drive south on U.S. Route 209 for about 2 miles, then turn left onto an asphalt road that also leads to the marsh. Observe from suitable locations around the marsh. Do not attempt to approach eagles closely.

References: *Birding*, 1977, 9 (6): 264s–264t; *A Guide to Hawk Watching in North America* (Pennsylvania State University Press, 1979).

Callicoon

Raptors: Bald Eagles.

Viewing Season: Winter.

Watch Site Description: The confluence of Callicoon Creek and the Delaware River at Callicoon.

Access: From Callicoon, drive south on State Route 97 for a short distance to the confluence of Callicoon Creek and the Delaware River.

Reference: *Bald Eagles on the Upper Delaware* (Delaware Water Gap National Recreation Area information sheet, 1998).

Hudson River (Kingston to Croton-on-Hudson)

Raptors: Bald Eagles.

Viewing Season: December to mid-March, with peak numbers in January and February.

Watch Site Description: Various locations along the Hudson River and its shorelines, and on commuter trains running beside the Hudson River from Albany and Croton-on-Hudson.

- Norrie Point State Park near Hyde Park.
- West Point (Constitution Island from North Dock).
- Iona Island Overlook from U.S. Route 202.
- Riverfront Park in Peekskill.
- Charles Point and China Pier in Peekskill.
- Verplanck waterfront.
- George's Island Park parking area in Verplanck.
- Commuter trains running along the Hudson River between Albany and Croton-on-Hudson.

Access: Various roads parallel parts of the Hudson River between Kingston and Croton-on-Hudson. Consult a New York State road map, and also explore local side roads leading to the river. Riding commuter trains between Albany and Croton-on-Hudson also provides Bald Eagle watching opportunities during late autumn and winter.

Reference: New York State Department of Environmental Conservation at www.dec.state.ny.us.

Minisink Ford (opposite Lackawaxen, Pennsylvania)

Raptors: Bald Eagles.

Viewing Season: Winter.

**Watch Site
Description:** The Delaware River at Minisink Ford, at the southern end of State Route 97 and the confluence of the Delaware and Lackawaxen Rivers.

Access: At Minisink Ford on State Route 97, drive to any vantage point near the confluence of the Delaware and Lackawaxen Rivers and observe from there, or drive across the Delaware River into Pennsylvania and observe from the public access area to the river along Pennsylvania State Route 590.

Reference: *Bald Eagles on the Upper Delaware* (Delaware Water Gap National Recreation Area information sheet, 1998).

Mongaup Valley (between Rio and Mongaup Falls)

Raptors: Bald Eagles.

Viewing Season: Winter.

**Watch Site
Description:** Rio Reservoir and Mongaup Falls Reservoir along Plank Road northwest of State Route 42 in the Mongaup Valley between Mongaup and Mongaup Falls.

Access: From the junction of State Routes 42 and 97 north of Sparrowbush, drive north on Route 42 to the junction with Plank Road. Turn left onto Plank Road and continue to eagle viewing locations along the Rio and Mongaup Falls Reservoirs. There is an information and observation structure at the northern end of the Mongaup Falls Reservoir.

References: *Bald Eagles on the Upper Delaware* (Delaware Water Gap National Recreation Area information sheet, 1998); *New York Wildlife Viewing Guide* (Falcon Publishing, 1998).

Narrowsburg

Raptors: Bald Eagles.

Viewing Season: Winter.

Watch Site Description: The Delaware River at Narrowsburg.

Access: At Narrowsburg, drive to areas along State Routes 97 and 652 close to the Delaware River from which eagles can be seen.

References: *Bald Eagles on the Upper Delaware* (Delaware Water Gap National Recreation Area information sheet, 1998); *Eagles Among Us* (Eagle Institute, no date).

Pond Eddy

Raptors: Bald Eagles.

Viewing Season: Winter.

Watch Site Description: A public access area to the Delaware River, allowing observation of Bald Eagles along the river.

Access: From State Route 97 at Pond Eddy, drive to the Delaware River public access area.

Reference: *Bald Eagles on the Upper Delaware* (Delaware Water Gap National Recreation Area information sheet, 1998).

Rondout Reservoir (near Ellenville)

Raptors: Wintering Bald Eagles.

Viewing Season: Mid-December to mid-March.

Watch Site Description: Either of two state roads closely paralleling the shoreline of the Rondout Reservoir. Eagles perch in trees along the shoreline of the reservoir at the northwest end, or fish in open water at the nearby power plant.

Access: From Ellenville, drive north on U.S. Route 209 to the junction with State Route 55 at Napanoch. Then turn left (northwest) onto Route 55 and continue for about 5 miles to a Y junction of State Routes 55 and 55A. Take either route and drive along the reservoir shoreline, looking for eagles at the northwest end. *Warning:* Do not attempt to approach eagles on foot. There are severe state and federal penalties for molesting these birds.

Reference: *A Guide to Hawk Watching in North America* (Pennsylvania State University Press, 1979).

Oklahoma

Beavers Bend State Park (near Broken Bow)

Raptors: Bald Eagles.

Viewing Season: November through February.

Watch Site Description: A complex of 14,240 combined lake acres consisting of part of the Mountain Fork River, and other areas, from which Bald Eagles are observed during winter. Eagle watchers gather at the area's nature center, which coordinates eagle watching activities.

Access: From Broken Bow, drive north on U.S. Route 259 to the junction with State Route 259A. Turn right (east) onto Route 259A and continue to the entrance to Beavers Bend State Park. Enter, go to the headquarters or ranger station, and secure directions to the nature center, where current information about Bald Eagle viewing is available. You can telephone the nature center at (580) 494–6556.

Reference: Oklahoma Department of Wildlife Conservation at www.wildlifedepartment.com/eag.htm.

Chickasaw National Recreation Area (near Sulphur)

Raptors: Bald Eagles.

Viewing Season: January.

Watch Site Description: The Travertine Nature Center in the Chickasaw National Recreation Area offers a two-part Bald Eagle viewing program that includes an indoor eagle introduction presentation followed by eagle viewing field trips to nearby Lake Arbuckle.

Access: From U.S. Route 177 in Sulphur, follow directional signs to the nearby Travertine Nature Center in the Chickasaw National Recreation Area. Telephone the Travertine Nature Center at (405) 622–3165 for current details on Bald Eagle watching tours.

Reference: Oklahoma Department of Wildlife Conservation at www.wildlifedepartment.com/eag.htm.

Fort Gibson Dam and Reservoir (near Okay)

Raptors: Bald Eagles.

Viewing Season: January.

Watch Site Description: The parking area below the long Fort Gibson Dam. On selected dates in mid-January, the Indian Nations Audubon Society has representatives present with spotting scopes to assist eagle watchers in seeing and understanding these birds, which feed in open water below the dam and roost in trees beside the river below the reservoir.

Access: From Okay, drive east on State Route 251 for about 6 miles to the parking area below the dam.

Reference: Oklahoma Department of Wildlife Conservation at www.wildlifedepartment.com/eag.htm.

Kaw Lake (near Ponca City)

Raptors: Bald Eagles.

Viewing Season: January.

Watch Site Description: The shoreline of Kaw Lake as viewed from roads adjacent to the lake. Various state and federal governmental agencies, and nonprofit wildlife organizations, assist visitors wanting to see Bald Eagles.

Access: Kaw Lake is located east of Ponca City and is reached by local roads. Secure further directions in Ponca City or Kaw City. Telephone the Oklahoma Wildlife Diversity

Program at (405) 521–4616 for current details regarding formal Bald Eagle watching programs at Kaw Lake.

Reference: Oklahoma Department of Wildlife Conservation at www.wildlifedepartment.com/eag.htm.

Keystone Reservoir Dam (near Sand Springs)

Raptors: Bald Eagles.

Viewing Season: January.

Watch Site Description: A large flood-control facility. Bald Eagle viewing is done from the parking lot of the Watchable Wildlife Area near the office of the U.S. Army Corps of Engineers, located on the north side of the Arkansas River near the Keystone Reservoir Dam. Representatives of the Tulsa Audubon Society are present on selected dates with spotting scopes to assist eagle watchers seeing the birds and understanding them.

Access: From Tulsa, drive west on U.S. Route 64 for approximately 15 miles to Keystone State Park and the Keystone Reservoir Dam, operated by the U.S. Army Corps of Engineers. The parking lot of the wildlife management area is located east of the office of the Army Corps of Engineers. For further information call the Corps of Engineers office at (918) 865–2621.

Reference: Oklahoma Department of Wildlife Conservation at www.wildlifedepartment.com/eag.htm.

Lake Texoma State Park (near Madill)

Raptors: Bald Eagles.

Viewing Season: January.

Watch Site Description: Created by the U.S. Army Corps of Engineers, this large lake attracts migrant and wintering Bald Eagles. The staff of the Two Rivers Nature Center, located in the park, coordinates Saturday Bald Eagle watching tours for which a fee and reservations are required. All tours depend upon favorable prevailing weather conditions.

Access: From Madill, drive south on U.S. Route 177 to the junction with State Route 106. Turn east onto State Route 106 and continue a few miles to Lake Texoma State Park, where further details about Bald Eagle watching can be secured. Telephone the Two Rivers Nature Center at (580) 564–2311, ext. 157, for additional details.

Reference: Oklahoma Department of Wildlife Conservation at www.wildlifedepartment.com/eag.htm.

Salt Plains National Wildlife Refuge (near Jet)

Raptors: Concentrations of Bald Eagles and Golden Eagles.

Viewing Season: Winter.

Watch Site Description: Marshes, ponds, and fields in a wildlife refuge.

Access: From the junction of U.S. Route 64 and State Route 38 at the town of Jet, drive north on State Route 38 to a point 2 miles south of its junction with State Route 11, then turn west and continue for a mile to the refuge headquarters. Signs direct visitors to the refuge. Secure current eagle watching information at the headquarters.

Reference: *A Guide to Hawk Watching in North America* (Pennsylvania State University Press, 1979).

Sequoyah National Wildlife Refuge (near Keota)

Raptors: Bald Eagles.

Viewing Season: Autumn through spring.

Watch Site Description: A large wildlife refuge that attracts considerable numbers of migrant, and sometimes wintering, Bald Eagles. These feed on the huge numbers of migrant waterfowl attracted to the refuge's habitat.

Access: From Keota on State Route 9, drive north on a local road following signs into the refuge.

References: None.

Oregon

Bear Valley National Wildlife Refuge (near Worden)

Raptors: Bald Eagles.

Viewing Season: December to mid-March.

**Watch Site
Description:** A 4,200-acre old-growth, forested hillside used by as many as 300 Bald Eagles as a major roost site. *The refuge is closed to public entry.* Observe from the adjacent shoulder of the road, *outside* the refuge, looking toward the west and Hamaker Mountain. Bald Eagles will approach you heading east, passing overhead and along adjacent ridges. The best eagle viewing times are from approximately half an hour before sunrise to one hour after sunrise.

Access: From Worden, drive south on U.S. Route 97 a short distance to the junction with Keno–Worden Road. Turn west onto Keno–Worden Road and continue to a railroad crossing. Cross the tracks and after a short distance turn left onto an unpaved road. Continue ahead on this unpaved road for about 0.5 mile, then park on the shoulder of the road. Observe from there.

Reference: www.klamathnwr.org/eagle.html.

Pennsylvania

Delaware Water Gap National Recreation Area (north of Stroudsburg)

Raptors: Bald Eagles.

Viewing Season: Winter.

**Watch Site
Description:** Several Bald Eagle watching locations with public access to the Delaware River are located in the Pennsylvania portion of the Delaware Water Gap National Recreation Area:

- Bushkill boat access area.

- Dingmans Ferry public access area.

- Milford Beach public access area.

- Smithfield Beach public access area.

Access: In Pennsylvania, U.S. Route 209 north of Stroudsburg provides public access areas to several sections of the Delaware Water Gap National Recreation Area.

Reference: *Bald Eagles on the Upper Delaware* (Delaware Water Gap National Recreation Area information sheet, 1998).

Lackawaxen (opposite Minisink Ford, New York)

Raptors: Bald Eagles.

Viewing Season: Winter.

Watch Site Description: The confluence of the Delaware and Lackawaxen Rivers near Lackawaxen, Pennsylvania, where Bald Eagles gather to feed in open water during winter.

Access: In Lackawaxen on State Route 590, drive north to the confluence of the Delaware and Lackawaxen Rivers and public access areas from which eagle watching is possible.

Reference: *Bald Eagles on the Upper Delaware* (Delaware Water Gap National Recreation Area information sheet, 1998).

Middle Creek Wildlife Management Area (near Kleinfeltersville)

Raptors: Nesting Bald Eagles.

Viewing Season: Late winter through summer.

Watch Site Description: A 6,254-acre area of ponds, fields, woodland, creeks, and other wetlands owned and managed by the Pennsylvania Game Commission. At least one pair of Bald Eagles nest on the property. Inquire at the visitor center and head-quarters about current eagle viewing opportunities and locations.

Access: From the junction of State Routes 501 and 897 at Schaefferstown, drive east on Route 897 for several miles to the village of Kleinfeltersville. Turn right at the sign pointing to the Middle Creek Wildlife Management Area and continue a few miles to a sign on the right pointing to the headquarters and visitor center. Turn right and follow the access road to the parking lot. Ask in the visitor center about current Bald Eagle viewing opportunities and locations. Excellent restroom facilities are available in this building, which also contains a small museum. The building is open Tuesday through Saturday 8:00 A.M. to 4:00 P.M., and on Sunday from noon to 5:00 P.M., February 1 to Thanksgiving. The visitor center is closed on Monday.

References: None.

Pymatuning Waterfowl Area (near Linesville)

Raptors: Nesting Bald Eagles.

Viewing Season: Spring and summer.

Watch Site Description: Large dead trees in the vicinity of the Pennsylvania Game Commission's waterfowl museum on Ford Island.

Access: From Linesville, drive south on an unnumbered road to the waterfowl museum on Ford Island. Here you can secure information on current Bald Eagle watching opportunities.

Reference: *A Guide to Hawk Watching in North America* (Pennsylvania State University Press, 1979).

Shohola Recreation Area (near Shohola Falls)

Raptors: Bald Eagles.

Viewing Season: Winter.

Watch Site Description: A Pennsylvania Game Commission recreation area with a lake that attracts Bald Eagles during winter when the lake is not frozen.

Access: From Shohola Falls, drive south a few miles on U.S. Route 6 to the Shohola Recreation Area operated by the Pennsylvania Game Commission. Enter the area and check for Bald Eagles along the shoreline of the lake, perched on trees near the shoreline, or flying overhead.

Reference: *Bald Eagles on the Upper Delaware* (Delaware Water Gap National Recreation Area information sheet, 1998).

South Dakota

Fort Randall Dam (near Pickstown)

Raptors: Large concentrations of Bald Eagles. Golden Eagles and Ferruginous Hawks are also seen, along with lesser numbers of Northern Harriers, Sharp-shinned Hawks, Red-tailed Hawks, Rough-legged Hawks, and American Kestrels.

Viewing Season: November through March, particularly December and early January for Bald Eagles.

Watch Site Description: Areas immediately below the Fort Randall Dam, trees on the eastern bank adjacent to the Spillway Road, large trees on the western bank near the Randall Creek Campground, and the tailraces visible from Tailrace Road. *Do not leave your vehicle or attempt to approach Bald Eagles closely.*

Access: From Pickstown, drive west on U.S. Routes 18/281 for a short distance to the dam. Stop at the Army Corps of Engineers Ranger Station for additional information and maps of the area, as well as current eagle watching opportunities.

References: *A Guide to Hawk Watching in North America* (Pennsylvania State University Press, 1979); *Eyeing Eagles in South Dakota* (Bald Eagle Awareness Day Committee and South Dakota Department of Game, Fish and Parks, 2003).

Lake Andes National Wildlife Refuge (near Lake Andes)

Raptors: Wintering Bald Eagles.

Viewing Season: October through March.

Watch Site Description: A nationally significant winter habitat for Bald Eagles. Eagle viewing is done from the east shore of Lake Andes amid cottonwood bottomlands. *Do not leave your vehicle or attempt to approach Bald Eagles closely.*

Access: From Lake Andes, drive north for 1 mile, passing grain elevators, then turn east and continue for 6 miles on a hard-surfaced county road that crosses Lake Andes from west to east and continues to the refuge visitor center. Obtain current eagle viewing information at the visitor center.

Reference: *Eyeing Eagles in South Dakota* (Bald Eagle Awareness Day Committee and South Dakota Department of Game, Fish and Parks, 2003).

Lake Sharpe (near Pierre)

Raptors: Wintering Bald Eagles.

Viewing Season: October through March.

Watch Site Description: An eagle viewing driving route marked by directional signs through a remnant cottonwood forest ecosystem.

Access: From Pierre, drive north on State Route 1804 on the left side of the Missouri River to the South Dakota Game, Fish and Parks Downstream Area below Oahe Dam. Then follow the EAGLE VIEWING ROUTE signs.

Reference: *Eyeing Eagles in South Dakota* (Bald Eagle Awareness Day Committee and South Dakota Department of Game, Fish and Parks, 2003).

Tennessee

Cross Creeks National Wildlife Refuge (near Dover)

Raptors: Small numbers of wintering Bald Eagles.

Viewing Season: Winter.

Watch Site Description: A large refuge consisting of Barkley Lake, sections of the Cumberland River, ponds, marshes, and fields.

Access: From Dover, drive east on State Route 49 for about 2 miles, then continue north for about 1 mile on a county road. Signs point to the refuge.

References: *A Guide to Bird Finding East of the Mississippi* (Oxford University Press, 1977); *A Guide to Hawk Watching in North America* (Pennsylvania State University Press, 1979).

Reelfoot Lake State Park and Reelfoot National Wildlife Refuge (near Tiptonville)

Raptors: Concentrations of wintering Bald Eagles.

Viewing Season: November to mid-March; the greatest numbers of eagles are usually seen in January and February.

Watch Site Description: A large lake with islands, wooded swamps, and other aquatic habitats. Eagles occur anywhere at the lake, especially along the shoreline and soaring over open water.

Access: From the town of Tiptonville, follow State Routes 21 and 22 around the lake, keeping watch for Bald Eagles aloft or along the shoreline. Formal eagle viewing tours are organized by naturalists at Reelfoot State Park daily and on weekends in winter. For details, contact the naturalist at Reelfoot Lake State Park, Tiptonville, TN 38079.

References: *Wintering of the Migrant Bald Eagle in the Lower 48 States* (National Agricultural Chemicals Association, 1976); *A Guide to Hawk Watching in North America* (Pennsylvania State University Press, 1979); *Guide to Birdwatching Sites/Eastern U.S.* (National Geographic Society, 1999).

Texas

Fairfield Lake State Park (near Fairfield)

Raptors: Bald Eagles.

Viewing Season: November through February.

Watch Site Description: A park containing a 2,400-acre lake and surrounding woodland, pastures, and fields. Warm-water discharges from an outlet from a steam electrical generation facility on the north shore of the lake attract fifteen to twenty Bald Eagles from November through February, with largest eagle concentrations occurring during December. Free Bald Eagle Boat Tours are offered by the park staff to the public four or more times each month (November through February), thus providing birders and other interested persons opportunities to see eagles without disturbing these majestic birds. For detailed information regarding the boat tour schedules, contact Fairfield Lake State Park, Route 2, Box 912, Fairfield, TX 75840; (903) 389–2130.

Access: From the junction of U.S. Route 84 and Farm-to-Market (FM) Road 488, near Fairfield, drive east on FM 488 to the junction with FM 2570 and continue north on it to the junction with FM 3285. Turn east onto FM 3285 and continue to the park entrance. Enter the park and follow directions provided by the park staff for participating on Bald Eagle Boat Tours.

Reference: *Birding Texas* (Falcon/Globe Pequot Press, 1998).

Lake O'the Pines (near Jefferson)

Raptors: Bald Eagles.

Viewing Season: Winter.

Watch Site Description: The overlook from which observers look down on the Ferrells Bridge Dam at the Buckhorn Creek area of Lake O'the Pines.

Access: From Jefferson, drive west for about 9 miles on Farm-to-Market (FM) Road 729 to its junction with FM 726, then continue south on FM 726 to the Ferrells Bridge Dam overlook at Buckhorn Creek.

Reference: *Birding Texas* (Falcon/Globe Pequot Press, 1998).

Wright Patman Lake (near Texarkana)

Raptors: Wintering Bald Eagles.

Viewing Season: January.

Watch Site
Description: A U.S. Army Corps of Engineers lake and dam with various parks adjacent to parts of the lake. Wintering eagles are seen in the vicinity of the dam.

Access: From Texarkana, drive south for about 9 miles on State Route 59 to the entrance to the lake's dam area. A local Audubon chapter monitors Bald Eagle numbers each January.

Reference: *Birding Texas* (Falcon/Globe Pequot Press, 1998).

Utah

Bear River Migratory Bird Refuge (near Brigham City)

Raptors: Wintering Bald Eagles.

Viewing Season: Early November through April, with peak numbers being seen in early December and again in February and March.

Watch Site
Description: Ice floes and open-water channels where Carp gather along the refuge's tour route.

Access: From Brigham City, drive west for about 15 miles to the refuge headquarters, where the 12-mile-long tour route through the refuge begins. Stop at the headquarters and secure current eagle watching information before beginning the tour.

References: *Wintering of the Migrant Bald Eagle in the Lower 48 States* (National Agricultural Chemicals Association, 1976); *A*

Guide to Hawk Watching in North America (Pennsylvania State University Press, 1979).

Willard Canyon Bald Eagle Roost

Raptors: Concentrations of Bald Eagles.

Viewing Season: Mid-November to late March, with the best eagle viewing from late February to mid-March.

Watch Site Description: Dense stands of Douglas fir on the 6,000- to 9,000-foot slopes of rugged Willard Canyon. Eagle watchers should always exercise great caution and restraint. Watch the birds from safe distances (0.25 mile or more away) to avoid disturbing them at their roost site. The best eagle watching opportunities can be enjoyed during the afternoon and early evening before sunset.

Access: From Brigham City, drive south on U.S. Route 89 for about 6 miles to the town of Willard. Turn left (east) onto 200 South Street and drive through town. Continue on the paved road (1 mile or less) as it winds northeastward toward the mouth of Willard Canyon Park. Park along the side of the road at a creekbed. Then hike up the narrow portion of the canyon, or observe from the bench region (an elevated area) just north of the canyon's mouth.

References: *Wilson Bulletin*, 1964, 76 (2): 186–187; *A Guide to Hawk Watching in North America* (Pennsylvania State University Press, 1979).

Vermont

Button Bay (near Vergennes)

Raptors: Bald Eagles, Northern Harriers, Red-tailed Hawks, Rough-legged Hawks, and American Kestrels.

Viewing Season: March.

Watch Site Description: A boat-launch overlook providing views of Button Bay and Bald Eagles perched on trees along the shore of the bay, on ice in the bay, or sometimes flying overhead. Other raptors frequent fields near the bay.

Access: From Vergennes, drive south for 0.2 mile on State Route 22A from the Otter Creek Bridge to the junction with Panton Road. Turn right (west) onto Panton Road and continue for 1.4 miles to the junction with Basin Harbor Road. Turn right onto Basin Harbor Road and continue to the entrance to Button Bay State Park. Then drive 0.4 mile farther to the entrance road. A boat launch and overlook on the right provide views of the bay and Bald Eagles in the bay area.

Reference: *Birdwatching in Vermont* (University Press of New England, 2002).

Virginia

Caledon Natural Area (near Fredericksburg)

Raptors: Bald Eagles.

Viewing Season: Mid-June to Labor Day.

Watch Site Description: A 2,579-acre natural area containing part of the Potomac River, marshland, and upland woodland. Guided Bald Eagle viewing tours are available by reservation. Some areas of the Caledon Natural Area are closed to public entry; please do not enter these areas.

Access: From Fredericksburg, drive east on State Route 218 to the Caledon Natural Area. Telephone the Virginia Department of Conservation and Recreation at (703) 663–3861 for additional information and Bald Eagle viewing tour reservations.

Reference: *Virginia Wildlife Viewing Guide* (Falcon Press Publishing, 1994).

John H. Kerr Reservoir (near Boydton)

Raptors: Bald Eagles.

Viewing Season: Winter.

Watch Site
Description: Open water in the area below the U.S. Army Corps of Engineers' John H. Kerr Reservoir Dam. The best eagle viewing time is early in the morning.

Access: From Boydton, drive east on U.S. Route 58 for 6 miles to the junction with State Route 4. Turn onto Route 4 and continue south to the dam. For current eagle watching and other information, drive to the visitor center located on State Route 678 about 0.5 mile southwest of the dam.

Reference: *Virginia Wildlife Viewing Guide* (Falcon Press Publishing, 1994).

Mason Neck National Wildlife Refuge (near Lorton)

Raptors: Bald Eagles.

Viewing Season: Winter.

Watch Site
Description: A 2,227-acre wildlife refuge that is part of a peninsula on the shore of the Potomac River with upland and marsh habitats. Dozens of Bald Eagles inhabit the area during winter, providing favorable eagle watching opportunities.

Access: From the junction of U.S. Route 1 and Gunston Hall Road (State Route 242), drive east on Route 242 for approximately 5 miles to the refuge entrance. Enter and stop at the refuge office for current Bald Eagle viewing information and literature about the refuge.

Reference: *Virginia Wildlife Viewing Guide* (Falcon Press Publishing, 1994).

Washington

North Cascades National Park Service Complex (near Burlington)

Raptors: Wintering Bald Eagles.

Viewing Season: Late October to mid-March, with the largest numbers of eagles appearing in late December and January.

Watch Site
Description: The shoreline of the Skagit River in the western corridor of North Cascades National Park Complex, as well as portions of the river just west of the park. *Warning:* There are severe federal and state penalties for molesting eagles. Do *not* approach them closely.

Access: From the junction of Interstate 5 and State Route 20 at Burlington, drive east on Route 20 to North Cascades National Park. This road parallels the Skagit River for some 43 miles and provides good eagle watching opportunities at various locations along the shore. See information for the Skagit River Bald Eagle Natural Area and Upper Skagit Bald Eagle Festival (below) for additional eagle viewing opportunities.

References: *Wintering of the Migrant Bald Eagle in the Lower 48 States* (National Agricultural Chemicals Association, 1976); *Washington Wildlife*, 1977, 29 (3): 9–13; *A Guide to Hawk Watching in North America* (Pennsylvania State University Press, 1979).

Olympic National Park Area (Olympic Peninsula)

Raptors: Wintering Bald Eagles.

Viewing Season: Mid-November to late February.

Watch Site
Description: An unusually wild and scenic ocean coastline along the Olympic Peninsula, especially between Rialto Beach and Cape Alava where large numbers of Bald Eagles occur. The shorelines of the Bogachiel, Hoh, Queets, and Quinault Rivers—which flow westward from the Olympic Mountains into the Pacific Ocean—are also suitable eagle watching areas.

Access: U.S. Route 101 circles part of the peninsula and the Olympic National Park area, and provides access to various parts of the peninsula via interconnecting roads.

• *Rialto Beach.* From Forks, drive north on U.S. 101 for about 2 miles, then turn left (west) onto the county road leading to Mora. This road also leads to Rialto Beach.

• *Cape Alava.* From Port Angeles, drive west on State Route 112 for about 53 miles, then turn southwest on the Ozette Road and follow it for another 20 miles to the Lake Ozette Ranger Station. From there, walk for about 3 miles to Cape Alava. *Caution:* When hiking the beaches in winter, be alert for weather changes, which frequently bring gales and severe drops in temperatures. Particular care also should be taken to avoid being trapped between headland cliffs and incoming tides that provide no escape. Always consult local tide schedules before attempting to hike long distances on the beach.

- *Rivers.* Those flowing into the Pacific Ocean within the park can be reached by driving north or south on U.S. 101 and turning east or west, as appropriate for visiting eagle watching sites at river shorelines.

References: *Wintering of the Migrant Bald Eagle in the Lower 48 States* (National Agricultural Chemicals Association, 1976); *A Guide to Hawk Watching in North America* (Pennsylvania State University Press, 1979).

San Juan Islands National Historic Park

Raptors: Bald Eagles and seventeen other raptor species.

Viewing Season: Mid-November through late February, with the largest numbers of Bald Eagles seen in mid-January. Some eagles can also be seen during other seasons.

Watch Site Description: Open grassland around the American Camp Unit bounded by forest and seacoast.

Access: From Anacortes, Washington, or Sidney, British Columbia, board the Washington State Ferry and cross to San Juan Island. At the island town of Friday Harbor, drive south on a well-marked county road for 6.25 miles to the park's American Camp Unit, where Bald Eagles can be observed. Eagle watching also can be enjoyed on other sections of the island, which is reachable by airplane and private boat as well.

References: *Wintering of the Migrant Bald Eagle in the Lower 48 States* (National Agricultural Chemicals Association, 1976); *Washington Wildlife*, 1977, 29 (3): 9–13; *A Guide to Hawk Watching in North America* (Pennsylvania State University Press, 1979).

Skagit River Bald Eagle Natural Area (near Rockport)

Raptors: Large numbers of wintering Bald Eagles feeding on carcasses of spawned-out salmon.

Viewing Season: Late October to mid-March, with the largest numbers of birds appearing from late December to mid-February.

Watch Site Description: A 1,500-acre refuge located in northwestern Washington along a 7-mile-long protected corridor of the Skagit River between Rockport and Marblemount. The following are designated Bald Eagle watching locations:

- *Howard Miller Steelhead Park* in Rockport. Observe from the sidewalk of the bridge over the Skagit River when eagles are feeding on a gravel bed of the river, or perched on trees on the south side of the river. "Eagle Watcher" volunteers are present here on weekends during Bald Eagle viewing season to assist visitors and answer questions. Look for yellow EAGLE WATCHER signs marking their stations.

- *Marblemount Fish Hatchery.* Bald Eagle watching tours are offered at the fish hatchery on Saturday and Sunday from the last weekend in December through mid-February. Eagle Watcher volunteers are present here on weekends during Bald Eagle viewing season to assist visitors and answer questions. Look for yellow EAGLE WATCHER signs marking their stations.

- *Newhalem Visitor Center.* A visitor center with geology and plant exhibits, hiking trails, a scenic vista, a gift shop, and more.

- *Sutter Creek Rest Area.* This roadside rest area parallels the Skagit River and provides excellent Bald Eagle viewing when the birds are on gravel beds, or perching on trees, along the south side of the river. Eagle Watcher volunteers are present here on weekends during Bald Eagle viewing season to assist visitors and answer questions. Look for yellow EAGLE WATCHER signs marking their stations.

Bald Eagles generally feed from dawn to about 11:00 A.M. at various locations along the Skagit River, and return to roosting areas (which should *not* be visited, nor the birds disturbed) late in the afternoon. On cloudy days the birds tend to perch for many hours loafing and conserving energy. On sunny afternoons, however, eagles are active and sometimes thermal soar overhead.

Access: The entrance to Howard Miller Steelhead Park is in Rockport along State Route 530, where parking near the entrance also is available. The Marblemount Fish Hatchery is reached by driving to Marblemount, crossing the bridge over the Skagit River, then following Cascade River Road north for 1 mile to Rockport Cascade Road. Turn right onto Rockport Cascade Road and continue across the Cascade River to the next road to the right. Turn right and continue to the Marblemount Fish Hatchery. To visit the Newhalem Visitor Center, drive east from Rockport on State Route 20, following the Skagit River, to the Ross Lake Recreation Area and the Newhalem Visitor Center about 13 miles east of Marblemount. Drive carefully due to ice and snow conditions. The Sutter Creek Rest Area is located near Rockport along Route 20 at milepost 100. *Warning:* Do not park on narrow road shoulders or block road traffic.

References: *Wintering of the Migrant Bald Eagle in the Lower 48 States* (National Agricultural Chemicals Association, 1976); *Washington Wildlife*, 1977, 29 (3): 9–13; *A Guide to Hawk Watching in North America* (Pennsylvania State University Press, 1979); *The Bald Eagle of Alaska, BC and Washington* (Hancock House Publishers, 2003); Upper Skagit Bald Eagle Festival at www.skagiteagle.org.

Upper Skagit Bald Eagle Festival (in Rockport)

Raptors: Bald Eagles.

Viewing Season: Late December to mid-February.

Watch Site Description: The Upper Skagit Bald Eagle Festival takes place annually at the Skagit River Bald Eagle Interpretive Center from late December to mid-February. The center features photographs of Bald Eagles, exhibits, guest speakers, children's activities, and a gift shop.

Access: In Rockport at the junction of State Route 20 and Alfred Street, drive south on Alfred Street for 1 block to the Rockport Fire Hall in which the Upper Skagit Bald Eagle Festival is based. The center is open Friday through Monday, 10:00 A.M. to 4:00 P.M. For current details, call (360) 853–7283.

References: *The Bald Eagle of Alaska, BC and Washington* (Hancock House Publishers, 2003); Upper Skagit Bald Eagle Festival at www.skagiteagle.org.

West Virginia

Potomac Eagle Scenic Railroad Train (near Romney)

Raptors: Bald Eagles.

Viewing Season: Spring and autumn.

Watch Site Description: A three-hour train ride north along the South Branch of the Potomac River through a beautiful mountain landscape with historic farms and a narrow valley called "The Trough." There is a 90 percent chance of seeing at least one Bald Eagle, or at least several eagle nests, on these train rides.

Access: Tourist trains depart from the Wappocomo Station, located on State Route 28 about 1.5 miles north of the town of Romney. For more details, and tickets, contact the Potomac Eagle Ticket Office, 2306 35th Street, Parkersburg, WV 26104-2242; (304) 424–0736.

References: *West Virginia Wildlife Viewing Guide* (Falcon Publishing, 1999); Potomac Eagle Scenic Railroad at http://wvweb.com/potomaceagle/textonly.html.

Wisconsin

Cassville

Raptors: Concentrations of Bald Eagles.

Viewing Season: Mid-December through early March (especially January and February).

Watch Site Description: There are several suitable Bald Eagle viewing areas in and near Cassville. Within Cassville, use an eagle observation deck or the nearby Riverside Park overlooking the Mississippi River. Alternatively, Nelson Dewey State Park north of Cassville provides additional Bald Eagle viewing opportunities.

Access: In Cassville, drive to the Mississippi River waterfront and the eagle observation deck just north of the Ferry Landing, or Riverside Park a short distance southeast of the Ferry Landing. To reach Nelson Dewey State Park, drive north from Cassville on County Route VV to the park and observe eagles on or near the Mississippi River from there.

References: *Wintering of the Migrant Bald Eagle in the Lower 48 States* (National Agricultural Chemicals Association, 1976); *A Guide to Hawk Watching in North America* (Pennsylvania State University Press, 1979).

Genoa–Prairie du Chien Area

Raptors: Bald Eagles.

Viewing Season: Late November to early December, or late February to early March.

Watch Site Description: Bluffs along State Route 35 and the nearby Mississippi River over which eagles soar.

Access: From Genoa, drive toward Prairie du Chien (or vice versa) along State Route 35. Watch for eagles soaring along the nearby bluffs.

References: *Wintering of the Migrant Bald Eagle in the Lower 48 States* (National Agricultural Chemicals Association, 1976); *A Guide to Hawk Watching in North America* (Pennsylvania State University Press, 1979).

Mississippi Lock & Dam No. 4 (near Alma)

Raptors: Bald Eagles.

Viewing Season: Early winter and mid-March.

**Watch Site
Description:** Open areas of the Mississippi River or along bluffs near the highway between Fountain City and Alma.

Access: From Alma, drive south on State Route 35 toward Fountain City. Look for eagles along or over the nearby river, or birds flying over nearby bluffs.

References: *Wintering of the Migrant Bald Eagle in the Lower 48 States* (National Agricultural Chemicals Association, 1976); *A Guide to Hawk Watching in North America* (Pennsylvania State University Press, 1979).

Nelson Dewey State Park (near Cassville)

Raptors: Bald Eagles and Red-shouldered Hawks.

Viewing Season: Winter.

**Watch Site
Description:** A drive-in lookout overlooking the Mississippi River. Observers can look down upon eagles feeding along the river or perched in trees nearby. Red-shouldered Hawks are sometimes seen in trees north of the parking lot.

Access: From Cassville, drive north on State Route 133 for a short distance, then turn onto County Route VV. Continue north on this road for 5 miles or more until you reach the park (which may be closed at certain times). Enter and drive to the lookout.

References: *Wintering of the Migrant Bald Eagle in the Lower 48 States* (National Agricultural Chemicals Association, 1976); *A Guide to Hawk Watching in North America* (Pennsylvania State University Press, 1979).

Prairie du Sac/Sauk City

Raptors: Bald Eagles.

Viewing Season: Mid-December through February.

Watch Site Description: Annual Bald Eagle Watching Days (over the weekend prior to Martin Luther King Jr. Day) provide excellent opportunities for the public to see Bald Eagles along the lower Wisconsin River. Early morning is the best time to engage in eagle watching. Eagle Watching Days also offer a range of related activities, exhibits, and programs in Prairie du Sac and Sauk City.

Several locations in the "Sauk–Prairie" area with views of the Wisconsin River are designated for Bald Eagle viewing while preventing disturbance of the birds:

- *Eagle Watching Bus Tours.* Provides experienced guides for eagle watching along the Wisconsin River. Stops are made at appropriate locations providing opportunities for eagle viewing. Check with the Ferry Bluff Eagle Council (P.O. Box 532, Sauk City, WI 53583; www.ferrybluffeaglecouncil.org) for current eagle watching bus tours and departure points.

- *Ferry Bluff Eagle Council Overlook.* Provides good views of Bald Eagles perched on Eagle Island or soaring overhead. Telescopes are available for the public so people have good views of the birds. Additional eagle information is available at the kiosk. The overlook is staffed with knowledgeable volunteers from 9:00 A.M. to 1:00 P.M. Saturday and Sunday in January and February.

- *Veterans Park.* Provides eagle viewing, but *only* from your vehicle to prevent disturbances to the birds.

- *Prairie du Sac Generating Station Dam.* Provides excellent eagle viewing, but also only from your vehicle to prevent disturbances to the birds. *You must use your vehicle as a blind at this important site to watch eagles flying and fishing.*

- *Wollersheim Winery Bluffs.* Located behind the winery, these bluffs also provide eagle watching opportunities.

Access: The Ferry Bluff Eagle Council Overlook is located across from the Mobil gas station at 540 Water Street, Prairie du

Sac. Veterans Park is located off Water Street (State Route 78) about 0.4 mile north of State Route 60 in Prairie du Sac. Look for a small sign pointing to the park. The Prairie du Sac Generating Station Dam is located about 1 mile north of Prairie du Sac on Route 78, then right onto Dam Road to the dam. The Wollersheim Winery bluffs are reached by driving east from Prairie du Sac on Route 60 across the Wisconsin River to the junction with State Route 188. Turn right (south) onto Route 188 and continue for about 1 mile to the Wollersheim Winery on the left. Please patronize this business before enjoying eagle watching from bluffs behind the winery.

References: *Eagle Watcher's Guide to Sauk City and Prairie du Sac Wisconsin* (Ferry Bluff Eagle Council, 2003); *Bald Eagle Watching Days* (Sauk Prairie Area Chamber of Commerce, no date).

British Columbia

Bald Eagles are exceptionally abundant raptors in British Columbia, with many thousands of pairs scattered throughout the province, especially along the coast. There are many locations where these birds can be observed. Most of those discussed here are easy to visit and noted for large numbers of eagles.

Active Pass (in the Gulf Islands)

Raptors: Bald Eagles.

Viewing Season: October through July.

Watch Site
Description: The vicinity of Helen Point at the southeastern end of Active Pass as well as the south side of the pass. Eagles also can be seen with binoculars circling over the western end of the pass and adjacent mountains.

Access: Active Pass is located in the Gulf Islands between Mayne and Galiano Islands. The area can be visited by riding the British Columbia government ferries between Vancouver or Tsawwassen and Victoria at Swartz Bay. Observers should stand on the ferry bow or starboard side for the best eagle viewing opportunities.

References: *Adventures with Eagles* (Hancock House, 1970); *A Guide to Hawk Watching in North America* (Pennsylvania State University Press, 1979).

Fraser Valley Bald Eagle Festival (near Mission)

Raptors: Bald Eagles.

Viewing Season: December through February.

Watch Site Description: The Harrison River area of the Fraser Valley of British Columbia is a major Bald Eagle watching area. Among the most favorable locations are the following:

- The Fraser Valley Bald Eagle Festival, held annually on the third weekend in November, in Mission. Special speakers and programs regarding eagles, a crafts fair, other events, and eagle watching field trips are scheduled during the festival.

- The shorelines of the Harrison and Pitt Rivers in the Fraser Valley. The Harrison River Bridge and its vicinity on Lougheed Highway 7 is a key Bald Eagle watching site, as is the area north of the bridge.

- Rowena's Inn On the River (14282 Morris Valley, Harrison Mills) also provides excellent eagle viewing opportunities.

- Kilby Provincial Park has picnic and boat-ramp facilities just southeast of the Harrison River Bridge. From the parking lot, walk about 0.5 mile south on the dike toward the Fraser River, from which eagles can be seen.

Access: From Mission, drive east for about 23 miles up the Fraser Valley on Lougheed Highway 7 to the Harrison River Bridge area.

References: *A Guide to Hawk Watching in North America* (Pennsylvania State University Press, 1979); *The Bald Eagle of Alaska, BC and Washington* (Hancock House Publishers, 2003); www.fraservalleyguide.com/eagle-festival/.

Greater Vancouver Area

Raptors: Bald Eagles.

Viewing Season: Year-round.

Watch Site Description: More than one hundred pairs of Bald Eagles now nest in urban settings, sometimes as close as 30 feet to occupied houses and above city streets, in the greater Vancouver area. Hawk watchers in this urban area should remain alert for some of these birds and their nesting activities. Never disturb nesting eagles, and never trespass on private property to secure very close views or photographs of nesting birds.

Access: Public roads throughout the greater Vancouver area.

Reference: *The Bald Eagle of Alaska, BC and Washington* (Hancock House Publishers, 2003).

Pacific Rim National Park (on Vancouver Island)

Raptors: Nesting Bald Eagles.

Viewing Season: Spring, summer, and autumn.

Watch Site Description: The islands and shorelines of Barkley Sound.

Access: By private boat from the towns of Ucluelet or Bamfield. Ucluelet can be reached by automobile via Provincial Route 4 on Vancouver Island. Private airplane charters from Vancouver and Victoria also can transport visitors to Barkley Sound in the park.

References: *Adventures with Eagles* (Hancock House, 1970); *A Guide to Hawk Watching in North America* (Pennsylvania State University Press, 1979).

Prince Rupert

Raptors: Bald Eagles.

Viewing Season: All year.

Watch Site
Description: The area around the harbor, or the Prince Rupert garbage dump where eagles feed.

Access: By ferry or automobile on Canadian Route 16.

Reference: *A Guide to Hawk Watching in North America* (Pennsylvania State University Press, 1979).

Squamish Valley (near Squamish and Brackendale)

Raptors: Wintering Bald Eagles (as many as 3,701 in one day).

Viewing Season: Late November through February (especially December and January).

Watch Site
Description: Concentrations of Bald Eagles feeding on spawning salmon in the Cheakamus, Mamquam, and Squamish Rivers flowing into Howe Sound.

Access: There are several ways of seeing Bald Eagles in the Squamish Valley area:

- Bald Eagle watching by raft trips on the Cheakamus River near Brackendale are available from commercial companies in the Brackendale–Squamish area. Contact the Squamish Chamber of Commerce for current information, as well as names and contact information for companies offering these trips.

- Bald Eagle viewing also is possible between Brackendale and Squamish from the Eagle Viewing Dike opposite the Easter Seal Camp on Government Road. During December and January, volunteers are on site from 9:30 A.M. to 3:30 P.M. on Saturday and Sunday to answer questions.

- The Tenderfoot Creek Fish Hatchery in the Cheakamus Valley.

References: *The Bald Eagle of Alaska, BC and Washington* (Hancock House Publishers, 2003); Squamish Chamber of Commerce, Box 1009, Squamish, BC V0N 3G0, (604) 892–9244; www.squamishchamber.bc.ca; www.nusalya.com/grackendale; www.explorenorth.com/library/weekly/aa112098-3.htm.

Other Raptor Viewing Areas

The raptor viewing areas discussed in this section are mostly short-term stopover habitat sites, winter areas, or summer locations. They are representative of places where raptors can be seen relatively easily.

Alaska

Alaska Highway (State Route 1)

Raptors: Bald Eagles, Northern Harriers, Northern Goshawks, Red-tailed Hawks (Harlan's subspecies), Golden Eagles, Gyrfalcons, Peregrine Falcons, Northern Hawk Owls, Great Gray Owls, and Short-eared Owls. Rough-legged Hawks can sometimes be seen during autumn migration. Other notable viewable wildlife includes bears, Dall Sheep, Mountain Goats, Caribou, and White-tailed Ptarmigan.

Viewing Season: Year-round.

Watch Site Description: The Alaska Highway is an extremely beautiful road passing through pristine mountain, lake, and stream ecosystems rich in wildlife. Raptor watching, as well as other wildlife watching, is excellent and very productive.

Access: The Alaska Highway connects Fairbanks, Alaska, with Dawson Creek, British Columbia. Between Dawson Creek and the border with Canada's Yukon Territory, it is Highway 97, but in the Yukon Territory and Alaska it is State Route 1. Everyone driving this highway should have a full tank of gasoline when entering the road, have a good spare tire, and remain alert for wildlife on the road or crossing it.

References: None.

Denali Highway (State Route 8)

Raptors: Northern Harriers, Golden Eagles, and Gyrfalcons.

Viewing Season: Spring through early autumn.

Watch Site Description: An important highway connecting Paxson on the east with Cantwell and the eastern side of Denali National Park on the west. Remain alert for raptors while driving this road.

Access: The Denali Highway is accessed from Paxson on the east or Cantwell on the west. The road is closed during winter.

Reference: *A Birder's Guide to Alaska* (American Birding Association, 2002).

California

Yolo Farmlands Loop (near Woodland)

Raptors: White-tailed Kites, Northern Harriers, Swainson's Hawks (summer), Red-tailed Hawks, Ferruginous Hawks, Rough-legged Hawks, American Kestrels, and rarely Merlins, Peregrine Falcons, and Prairie Falcons.

Viewing Season: Winter; summer for Swainson's Hawks.

Watch Site Description: A loop of rural roads around, and through, agricultural fields and grasslands where raptors winter.

Access: From the junction of Interstate 505 and County Route 29A southwest of Woodland, drive east on Route 29A and continue to the junction with County Route 99. Turn north on Route 99 and continue to County Route 27. Turn left (west) on Route 27 and return to I–505. You can also explore other county roads in this general area while looking for raptors.

Reference: *Birding Northern California* (Falcon/Globe Pequot Press, 1999).

Florida

Big Bend Wildlife Management Area/Hickory Mound Impoundment (near Perry)

Raptors: Ospreys, Swallow-tailed Kites (spring and summer), Mississippi Kites, and Bald Eagles.

Viewing Season: Year-round.

Watch Site Description: A 6.5-mile dike around a brackish impoundment and pine and palm hammocks.

Access: From Perry, drive west on U.S. Route 98 for 18 miles to Cow Creek Grade. Turn left on Cow Creek Grade and continue for 6 miles to the check station. Stop and secure a map at the station, then continue another 2 miles to the impoundment.

Reference: www.floridaconservation.org.

T. M. Goodwin Waterfowl Management Area

Raptors: Swallow-tailed Kites (summer), Northern Harriers, and—during October—migrant Red-shouldered Hawks, Red-tailed Hawks, American Kestrels, Merlins, and Peregrine Falcons.

Viewing Season: Year-round.

Watch Site Description: Part of the upper basin of the St. Johns River, with ten impoundments, a semipermanent marsh flooded as a reservoir, and dikes from which raptor watching can be done.

Access: From the junction of Interstate 95 and County Route 512 north of Vero Beach, drive west on Route 512 for 3 miles to County Route 507 (Babcock Street) south of the C-54 canal. Signs direct visitors from the Stick Marsh boat ramp to the entrance to the Goodwin management area.

Reference: www.floridaconservation.org.

Joe Overstreet Landing (near St. Cloud)

Raptors: Swallow-tailed Kites (spring and summer), Snail Kites, Bald Eagles, Crested Caracaras, and Burrowing Owls.

Viewing Season: Year-round.

Watch Site Description: A small county park at the southern end of Lake Kissimmee, providing views of the lake and adjacent habitats, including open pastures and prairies. Search for Swallow-tailed Kites, Crested Caracaras, and Burrowing Owls in pasture and prairie habitat on the way to the park, and in the park. Bald Eagles and Snail Kites can sometimes be seen from the park's boat landing.

Access: From U.S. Route 192 in St. Cloud, drive south on County Road 523 (Vermont Avenue, which becomes Canoe Creek Road) for about 20 miles, at which point it becomes unpaved Joe Overstreet Road. Continue for another 5.4 miles to the end of the road and the entrance to the park. Enter, and explore the park looking for raptors.

Reference: www.floridaconservation.org.

Little-Big Econ State Forest and Wildlife Management Area (near Oviedo)

Raptors: Ospreys, Swallow-tailed Kites (spring and summer), Bald Eagles, and other hawks.

Viewing Season: Year-round.

Watch Site Description: A canoe trail providing access to the Econlockhatchee River, and hiking trails extending through river swamp, oak hammock, and prairie habitats.

Access: From Oviedo, drive east on County Route 426 for 3.3 miles to the entrance to Little-Big Econ State Forest. Enter, park your vehicle in areas provided, and secure current information regarding raptor viewing from park officials. *Caution:* Do *not* use the separate Kilbee Tract, on which hunting is permitted.

Reference: www.floridaconservation.org.

Loxahatchee National Wildlife Refuge (near West Palm Beach)

Raptors: Black Vultures, Turkey Vultures, Ospreys, Swallow-tailed Kites, Snail Kites, Bald Eagles, Northern Harriers, Sharp-shinned Hawks, Cooper's Hawks, Red-shouldered Hawks, Broad-winged Hawks, Red-tailed Hawks, Short-tailed Hawks, American Kestrels, Merlins, and Peregrine Falcons.

Viewing Season: All year.

Watch Site Description: A 145,635-acre refuge containing portions of the Everglades, saw grass marsh, wet prairies, tree islands, and sloughs.

Access: From the junction of U.S. Route 1 and State Route 80 near West Palm Beach, drive west on Route 80 to the junction with U.S. Route 441. Turn onto U.S. 441 and drive south for several miles to the refuge entrance road.

Reference: *A Guide to Hawk Watching in North America* (Pennsylvania State University Press, 1979).

Turkey Vultures are among the raptors seen at the Loxahatchee National Wildlife Refuge, Florida.

Merritt Island National Wildlife Refuge (near Titusville)

Raptors: Ospreys, Bald Eagles (nesting in November), Sharp-shinned Hawks, Red-shouldered Hawks, Red-tailed Hawks, American Kestrels, and Merlins.

Viewing Season: Year-round.

Watch Site Description: Ecosystems include part of the Indian River, Mosquito Lagoon, other saltwater lagoons with Red Mangroves, marshes, and palmetto-oak hammocks in upland areas. Sharp-shinned Hawks and falcons are common spring and autumn migrants.

Access: From Titusville, drive east on State Route 406 to the refuge (which is also the Kennedy Space Center).

Reference: www.floridaconservation.org.

Tosohatchee State Reserve (near Christmas)

Raptors: Ospreys, Bald Eagles, and Red-shouldered Hawks.

Viewing Season: Year-round.

Watch Site Description: Cypress swamps, freshwater marshes, hammocks, and Slash Pine upland woodlands bordering the St. Johns River.

Access: From State Route 50 in Christmas, turn south onto Taylor Creek Road and continue for 3 miles to the entrance on the left to Tosohatchee State Reserve.

Reference: www.floridaconservation.org.

Idaho

Snake River Birds of Prey National Conservation Area (near Boise)

Raptors: Numerous raptor species occur in the Snake River Birds of Prey National Conservation Area as nesting birds or migrants.

Nesting raptors include: Turkey Vultures, Ospreys, Northern Harriers, Swainson's Hawks, Red-tailed Hawks, Ferruginous Hawks, Golden Eagles, American Kestrels, Prairie Falcons, Barn Owls, Great Horned Owls, Western Screech-Owls, Burrowing Owls, Long-eared Owls, Short-eared Owls, and Northern Saw-whet Owls.

Migrating raptors include: Ospreys, Bald Eagles, Sharp-shinned Hawks, Cooper's Hawks, Northern Goshawks, Rough-legged Hawks, Merlins, Gyrfalcons, and Peregrine Falcons.

Viewing Season: All seasons, but particularly during spring, summer, and autumn.

Watch Site Description: A unique 485,000-acre natural area containing 81 miles of rugged Snake River canyons and cliffs that provide nest sites for large numbers of hawks, eagles, falcons, and owls in southwestern Idaho. The area is noted for impressive numbers of nesting Golden Eagles and Prairie Falcons (nearly 200 pairs).

Access: From Boise, drive west on Interstate 84 to exit 44 for Meridan, then continue south on State Route 69 to Kuna. Procure adequate supplies of gasoline, food, and water in Kuna. From Kuna, drive south on the Swan Falls Road to the Kuna Visitor Center, where you can obtain NCA maps, circulars, and other current information. You can drive a 56-mile tour loop of the Snake River Birds of Prey National Conservation Area, starting at the Kuna Visitor Center, which includes stops at scenic vistas and offers excellent wildlife viewing opportunities. Information is also available at the Swan Falls Dam and Visitor Center. Alternatively, write to the Bureau of Land Management office for copies of circulars, maps, and current information: Manager, Lower Snake River District, Bureau of Land Management, 3948 Development Avenue, Boise, ID 83709.

References: *A Guide to Hawk Watching in North America* (Pennsylvania State University Press, 1979); *Snake River Birds of Prey National Conservation Area 1994 Annual Report* (Bureau of Land Management, 1994); *Snake River Birds of Prey National Conservation Area/Idaho Visitor's Guide* (Bureau of Land Management, 1997).

World Center for Birds of Prey (in Boise)

Raptors: Captive breeding of Peregrine Falcons and selected other species.

Viewing Season: Open daily, except certain holidays, from 9:00 A.M. to 4:30 P.M. in summer, and 10:00 A.M. to 4:00 P.M. in winter (November through February).

Watch Site Description: The Velma Morrison Interpretive Center provides multi-media displays and exhibits, and live bird presentations.

Access: From exit 50 off Interstate 84 at Boise, drive south following directional signs to South Cole Road, then continue south on South Cole Road for approximately 6 miles to Flying Hawk Lane. Turn uphill onto Flying Hawk Lane and continue to the World Center for Birds of Prey at 5666 Flying Hawk Lane.

Reference: *Snake River Birds of Prey National Conservation Area/Idaho Visitor's Guide* (Bureau of Land Management, 1997).

Indiana

Buzzard's Roost Overlook (near Magnet)

Raptors: Turkey Vultures and various hawks (summer); Bald Eagles (winter).

Viewing Season: Summer and winter.

Watch Site Description: A high roadside overlook providing excellent views of a section of the Ohio River.

Access: From Magnet, drive north on State Route 27 and look for signs for the turnoff road going to the Buzzard's Roost Overlook. Drive to the overlook and look for raptors from there.

Reference: *Indiana Wildlife Viewing Guide* (Falcon Press Publishing, 1992).

Kentucky

Taylorsville Lake State Park (near Taylorsville)

Raptors: Ospreys and Red-shouldered Hawks.

Viewing Season: Spring through autumn.

Watch Site Description: An 11,672-acre park and wildlife management area consisting mostly of woodland, abandoned farmland, and several lakes. During April to June, Ospreys nest on the shoreline of Lake Barkley and are seen commonly at other nearby lakes.

Access: From the junction of State Routes 44 and 55 at Taylorsville, drive east on Route 44 for 5 miles to the junction with State Route 248. Continue on Route 248 for 2 miles to the park's entrance. Explore the park by driving the park roads looking for raptors. Inquire at the park headquarters for updated raptor viewing information and opportunities.

Reference: *Kentucky Wildlife Viewing Guide* (Falcon Press Publishing, 1994).

Maryland

Eastern Neck National Wildlife Refuge (near Rock Hall)

Raptors: Black Vultures, Turkey Vultures, Northern Harriers, Cooper's Hawks, Red-tailed Hawks, and American Kestrels; sometimes to rarely Bald Eagles, Red-shouldered Hawks, Rough-legged Hawks, and Golden Eagles.

Viewing Season: Winter.

Watch Site Description: A 2,285-acre island wildlife refuge where a variety of raptors winter. Explore the various roads and trails of the refuge remaining alert for raptors perched on in flight. The refuge is open daily 7:30 A.M. to half an hour after sunset, when the gate is locked for the night. There is no entrance fee.

From the blinking red light in Rock Hall on the eastern shore of the Chesapeake Bay in Maryland, turn left onto State Route 445 and continue south for about 8 miles to the entrance bridge to the refuge. Cross the bridge and explore the refuge.

References: *Finding Birds in the National Capital Area* (Smithsonian Institution Press, 1983); http://easternneck.fws.gov/general.html.

Mississippi

Lucky's Corner (near Lakeshore)

Raptors: Northern Harriers, Red-tailed Hawks, and American Kestrels. Rarely White-tailed Kites, Sharp-shinned Hawks, Cooper's Hawks, Swainson's Hawks, Ferruginous Hawks, Merlins, and Peregrine Falcons.

Viewing Season: Winter.

Watch Site
Description: A pine plantation surrounding a pasture.

Access: From the town of Lakeshore, drive north on Lakeshore Drive to the junction with the Pearlington-Ansley Road. Turn left (southwest) onto the Pearlington-Ansley Road and continue for several miles until you reach Luxich's Auto Repair on the left side of the road. Turn left here onto an unpaved road, and explore the landscape along the road for raptors.

Reference: *Birds and Birding on the Mississippi Coast* (University Press of Mississippi, 1987).

Nebraska

Agate Fossil Beds National Monument (near Harrison)

Raptors: Swainson's Hawks and Ferruginous Hawks.

Viewing Season: Summer.

Description: An undisturbed mixed-grass and shortgrass prairie famous for its fossils. Swainson's Hawks and Ferruginous Hawks are sometimes observed flying overhead by people at the visitor center or driving along roads. Ask at the interpretive center for current Swainson's Hawk and Ferruginous Hawk watching information.

Access: From the junction of U.S. Route 20 and State Route 29 at Harrison, drive south on Route 29 for at least 15 miles to the junction with River Road (which extends east). Turn east onto River Road and continue for approximately 2.5 miles to the interpretive center.

Reference: *Nebraska Wildlife Viewing Guide* (Falcon Press Publishing, 1997).

Nevada

Great Basin National Park (near Baker).

Raptors: Sharp-shinned Hawks, Golden Eagles, and Prairie Falcons.

Viewing Season: Spring through autumn.

**Watch Site
Description:** Alpine lakes, high-desert Sagebrush, cliffs, meadows, and Bristlecone Pine and other forested areas. Look for raptors from roadsides or while hiking trails in the park.

Access: From Baker, drive west on State Route 488 for about 5 miles to the park visitor center, where current raptor viewing information can be secured along with handout literature and maps of the park.

Reference: *Nevada Wildlife Viewing Guide* (Falcon Press Publishing, 1993).

Jacks Valley Road (near Carson City)

Raptors: Bald Eagles, Northern Harriers, Swainson's Hawks, and Red-tailed Hawks.

Viewing Season: Year-round, with the greatest raptor numbers during winter.

**Watch Site
Description:** A 22-mile-long drive along State Route 206 passing through a scenic valley containing agricultural fields, Sagebrush, and Bitterbrush. Raptors perch on utility poles and fence posts, offering favorable roadside raptor watching opportunities.

Access: From Carson City, drive south on U.S. Route 395 for 3 miles to the junction with State Route 206. Turn west onto Route 206 and follow it for the next 22 miles, looking for raptors along the road. When Route 206 meets State Route 88, you can go north again on Route 88, which eventually links into U.S. 395 and Carson City to the north.

Reference: *Nevada Wildlife Viewing Guide* (Falcon Press Publishing, 1993).

Lovelock Valley Raptor Viewing Tour (near Lovelock)

Raptors: Northern Harriers, Red-tailed Hawks, Ferruginous Hawks, Rough-legged Hawks, Golden Eagles, and Prairie Falcons; also Great Horned Owls and Short-eared Owls.

Viewing Season: Winter.

**Watch Site
Description:** Rural roads bordered by ranches and farms with cottonwood hedgerows. Diurnal raptors often perch in tall trees and on utility poles, making hawk watching easy and productive.

Access: From Interstate 80 at Lovelock, take exit 107, drive south into town, and turn right onto 14th Street. Continue to Lovelock Valley Road, turn left onto it, and continue for 1.3 miles to Loorz Road. Turn northwest onto Loorz Road, where the raptor viewing route begins. Continue for another mile to Fairview Road, turn left onto Fairview, and continue for 1 mile to North Meridian Road. Turn left onto North Meridian Road and continue for 2 miles back into Lovelock.

Reference: *Nevada Wildlife Viewing Guide* (Falcon Press Publishing, 1993).

New Jersey

Brigantine (Edwin B. Forsythe) National Wildlife Refuge

Raptors: Ospreys, Bald Eagles, Northern Harriers, Rough-legged Hawks, Golden Eagles, Peregrine Falcons, and rarely Gyrfalcons and Snowy Owls.

Viewing Season: Autumn, winter, and spring—especially during winter. Many birders avoid visiting Brigantine during July and August because of large numbers of disagreeable Green-headed Flies during those months.

Watch Site Description: A large wildlife refuge containing some 20,000 acres of coastal salt marsh along with channels and bays, islands, two large impoundments (East Pool and West Pool), upland fields, and woodland. An auto tour route enables visitors to drive around the edges of the impoundments and other upland parts of the refuge.

Golden Eagles are sometimes seen at Brigantine (Edwin B. Forsythe) National Wildlife Refuge.

Access: At Oceanville on U.S. Route 9, look for the refuge sign and drive east on the road leading into the refuge. Stop at the information center (with restrooms) near the refuge headquarters to pick up free literature and a bird checklist, and to check recent bird sightings in the log. Then continue on the refuge's auto tour route following directional arrows, looking for raptors and other species of waterbirds and upland birds.

Reference: *A Guide to Bird Finding in New Jersey* (Rutgers University Press, 2002).

Island Beach State Park (near Seaside Heights)

Raptors: Ospreys, Merlins, and Peregrine Falcons.

Viewing Season: Spring and autumn.

Watch Site Description: An undisturbed barrier beach island. Ospreys nest on dead cedar trees, platforms designed for this purpose, and other elevated structures in various sections of the park, giving visitors opportunities to see these spectacular raptors without disturbing them. During autumn, migrating falcons (especially Merlins and Peregrines) as well as limited numbers of other hawks are seen from the ocean or bay side of the island.

Access: From Toms River, drive east on State Route 37 to Seaside Heights. Turn right and follow the island's main road south for a few miles to the Island Beach State Park entrance. An entrance fee is charged. After entering the park, continue south on the main park road to the headquarters. Stop here and secure additional information about the park, and updated information for visiting the most favorable locations for seeing nesting Ospreys. Not all sections of the park are open to public use. *Warning:* Do not walk on dunes or fragile dune vegetation!

References: *A Guide to Hawk Watching in North America* (Pennsylvania State University Press, 1979); *The Migrations of Hawks* (Indiana University Press, 1986).

Jakes Landing Road (near Dennisville)

Raptors: Bald Eagles, Northern Harriers, Rough-legged Hawks, Golden Eagles, and Short-eared Owls.

Viewing Season: Winter.

Watch Site Description: A 1.4-mile-long road extending through deciduous woodland (part of Belleplain State Forest), as well as an area planted with pine and spruce trees along the final 0.25 mile of the road. Raptors such as Northern Harriers and Rough-legged Hawks commonly are seen along this road and its adjacent terrain during winter. Sometimes Bald Eagles and Golden Eagles are also observed.

Access: From Dennisville, drive west on State Route 47 for 1.4 miles to Jakes Landing Road. Turn south onto that road and continue for 1.4 miles to the parking lot at its end. Look for raptors anywhere along this road

Reference: *A Guide to Bird Finding in New Jersey* (Rutgers University Press, 2002).

The Raptor Trust

Raptors: Various permanently disabled hawks, eagles, falcons, and owls.

Viewing Season: Year-round.

Watch Site Description: A nonprofit raptor rehabilitation and education center providing public access to permanently disabled hawks, eagles, falcons, and owls.

Access: From exit 30A at the junction of Interstate 287 and North Maple Avenue near Basking Ridge, drive south on North Maple Avenue to Basking Ridge. Continue south on what becomes South Maple Avenue to the junction with Lord Stirling Road. Turn east onto Lord Stirling Road (which becomes White Bridge Road) and continue to The Raptor Trust at 1390 White Bridge Road in Millington. Visiting hours are daily 9:00 A.M. to dusk.

References: *The Raptor Trust* (The Raptor Trust, no date); *Hawks and Owls of Eastern North America* (Rutgers University Press, 2004).

Tuckerton Marshes (near Tuckerton)

Raptors: Ospreys, Northern Harriers, Rough-legged Hawks, and Short-eared Owls.

Viewing Season: Spring, autumn, and winter.

Watch Site Description: A narrow road, crossing five small bridges, extending across a very large salt marsh as part of the Great Bay Wildlife Management Area. Ospreys nest on utility poles and other elevated structures in various parts of the area— especially after the first two bridges are crossed. During winter, Northern Harriers, Rough-legged Hawks, and occasionally Short-eared Owls are seen in various spots on the Tuckerton Marshes.

Access: From the traffic light at the junction of County Route 539 and U.S. Route 9 in Tuckerton, turn west and continue for about 0.2 mile to a fork in the road across from a large lake. Leave U.S. 9 at this point and follow Great Bay Boulevard for 1.6 miles to the beginning of the Tuckerton Marshes. Continue following the road to its end, looking for nesting Ospreys after the first two small bridges during spring and early summer, or Northern Harriers, Rough-legged Hawks, and occasionally Short-eared Owls during winter.

Reference: *A Guide to Bird Finding in New Jersey* (Rutgers University Press, 2002).

New Mexico

Ocate–Wagon Mound Road

Raptors: Northern Harriers, Swainson's Hawks, Red-tailed Hawks, Ferruginous Hawks, Golden Eagles, and American Kestrels.

Viewing Season: Summer.

Watch Site

Description: A section of highway between Ocate and Wagon Mound. Raptor viewing is done only from the roadside; adjacent land is private property and closed to public access.

Access: From Ocate, drive toward Wagon Mound on State Route 120, looking for raptors between mile markers 22 and 38.

Reference: *New Mexico Wildlife Viewing Guide* (Falcon Publishing, second edition, 2000).

Wild Rivers Recreation Area (near Questa)

Raptors: Turkey Vultures, Bald Eagles (winter), Red-tailed Hawks, and Golden Eagles.

Viewing Season: Year-round.

Watch Site

Description: A loop road providing views over the nationally scenic Red River and Rio Grande and the gorge into which they converge.

Access: From Questa, drive north for 2.6 miles on State Routes 522/378 and follow directional signs to the entrance to the Wild Rivers Recreation Area. Enter the recreation area and continue for another 5.4 miles to the visitor center, where you can obtain current raptor viewing information.

Reference: *New Mexico Wildlife Viewing Guide* (Falcon Publishing, second edition, 2000).

Pennsylvania

John Heinz National Wildlife Refuge at Tinicum (in Philadelphia)

Raptors: Northern Harriers, Red-tailed Hawks, Rough-legged Hawks, and American Kestrels; also Eastern Screech-Owls, Long-eared Owls, and Short-eared Owls.

Viewing Season: Winter.

Watch Site

Description: Hundreds of acres of freshwater tidal marsh, ponds, and trails near Philadelphia International Airport, plus the

American Kestrels are among the raptors sometimes seen in the John Heinz National Wildlife Refuge, Pennsylvania.

Cusano Environmental Education Center. The refuge grounds are open year-round from 8:00 A.M. to sunset, without charge; the education center is open daily from 8:30 A.M. to 4:00 P.M., also without charge.

Access: Access differs depending on the direction from which you approach the refuge. Traffic in this area is heavy, and often fast moving, so drive carefully.

- *From the North.* Drive south on Interstate 95 to exit 14 (Bartram Avenue). Take exit 14 and follow the right exiting for State Route 291 (Lester). At the traffic light, turn right onto Bartram Avenue and continue to the second traffic light. Turn left onto 84th Street and again continue to the second traffic light. Then turn left onto Lindberg Boulevard to the refuge entrance.

- *From the South.* Drive north on Interstate 95 to exit 10, (State Route 291). Take exit 10 and continue to the first traffic light, then turn left onto Bartram Avenue. Continue on Bartram to the third traffic light and turn left onto 84th Street. Continue on 84th Street to the second traffic light, then turn left onto Lindberg Boulevard and continue to the refuge entrance.

- *From the Schuylkill Expressway.* Driving east on Interstate 75, stay in the left lane and follow signs for State Route 291/West I–95 South/Airport. At the traffic light, turn right onto Route 291 west. Continue on Route 291, following signs to Interstate 95 south. Exit onto I–95 south and continue to exit 10, Route 291/Airport. Take this exit and follow the right fork. Exit at Route 291/Lester. Continue to the first traffic light, then turn right onto Bartram Avenue. Continue on Bartram to the second traffic light, then turn onto 84th Street. Continue on 84th to the second traffic light, then turn left onto Lindberg Boulevard and continue to the refuge entrance.

- *From the Blue Route.* Driving on Interstate 475 south, follow signs for Interstate 95 north. Exit onto I–95 north and continue to the State Route 291/Airport exit. Take this exit and continue to the first traffic light, then turn left onto Bartram Avenue. Continue on Bartram to the third traffic light, then turn left onto 84th Street. Continue on 84th to the second traffic light, then turn left onto Lindberg Boulevard. Continue on Lindberg to the refuge entrance.

References: *Birding the Delaware Valley Region* (Temple University Press, 1980); John Heinz National Wildlife Refuge at Tinicum at www.heinz.fws.gov.

Texas

Attwater Prairie Chicken National Wildlife Refuge (near Eagle Lake)

Raptors: White-tailed Kites, Bald Eagles, Northern Harriers, Ferruginous Hawks, Rough-legged Hawks (occasionally), Crested Caracaras, American Kestrels, Merlins, Peregrine Falcons, and Prairie Falcons. White-tailed Hawks and Crested Caracaras also nest in spring in the area encompassed by the auto tour loop.

Viewing Season: Winter; spring for White-tailed Hawks and Crested Caracaras.

Watch Site Description: An auto tour loop extending for 5 miles around the LaFitte Prairie and Pintail Marsh.

Access: From the town of Eagle Lake, drive northeast for about 7 miles on Farm-to-Market (FM) Road 3013 to the entrance road into the refuge. Look for a sign for the entrance road.

Reference: *Birding Texas* (Falcon/Globe Pequot Press, 1998).

Bentsen–Rio Grande Valley State Park (near Mission)

Raptors: Hook-billed Kites, White-tailed Kites, Gray Hawks, Harris's Hawks, White-tailed Hawks, Merlins, and Peregrine Falcons.

Viewing Season: Year-round, especially November through May.

Watch Site Description: A 588-acre park along the Rio Grande in the Rio Grande Valley with mesquite grassland, fields, Tamaulipan scrub, thorn forest, riparian woodland, and various aquatic habitats.

Access: From the junction of U.S. Business Route 83 and the Inspiration Road exit west of Mission, drive south on Farm-to-Market (FM) Road 2063 for 3 miles to the entrance to the park. Enter, park at appropriate locations, and explore the area for raptors and other birds.

Reference: *Birding Texas* (Falcon/Globe Pequot Press, 1998).

Boca Chica Area (near Brownsville)

Raptors: Ospreys, Northern Harriers, White-tailed Hawks, American Kestrels, Merlins, and Peregrine Falcons.

Viewing Season: Winter.

Description: Tidal flats adjacent to State Route 4 between Brownsville and the Gulf of Mexico. Watch for raptors, including White-tailed Hawks, perched or flying overhead.

Access: From Brownsville and the junction of U.S. Route 77 and State Route 4, drive east on Route 4 (Boca Chica Boulevard) for about 16 miles to the Gulf of Mexico.

Reference: *Birding Texas* (Falcon/Globe Pequot Press, 1998).

Franklin Mountain State Park (near El Paso)

Raptors: Turkey Vultures, Red-tailed Hawks, Golden Eagles, American Kestrels, and Prairie Falcons.

Viewing Season: Winter.

Watch Site Description: A 24,000-acre park within the city of El Paso. Chihuahuan Desert vegetation predominates in the park.

Access: Take exit 6 off Interstate 10 near El Paso and follow Trans-Mountain Road (Loop 375) east for 3.3 miles to the park entrance. Enter and explore the park, looking for raptors overhead or perched.

Reference: *Birding Texas* (Falcon/Globe Pequot Press, 1998).

Lake Texana (near Edna)

Raptors: Bald Eagles, Northern Harriers, Sharp-shinned Hawks, Cooper's Hawks, White-tailed Hawks, Red-tailed Hawks, Crested Caracaras, American Kestrels, Merlins, and Peregrine Falcons.

Viewing Season: Winter.

Watch Site Description: Fields and pastures, cropland, coastal prairie, scrubland, wetlands, and Lake Texana adjacent to a loop of roads around the southern half of Lake Texana. Watch for raptors on perches along the road or in adjacent habitat, as well as flying overhead.

Access: From the town of Edna, drive east on State Route 111 to the junction with Farm-to-Market (FM) Road 3131. Turn south onto FM 3131 and continue to the junction with FM 1593. Turn north onto FM 1593 and continue to the junction with Route 111. Turn west onto Route 111 and return to Edna.

Reference: *Birding Texas* (Falcon/Globe Pequot Press, 1998).

Lost Maples State Park (near Vanderpool)

Raptors: Summer raptors include Black Vultures, Turkey Vultures, Red-shouldered Hawks, Zone-tailed Hawks, and Red-tailed Hawks. Winter raptors include Bald Eagles and Ferruginous Hawks.

Viewing Season: Summer and winter.

Watch Site Description: A 2,208-acre park with numerous Big-tooth Maples, juniper and oak-juniper woodlands, canyons, overlooks, and wetlands (pond, creek, and river). You will also find an interpretive center and store, and other visitor facilities.

Access: From Vanderpool, drive north on Farm-to-Market (FM) Road 187 for 5 miles to the park.

Reference: *Birding Texas* (Falcon/Globe Pequot Press, 1998).

Muleshoe National Wildlife Refuge (near Littlefield)

Raptors: Bald Eagles, Red-tailed Hawks, Ferruginous Hawks, Rough-legged Hawks, Golden Eagles, American Kestrels, Peregrine Falcons, and Prairie Falcons.

Viewing Season: November to mid-February.

Watch Site Description: A 5,809-acre wildlife refuge containing prairie, mesquite grassland, woodland, and creek and lake wetlands.

Access: From Littlefield, drive west on Farm-to-Market (FM) Roads 54 and 37 for 30 miles to the junction with State Route 214, then continue north on Route 214 for 2.5 miles to the refuge entrance. Enter and drive various refuge roads to explore the area for raptors and other birds.

Reference: *Birding Texas* (Falcon/Globe Pequot Press, 1998).

Port O'Connor–Seadrift Area

Raptors: White-tailed Hawks.

Viewing Season: Year-round.

Watch Site Description: Utility poles and wires, and other elevated perches, along State Route 185 between Port O'Connor and Seadrift, as well as along Farm-to-Market (FM) Road 1289 north.

Access: From the town of Port O'Connor, drive east on State Route 185 to Seadrift, then drive back on Route 185 to the junction with FM 1289. Turn north onto FM 1289, continue on it for a number of miles, and leave the area or retrace your route. Remain alert for White-tailed Hawks perched on poles, wires, trees, and other elevated structures or flying overhead.

Reference: *Birding Texas* (Falcon/Globe Pequot Press, 1998).

Santa Ana National Wildlife Refuge (near McAllen)

Raptors: Black Vultures, Turkey Vultures, Ospreys, Hook-billed Kites, Swallow-tailed Kites, White-tailed Kites, Mississippi Kites, Northern Harriers, Sharp-shinned Hawks, Cooper's Hawks, Crane Hawks (accidental), Gray Hawks, Common Black-Hawks, Harris' Hawks, Roadside Hawks (accidental), Red-shouldered Hawks, Broad-winged Hawks, Short-tailed Hawks, Swainson's Hawks, White-tailed Hawks, Zone-tailed Hawks, Red-tailed Hawks, Crested Caracaras, American Kestrels, Merlins, Peregrine Falcons, and Prairie Falcons.

Viewing Season: All months.

Watch Site Description: Subtropical forest, lakes, and marshes covering 2,000 acres along the Rio Grande.

Access: From McAllen, drive south on 10th Street (which becomes State Route 336) for about 6 miles to the junction with U.S. Route 281 (Old Military Road). Turn left (east) onto U.S. 281 and continue for another 10 miles toward Brownsville. Then look for the refuge sign along the right side of the highway. Turn right and drive into the refuge. Literature and information can be secured at the headquarters.

References: *A Birder's Guide to the Rio Grande Valley of Texas* (L & P Photography, 1971); *A Guide to Hawk Watching in North America* (Pennsylvania State University Press, 1979); *Birding Texas* (Falcon/Globe Pequot Press, 1998).

Vermont

Vermont Institute of Natural Science (near Woodstock)

Raptors: Various permanently disabled hawks, eagles, and falcons.

Viewing Season: Year-round.

Watch Site Description: An environmental education facility that includes The Raptor Center, where permanently disabled raptors are housed and displayed to the public, and injured raptors are rehabilitated.

Access: At the junction of U.S. Route 4 and Church Hill Road in Woodstock (look for a large stone church), turn onto Church Hill Road and continue for 1.8 miles to the sign for the Vermont Institute of Natural Science. Turn into the property and go to The Raptor Center (entry fee charged) to see their educational raptor exhibits.

Reference: *Vermont Wildlife Viewing Guide* (Falcon Press Publishing, 1994).

Ontario

Amherst Island (opposite Millhaven)

Raptors: Rough-legged Hawks and various northern owl species.

Viewing Season: Winter.

Watch Site Description: An island in the St. Lawrence River with unpaved roads crossing private farmland and wooded areas. During some winters as many as ten owl species, including impressive numbers of rare northern owls, concentrate on the island to feed on voles and other prey. Observations are made from public roads. *Do not trespass on private land.*

Access: From Millhaven on Provincial Route 33, take the ferry to Amherst Island. Check locally for the current ferry schedule.

Reference: *A Bird-Finding Guide to Ontario* (University of Toronto Press, 1982).

Wolfe Island (opposite Kingston)

Raptors: Rough-legged Hawks and various northern owl species.

Viewing Season: Winter.

Watch Site Description: An island in the St. Lawrence River opposite Kingston with unpaved roads crossing private farmland and wooded areas. During some winters as many as ten owl species, including impressive numbers of rare northern owls, concentrate on the island to feed on voles and other prey. Observations are made from public roads. *Do not trespass on private land.*

Access: From exit 613 or 617 off Provincial Route 401 at Kingston, drive to the foot of Brock Street where the ferry departs to Wolfe Island. Check locally for the current ferry schedule.

Reference: *A Bird-Finding Guide to Ontario* (University of Toronto Press, 1982).

Yukon

North Klondike Highway

Raptors: Bald Eagles (usually seen along lakes and rivers), Northern Goshawks, Red-tailed Hawks (dark morph Harlan's are most common, but some intermediate and rarely light morph individuals also occur, as do some Western Red-tails), Golden Eagles (often seen by scanning ridges with binoculars), Gyrfalcons, Peregrine Falcons, Northern Hawk Owls, Great Gray Owls, and Short-eared Owls. Rough-legged Hawks may be seen during autumn migration. Other notable viewable wildlife includes bears, Dall Sheep, Mountain Goats, Caribou, and White-tailed Ptarmigan.

Viewing Season: Year-round.

Watch Site Description: The northern section of the Klondike Highway (Provincial Route 2) connecting Whitehorse with Dawson City. The road runs through pristine mountain, lake, and river and stream ecosystems rich in wildlife.

Access: The northern section of the Klondike Highway connecting Whitehorse with Dawson City is a well-maintained road open year-round, although winter weather and driving conditions can occur anytime except perhaps in midsummer. Everyone driving this highway should have a full tank of gasoline when entering the road, have a good spare tire, and remain alert for wildlife on the road or crossing it. Motorists in the Yukon Territory can call (877) 456–7623 for current road conditions. Gas stations and other services are available in Whitehorse and Dawson City.

References: None.

South Klondike Highway

Raptors: Bald Eagles, Northern Harriers, Northern Goshawks, Red-tailed Hawks (Harlan's subspecies), Golden Eagles, Gyrfalcons, Peregrine Falcons, Northern Hawk Owls, Great Gray Owls, and Short-eared Owls. Rough-legged

Hawks may be seen during autumn migration. Other notable viewable wildlife includes bears, Dall Sheep, Mountain Goats, Caribou, and White-tailed Ptarmigan.

Viewing Season: Year-round.

Watch Site Description: The main highway connecting Skagway with Whitehorse is one of the most beautiful drives in North America. The road runs through coastal temperate rain forest, the alpine zone at White Pass, and interior boreal forest along the interior parts of the highway.

Access: The southern part of the Klondike Highway (Provincial Route 2) connecting Skagway, Alaska, with Canada's Whitehorse in the Yukon Territory is a well-maintained road open year-round, although winter weather and driving conditions can occur anytime except perhaps in midsummer. Everyone driving this highway should have a full tank of gasoline when entering the road, have a good spare tire, and remain alert for wildlife on the road or crossing it. Motorists in the Yukon Territory can call (877) 456–7623 for current road conditions. Gas stations and other services are available in Skagway, Carcross, and Whitehorse.

References: None.

Appendix: Vagrant North American Raptor Sightings

In addition to the species described earlier in this guide, a few others have been observed as vagrants in North America. They occurred here unexpectedly far from their normal geographic ranges or at the extreme limit of their geographic ranges.

Steller's Sea Eagle (Haliaeetus pelagicus)

Alaskan records include birds on Attu, Kodiak, Simeonof, and Unimak Islands, and along the Taku River near Juneau.

Crane Hawk (Geranospiza caerulescens)

Photographed in 1987–1988 in Santa Ana National Wildlife Refuge, Texas.

Roadside Hawk (Buteo magnirostris)

This species occurs very rarely in the Rio Grande Valley of Texas. A specimen was secured in 1901 in Cameron County, another overwintered in 1982–1983 in Bentsen–Rio Grande Valley State Park, and there are at least ten questionable sight records.

Collared Forest-Falcon (Micrastur semitorquatus)

One photographic record from Bentsen–Rio Grande Valley State Park, Texas.

Eurasian Kestrel (Falco tinnunculus)

An Old World falcon resembling the American Kestrel. There are records from Alaska, Massachusetts, and New Jersey, and in Canada from British Columbia, New Brunswick, and Nova Scotia.

Eurasian Hobby (Falco subbuteo)

Reported in Alaska from the Aleutian Islands (Agattu, Attu) and Pribilof Islands (St. George).

References and Suggested Reading

American Ornithologists' Union
  1998   *Check-list of North American Birds.* Seventh edition. American Ornithologists' Union, Washington, DC.
  2000   Forty-second Supplement to the American Ornithologists' Union *Check-list of North American Birds. Auk,* 117 (3): 847–858.

Anderson, S. H., and J. R. Squires
  1997   *The Prairie Falcon.* University of Texas Press, Austin, TX.

Anonymous
  1993–   *The Kittatinny Raptor Corridor Educational Handbook.* Wildlife Information Center, Inc., Allentown [now Slatington], PA.

Arnold, C.
  1997   *Hawk Highway in the Sky: Watching Raptor Migration.* Harcourt Brace, New York, NY.

Austing, G. R.
  1964   *The World of the Red-tailed Hawk.* L. B. Lippincott, Philadelphia, PA.

Bailey, B. H.
  1918   *The Raptorial Birds of Iowa.* Bulletin No. 6. Iowa Geological Survey, Des Moines, IA.

Baker, J.
  1967   *The Peregrine.* University of Idaho Press, Boise, ID.

Barber, D. R., C. R. Fosdick, L. J. Goodrich, and S. Luke
  2001   *Hawk Mountain Sanctuary Migration Count Manual.* First edition. Hawk Mountain Sanctuary Association, Kempton, PA.

Beans, B. E.
  1996   *Eagle's Plume: Preserving the Life and Habit of America's Bald Eagle.* Charles Scribner's Sons, New York, NY.

Beebe, F. L.
  1974   *Field Studies of the Falconiformes of British Columbia.*
          Occasional Paper Series No. 17. British Columbia
          Provincial Museum, Victoria, BC, Canada.

Bent, A. C.
  1937   *Life Histories of North American Birds of Prey.* Part 1.
          Bulletin 167. U.S. National Museum, Washington, DC.
  1938   *Life Histories of North American Birds of Prey.* Part 2.
          Bulletin 170. U.S. National Museum, Washington, DC.

Bijleveld, M.
  1974   *Birds of Prey in Europe.* Macmillan Press, Ltd., London,
          England.

Bildstein, K. L., and D. Klem Jr.
  2001   *Hawkwatching in the Americas.* Hawk Migration
          Association of North America, North Wales, PA.

Bildstein, K. L., and K. Meyer
  2000   Sharp-shinned Hawk *(Accipiter striatus). In* The Birds of
          North America, No. 482 (A. Poole and F. Gill, eds.).
          The Birds of North America, Inc., Philadelphia, PA.

Billings, G.
  1990   *Birds of Prey of Connecticut.* Published by the author,
          Norfolk, CT.

Bird, D. M. (ed.)
  1983   *Biology and Management of Bald Eagles and Ospreys.*
          MacDonald Raptor Research Center, McGill University,
          Montreal, Quebec, Canada.

Bird, D., D. Varland, and J. Negro
  1996   *Raptor in Human Landscapes: Adaptations to Built
          and Cultivated Environments.* Academic Press, Inc.,
          San Diego, CA.

Block, W. M., M. L. Morrison, and M. H. Reiser (eds.)
  1994   *The Northern Goshawk: Ecology and Management.* Studies
         in Avian Biology No. 16. Cooper Ornithological Society,
         Lawrence, KS.

Bolen, E. G., and D. Flores
  1993   *The Mississippi Kite: Portrait of a Southern Hawk.*
         University of Texas Press, Austin, TX.

Bosakowski, T.
  1999   *The Northern Goshawk: Ecology, Behavior, and Management
         in North America.* Hancock House, Blaine, WA.

Brashear, C. B. and P. K. Stoddard
  2001   *Autumn Raptor Migration Through the Florida Keys with
         Special Focus on the Peregrine Falcon.* Final Report Project
         NG96-101. Bureau of Wildlife Diversity Conservation,
         Florida Fish and Wildlife Conservation Commission,
         Tallahassee, FL.

Brett, J. J.
  1991   *The Mountain and the Migration.* Revised and expanded
         edition. Cornell University Press, Ithaca, NY.

Broley, M. J.
  1952   *Eagle Man: Charles L. Broley's Field Adventures with
         American Eagles.* Pellegrini & Cudahy, Publishers,
         New York, NY.

Broun, M.
  1948   *Hawks Aloft: The Story of Hawk Mountain.* Dodd,
         Mead Co., New York, NY.

Brown, L.
  1970   *Eagles.* Arco Publishing, New York, NY.
  1976   *Eagles of the World.* Universe Books, New York, NY.

Brown, L., and D. Amadon
  1968   *Eagles, Hawks and Falcons of the World.* Two volumes.
         McGraw-Hill Book Co., New York, NY.

Buehler, D. A.

   2000   Bald Eagle *(Haliaeetus leucocephalus). In* The Birds of
          North America, No. 506 (A. Poole and F. Gill, eds.).
          The Birds of North America, Inc., Philadelphia, PA.

Bureau of Land Management

   1997   *Snake River Birds of Prey National Conservation Area/Idaho
          Visitor's Guide.* Bureau of Land Management, Boise, ID.

Cade, T. J.

   1982   *The Falcons of the World.* Comstock/Cornell University
          Press, Ithaca, NY.

Cade, T. J., J. H. Enderson, C. G. Thelander, and C. M. White

   1988   *Peregrine Falcon Populations: Their Management and
          Recovery.* The Peregrine Fund, Inc., Boise, ID.

Chartier, A., and D. Stimac

   2002   *Hawks of Holiday Beach.* Second edition. Holiday Beach
          Migration Observatory, Holiday Beach Conservation Area,
          Ontario, Canada.

Clark, N.

   1983   *Eastern Birds of Prey: A Guide to the Private Lives of Eastern
          Raptors.* Thorndike Press, Thorndike, ME.

Clark, William S., and Brian K. Wheeler

   2001   *A Field Guide to Hawks of North America.* Second edition.
          Houghton Mifflin Co., Boston, MA.

Clum, N. J., and T. J. Cade

   1994   Gyrfalcon *(Falco rusticolus). In* The Birds of North
          America, No. 114 (A. Poole and F. Gill, eds.). The Birds
          of North America, Inc., Philadelphia, PA.

Craighead, J. J., and F. C. Craighead Jr.

   1956   *Hawks, Owls and Wildlife.* Stackpole Books, Harrisburg, PA.
   1966   Raptors. *In* Birds In Our Lives. U.S. Department of the
          Interior, Washington, DC. Pages 200–217.

Crocoll, S. T.
  1994   Red-shouldered Hawk *(Buteo lineatus)*. *In* The Birds of
          North America, No. 107 (A. Poole and F. Gill, eds.).
          The Birds of North America, Inc., Philadelphia, PA.

Darlington, D.
  1987   *In Condor Country.* Houghton Mifflin Co., Boston, MA.

Davis, K.
  2002   *Raptors of the Rockies.* Mountain Press Publishing
          Company, Missoula, MT.

Dekker, D.
  1996   *Hawks: Hunters on the Wing.* NorthWord Press,
          Chicago, IL.
  1999   *Bolt from the Blue: Wild Peregrines on the Hunt.* Hancock
          House Publishers, Blaine, WA.

Del Hoyo, J., A. Elliott, and J. Sargatal
  1994   *Handbook of the Birds of the World: New World Vultures to
          Guineafowl.* Volume 2. Lynx Edicions, Barcelona, Spain.

Dunne, P., D. Sibley, and C. Sutton
  1988   *Hawks in Flight.* Houghton Mifflin Co., Boston, MA.

Dunk, J. R.
  1995   White-tailed Kite *(Elanus leucurus)*. *In* The Birds of North
          America, No. 178 (A. Poole and F. Gill, eds.). The Birds of
          North America, Inc., Philadelphia, PA.

England, A. S., M. J. Bechard, and C. S. Houston
  1997   Swainson's Hawk *(Buteo swainsoni)*. *In* The Birds of North
          America, No. 265 (A. Poole and F. Gill, eds.). The Birds of
          North America, Inc., Philadelphia, PA.

Everett, M.
  1975   *Birds of Prey.* G. P. Putnam's Sons, New York, NY.

Ferguson-Lees, J., and D. A. Christie
  2001   *Raptors of the World.* Houghton Mifflin Co., Boston, MA.

Fisher, A. K.

    1893   *The Hawks and Owls of the United States in their Relation to Agriculture.* Bulletin 3. Division of Ornithology and Mammalogy, U.S. Department of Agriculture, Washington, DC.

Fox, N.

    1995   *Understanding the Birds of Prey.* Hancock House Publishers, Blaine, WA.

Frank, S.

    1994   *City Peregrines: A Ten-year Saga of New York City Falcons.* Hancock House Publishers, Blaine, WA.

Gerrard, J. M., and G. R. Bortolotti

    1988   *The Bald Eagle.* Smithsonian Institution Press, Washington, DC.

Glinski, R. L. (ed.)

    1998   *The Raptors of Arizona.* University of Arizona Press, Tucson, AZ.

Goodrich, L. J., S. C. Crocoll, and S. E. Senner

    1996   Broad-winged Hawk *(Buteo platypterus). In* The Birds of North America, No. 218 (A. Poole and F. Gill, eds.). The Birds of North America, Inc., Philadelphia, PA.

Grady, W.

    1997   *Vulture: Nature's Ghastly Gourmet.* Sierra Club Books, San Francisco, CA.

Grambo, R. L.

    1999   *Eagles.* Voyageur Press, Inc., Stillwater, MN.

Grossman, M. L., and J. Hamlet

    1964   *Birds of Prey of the World.* Clarkson N. Potter, New York, NY.

Haak, B. A.

    1995   *Pirate of the Plains: Adventures with Prairie Falcons in the High Desert.* Hancock House Publishers, Blaine, WA.

Hamerstrom, F.

   1970   *An Eagle to the Sky.* Iowa State University Press, Ames, IA.

   1972   *Birds of Prey of Wisconsin.* Wisconsin Department of
          Natural Resources, Madison, WI.

   1984   *Birding with a Purpose.* Iowa State University Press,
          Ames, IA.

   1986   *Harrier: Hawk of the Marshes.* Smithsonian Institution
          Press, Washington, DC.

Hancock, D.

   2003   *The Bald Eagle of Alaska, BC and Washington.* Hancock
          House Publishers, Blaine, WA.

Harwood, M.

   1973   *The View from Hawk Mountain.* Scribner's, New York, NY.

Heintzelman, D. S.

   1970   *The Hawks of New Jersey.* Bulletin 13. New Jersey State
          Museum, Trenton, NJ.

   1975   *Autumn Hawk Flights: The Migrations in Eastern North
          America.* Rutgers University Press, New Brunswick, NJ.

   1979a *A Guide to Hawk Watching in North America.* Keystone
          Books [Pennsylvania State University Press], University
          Park, PA.

   1979b *Hawks and Owls of North America.* Universe Books,
          New York, NY.

   1986   *The Migrations of Hawks.* Indiana University Press,
          Bloomington, IN.

   2002   *All-Weather Hawk Watcher's Field Journal.* J. L. Darling
          Corporation, Tacoma, WA.

   2004   *Hawks and Owls of Eastern North America.* Rutgers
          University Press, New Brunswick, NJ.

Hickey, J. J. (ed.)

   1969   *Peregrine Falcon Populations: Their Biology and Decline.*
          University of Wisconsin Press, Madison, WI.

Houle, M. C.
: 1991 *Wings for My Flight: The Peregrine Falcons of Chimney Rock.*
  Addison-Wesley Publishing Co., Inc., Reading, MA.

Houston, D.
: 2001 *Condors and Vultures.* Voyageur Press, Stillwater, MN.

Ingram, T. N.
: 1965 *A Field Guide for Locating Bald Eagles at Cassville,
  Wisconsin.* Southwestern Wisconsin Audubon Club.

Johnsgard, P. A.
: 1990 *Hawks, Eagles, & Falcons of North America: Biology and
  Natural History.* Smithsonian Institution Press,
  Washington, DC.

Johnson, D. R.
: 1981 *The Study of Raptor Populations.* Revised edition.
  University Press of Idaho, Moscow, ID.

Jones, D.
: 1996 *Eagles.* Whitecap Books, Vancouver, BC, Canada.

Kaufman, J., and H. Meng
: 1975 *Falcons Return: Restoring An Endangered Species.* William
  Morrow and Company, New York, NY.

Keith, L. B.
: 1963 *Wildlife's Ten-year Cycle.* University of Wisconsin Press,
  Madison, WI.

Kerlinger, P.
: 1989 *Flight Strategies of Migrating Hawks.* University of Chicago
  Press, Chicago, IL.

Koford, C. B.
: 1953 *The California Condor.* Research Report No. 4. National
  Audubon Society, New York, NY.

Kunkle, D.
>   2002   *Bake Oven Knob Autumn Hawk Count Manual.*
>   Wildlife Information Center, Inc., Slatington, PA.

Laycock, G.
>   1973   *Autumn of the Eagle.* Scribner's, New York, NY.

Lloyd, G., and D. Lloyd
>   1970   *Birds of Prey.* Grosset & Dunlap, New York, NY.

Lockyer, J.
>   2003   *Rose Tree Park HawkWatch Site Manual.* Jl-studioArt &
>   Design, Media, PA.

MacWhirter, R. B., and K. L. Bildstein
>   1996   Northern Harrier *(Circus cyaneus). In* The Birds of North
>   America, No. 210 (A. Poole and F. Gill, eds.). The Birds of
>   North America, Inc., Philadelphia, PA.

McDowell, R. D., and L. A. Luttringer Jr.
>   1948   *Pennsylvania Birds of Prey.* Pennsylvania Game
>   Commission, Harrisburg, PA.

Marti, C. D.
>   2002   *Enhancing Raptor Populations: A Techniques Manual.*
>   The Peregrine Fund, Boise, ID.

May, J. B.
>   1935   *The Hawks of North America: Their Field Identification and
>   Feeding Habits.* National Association of Audubon Societies,
>   New York, NY.

McMillan, I.
>   1968   *Man and the California Condor.* Dutton, New York, NY.

Meyer, K. D.
>   1995   Swallow-tailed Kite *(Elanoides forficatus). In* The Birds of
>   North America, No. 138 (A. Poole and F. Gill, eds.).
>   The Birds of North America, Inc., Philadelphia, PA.

Miller, A. H., I. I. McMillan, and E. McMillan
  1965 *The Current Status and Welfare of the California Condor.*
        Research Report No. 6. National Audubon Society,
        New York, NY.

Morrison, J. L.
  1996 Crested Caracara *(Caracara plancus). In* The Birds of
        North America, No. 249 (A. Poole and F. Gill, eds.).
        The Birds of North America, Inc., Philadelphia, PA.

Newton, I.
  1979 *Population Ecology of Raptors.* Buteo Books, Vermillion, SD.
  1990 *Birds of Prey.* Facts On File, Inc., New York, NY.

Olendorff, R. R.
  1975 *Golden Eagle Country.* Alfred Knopf, New York, NY.

Ovington, R.
  1975 *[Florida's] Birds of Prey.* Great Outdoors Publishing Co.,
        St. Petersburg, FL.

Palmer, R. S. (ed.)
  1988a *Handbook of North American Birds.* Volume 4.
        Yale University Press, New Haven, CT.
  1988b *Handbook of North American Birds.* Volume 5.
        Yale University Press, New Haven, CT.

Parker, J. W.
  1999 Mississippi Kite *(Ictinia mississippiensis). In* The Birds of
        North America, No. 402 (A. Poole and F. Gill, eds.). The
        Birds of North America, Inc., Philadelphia, PA.

Patuxent Wildlife Research Center
  2002 AOU 2890-3880 Longevity Records. Web site:
        www.pwrc.usgs.gov/BBL/homepage/long2890.htm.

Peterson, R. T., and V. M. Peterson
  2002 *A Field Guide to the Birds of Eastern and Central North
        America.* Fifth edition. Houghton Mifflin Co., Boston, MA.

Phillips, R. E., and C. M. Kirkpatrick

    1964   *Indiana Hawks and Owls.* Bulletin No. 8. Indiana Department of Conservation, Indianapolis, IN.

Poole, A. F.

    1989   *Ospreys: A Natural and Unnatural History.* Cambridge University Press, Cambridge, England.

Porter, R. F., I. Willis, S. Christensen, and B. P. Nielsen

    1981   *Flight Identification of European Raptors.* Third edition. Poyser, Calton, England.

Preston, C. R.

    2000   *Wild Bird Guides/Red-tailed Hawk.* Stackpole Books, Mechanicsburg, PA.

Preston, C. R., and R. D. Beane

    1993   Red-tailed Hawk *(Buteo jamaicensis). In* The Birds of North America, No. 52 (A. Poole and F. Gill, eds.). The Birds of North America, Inc., Philadelphia, PA.

Ratcliff, D.

    1980   *The Peregrine Falcon.* Buteo Books, Vermillion, SD.

Rosenfield, R. N., and J. Bielefeldt

    1993   Cooper's Hawk *(Accipiter cooperii). In* The Birds of North America, No. 75 (A. Poole and F. Gill, eds.). The Birds of North America, Inc., Philadelphia, PA.

Saul, F.

    1994   *City Peregrines: A Ten-Year Saga of New York City Falcons.* Hancock House, Blaine, WA.

Savage, C.

    1987   *Eagles of North America.* NorthWord, Inc., Ashland, WI.

    1992   *Peregrine Falcons.* Sierra Club Books, San Francisco, CA.

Schueler, D. G.

    1991   *Incident at Eagle Ranch: Predators as Prey in the American West.* University of Arizona Press, Tucson, AZ.

Sibley, D. A.

    2003a *The Sibley Field Guide to Birds of Eastern North America.*
          Alfred A. Knopf, New York, NY.

    2003b *The Sibley Field Guide to Birds of Western North America.*
          Alfred A. Knopf, New York, NY.

Simmons, R. E.

    2000 *Harriers of the World: Their Behaviour and Ecology.* Oxford
        University Press, New York, NY.

Smallwood, J. A., and D. M. Bird

    2002 American Kestrel *(Falco sparverius). In* The Birds of North
        America, No. 602 (A. Poole and F. Gill, eds.). The Birds of
        North America, Inc., Philadelphia, PA.

Snyder, N., and H. Snyder

    1997 *Raptors: North American Birds of Prey.* Voyageur Press,
        Stillwater, MN.

    2000 *The California Condor: A Saga of Natural History and
        Conservation.* Academic Press, San Diego, CA.

Sodhi, N. S., *et al.*

    1993 Merlin *(Falco columbarius). In* The Birds of North
        America, No. 44 (A. Poole and F. Gill, eds.). The Birds of
        North America, Inc., Philadelphia, PA.

Spencer, D. A.

    1976 *Wintering of the Migrant Bald Eagle in the Lower 48 States.*
        National Agricultural Chemicals Association,
        Washington, DC.

Sprunt, A., Jr.

    1955 *North American Birds of Prey.* Harper & Brothers,
        New York, NY.

Stalmaster, M.

    1987 *The Bald Eagle.* Universe Books, New York, NY.

Steenhof, K. (ed.)
> 1994   *Snake River Birds of Prey National Conservation Area 1994
> Annual Report.* Bureau of Land Management, Boise, ID.

Stone, W.
> 1937   *Bird Studies at Old Cape May.* Volume 1. Delaware Valley
> Ornithological Club/Academy of Natural Sciences of
> Philadelphia, Philadelphia, PA.

Stuebner, S.
> 2002   *Cool North Wind: Morley Nelson's Life with Birds of Prey.*
> Caxton Press, Caldwell, ID.

Sutton, P., and C. Sutton
> 1996   *How to Spot a Hawk.* Chapters, Shelburne, VT.

Swann, H. K.
> 1924–   *A Monograph of the Birds of Prey.* Two volumes. Sheldon &
> Wesley, Ltd., London, England.

Sykes, P. W. Jr., J. A. Rodgers Jr., and R. E. Bennets
> 1995   Snail Kite *(Rostrhamus sociabilis). In* The Birds of North
> America, No. 171 (A. Poole and F. Gill, eds.). The Birds of
> North America, Inc., Philadelphia, PA.

Turner, A. E.
> 1999   *Enjoying Hawk Mountain: Teacher Guide (Raptors and the
> Central Appalachian Forest).* Hawk Mountain Sanctuary
> Association, Kempton, PA.

Vezo, T., and R. L. Glinski
> 2002   *Birds of Prey of the American West.* Nuevo Publishers,
> Tucson, AZ.

Watson, D.
> 1977   *The Hen Harrier.* Buteo Books, Vermillion, SD.

Watson, J.
> 1997   *The Golden Eagle.* T & AD Poyser, London, England.

Weick, F.
    1980   *Birds of Prey of the World.* Paul Parey, Hamburg, Germany.

Weidensaul, S.
    2000   *The Raptor Almanac.* The Lyons Press, New York, NY.

Welch, B.
    1987   *Wings at My Wingtip.* North Country Press,
          Thorndike, ME.

Wheeler, B. K.
    2003a *Raptors of Eastern North America.* Princeton University
          Press, Princeton, NJ.
    2003b *Raptors of Western North America.* Princeton University
          Press, Princeton, NJ.

Wheeler, B. K., and W. S. Clark
    1995   *A Photographic Guide to North American Raptors.* Academic
          Press, San Diego, CA.

White, T. H.
    1979   *The Goshawk.* Lyons & Burford, New York, NY.

Wilbur, S. R.
    1978   The California Condor, 1966–76: A Look at Its Past and
          Future. *North American Fauna* 72: 1–136.

Wilbur, S. R., and J. A. Jackson
    1983   *Vulture Biology and Management.* University of California
          Press, Berkeley, CA.

Zalles, J. I., and K. L. Bildstein
    2000   *Raptor Watch: A Global Directory of Raptor Migration Sites.*
          BirdLife International, Cambridge, England, and Hawk
          Mountain Sanctuary, Kempton, PA.

Index

Acadia National Park (ME),
114–15

Accipiter
  cooperii, 27–29
  gentilis, 29–31
  striatus, 24–27
Active Pass (British Columbia),
  362–63
Agate Fossil Beds National
  Monument (NE), 376–77,
Alabama, 89–90
Alaska, 90–92, 289–97, 367–68
Alaska Chilkat Bald Eagle Preserve
  (AK), 289–91
Alaska Highway (AK), 367
Alberta, 269
*All-Weather Hawk Watcher's Field
  Journal,* 76
Alpine Boat Basin (Palisades
  Interstate Parkway, NJ), 150
Amherstburg (Ontario), 274
Amherst Island (Ontario), 391
Apple Orchard Mountain
  Overlook (Blue Ridge
  Parkway, VA), 233
Aquila chrysaetos, 50–52
Aransas and Copano Bay Area
  (TX), 219
Arizona, 92–94
Arkansas, 94
Assateague Island National
  Seashore (MD), 116
Asturina nitida, 31–32
Attwater Prairie Chicken National
  Wildlife Refuge (TX), 385–86

Audubon Center of Greenwich
  (CT), 100

Backbone Mountain (WV),
  259–60
Bacon Hollow Overlook
  (Shenandoah National
  Park, VA), 252–53
Bake Oven Knob (PA), 191–93
Bald Eagle Viewing Areas, 287–365
  Canada, 362–65
  United States, 287–362
Bald Peak (CT), 98
Bark Point (WI), 264
Barre Falls (MA), 124
Barryville (NY), 335
Basherkill Marsh (NY), 335
Bay Hundred Peninsula (MD), 117
Bear Den Overlook (Blue Ridge
  Parkway, NC), 176
Bear Head Lake State Park
  (MN), 322–23
Bear Mountain State Park
  (NY), 159–60
Bear River Migratory Bird Refuge
  (UT), 350–51
Bear Rocks (PA), 193–94
Bear Rocks (WV), 260
Bear Valley National Wildlife
  Refuge (OR), 343
Beavers Bend State Park (OK), 339
Becher Bay Headlands (British
  Columbia), 269–70
Beech Mountain (ME), 111
Bellevue (IA), 311–12

Belvedere Castle (NY), 160
Bentsen–Rio Grande Valley State
    Park (TX), 219–20, 386
Berners Bay (AK), 289
Big Bend Wildlife Management
    Area (FL), 369
Big Schloss (VA), 231
Black-Hawk, Common, 32–33
Blackwater National Wildlife
    Refuge (MD), 321
Blueberry Hill (MA), 124
Blue Ridge Parkway (NC), 173–84
Blue Ridge Parkway (VA), 231–37
Bluff Head (CT), 98–99
Boca Chica Area (TX), 386–87
Bodie Island Lighthouse (NC), 184
Bolton Flats Hawk Watch
    (MA), 125
Bombay Hook National Wildlife
    Refuge (DE), 301
Bonney Butte (OR), 190
Bonticou Crag (NY), 160–61
Borrego Valley Hawk Watch
    (CA), 94–95
Braddock Bay State Park (NY), 161
Bradbury Mountain State Park
    (ME), 112
Brady's Bend Hawk Watch
    (PA), 194–95
Brandywine Creek State Park
    (DE), 101–02
Bridger Mountains Hawk Watch
    (MT), 140–41
Brier Island (Nova Scotia), 273–74
Brigantine (Edwin B. Forsythe)
    National Wildlife Refuge
    (NJ), 379–80
British Columbia, 269–70, 362–65

Brockway Mountain (MI), 133
Browntown Valley Overlook
    (Shenandoah National Park,
    VA), 243
Bunker Hill (Golden Gate Raptor
    Observatory, CA), 95–96
Bushkill Boat Area (Delaware
    Water Gap National Recreation
    Area, PA), 344
Buteo
    albicaudatus, 41–42
    albonotatus, 42–43
    brachyurus, 39–40
    jamaicensis, 43–45
    lagopus, 47–49
    lineatus, 35–36
    magnirostris, 395
    platypterus, 37–38
    regalis, 46–47
    swainsoni, 40–41
Buteogallus anthracinus, 32–33
Button Bay (VT), 351–52
Buxton Woods (NC), 185
Buzzard's Roost Overlook
    (IN), 374

Caballo Lake State Park (NM),
    333–34
Caesars Head State Park (SC), 216
Caledon Natural Area (VA), 352
California, 94–97, 297–99, 368
Callicoon (NY), 336
Camel's Hump (VT), 227
Camp Lacupolis to Read's Landing
    Area (MN), 323
Canada, 269–85, 391–93
Canaveral National Seashore
    (FL), 103

Canmore Collegiate High School (Alberta), 269

Canyon Ferry Bald Eagle Watch (MT), 330–31

Cape Alava (Olympic National Park Area, WA), 354–55

Cape Henlopen State Park (DE), 102–03

Cape May Point State Park (NJ), 145–46

Caracara cheriway, 52–53

Caracara, Crested, 52–53

Casco Bay Area (ME), 112

Cass Lake (Chippewa National Forest Area, MN), 324

Cass Lake Wayside Rest (Chippewa National Forest Area, MN), 324

Cassville (WI), 359

Cathartes aura, 3–4

Cattaraugus Creek (NY), 162

Cedar Grove Ornithological Station (WI), 264–65

Charles Point in Peekskill (NY), 336

Charlotte Harbor Environmental Center (FL), 302

Cheat Mountain (WV), 261

Chelan Ridge (WA), 258

Chequamegon Bay Hawk Watch (WI), 265–66

Chicago (IL), 107–08

Chickasaw National Recreation Area (OK), 339–40

Chickies Rock (PA), 195–96

Chimney Rock Hawk Watch (NJ), 146

China Pier in Peekskill (NY), 336

Chincoteague National Wildlife Refuge (VA), 237–38

Chippewa National Forest Area (MN), 323–24

Chondrohierax uncinatus, 12–13

Circus cyaneus, 22–24

Cobourg (Ontario), 274–75

Cold Knob Scenic Area (WV), 261

College Hill Hawk Watch (PA), 196–97

Colorado, 97–98, 299

Commuter Trains (Along Hudson River, NY), 336

Concordia University (WI), 266

Condor, California, 4–8

Connecticut, 98–101, 300–301

Connecticut River Eagle Festival (CT), 300

Cook Inlet (AK), 291

Coragyps atratus, 1–2

Council Cup Hawk Watch (PA), 197

Crab Orchard National Wildlife Refuge (IL), 306

Craggy Dome Overlook (Blue Ridge Parkway, NC), 180

Craggy Gardens Visitor Center (Blue Ridge Parkway, NC), 180–81

Cranberry Marsh Raptor Watch (Ontario), 275

Crane Creek State Park (OH), 188

Crescent Rock Overlook (Shenandoah National Park, VA), 250

Cross Creeks National Wildlife Refuge (TN), 348

Cross Hill (Golden Gate Raptor Observatory, CA), 95–96

Cross Lake (MN), 324

Cumberland Island National Seashore (GA), 106

Cutler Area (ME), 113

Daingerfield State Park (TX), 220

Dauphin Island (AL), 89

Davenport Area (IA), 312

Deep Creek State Recreation Area (Kenai Peninsula, AK), 292

Delaware, 101–03, 301

Delaware Water Gap National Recreation Area (PA), 343–44

Denali Highway (AK), 368

Derby Hill (NY), 162–63

DeSoto National Wildlife Refuge (IA), 312–13

Destin (FL), 104

Devil's Backbone Overlook (Blue Ridge Parkway, VA), 237

Devil's Courthouse (Blue Ridge Parkway, NC), 182–83

Dickey Ridge Visitor Center (Shenandoah National Park, VA), 240–41

Dingmans Ferry (Delaware Water Gap National Recreation Area, PA), 344

Dinosaur Ridge Raptor Migration Station (CO), 97–98

Dunlap Fire Tower (TN), 217–18

Dutchman's Peak (OR), 190–91

Eagle
Bald, 18–21
Golden, 50–52
Steller's Sea, 395
White-tailed, 21–22

Eagle Ridge (MN), 137

Eagle Valley Nature Preserve (WI), 267

Eagle Watching Bus Tours (Prairie du Sac/Sauk City, WI), 361

Eagle Watching Etiquette, 288

East Fork Overlook (Blue Ridge Parkway, NC), 181–82

Eastern Neck National Wildlife Refuge (MD), 375–76

Eaton Hollow Overlook (Shenandoah National Park, VA), 253

Effigy Mounds National Monument (IA), 109–10

Elanoides forficatus, 13–14

Elanus leucurus, 14–15

Emeralda Marsh Conservation Area (FL), 302

Everglades National Park (FL), 104–05

Fairfield Lake State Park (TX), 349

Falco
columbarius, 56–57
femoralis, 57–58
mexicanus, 61–62
peregrinus, 60–61
rusticolus, 58–59
sparverius, 54–55
subbuteo, 395
tinnunculus, 395

Falcon
Aplomado, 57–58
Peregrine, 60–61
Prairie, 61–62

Fall Creek Falls State Park (TN), 218

Federal Dam (Chippewa National
  Forest Area, MN), 324
Ferry Bluff Eagle Council
  Overlook (Prairie du Sac/
  Sauk City, WI), 361
Field Equipment, 73–76
  All-Weather Hawk Watcher's
    Field Journal, 76
  Binoculars, 73
  Cameras and Video Cameras, 75
  Decoys, 74
  Field Clothing, 75
  Other Equipment, 75–76
  Telescopes, 74
Fire Island (NY), 164
Fisher Hill (MA), 125–26
Fishers Island (NY), 164
Florida, 103–06, 302–06, 369–72
Forest-Falcon, Collared, 395
Forney Lake Wildlife Area
  (IA), 313
Fort Edwards (IL), 307
Fort Gibson Dam and Reservoir
  (OK), 340
Fort Hill (MN), 140
Fort Macon State Park (NC),
  185–86
Fort Morgan State Park (AL),
  89–90
Fort Randall Dam (SD), 346
Fort Smallwood Park (MD),
  117–18
Fort Tilden (NY), 165
Four Mile Creek State Park
  (NY), 165
Franklin Cliffs Overlook
  (Shenandoah National Park,
  VA), 251–52

Franklin Mountain Hawkwatch
  (NY), 166
Franklin Mountain State Park
  (TX), 387
Fraser Valley Bald Eagle Festival
  (British Columbia), 363
Fulton Bald Eagle Watch (IL), 307
Fundy National Park (New
  Brunswick), 271–72

Gavins Point Dam (NE), 331
Genoa to Prairie Du Chien Area
  (WI), 359–60
George's Island Park in Verplank
  (NY), 336
Georgia, 106
Geranospiza caerulescens, 395
Glacier Bay National Monument
  (AK), 291–92
Glebe Mountain (VT), 227
Glenn Highway (AK), 90–91
Golden Gate Raptor Observatory
  (CA), 95–96
Gooney Run and Gooney Manor
  Overlooks (Shenandoah
  National Park, VA), 241–42
Goshawk, Northern, 29–31
Goshute Mountain (NV),
  141–42
Grand Canyon National Park
  (AZ), 92–94
Grand Manan (New Brunswick),
  272
Grassy Key (FL), 105
Great Basin National Park
  (NV), 377,
Great Valley Overlook (Blue Ridge
  Parkway, VA), 236–37

Greater Vancouver Area (British Columbia), 364
Greenbrook Sanctuary (NJ), 147
Green Knob Overlook (Blue Ridge Parkway, NC), 178
Gunsight Mountain Hawkwatch (AK), 91–92
Gunsight Peak (UT), 223–24
Gymnogyps californianus, 4–8
Gyrfalcon, 58–59

Haliaeetus
    albicilla, 21–22
    leucocephalus, 18–21
    pelagicus, 395
Hamburg Hawk Watch (NY), 166–67
Hamilton Area (Ontario), 275–76
Hammonasset Beach State Park (CT), 99
Hanging Rock Raptor Observatory (WV), 262, 263
Harrier, Northern, 22–24
Harrington Beach State Park (WI), 267
Harvey's Knob Overlook (Blue Ridge Parkway, VA), 235–36
Hatteras Island (NC), 186
Hawk
    Broad-winged, 37–38
    Cooper's, 27–29
    Crane, 395
    Ferruginous, 46–47
    Gray, 31–32
    Harris's, 33–35
    Red-shouldered, 35–36
    Red-tailed, 43–45
    Roadside, 395

    Rough-legged, 47–49
    Sharp–shinned, 24–27
    Short-tailed, 39–40
    Swainson's, 40–41
    White-tailed, 41–42
    Zone-tailed, 42–43
Hawk Cliff (Ontario), 276
Hawk Identification and Study, 63–69
    Date, 69
    Distance from Observer, 67–68
    Experience of Observer, 69
    Flight Style and Behavior, 65–67
    Geographic Range and Location, 68
    Habitat, 68
    Length of Observation Period, 69
    Light Conditions, 68
    Miscellaneous Factors, 69
    Shape, 63–65
    Size, 63
    Viewing Angle, 67–68
Hawk Migration Watch Sites, 89–285
    Canada, 269–85
    United States, 89–268
Hawk Mountain Sanctuary (PA), 198–200
Hawk Ridge Nature Reserve (MN), 137–38
Hawk Watching, Types of, 71–72
    Summer Hawk Watching, 71–72
    Watching Hawks Migrate, 71
    Winter Hawk Watching, 72
Hawksbill Mountain (Shenandoah National Park, VA), 251

Hazel Bazemore County Park
    Hawk Watch (TX), 220–21
Heron Bend Conservation Area
    (IA), 313
Higbee Beach Wildlife Manage-
    ment Area (NJ), 147–48
High Knob (VA), 238
High Park (Ontario), 276–77
High Point State Park (NJ), 148
High Rocks (KY), 111
Hilton Head Island (SC), 217
Hitchcock Nature Area (IA), 110
Hobby, Eurasian, 395
Hogback Overlook (Shenandoah
    National Park, VA), 245
Hogback Mountain (VT), 228
Hogwallow Flats Overlook
    (Shenandoah National Park,
    VA), 242–43
Holiday Beach Migration
    Observatory (Ontario), 277–78
Homer (Kenai Peninsula, AK), 293
Hook Mountain (NY), 167–68
Hooper Island (MD), 119
Hornsby Bend Hawk Watch
    (TX), 221
Horseshoe Lake Conservation
    Area (IL), 308
Howard Miller Steelhead Park
    (Skagit River Bald Eagle Natural
    Area, WA), 356
Hudson River (NY), 336–37
Hudson River Commuter Trains
    (NY), 336
Hyde Park Knoll (UT), 224

Ictinia mississippiensis, 17–18
Idaho, 107, 306, 372–74

Ile Perrot (Quebec), 282–83
Illinois, 107–08, 306–11
Illinois Beach State Park (IL), 108
Indian Medicine Wheel (WY), 268
Indiana, 108–09, 374
Indiana Dunes National Lakeshore
    (IN), 108–09
Indiana Dunes State Park (IN), 109
Interior of the Peninsula (Kenai
    Peninsula, AK), 293
Iona Island Overlook (NY), 336
Iowa, 109–10, 311–19
Island Beach State Park (NJ), 380
Ivy Creek Overlook (Shenandoah
    National Park, VA), 254

Jacks Valley Road (NV), 377–78,
Jack's Mountain (PA), 200
Jakes Landing Road (NJ), 381
Jewell Hollow Overlook
    (Shenandoah National Park,
    VA), 246–47
Joe Overstreet Landing (FL), 370
John Heinz National Wildlife
    Refuge (PA), 383–85
Jones Beach (NY), 168–69
Jordanelle Hawk Watch (UT), 225

Kansas, 320
Katmai National Park and Preserve
    (AK), 292
Kaw Lake (OK), 340–41
Kenai Peninsula (AK), 292–93
Kenai River and Flats (Kenai
    Peninsula, AK), 293
Kennedy Peak (VA), 238–39
Kent Island (MD), 119–20
Kentucky, 111, 320–21, 375

Kern Valley Turkey Vulture Festival
(CA), 96–97
Kern Valley Vulture Watch
(CA), 97
John H. Kerr Reservoir (VA),
352–53
Kestrel
American, 54–55
Eurasian, 395
Key West Area (FL), 105–06
Keystone Reservoir Dam
(OK), 341
Kilby Provincial Park (Fraser Valley
Bald Eagle Festival, British
Columbia), 363
Killarney Provincial Park
(Ontario), 279
Kiptopeke State Park (VA), 239
Kite
Hook-billed, 12–13
Mississippi, 17–18
Snail (Everglade), 15–17
Swallow-tailed, 13–14
White-tailed, 14–15
Kittatinny Point Visitor Center
(Delaware Water Gap National
Recreation Area, NJ), 333
Kittery Point (ME), 113
Klamath Basin National Wildlife
Refuges (CA), 297–98
Klondike Gold Rush National
Historical Park (AK), 293–94
Knutson Dam (Chippewa National
Forest Area, MN), 324
Kodiak National Wildlife Refuge
(AK), 294

Lackawaxen (PA), 344

Lake Andes National Wildlife
Refuge (SD), 347
Lake Barkley State Resort Park
and Land Between the Lakes
Recreation Area (KY), 320–21
Lake Chautauqua National
Wildlife Refuge (IL), 308
Lake Erie Metropark (MI), 133–34
Lake Kissimmee State Park (FL),
302–03
Lake Manawa State Park
(IA), 314
Lake Ogallala (NE), 331–32
Lake O'the Pines (TX), 349–50
Lake Sharpe (SD), 347
Lake Taneycomo (MO), 328
Lake Texana (TX), 387–88
Lake Texoma State Park (OK),
341–42
Lakeport State Park (MI), 134–35
Lakewood Park (OH), 188
Le Claire–Princeton Area
(IA), 314
Lehigh Furnace Gap (PA), 201
Lehigh Gap—East-Side Parking
Lot (PA), 201–02
Lehigh Gap—West Side at Osprey
House (PA), 202–03
Lenoir Hawk Watch (NY), 169
Lighthouse Point Park (CT), 100
Lipan Point (Grand Canyon,
AZ), 92
Little-Big Econ State Forest and
Wildlife Management Area
(FL), 370
Little Gap (PA), 203–05
Little Round Top (NH), 142–43
Long Lake Cliffs (AK), 92

Lost Maples State Park (TX), 388

Lovelock Valley Raptor Viewing
Tour (NE), 378

Lower Suwannee National Wildlife
Refuge (FL), 303

Loxahatchee National Wildlife
Refuge (FL), 371

Lucky Peak (ID), 107

Lucky's Corner (MS), 376

Mahogany Rock (Blue Ridge
Parkway, NC), 174

Maine, 111–16

Manitoba, 270–71

Manzanos Mountains Hawk
Watch (NM), 158

Marblemount Fish Hatchery
(Skagit River Bald Eagle
Natural Area, WA), 356

Martha's Vineyard (MA), 126

Maryland, 116–23, 321, 375–76

Mason Neck National Wildlife
Refuge (VA), 353

Massachusetts, 124–32, 322

Maxwell National Wildlife Refuge
(NM), 334

Mechanics of Hawk Flights, 83–88
Deflective Updrafts, 83–84
General Weather Conditions, 83
Leading–Lines, 86–88
Lee Waves, 84
Squall Lines, 86
Thermals, 85–86
Thermal Streets, 86

Mendota Fire Tower (VA), 240

Merck Forest & Farmland Center
(VT), 228

Merlin, 56–57

Merritt Island National Wildlife
Refuge (FL), 372

Michigan, 133–36

Micrastur semitorquatus, 395

Middle Creek Wildlife
Management Area
(PA), 344–45

Migration Seasons, 77–81
Autumn Hawk Migrations, 77
Spring Hawk Migrations, 77–81

Milford Beach (Delaware Water
Gap National Recreation Area,
PA), 344

Militia Hill Hawk Watch (PA),
205–06

Minidoka National Wildlife
Refuge (ID), 306

Minisink Ford (NY), 337

Minnesota, 137–40, 322–27

Mississippi, 140, 376

Mississippi Lock & Dam 2 (MN),
324–25

Mississippi Lock & Dam No. 4
(WI), 360

Mississippi Lock & Dam No. 9
(IA), 314–15

Mississippi Lock & Dam No. 10
(IA), 315

Mississippi Lock & Dam No. 11
(IA), 315–16

Mississippi Lock & Dam No. 12
(IA), 316

Mississippi Lock & Dam No. 14
(IL), 309

Mississippi Lock & Dam No. 14
(IA), 317

Mississippi Lock & Dam No. 15
(IA), 317

Mississippi Lock & Dam No. 16 (IL), 309

Mississippi Lock & Dam No. 17 (IL), 309–10

Mississippi Lock & Dam No. 19 (IA), 318

Mississippi Lock & Dam No. 24 (MO), 328

Mississippi Palisades State Park (IL), 310

Missouri, 328–30

Modoc National Wildlife Refuge (CA), 298–99

Mongaup Valley (NY), 337

Monhegan Island (ME), 113–14

Montana, 140–41, 330–31

Montclair Hawk Lookout Sanctuary (NJ), 148–50

Montebello Conservation Area (IL), 310–11

Monte Vista National Wildlife Refuge (CO), 299

Morgan Arboretum (Quebec), 283

Mount Agamenticus (ME), 114

Mount Ascutney (VT), 228–29

Mount Cadillac (ME), 114–15

Mount Everett State Reservation (MA), 126–27

Mount Mitchell (NC), 178–79

Mount Peter (NY), 169–70

Mount Philo State Park (VT), 229

Mount Royal (Quebec), 283–84

Mount Tom State Reservation (MA), 127–28

Mount Wachusett State Reservation (MA), 128–29

Mount Watatic (MA), 129

Muleshoe National Wildlife Refuge (TX), 388–89

Napatree Point (RI), 216

Narrowsburg (NY), 338

National Forest Scenic Byway (Chippewa National Forest Area, MN), 323

Navajo Lake State Park (NM), 334–35

Nebraska, 331–32, 376–77

Nelson Dewey State Park (WI), 360

New Brunswick, 271–73

New Hampshire, 142–44

New Jersey, 145–57, 333, 379–82

New Mexico, 158–59, 333–35, 382–83

New Trapps Watch Site (NY), 171

New York, 159–73, 335–39

Newhalem Visitor Center (Skagit River Bald Eagle Natural Area, WA), 356

Nevada, 141–42, 332–33, 377,

Niagara Peninsula Hawk Watch (Ontario), 279–80

Norrie Point State Park (NY), 336

North Carolina, 173–87

North Cascades National Park Service Complex (WA), 353–54

North Cove Overlook (Blue Ridge Parkway, NC), 177

North Klondike Highway (Yukon), 392

Northern Great Lakes Visitor Center (WI), 265–66

Nova Scotia, 273–74

Ocate–Wagon Mound Road
    (NM), 382–83
Ohio, 188–89
Oklahoma, 339–42
Olympic National Park Area
    (WA), 354–55
Oneida Watch Site (NY), 171–72
Ontario, 274–82, 391
Oregon, 190–91, 343
Osprey, 9–11
Other Raptor Viewing Areas,
    367–93

Pacific Rim National Park (British
    Columbia), 364
Palisades Interstate Parkway
    (NJ), 150
Pandion haliaetus, 9–11
Parabuteo unicinctus, 33–35
Paradise Point (MN), 138–39
Parker River National Wildlife
    Refuge (MA), 130
Patricia Beach Provincial Park
    (Manitoba), 270
Paxson Alpine Tours and Denali
    Highway Cabins (AK), 295
Pea Island (NC), 186–87
Peaked Hill (NH), 143
Pembina Valley Wildlife Manage-
    ment Area (Manitoba), 270–71
Pennsylvania, 191–215, 343–46,
    383–85
Pere Marquette State Park (IL), 311
Perkins Beach (OH), 189
Petit Jean State Park (AR), 94
Pilgrim Heights (MA), 130–31
Pilot Mountain State Park
    (NC), 187

Pine Tree Overlook (Blue Ridge
    Parkway, VA), 235
Pipestem State Park (WV),
    262, 264
Pitcher Mountain (NH), 143–44
Point Diablo (CA), 95
Point Mouille State Game Area
    (MI), 135
Point Pelee National Park
    (Ontario), 281
Ponca State Park (NE), 332
Pond Eddy (NY), 338
Popham Beach State Park
    (ME), 116
Port Burwell Provincial Park
    (Ontario), 280
Port Credit (Ontario), 280
Port Jervis Watch Site (NY), 172
Port O'Connor-to-Seadrift Area
    (TX), 389
Potomac Eagle Scenic Railroad
    Train (WV), 358
Prairie du Sac Generating Station
    Dam (Prairie du Sac/Sauk City,
    WI), 361
Prairie du Sac/Sauk City
    (WI), 361–62
Presque Isle State Park (PA), 206
Prince Rupert (British Columbia),
    364–65
Prince William Sound (AK), 296
Province Lands State Reservation
    (MA), 131
Purgatory Mountain Overlook
    (Blue Ridge Parkway, VA), 234
Putney Mountain (VT), 230
Pymatuning Waterfowl Area
    (PA), 345

Quabbin Reservoir (MA), 132, 322
Quaker Ridge (CT), 100–101
Quebec, 282–85
Quivira National Wildlife Refuge
  (KS), 320

Raccoon Ridge (NJ), 151–52
Range View Overlook
  (Shenandoah National
  Park, VA), 244
Raptor Trust, The (NJ), 381–82
Rathbun Lake and Wildlife Area
  (IA), 318
Read's Landing (MN), 325
Red Wing (MN), 325
Reelfoot Lake State Park &
  Reelfoot National Wildlife
  Refuge (TN), 348
References and Suggested Reading,
  396–409
Rhode Island, 216
Rialto Beach (Olympic National
  Park Area, WA), 354
Richardson Highway (AK),
  295–96
Richland Balsam Overlook (Blue
  Ridge Parkway, NC), 183
Ridge Junction Overlook (Blue
  Ridge Parkway, NC), 178
Rifle Camp Park (NJ), 152
Riverfront Park in Peekskill
  (NY), 336
Robstown (TX), 222
Rockfish Gap (Blue Ridge Parkway,
  VA), 232
Rocky Ridge County Park (PA),
  206–07
Rogers Pass Overlook (MT), 141

Rogersville–Kyles Ford Fire Tower
  (SC), 218
Rondeau Provincial Park
  (Ontario), 281
Rondout Reservoir (NY), 338–39
Rose Tree Park Hawk Watch
  (PA), 207
Rostrhamus sociabilis, 15–17
Roth Rock Fire Tower (MD), 120
Round Top (MA), 132
Route 183 (PA), 208
Route 309 (PA), 209
Rowena's Inn On the River (Fraser
  Valley Bald Eagle Festival,
  British Columbia), 363
Saint Adolphe Bridge
  (Manitoba), 271
Saint Andrews (New
  Brunswick), 273
Saint Croix National Scenic
  Riverway (MN), 326
Saint Marks National Wildlife
  Refuge (FL), 303–04
Saint Vincent Island National
  Wildlife Refuge (FL), 304
Salaberry-de-Valleyfield
  (Quebec), 284–85
Salt Creek Recreation Area County
  Park (WA), 259
Salt Plains National Wildlife
  Refuge (OK), 342
San Juan Islands National Historic
  Park (WA), 355
Sandia Mountains Hawk Watch
  (NM), 158–59
Sandy Hook (NJ), 153
Sandy Point State Park
  (MD), 120–21

Santa Ana National Wildlife
    Refuge (TX), 222–23, 389–90
Schlitz Audubon Center (WI), 268
Scott's Mountain Hawk Watch
    (NJ), 153–54
Second Mountain Hawk Watch
    (PA), 209–10
Sequoyah National Wildlife Refuge
    (OK), 342
Seward Area (Kenai Peninsula,
    AK), 293
Seymour Eagle Management
    Area (AK), 296
Shepaug Eagle Observation Area
    (CT), 300–301
Sherburne National Wildlife
    Refuge (MN), 326
Shohola Recreation Area (PA),
    345–46
Sitka National Historical Park
    (AK), 297
Skagit River Bald Eagle Natural
    Area (WA), 356
Skyline Drive (Shenandoah
    National Park, VA), 240–54
Skyline Ridge (NJ), 155
Smithfield Beach (Delaware Water
    Gap National Recreation Area,
    PA), 344
Smith Point Hawk Watch
    (TX), 223
Smugglers Notch State Park
    (VT), 230
Snake River Birds of Prey
    National Conservation Area
    (ID), 372–73
Snicker's Gap Hawk Watch
    (VA), 255

Soldotna-to-Homer Area (Kenai
    Peninsula, AK), 293
South Bass Island (OH), 189
South Carolina, 216–17
South Dakota, 346–47
South Klondike Highway
    (Yukon), 392–93
South Pack Monadnock Mountain
    (NH), 144
Squamish Valley (British
    Columbia), 365
Squaw Creek National Wildlife
    Refuge (MO), 328–29
State Hill Hawk Watch (PA), 210
State Line Lookout (Palisades
    Interstate Parkway, NJ), 150
State Route 38 (Chippewa
    National Forest Area, MN), 323
Sterrett's Gap (PA), 211
Stikine River (AK), 297
Stillwater Wildlife Management
    Area (NV), 332–33
Stone Mountain (PA), 211–12
Stony Man Mountain
    (Shenandoah National
    Park, VA), 248
Stony Man Overlook (Shenandoah
    National Park, VA), 247–48
Storm King Mountain (NY),
    172–73
Straits of Mackinac (MI), 136
Sullivans Island (SC), 217
Sunrise Mountain (NJ), 155–56
Sutter Creek Rest Area (Skagit
    River Bald Eagle Natural Area,
    WA), 356
Swan Lake National Wildlife
    Refuge (MO), 329–30

T. M. Goodwin Waterfowl
Management Area (FL), 369
Table Rock (MD), 121
Table Rock Lake (MO), 330
Tamarac National Wildlife Refuge
(MN), 327
Tamarack Point (Chippewa
National Forest Area, MN), 324
Taylorsville Lake State Park
(KY), 375
Tenderfoot Creek Fish Hatchery
(Squamish Valley, British
Columbia), 365
Tennessee, 217–18, 348
Texas, 219–23, 349–50, 385–90
Three Lakes Wildlife Management
Area (FL), 304–05
Thunder Hill Overlook (Blue
Ridge Parkway, NC), 174–75
Timber Hollow Overlook
(Shenandoah National
Park, VA), 249
Tobermory (Ontario), 281–82
Tosohatchee State Reserve
(FL), 372
Town Hill Hawk Watch
(MD), 121
Tuckerton Marshes and Meadows
(NJ), 382
Tunnel Parking Overlook
(Shenandoah National
Park, VA), 245–46
Turkey Mountain (VA), 255
Turkey Point (in Elk Neck State
Park, MD), 122
Tuscarora Mountain (PA), 212
Tussey Mountain Hawk Watch
(PA), 213

Uncanoonuc Mountain (NH), 144
Upper Skagit Bald Eagle Festival
(WA), 357–58
Utah, 223–26, 350–51
Utah Valley Hawk Migration
Lookouts (UT), 225–26

Vagrant North American Raptor
Sightings, 395
Vera Carter Environmental Center
(FL), 305
Vermont, 227–30, 351–52, 390
Vermont Institute of Natural
Science (VT), 390
Verplank (NY), 336
Veterans Park (Prairie du Sac/Sauk
City, WI), 361
Victory Park (IA), 319
Virginia, 221–58, 352–53
Virginia Coast Reserve (VA), 256
Virginia National Wildlife Refuge
(VA), 256–58
Vulture
Black, 1–2
Turkey, 3–4

Wabasha EagleWatch (MN), 327
Waggoner's Gap (PA), 213–14
Washington, 258–59, 353–58
Washington Monument State Park
(MD), 122–23
Wasp Environmental Center
(IA), 319
Wellsville Mountain Hawk
Lookout (UT), 226
West Lake Middle School
(PA), 215
West Point (NY), 336

West Skyline Hawk Count (MN), 139–40

West Virginia, 259–64, 358

White Deer Ridge Hawk Watch (PA), 215

Whitefish Point Bird Observatory (MI), 136

Wild Rivers Recreation Area (NM), 383

Wildcat Ridge Hawk Watch (NJ), 157

Willard Canyon Bald Eagle Roost (UT), 351

Wisconsin, 264–68, 359–62

Wolfe Island (Ontario), 391

Wollersheim Winery Bluffs (Prairie du Sac/Sauk City, WI), 361

World Center for Birds of Prey (ID), 374

Wright Patman Lake (TX), 350

Wyoming, 268

Yaki Point (Grand Canyon, AZ), 92

Yellow Face Overlook (NC), 184

Yolo Farmlands Loop (CA), 368

Yukon, 392–93

About the Author

Donald S. Heintzelman was an associate curator of natural science at the William Penn Memorial Museum (now the State Museum of Pennsylvania) and was for some years curator of ornithology at the New Jersey State Museum. He has traveled widely in eastern North America, the West Indies, South America, the Falkland and Galapagos Islands, East Africa, and the Antarctic, studying and photographing wildlife. He was also a wildlife film lecturer for the National Audubon Society and was ornithologist on the ecotourism ship MS *Lindblad Explorer* on expeditions to Amazonia, the Antarctic, and Galapagos. For nearly fifty years he has studied birds of prey and their migrations, and has published extensively on these birds in books, newspapers, and leading national and international ornithology, wildlife, and conservation magazines. His most recent books include the *All-Weather Hawk Watcher's Field Journal, Hawks and Owls of Eastern North America,* and *The Complete Backyard Birdwatcher's Home Companion.* He lives near the famous Kittatinny Raptor Corridor in eastern Pennsylvania.